Social Movements for Global Democracy

Social Movements for Global Democracy

JACKIE SMITH

The Johns Hopkins University Press

Baltimore

© 2008 The Johns Hopkins University Press
All rights reserved. Published 2008
Printed in the United States of America on acid-free paper
2 4 6 8 9 7 5 3

The Johns Hopkins University Press
2715 North Charles Street
Baltimore, Maryland 21218-4363
www.press.jhu.edu

Library of Congress Cataloging-in-Publication Data

Smith, Jackie, 1968–
Social Movements for Global Democracy / Jackie Smith.
p.   cm.
Includes bibliographical references and index.
ISBN-13: 978-0-8018-8743-7 (hardcover alk. paper)
ISBN-13: 978-0-8018-8744-4 (pbk. : alk. paper)
ISBN-10: 0-8018-8743-7 (hardcover alk. paper)
ISBN-10: 0-8018-8744-5 (pbk. : alk. paper)
1. Social movements. 2. Globalization. I. Title.
HN17.5.S586 2008
327—dc22
2007024502

A catalog record for this book is available from the British Library.

Special discounts are available for bulk purchases of this book. For more information,
please contact Special Sales at 410-516-6936 or specialsales@press.jhu.edu.

CONTENTS

TABLES

FIGURES

For many, *globalization* refers to the increasing expansion of global markets and the subordination of national economies to a global free market system. This vision of globalization, known as neoliberalism, is presented as the only way toward progress and development. As former British prime minister Margaret Thatcher claimed, "there is no alternative" to economic globalization. But citizens' groups and their allies have long demanded a completely different vision of global integration—one that begins not with markets but with human beings. They have worked to build democratic structures to govern markets, making them responsive to social needs rather than to the laws of supply and demand. This book documents some of these struggles to build a more democratic and humane world, demonstrating how contemporary activism for global justice builds upon a rich history of transnational political action.

A more just and peaceful world requires more effective cooperation among those who support a democratic vision of globalization. It also requires greater attention to questions about how global institutions can be transformed to better serve the interests of all of the world's people. I am increasingly convinced that people who want a democratic, peaceful, and environmentally sustainable world must devote greater attention to the work of both strengthening and democratizing the UN system. By neglecting the UN, democratic globalizers relinquish a key resource and ally in the struggle to define how our world is organized. And neoliberals will continue to fill this vacuum. Achieving this will require cooperation among a diverse array of people and organizations, and supporters of democracy must develop new ways to manage their differences so that they can work together more effectively.

This book is as much a political project as an intellectual one. It takes sides in favor of pro-democracy forces. Given the enormous inequalities of our day, I find it hard to even fathom the notion that any scholar might want to remain a neutral analyst of social reality, even if this were possible. Fortunately, and at least partly as a result of the movement actors analyzed in this book, numerous scholarly disciplines in the United States have revived attention to questions of their disciplines' social responsibility. The pages that follow are an attempt by this sociologist to take to heart former American Sociological Association president Michael Burawoy's call for us to use our knowledge to "represent humanity's interest in containing the unbridled tyranny of market and state" (2004: 4).

The process of writing this book began more than ten years ago. As I completed my dissertation on how transnational social movements were working to shape global human rights, peace, and environmental treaties, I realized that changes such as the creation of the World Trade Organization (WTO) in 1995 threatened to reverse the hard-won gains of transnational activists. At the same time, I saw that these earlier UN-oriented campaigns provided activists with important skills, relationships, and templates for action that would be used to resist the policies of economic globalization. I went to Seattle for the 1999 WTO meeting on the hunch that something big was about to happen there. Subsequently, I traveled to other global financial meetings in Washington, D.C., Prague, and Quebec City to observe the variety of protest forms used in these settings, to talk with participants, and to listen to the ways activists framed their struggles and responded to the various new challenges they confronted.

When the energy of the movement shifted away from official meetings and toward more autonomous global meetings of civil society actors, I headed south in 2001 and again in 2005 to attend the World Social Forum (WSF) meetings in Porto Alegre, Brazil. Local social forums in New York and Boston allowed me to examine how the global discourses and activities of this movement were interpreted in local contexts. In addition to participant observation and informal interviews, I reviewed published, online, and other electronic materials reflecting activists' analyses of evolving political developments (such as the biannual meetings of the WTO) and internal strategic and organizational debates of groups closely and tangentially involved in the major actions of what had come to be known as the global justice movement. As a participant-observer, I wore several hats. I attended various meetings as a consultant and researcher with a transnational organization called EarthAction, as well as in my role as a delegate in the United University Professions, my faculty union at Stony Brook University. Each role provided important lenses through which I could examine the impacts of global economic integration and its effects on various groups of people, including my colleagues and students. Later, I became a member of Sociologists without Borders, which helped put me in touch with other social scientists interested in progressive activism and has supported new ways of thinking about and building transborder cooperation. I am grateful for the tireless work of Judith Blau and Alberto Moncada, who have built and helped sustain this organization of globally oriented scholar-activists.

This qualitative work is complemented by my research on patterns of transnational organizing, which draws from records in the *Yearbook of International Associations* to explore how the formal organizations that support transnational activism have changed over time. I draw from this work in chapter 6, but my overall understanding of the infrastructures of the democratic globalization network has emerged from close attention to the macro-level organizing patterns among transnational social movement organizations.

Research on globalization necessarily draws from multiple disciplines, and my original dissertation project sought to begin building a bridge between international relations theory and research in the sociology of social movements. That bridge has become much better developed (and well traversed!) since then, and the work by constructivist theorists in international relations and world culture theorists in sociology have contributed much to our understandings of social movements and global change. Social movement scholarship, too, has evolved in important ways, placing greater emphasis on the interactions between social movement actors and others in the political environment. More and more analysts are adopting the concept of networks to characterize the mobilizing structures that make up social movements. This book starts with some of the lessons that have emerged from crossing disciplinary boundaries, and hopefully moves our thinking forward in the process.

I have incurred many debts in the course of researching and writing this book, and the ideas I present here are ones for which I alone cannot take credit. They have emerged through countless discussions with activists and other analysts, and they build upon insights I gained from attending movement forums, rallies, and protest actions. I am grateful to colleagues and friends in the worlds of political activism and in academia who have been a part of my effort to make sense of a complex and ever-evolving global political reality.

The sociology department at the Stony Brook University provided me with leave time and intellectual support throughout much of this research. The Dr. Nuala McGann Drescher Affirmative Action/Diversity Leave Grant from the State of New York United University Professions enabled me to travel to Prague, Quebec City, and Porto Alegre and to begin writing about this emerging "movement of movements," which I call in this book the democratic globalization network.

A grant from the World Society Foundation supported my travel to Porto Alegre in 2001 as well as my library and computer-based organizational research. Additional support for my research on transnational social movement organizations in the late twentieth century came from the National Science Foundation (#SES 03–24735). The Office of the Vice President of Research and the Dean of Arts and Sciences at Stony Brook University supported some of my research travel. And I am grateful to the University of Notre Dame's Graduate School, College of Arts and Letters, and the Joan B. Kroc Institute for International Peace Studies for supporting my sabbatical leave in 2004–2005.

Much of the writing of this book was done while I was a visiting scholar at McMaster University's Institute on Globalization and the Human Condition in Hamilton, Ontario. The project benefited immensely from my cross-border year, and the opportunity to discuss these ideas with my Canadian colleagues certainly has sharpened my arguments about transnational politics. I am grateful to Will Coleman, Robert O'Brien, Tony Porter, Neil McLaughlin, and Graham Knight for sharing their ideas, commenting on drafts, and helping make my year in Hamilton an intellectually rewarding one. And Jennifer Clark provided invaluable logistical support while also making sure I found some time to enjoy some beautiful spots in southern Ontario. Special thanks go to my McMaster office mate, Nancy Cook, and to Tina Fetner, both of whom read through several of the very early and very rough chapters and provided invaluable feedback and encouragement. I doubt this book would be half as good—if it even got finished—without their input and those Monday evenings with Tina and Maxwell. I am especially grateful to John McCarthy, who read the entire manuscript twice, offering extremely helpful advice and encouragement that have been invaluable to the project. Carol Mueller, Sidney Tarrow, and Leslie Sklair should be credited for prodding me to finally sit down and pull this book together. I am also grateful to my many coeditors and other collaborators on the various book projects to which I have contributed.

My understanding of the complex world of transnational activism has been enhanced by the opportunity to work with an outstanding group of scholars with practical knowledge and experience of different national contexts and conflicts. Dawn Wiest has been an invaluable colleague, and I am grateful for her tireless work, first as a graduate assistant and now as a colleague and collaborator to help me better understand how transnational social movements develop over time. Patrick Gillham, Naomi Rosenthal, Michael Schwartz, and Sidney Tarrow all read and offered very helpful advice on large portions of the book manuscript. I am also grateful for input and encouragement from numerous colleagues, including Tristan Ann Borer, Ann Marie Clark (and the Purdue University social movements seminar), Chris Chase-Dunn, Charles Chatfield, Donatella della Porta, Ivana Eterović, Peter Evans, Felix Kolb, John W. Foster, Jeffrey Juris, Alex Khasnabish, Dave Maynard, Rachel Kutz-Flamenbaum, Laura Macdonald, Greg Maney, John Markoff, Kiyoteru Tsutsui, and Peter Waterman. The project benefited from opportunities to share work-in-progress at Sidney Tarrow's workshop on transnational contention, at the Institute on Globalization and the Human Condition at McMaster University, in Laura Macdonald's seminar at Carleton University, and in my own graduate seminars at the University of Notre Dame.

PART I

FOUNDATIONS

CHAPTER ONE

Contested Globalizations

[Global justice activists] reject as absurd the argument that the
poor must be exploited and the environment destroyed to make the
money necessary to end poverty and save the planet.

(International Forum on Globalization 2002: 8)

International economic integration is not an ineluctable process, as
many of its most enthusiastic advocates appear to believe. It is only
one, the best, of many possible futures for the world economy . . .
But is defending globalisation boldly on its merits as a truly moral
cause—against a mere rabble of exuberant irrationalists on the
streets . . . —entirely out of the question? If it is, as it seems to be,
that is dismal news for the world's poor.

(The Economist, 23 September 2000: 17–18)

Contemporary debates about how the world should be organized center
around two conflicting visions. On the one hand are policies and practices supported by the world's most powerful governments and driven by the needs of
increasingly globalized capitalism. Transnational corporate actors and the politicians supporting them work constantly to gain access to cheap sources of labor,
natural resources, and markets for selling the goods they produce. On the other
side are workers and citizens who argue that expanding global markets generate
a host of ecological problems, exacerbate social inequities, and threaten traditional cultures. These actors want a world order that focuses less on markets and
more on people. They thus seek a stronger voice in global policy arenas that are
largely insulated from public input and scrutiny.

With the end of the Cold War, these competing visions of world order have
come more sharply into focus. As tensions between the United States and the Soviet Union declined, concerns about global military security receded while other

social and economic issues came to the fore of global policy agendas. Many in the West saw the demise of the Soviet Union as a triumph for capitalist ideology and policy, and, after declaring the "end of history," they aggressively promoted this vision around the world. Without a countervailing superpower, as with the Cold War, they could show the world the benefits of truly globalized capitalism. From their privileged positions within governments and international organizations like the World Bank and the International Monetary Fund (IMF), they advocated open markets to promote global trade while reducing public spending and enacting fiscal policies that would enhance international investment.

While proponents of what is known as neoliberalism carried out a radical program to integrate local and national economies into a single, global one,[1] other people were mobilizing to defend established rights and to promote more people-centered rather than market-centered forms of global governance. They worked mainly within the UN, but by the late 1990s, growing numbers were focusing their attention on international economic institutions such as the World Bank, the IMF, and the World Trade Organization (WTO). Defenders of economic globalization labeled these protesters "anti-globalization," arguing, "we know what you're *against*, but what are you *for?*" Global economic planners envisioned a legal-technical order that would harmonize national policies and manage trade conflicts. Protesters spoke of human rights and sustainability, and they resisted the technical language of global economic management, but they appeared to lack a comprehensive alternative vision of how to organize global affairs to ensure widespread prosperity and peace.

What many activists and observers have failed to appreciate, however, is that citizens' groups have been working to shape the global economic and political order long before the 1990s. By tracing connections between protest groups and ideologies of the past and present, we see that popular groups have long promoted visions of global order to compete with that of globalized capitalism.[2] Moreover, the vision of global capitalism that is predominant today has itself changed with time, its current form reflecting a long trajectory of interactions between capitalists and their challengers as well as among proponents of either vision. This struggle might be seen in terms of a global society versus a world economic system. A global society is a community of citizens and states organized around a shared human identity and common norms that promote cooperation and social cohesion. Advocates of a world economy are not necessarily opposed to such a vision of global society, but in their view the most efficient way to allocate the world's resources is through markets. Global markets are seen as the key to the prosperity that will bring peace to the human community. Thus, while advocates of global society seek to socialize states and other actors in ways that place human rights norms at the center of policy, those advocating a world economy want to subordinate societies and states to market forces.

In this book I examine how people have come together to articulate and promote ideas of a global society that differ dramatically from the world economy promoted by far more powerful corporate and political actors. These people and the movement they comprise have been labeled "anti-globalization," but as we will see, in reality they are not anti-global but rather they work toward a vision of globalization based on cooperation and inclusion rather than economic competition. In the course of working to shape and promote their vision of globalization, these actors have innovated new ways of doing politics. And in the process they have helped democratize the global political system.

Throughout history, social movements have promoted their own vision of global integration by expanding global agendas, promoting multilateral initiatives, encouraging national implementation of international law, reconciling competing visions of globalization, and generating alternatives to the programs of governments and corporations. Although conventional accounts of global politics and history overlook much of this work, it has been and remains an important force shaping global institutions and processes. As the limits of economic globalization become increasingly apparent, citizens' groups have worked to make global institutions more responsive to the needs of the world's people. By exploring some of the relations between social change advocates and global institutional processes, this book aims to demonstrate possibilities for advancing a more coherent vision of a democratic global order that can compete more effectively with the neoliberal one.

We might usefully think of this struggle as one between two major transnational networks: a neoliberal network more densely linked and rich in material resources, and a democratic one that is loosely integrated around somewhat diffuse and vaguely conceptualized goals. While this latter network pales in comparison to its rival in terms of financial and material resources, its power lies mainly in its ability to challenge the legitimacy of dominant institutions and corporate actors. As diverse groups promote an even more diverse array of social change goals, they affect the constellation of actors mobilized for a more democratic global polity while altering the relative balance of power between the two rival networks. By more clearly articulating a global vision that can help unify the many causes they promote, opponents of neoliberalism might deepen and broaden their network and its possibilities for changing the world. Table 1.1 summarizes the key actors and ideas associated with each of these visions.

TABLE I.I
Neoliberal and Democratic Globalizers

Actors	Arguments/Claims	Policy Proposals
Democratic Globalizers		
* Civil society groups (e.g., unions, school groups, church groups) * Local, national, and transnational social movement organizations (e.g., Amnesty International, Greenpeace, Public Citizen) * Independent (noncommercial) media organizations * Internet Web sites	* Economic globalization forces a "race to the bottom," by limiting labor and environmental regulation * Global economy undermines democratic institutions * Global economy concentrates power in a small number of countries and companies * Global economy lacks transparency * Dominant form of economic globalization is not inevitable; it is advanced by a small elite and it benefits a limited group * Economic globalization prioritizes profit making over other social aims	* "Shrink or sink" global financial institutions to eliminate unfair advantage of rich countries and corporations * Strengthen economic governance at global level through, for example, "Tobin tax" on international financial transfers[1] * Debt relief for poor countries * Strengthen state sovereignty (economic) * "Deglobalize"[2] by emphasizing local economic empowerment and governance * Promote global culture-ideology of human rights
Neoliberal Globalizers		
* Some national government ministries (primarily the United States, Europe)[3] * Transnational corporations * Currency speculators * Commercial media outlets * Global financial institutions (IMF/World Bank/WTO)	* TINA (there is no alternative) to economic globalization model * Dominant economic model is inevitable, desirable, benevolent * Current form of global economic integration is irreversible * Economic globalization is the best route to development for all people	* Promote sustained economic growth * Enhance openness to international trade and investment * Reduce role of politics and the state in the economy; increase role of markets * Promote global culture-ideology of consumerism

SOURCES: Adapted from Ayres (2004) and Sklair (2002: 311).

1. The Tobin tax would place a small tax on international financial transactions to limit cross-border currency speculation and fund economic development in poor countries.

2. Bello (2003).

3. Ministries of finance and trade are likely to be proponents of neoliberal globalization, but other ministries, such as public health, agriculture, or education, are less likely to be so. Many local and provincial governments are also critical of neoliberal globalization, since it diminishes their own authority.

The neoliberal perspective envisions a world ordered according to market principles. It assumes that markets generate and distribute wealth most efficiently. Thus, while few neoliberals are explicitly opposed to equity, they believe that a single-minded focus on markets is the best approach to improving the lives of most people. But capitalist markets are inherently exclusive in nature.

They require inequalities in the distribution of resources to ensure a readily available pool of workers and to maximize profits. Neoliberals frequently argue that the creation of a globalized economic order will produce economic growth and technological innovation that will eventually benefit all people. But the evidence to date suggests that "eventually" can mean several lifetimes, and at least in the short and medium terms neoliberal policies contribute to considerable deprivation and suffering for large numbers of people (Babones and Turner 2003; World Commission on the Social Dimensions of Globalization 2004). By allowing the end goal of economic growth to justify the means or the policy prescriptions believed to produce such growth, neoliberals have supported a global political order that is neither equitable nor democratic.

In contrast, democratic globalism, or what Herman Daly (2002) has called "internationalization," offers a response to this economy-centered model for global integration by proposing not selfish or xenophobic reactions typical of proponents of neoliberalism as well as anti-globalists, but rather a vision that accepts and even celebrates "the increasing importance of relations between nations: international trade, international treaties, alliances, protocols, etc." (2002). Such global arrangements are seen as essential to confronting challenges that defy national borders and cause mutual vulnerabilities. They help address the interdependencies among national communities by recognizing that, despite differences, humans live on a single planet and therefore share a common fate. The World Commission on the Social Dimensions of Globalization describes this in terms of "solidarity": "Solidarity is the awareness of a common humanity and global citizenship and the voluntary acceptance of the responsibilities which go with it. It is the conscious commitment to redress inequalities both within and between countries. It is based on recognition that in an interdependent world, poverty or oppression anywhere is a threat to prosperity and stability everywhere" (2004: 8).

This way of thinking emphasizes democratic values as the means for addressing contemporary global problems. Thus, it does not seek to break down national and local political arrangements, but rather to integrate them more directly into global political processes. As Daly argues, "the basic unit of community and policy remains the nation, even as relations among nations, and among individuals in different nations, become increasingly necessary and important" (Daly 2002). Democratic globalism therefore emphasizes the legal principle that is common to many international treaties, namely subsidiarity, or the idea that "all decisions should be made at the lowest level of governing authority competent to deal with them" (Cavanagh and Mander 2004: 149). Subsidiarity helps to ensure democratic accountability while allowing people to address interdependencies across diverse communities.

It is important to note that this typology of approaches to globalization im-poses an order on the ideas of a vast array of global actors that may not be obvi-ous, even to the actors themselves. Many people pursue a particular project or agenda without considering how it fits within a broader context of meaning. Many stumble into political projects because of some personal experience or interpersonal connection, and they do not necessarily reflect upon how, for in-stance, their work on a campaign to free a political prisoner might imply a partic-ular vision of world order. Similarly, analyses of contemporary global capitalism view neoliberalism as a consciously global project that only emerged gradually since the mid-1970s (McMichael 2003; Sklair 1999). Many people who support capitalist ideologies and even passively reinforce them in their daily routines still may not consider their roles in shaping a global economic order. But political and ideological leaders cultivate support for and advance their visions of glo-balization by working to attract more conscious and explicit commitments and alliances. And regardless of whether or not actors themselves are conscious of their roles, their actions help to reproduce one vision or another. By exploring the possible scenarios for global integration and the constellation of actors asso-ciated with each scenario, we can identify ways to strengthen those approaches that best serve the needs of people struggling to share a single planet.

The two competing visions of global integration are not the only political vi-sions or projects that vie for popular support. Other alternatives include impe-rialist projects to advance the interests of a single country or coalition over the interests and security of all others. Imperialist visions have become more salient in recent years. Such projects undermine international law and multilateralism, and they threaten global peace and security. Countering both imperialism and neoliberalism are fundamentalist visions, which seek to protect traditional cul-tures and values from the onslaught of globalized capitalism and Western po-litical domination, sometimes generating militant forms of resistance (see, e.g., Barber 1995; Glasius and Kaldor 2002). My concern here, however, is with the competition between the neoliberal and democratic globalization projects, since I believe that this struggle will determine the extent to which other visions gain popular support.

Why Global Democracy?

The Universal Declaration of Human Rights states explicitly that "the will of the people shall be the basis of the authority of government." In doing so, it demonstrates the global resonance of democratic values and norms. However, many would argue that, even though they have been created by governments that, for the most part, are at least nominally democratic, international institutions fail to meet the most basic democratic criteria. Institutions like the UN and the World Bank were designed by and for governments that had little concern for ensuring that the people within their borders would wield much influence over the actual deliberations within these organizations. And they have demonstrated—through tough policing of public protests, among other efforts—a commitment to protecting these spaces from greater public scrutiny and input. Few governments have established routines for involving their populations in consultations about how their countries should be involved in the world. As a result, even though the world is more formally democratic than ever before (UNDP 2002: 2), people have less and less influence over decisions that affect their daily lives. In their report, the UN Secretary-General's High-Level Panel on Financing for Development wrote: "Despite recent worthy efforts, the world has no fully satisfactory mechanism to anticipate and counter global economic shocks. [. . . Furthermore, for] a range of common problems, the world has no formal institutional mechanism to ensure that voices representing all relevant parties are heard in the discussion" (quoted in World Commission on the Social Dimension of Globalization 2004: 118). Currently, citizens are "represented" in international institutions by officials who are appointed (only sometimes with legislative approval) by national government officials. But as the decisions taken in international arenas have increasingly important consequences for the day-to-day lives of citizens, some are demanding a more direct voice in these decisions.

Foreign policy tends to be the least democratic aspect of any nation's policy apparatus. In the United States, for instance, the executive branch of government wields considerable power in shaping the direction of foreign policy, and the legislative and judicial branches of government have little authority to check executive power over foreign policy. The U.S. Congress can ratify treaties and determine the budget for defense and other foreign policy–related expenses. It also is charged with authorizing declarations of war, but in practice this authority is of questionable significance (Pagnucco and Smith 1993). Once we move from the national decision-making context, citizens have even less say in the positions their governments take in international arenas. Although legislatures often have the right to approve the officials selected by executive branch officials to represent them in international bodies, these approval processes generate little in the way of a broad policy debate, and they do not guarantee that popular preferences are considered in government positions.

Historically, popular movements have sought to overcome their limited influence within their own domestic polities by cultivating transnational ties (Chatfield 2007: 5). Transnational alliances can serve as sources of material and moral support for people seeking to resist the policies of their own governments. They also provide alternative perspectives and analyses of policies to those offered by national governments. For instance, during the Cold War, U.S. peace groups established "sister city" programs to foster direct people-to-people contacts between U.S. citizens and people in the Soviet Union. Their aim was to build a sense of a shared humanity and a mutual interest in more peaceful international relations (Cortright 1993). Most important, transnational ties help emphasize the interests and identities of people that transcend the divisions constructed by national political boundaries.

Transnational alliances based on religious, professional, or ethnic identities foster ties that cut across nationalities, thereby deemphasizing national differences. Increasingly, transnational identities have assumed a more universal character, emphasizing a shared humanity over national or religious differences. The proliferation of ideas such as those expressed in the Universal Declaration of Human Rights, as well as expanded discussions of democratic values, contribute to this broadening basis for transnational alliance formation. And as we will see in greater detail later in this book, global institutions like the UN provide a common focal point where citizens can turn when their governments refuse to uphold international laws and norms (Keck and Sikkink 1998).

If people have limited capacity to influence their own nations' foreign policy positions, they have even less influence in international institutions. Aside from in the European Union (EU), there are no elections for international officials, and thus there are no political parties to help educate and mobilize voters around major international policy agendas. Even elected officials in national legislatures have very limited roles in ensuring that the policies advocated by their national governments are consistent with the needs and interests of their constituencies. This is a problem, because the authority of contemporary governments rests on the claim that they have been chosen by their people through fair, competitive, electoral processes. Global institutions therefore lack a credible claim to legitimate authority. As Markoff argues:

> As monarchical, aristocratic and corporate powers democratized, the new states aspired to the ceremonial majesty and legitimacy claims of the previous monarchical order, but now it was democratic majesty that was proclaimed . . . Elections are a dramatic ceremonial reminder of democratic legitimation. The emerging structures

of transnational decision-making, however, do not have such features, and much of their activity is even hidden. The inner processes of the World Bank and IMF, to take two conspicuously significant examples, are hardly publicized and positions taken by many national representatives to those organizations are not even made publicly available. Rather than legitimacy, it is invisibility that is sought. How such power might be democratized is the challenge of the twenty-first century. (1999: 254)

If international institutions lack what we might call external or popular legitimacy, they lack internal legitimacy as well, since they fail to represent equitably the voices of all the world's governments.

Growing numbers of public officials are echoing claims of social movement actors to demand efforts to strengthen democracy, at least between states if not within them. A key motivation for them is to maintain the popular acceptance, or legitimacy, of existing political institutions. Actors—including individuals and states—that do not have a stake in a given system have little interest in seeing that the system endures. They are unlikely to provide the support and cooperation required for the system's survival. While most systems can last for a time without universal or even widespread legitimacy, they cannot do so for long.

The 2002 edition of the UN Development Programme's *Human Development Report* demonstrates a growing concern in official circles with declining legitimacy in global institutions. This report focused on the challenges of democracy in the contemporary world, calling for two major reforms in international institutions, including the UN. First, it called for increased pluralism, or the expansion of the space for non-state actors (i.e., citizens' groups) to participate in global political processes and to hold powerful actors accountable. The report notes that these "powerful actors" are not just states, but also transnational corporations and other business groups. Second, the operations of international organizations must be made more democratic in the sense that member governments have an equitable voice in shaping policy. This means making international bodies more representative of members and increasing transparency and accountability in decision making (UNDP 2002). To these we should add that there is much room for improvement within countries—including those that are formally democratic—to enhance citizen participation and government accountability. This is particularly true in the area of foreign policy, where virtually all governments deny their citizens opportunities to participate in meaningful ways.

Democracy is widely seen as the best form of government for human societies concerned with improving the human condition and ensuring some minimal (and hopefully dignified) standard of living for all of their people (see, e.g., Sen 1999).[3] In any case, it is clear that no other form of government would be widely preferred to democracy, which Winston Churchill called "the worst form of government except for all those others that have been tried." There is also a practical argument for democracy. Government is easiest and least violent and costly where people accept the decisions of policy makers as legitimate and just. Governments that spend substantial resources to police and punish their own citizens have fewer material resources for carrying out other programs that would both meet the needs of their societies and cultivate the active support of their citizens.

Not only have a majority of the world's countries adopted this form of governance (often in minimalist ways), but also on the international stage even nondemocratic governments have demanded that democratic values be respected in global political arenas. Indeed, some of the least democratic states (e.g., China) have been the most vociferous defenders of equal rights for states in the international system. If they are to be bound by international agreements, all governments want to feel that they have a voice in shaping those agreements, that negotiations are open or transparent, and that they have a way to hold other governments and public officials accountable to those agreements. Without such protections, they would have little interest in seeing the continuation of global institutions. By creating a stake in the system for even the least powerful actors, democratic institutions can help ensure that political actors will use accepted procedures for resolving conflicts without recourse to violence. This logic is a guiding principle of both domestic and international law.

Elements of Global Democracy

Can a global political system be democratic? Moreover, should it be? And if so, should democratization precede or follow the construction of effective institutions? We lack a road map to global democracy, and history only tells us that democracy is the most acceptable form of government for diverse groups. We also know that in general, national states have only become democratic over long periods of time and struggle. Furthermore, even the most advanced democracies have room for improvement in achieving true democratic ideas. Given these observations, what can we say about the prospects for and the likely path toward a more democratic global order? John Markoff argues that global institutions will become more powerful before they become more democratic (Markoff 2004b). People will not mobilize to demand control over institutions that they do not see as affecting them. But international institutions have differing amounts of influence on the lives of people in diverse countries, and so it is impossible to say how powerful global institutions must become before they face pressures to democratize. And many opponents of international agreements base their dissent on claims that such agreements lack democratic legitimacy. So attempts to strengthen international institutions might require more extensive efforts to make these more accountable and open to citizen participation. What would global democracy entail?

The concept of democracy has been the subject of much debate,[4] and I do not intend to expand that discussion here. However, I outline some generally accepted views of what constitutes democracy so that we can evaluate the extent to which social movement participation in global politics helps democratize global institutions. Perhaps the most important element of democracy is the idea that political power should be widely dispersed rather than concentrated in the hands of a small number of individuals or groups. Inequality undermines democracy in important ways. As Mark Molloch Brown observed in his foreword to the 2002 *Human Development Report,* democratic politics involves "a set of principles and core values that allow poor people to gain power through participation while protecting them from arbitrary, unaccountable actions in their lives by governments, multinational corporations and other forces" (UNDP 2002: vi). In other words, democracy requires active efforts to create more equitable distributions of power in society.

Closely associated with this is the value of equality: that every voice should count equally in the political process, regardless of one's social status or economic standing. In democracies, minority groups must be protected from the potential for abuse by a system of basic rights and law that is applicable to all members of society on an equal and nondiscriminatory basis. To ensure the enjoyment of these basic human rights, democratic governance involves certain minimal institutional criteria: free and fair elections; independent media; a vibrant civil society; and checks and balances between executive, legislative, and judicial branches of government. While the forms of these arrangements can vary dramatically, some element of these features must be present for democracy to exist (Tilly 2004). And it is also clear that no existing society has implemented perfectly the ideals of democracy (Markoff 1996).

To achieve these broad aims, a democratic culture must be present so that citizens can learn to identify with the whole of the political community and to find common cause with others who may not share all of their views. This requires a broad acceptance of the values of tolerance of and respect for people with diverse opinions and practices, and a commitment to dialogue, compromise, and nonviolent forms of conflict resolution. Such values as well as the skills for practicing democracy can only be developed in societies that allow for what Evans and Boyt call "free spaces," or "environments in which people are able to learn a new self-respect, a deeper and more assertive group identity, public skills, and values of cooperation and civic virtue" (1986: 17). The importance of such spaces cannot be overestimated, even as these spaces disappear from the political landscapes (Wuthnow 1998). For instance, Gianpaolo Baiocchi's research in Porto Alegre, Brazil, found that local districts characterized by such free spaces were more effective participants in municipal participatory budgeting (2003).

Another important consideration is how the organization of economic life impacts the prospects for democratic politics in different countries and worldwide. Global economic change has brought a shift toward a more professionalized and information-savvy workforce in many places, but at the same time it has generated many low-paying and often insecure jobs requiring little training. The extent to which people's struggles for material survival consume their time and energy affects the prospects for political engagement by ordinary people. Thus, we must consider how the expansion of a global market economy shapes the possibilities for people to participate in politics as democracy requires.

A key argument of this book is that social movements have been essential to democratizing the global political system even though their work goes largely unnoticed in the mass media and historical accounts. An important feature of this has been their contributions to strengthening multilateral institutions. The following chapters examine how interactions among states, corporations, international organizations, and social movement actors have shaped global institutions and the foundations for transnational political action today. I argue as well that, just as they helped democratize national states, social movement actors and their allies are—consciously or not—strengthening possibilities for democracy in global institutions. Scholars exploring issues of democracy in global institutions identify the following criteria for assessing the impacts of social movements on global democratization:[5]

- Enhancing public awareness and debate on global problems and proposals for their solution (e.g., cultivating a global "public sphere")
- Enhancing the openness and representativeness of international institutions by promoting access and voice to excluded groups and by diminishing power inequities among states
- Enhancing transparency and accountability (both internally, among states, and externally, within the broader polity)

- Enhancing the fairness of global agreements based on shared principles of justice rather than on tradition, political expediency, or models of action
- Enhancing the effectiveness of international law and institutions

These criteria will be used in the following case studies of global activism to evaluate the contributions of social movement efforts to global democracy. They also suggest that any efforts to democratize the global system are inextricable from processes of building multilateral institutions. Governments will not join global institutions without a guarantee that they will have a voice and stake in the system, regardless of their relative power and wealth. In other words, there must be democracy *among states* for multilateral institutions to maintain the support of all the world's governments. All states must view the system of rules as fair and equitable. Similarly, democracy *within states*—that is, democratic relationships between national and multilateral officials and the citizens they are to represent—is required if these institutions are to be seen as legitimate by the people who must ultimately abide by their decisions. Without this, no version of multilateralism is sustainable in the long term.

Both democracy and multilateralism rely on the displacement of coercive and incentive-based forms of power by the rule of law, or persuasive forms of power. Both seek to curb action by individuals or states acting against the common interests by building more inclusive structures for cooperation and protection. Both systems assume that the participants in the system are interdependent. In other words, they have mutual interests and vulnerabilities that necessitate cooperative problem-solving approaches. Interdependence requires that these systems build from a notion of equality among members, and that they foster the values of tolerance and commitment to nonviolent forms of conflict resolution. This is because the failure of even small and relatively powerless actors to cooperate can threaten the whole system, as the post-9/11 era makes abundantly clear. Thus, even the weakest players must have a stake, or a reason, to participate in and support the existing order. Such shared visions of how the world should be governed can only emerge from routinized procedures for consultation and dialogue. Decision makers must be accountable to wider publics, including other states and the citizens they claim to represent. By exploring the connections between social movement activity and democracy, we will also come to better understand the operations and evolution of multilateral institutions.

Overview of the Book

The neoliberal vision of globalization that has been predominant in recent decades has been linked to ecological devastation and widening inequalities within and between nations. But as proponents of globalized capitalism have advanced their vision for global integration, ordinary people have worked to advance an alternative: a global society governed by norms of cooperation, inclusion, and participation. While they focus on a variety of issues, these groups tend to express ideas of a common, interdependent humanity and shared human values and norms. The following chapters develop a theoretical framework for understanding how groups advancing competing global visions mobilize resources and support. I explore in depth some of the specific ways democratic globalizers have worked to strengthen and democratize global institutions as they challenge neoliberal globalization.

Chapter 2 develops the concept of rival transnational networks, which I use to organize this analysis of contemporary global activism. It also explores the organizational bases of each of the key rival networks considered in this book, the neoliberal and democratic globalization networks. Chapter 3 outlines the key arenas of political action in which these rival networks compete. It explores relationships between national and international political processes, focusing in particular on global-level institutions including the UN, the World Bank, the IMF, and the WTO. It discusses the basic rules of the game that define the political opportunities and challenges for those seeking to advance particular visions of globalization. The idea that contemporary international politics is characterized by complex multilateralism is offered as a way of thinking about the many and multidirectional relationships between politics at local, national, and global levels.

Part II of the book introduces the central protagonists in the struggle to define the course of global integration, and it presents a general overview of the organizational bases and global strategies of each network. Since the key aim of the book is to understand how proponents of a more democratic world order might enhance their effectiveness, we begin by assessing the current state of affairs by examining how the broadly defined neoliberal globalization network has advanced its vision of global economic integration. Because challengers to neoliberalism must operate within a political space that is affected in important ways by those controlling the majority of the world's financial resources, it is crucial to understand the impacts of neoliberal globalizers on the institutions and processes that govern our world. Chapter 5 shines a spotlight on a less prominent but no less vital or important struggle to define a world order, namely those efforts by citizens' groups to advance models of global cooperation based on democracy and human rights rather than the maximization of profit. Democratic globalizers have long advocated for a system of global-level governance that protects citizens from abusive governments while also enhancing the capacities of states to address problems that transcend their borders. The chapter provides a brief overview of the history of transnational mobilization to demonstrate how social movements of the past helped shape the institutional arrangements and movement networks of today. It identifies key strategies challengers have used to strengthen multilateral institutions in the course of their efforts to change the world. Chapter 6 details the social infrastructures for global change reflected in the variety of organizations and informal groups that may be considered part of the democratic globalization network.

Part III provides more detailed explorations of how different sets of actors operating within the broadly defined democratic globalization network have influenced multilateral institutions in their particular efforts to promote a more democratic world order. Chapter 7 examines the agenda-setting work of transnational social movement actors, exploring in particular the work of the Independent Media Center and campaigns against climate change. The idea that multiple different agenda-setting processes are at work at different phases of the policy articulation and development process is crucial here, and we explore these agendas and the possibilities and limitations they define for each of our rival networks.

Chapter 8 explores ways that democratic globalizers help advance their vision of global integration by working to domesticate international law. It examines the Poor People's Economic Human Rights Campaign and the Inuit campaign to challenge U.S. environmental policies in international human rights courts as examples of how social movements help strengthen international law by bringing pressures on governments to conform to international standards.

Chapter 9 discusses how social movement campaigns have sought to strengthen democratic multilateralism by highlighting contradictions between different global economic and political institutions. While few groups have organized explicitly around this objective, some have made explicit calls to address fundamental conflicts between institutions designed to advance economic globalization—namely the World Bank, the IMF, and the WTO—and the UN system. Finally, chapter 10 explores a few of the ways that some democratic globalizers work outside of the formal institutional context to experiment with and develop alternative forms of political and economic participation.

The conclusion to the book seeks to draw out lessons from this study about how the democratic globalization network might more effectively mobilize support for its aims. A key theme here and in the book as a whole is that many activists focus their attention and energies on particular issues and causes without attempting to understand how their struggles relate to a much broader, global effort to create a world order that is conducive to the practice of democracy and human rights. As economic globalization has become a more pervasive force, more and more people are seeing that their local experiences are increasingly shaped by global processes. By envisioning particular struggles as part of a broader effort to create a more democratic and responsive system of multilateral governance, those working to promote global justice in all its forms might better unite their strength and coordinate their actions to change the world.

CHAPTER TWO

Rival Transnational Networks

Groups hoping to challenge predominant ways of organizing political and economic life must work to articulate and promote alternatives to what are generally viewed as logical or immutable institutional arrangements. Scholars have therefore focused considerable attention on "framing conflicts," since social change efforts typically begin when social movements mobilize people around ideas of the necessity and possibility for change. Movement organizers must convince large numbers of people that things they take for granted as normal, natural, or the result of their own personal failings are in fact the result of systemic and changeable conditions (Gamson and Meyer 1996; McCarthy 1994; Snow et al. 1986).

To do this, social movement actors must mobilize resources and support for their positions. The democratic foundations of modern governments mean that authority derives from the consent of the governed. Thus, elites frequently claim that their rule enjoys popular support. This invites challengers to provide contradictory evidence to this effect (Markoff 2004a; Tilly 2004). Authorities and other elites are better able to defend their interests, and challengers must therefore be constantly on the lookout for opportunities for contestation.

The concept of rival transnational networks seeks to convey the idea that most political struggles are contests between competing networks that are made up of diverse actors, and that these networks differ in their access to resources, organizing capacities, political opportunities, and intra-network relations. Those supporting the status quo tend to have more resources, but they still must act to defend existing practices from potential challengers. Thinking in terms of rival networks sensitizes analysts to the fact that much social movement activity involves efforts to cultivate and expand alliances while interacting with adversaries in both contentious and also non-confrontational ways (Kriesi 1996). Analysts have also used the terms *alliance system* and *conflict system* to capture this idea about how social conflicts operate (della Porta and Rucht 1995; Kriesi 2004; Rucht 1996). As Rucht observes, "from the viewpoint of a social movement engaged in a struggle with oppositional forces, it is more accurate to speak of a pairing of an internally differentiated alliance and conflict system. In a similar vein, the relations between these two systems can rarely be characterized as just being hostile. Rather, they include various kinds of interactions, ranging from bargaining to competition to open and possibly bloody confrontation" (2004: 212–213). This conceptualization helps move us away from reified notions of social movements, focusing on the diverse strategies people use to promote social and political change. It also directs more attention to how movement adversaries mobilize internally around their own agendas and identities than do approaches that emphasize contestation.[1]

Given that movements emerge from relatively powerless groups, in order to effectively voice their interests, movements must cultivate the support of other actors that can help enhance their political leverage and credibility. In fact, the mobilization of powerful networks of actors is probably equally if not more crucial in any struggle as the mobilization of ideas (see, e.g., Jenkins and Perrow 1977; Keck and Sikkink 1998; McAdam 1982; Tarrow 1988). Most successful movements have cultivated allies within government agencies, political parties, the mass media, and other groups in society. By winning the support of allies who can influence policy processes, movements can advance their goals in important ways. Moreover, it is important to remember that even as social change advocates seek support for their agendas, those defending the advantages of society's most powerful actors are also actively cultivating and sustaining their own connections to government and other elites. Thus, movements must seek to neutralize the influence of opponents over public officials. Figure 2.1 illustrates what Maney (2001) has called "rival transnational networks" contesting different visions of globalization. The idea of rival transnational networks highlights a number of important features of social movement struggles. Specifically, it emphasizes the fact that movement opponents, like movements themselves, must work to mobilize diverse collections of organizational and individual actors into loosely knit, network-like structures that advance their own claims.

The relative balance of a movement's alliance and conflict networks affects its political impact, and thus a substantial amount of energy must be devoted to building and sustaining the network as well as to confronting or otherwise engaging adversaries (see, e.g., della Porta and Rucht 1995; Goldstone 2003; Kriesi et al. 1995; Rucht 2004). Networks require conscious efforts to manage or coordinate the activities of widely varying members with highly unequal capacities, motivations, and political access. Network agents must also work diligently to manage strategically relations with their adversaries. In the course of any given struggle, actors in a network may defect from the network, or they might move

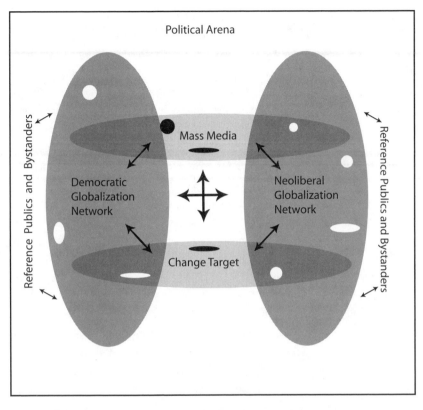

Figure 2.1. Rival Transnational Networks
Source: Adapted from Maney (2001: 107).

to the sidelines (to join the large ranks of bystanders) or into government or media positions, thereby hoping to advance their struggle in different ways.

It should be noted that the concept of rival networks as illustrated in figure 2.1 represents an ideal type. The boundaries and operations of each network are, in practice, often difficult to define. Networks are far from unitary actors, and by definition they are decentralized and fluid. Networks allow participants considerable autonomy to act, and the overall conflict must be understood as a collection of diverse and only loosely connected efforts. Thus, questions of how decisions are made and whether and how groups seek to influence other network players or coordinate their pressures on adversaries are important focal points. Analysts can identify central nodes of activity within each network, and they can draw from theories of social networks to gain insights into the relationships among different components of networks. The ideal type also helps analysts assess the potentials of and limitations on social movements. Its key advantage, however, is its emphasis on the ways interactions among diverse actors—including those within elite groups—shape trajectories of social conflict.

Maney's comparisons of rival transnational networks operating in localized contexts in different parts of South America led him to identify several key differences that helped explain the possibilities for a network's success in achieving its aims (2001). These included the resources available to the network, the political opportunities and constraints each network faces, and the nature of inter-organizational dynamics within the network. *Resources* include those controlled by members most directly involved in the work of the network as well as by its allies, although successful networks are those where the former group is relatively resourceful.

Political opportunities refer to the possibilities and limitations a network faces as it seeks to mobilize allies, popular support, and political attention around its concerns. As Maney points out, the opportunities for each network are distinct, but they are also affected by the activities of rival networks. Political opportunities consist of institutional rules and structures, the presence or absence of resourceful allies and opponents, and the division or unity of elites (Gamson and Meyer 1996; Meyer and Staggenborg 1996; Tarrow 1988).

Finally, *inter-organizational dynamics* refer to how well members of a network work together as they seek to promote similar interests. By their nature, networks are decentralized and loosely coordinated, so maintaining a unified focus and joint pressure is often very difficult, particularly where resources are scarce. Networks that experience little or limited conflict that is directed internally—toward other members of the network—can better focus their members' attention on rivals. Negative network dynamics see the energies of network members being focused on conflicts with those who share their aims. Such dynamics detract from the broader agenda of the network. Network dynamics are shaped by the density of network ties, the levels of dependence (inequality) versus interdependence (equality or mutual dependence) between network members, and the presence or absence of key leaders or "brokers." Brokers or bridge leaders foster communication and understanding between diverse network members, encouraging mutual trust and solidarity that is necessary for sustained cooperation (Bandy and Smith 2005; della Porta et al. 2006; Tarrow 2005). Bridge leaders can help broaden and deepen the network while reinforcing practices and skills that promote effective coalition work. They can help transform relationships viewed in terms of dependence into ones where actors are more sensitive to interdependencies, thereby creating what Maney calls "positive network dynamics." The network concept helps draw attention to the various types of identity-building and organizing work that is part of any social movement.

One rival network, the neoliberal globalization network, is populated primarily by transnational corporations and their officials, think tanks, and other business nongovernmental organizations (NGOs) formed to promote neoliberalism, individuals in business and government, mass media actors, businesses operating within countries, academics, and other professionals. Members of this network resemble what Sklair (2001) calls the "transnational capitalist class" (TCC), which he argues is made up of four complementary but only loosely connected fractions—the corporate, state, technical, and consumerist.[2] Table 2.1 describes these four fractions and their economic, organizational, and cultural foundations.

The corporate fraction consists of transnational corporate leadership, while the state fraction is made up of "globalizing politicians" who have espoused the ideology of neoliberalism and work to advance it in their governmental activities. These two fractions are prominent in two crucial nodes of the neoliberal globalization network, the International Chamber of Commerce and the Group of 8, or G8. The G8 is a group of leading core country governments that meet annually to plan and coordinate national economic policies. G8 policies have been central to the advancement of neoliberal aims. The International Chamber of Commerce is a business lobby that has played an important role in promoting neoliberal ideologies within government circles. The technical fraction is made up of skilled professionals such as economists and policy analysts who use their expertise to advance neoliberal aims. The work of this fraction is apparent in the global financial institutions described in the following chapter as well as in private bodies such as the Trilateral Commission, the Trans Atlantic Business Dialogue, and the World Economic Forum. The cultural (consumerist) fraction consists of mass media, policy organizations, and merchants who are most directly involved in cultural production such as marketing, public agenda shaping, and other forms of mass communication that advance a consumerist culture that sustains demand for the products of capitalist production. While these fractions differ in their emphases and activities, and while they may be organized either within or across national borders, their overall commitment is to a globalized system of capitalist production, and in this they complement and support each other, even if they do not do so explicitly.

TABLE 2.1
Fractions of the Transnational Capitalist Class

	Economic Base	Political Organization	Culture-ideology
Organizational Fraction	Corporate salaries, shares	Peak business organizations	Cohesive culture-ideology
Political Fraction	State salaries, perks	State and interstate agencies, corporatist organizations	Emergent global nationalism and economic neoliberalism
Technical Fraction	Salaries and fees, corporate financing (e.g., to universities), perks	Professional and corporatist organizations, researchers, think tanks	Economic neoliberalism
Cultural Fraction	Corporate salaries, perks, shares	Peak business organizations, mass media, selling spaces	Cohesive culture-ideology of consumerism

SOURCE: Sklair (2002: 22).

The democratic globalization network can be understood as operating with a network division of labor that resembles that of the transnational neoliberal network.[3] As will become clearer in later discussions of how these networks have operated, the corporate or organizational fraction of the democratic globalization network consists of organizations and coalitions that are most consciously devoted to advancing alternative visions of globalization, including social movement organizations and some (certainly not all) NGOs.[4] The state fraction consists of politicians working in national and sub-national governments as well as in international organizations that support policies that advance democratic over market forms of global integration. Like its neoliberal counterpart, the state fraction also includes numerous politicians working in local-level governments, many of whom have interests that diverge from those of national-level politicians.[5] The technical fraction is comprised of think tanks, academics, and other professionals (such as lawyers, physicians, etc.) who work on behalf of network aims. These individuals may or may not be formally affiliated with a formal social movement organization or NGO. The cultural fraction of the democratic globalization network includes the collection of civil society groups and individuals who may or may not be organized specifically around movement aims—such as school groups, recreational and professional groups, and the like—which help advance the cultural norms of the network by spreading the network's ideas to a variety of settings where people work and live. Non-movement actors help expand the connections between the democratic globalization network and a wider public, thereby enhancing the interest and participation in the network.

Thinking of movement dynamics in network terms sensitizes us to the organizational processes that are so much a part of routine movement activities. It also allows us to draw insights from a rich literature on the sociology of organizations and institutions (e.g., Campbell 2004; Davis et al. 2005; Hannan and Freeman 1977; Minkoff 1995; Powell and DiMaggio 1991). One important theme in this literature is the idea that organizations tend to adopt forms and practices that replicate others found in their environments, producing what is referred to as isomorphism within organizational fields. Thus, we would expect networks that interact—even if mostly in conflictual ways—to adopt similar profiles in terms of organizing structures and activities (Fetner 2001, Forthcoming). Thus, the similarities I have identified between the neoliberal globalization network and its democratic rivals are not unexpected and indeed can be explained as a result of their interactions and attempts to thrive in a similar global environment.

The network concept used here stresses the diversity of identities, structures, and organizational logics that characterize the participants in the global justice movement (Langman 2005; Schulz 1998; Waterman 1998). It also suggests a fluidity of boundaries, where actors can move in or out and be more or less active in the network over time and place. As Juris argues: "What many observers view as a single, unified 'anti-globalization movement' is actually a complex congeries of competing, yet sometimes overlapping social movement networks that differ according to issue addressed, political subjectivity, ideological framework, and perhaps most importantly, political culture and organizational logic" (Juris 2004: 70). This fluid and diverse global justice network contrasts with the rival neoliberal network, where the transnational capitalist class has substantial economic, organizational, and cultural resources at its disposal, and where a unifying logic of capitalism helps orient actors in complementary directions. Economically, the neoliberal network is supported by corporate salaries and other corporate funding for neoliberal lobbyists, think tanks, legal initiatives, advertising and promotion, and media relations. Significantly, the personal economic interests of individuals in this network are directly enhanced by their efforts to promote neoliberalism. By working to promote neoliberal globalization, they are also supporting themselves and their families.

This contrasts with many of the participants in the democratic globalization network, only a small percentage of whom are paid for their work. Moreover, those who work in this sector are typically compensated at rates far lower than those of their neoliberal counterparts.[6] A majority of actors in the democratic globalization network are not paid for their work at all, and they must therefore participate in their spare time. To attend meetings, many activists in the democratic globalization network must pay their own expenses, while neoliberal network participants have corporate expense accounts, child care benefits, and other support for their work to promote a neoliberal world order. Those democratic globalizers who are paid face far greater uncertainties than most of their neoliberal counterparts. They also are highly vulnerable to economic threats that may be brought on by their rivals through lawsuits or cuts in government or foundation support.

The political organization of the transnational capitalist class is also far more centralized and unified, partly because of the fact that it is supported by corporate resources and communications capacities. In contrast, those in the democratic globalization network draw from a much more diverse organizational base, and their organizational foundations are often precarious. They are more likely to be distracted from the primary aim of promoting network goals by the need to engage in efforts to mobilize resources to maintain their organizations.[7] For neoliberals, efforts to maintain their organizations generally complement both their personal economic interests and the broader interests of the network. Moreover, the commercial mass media can help reinforce their influence over political organizations while helping to maintain the positions of neoliberals within government offices.

Culturally, the consumerist logic of capitalism unifies the neoliberal network around a common ideology and set of organizing principles. The network seeks to promote a single economic model—globalized capitalism—and the immediate financial interests of actors in the network as well as bystanders are directly tied to the success of this model. Thus, politicians come to see their role as helping to advance capitalism by, for instance, limiting corporate taxation and regulation and encouraging consumption as a means of preserving jobs and economic growth (not to mention the profit margins of their corporate supporters). Workers who might prefer other ways of living see no option but to support the existing model if they are to both survive and expand their own consumption capacities.

The democratic globalization network has not yet found a comparably unifying culture around which to galvanize their supporters. A key element of their ideology is that one-size-fits-all economics does not work. Discussions among proponents of global democracy focus, for instance, on how progress is measured and on the failures of traditional economic indicators to capture the lived experiences of people (Daly 1996; South Commission 1989; ul Haq 1989). They also have documented the failures of markets to meet people's basic needs as well as the social and ecological destruction resulting from international development efforts (Cavanagh and Mander 2004; Korten 1996; Mander and Goldsmith

1996; Rich 1994). More recent discourses are influenced by indigenous peoples' voices, and one finds more references to the role of cultural diversity in helping to sustain human societies by allowing for adaptation and evolution, just as biological diversity has performed this role in nature (Indigenous Peoples' Caucus 2000; McMichael 2003; Shiva 2000). This can be a complicated message to convey, since it generates a host of possible alternatives to neoliberal economic models that are more-or-less applicable in different contexts. There is no single answer to the question of what opponents of neoliberalism want.

While there is widespread support for ideas of democracy and equality, these ideas cannot easily be linked to people's economic well-being, and, given existing distributions of wealth and power, these may directly conflict in the short term. Moreover, the alternatives to neoliberal models of economic organization are many, preventing a simple and readily conveyed message about viable alternatives to neoliberal globalization. The consumerist logic has the advantage that it generates the good sound-bites that mass commercial media demands, and thus can be frequently and forcefully conveyed through the mainstream media channels that are largely controlled by the neoliberal network.

The democratic globalization network's parallel to the cultural fraction of the TCC might be considered through the lens of the concept of "critical communities" advanced by Thomas Rochon. Critical communities are "relatively small communities of critical thinkers who have developed a sensitivity to some problem, an analysis of the sources of the problem, and a prescription for what should be done about the problem" (Rochon 1998: 22). They help incubate the ideas or ideologies that social movements then work to disseminate (Oliver and Johnston 2000: 45). They might be seen as important elements of what Wuthnow (1989) described as "communities of discourse." Wuthnow's analysis showed that in each of the major cultural transformations of the Protestant Reformation, the Enlightenment, and the rise of international socialism,

> the leading contributors to the new cultural motifs recognized the extent to which the institutional conditions of their day were flawed, constraining, oppressive, arbitrary. Their criticism of these conditions was often extreme and unrelenting. It was sharpened by an alternative vision, a vision constructed discursively, a vision that was pitted authoritatively against the established order, not as its replacement but as a conceptual space in which new modes of behavior could be considered. The strength of their discourse lay in going beyond negative criticism and beyond idealism to identify working models of individual and social action for the future. (1989: 582–583)

These notions of communities of discourse and critical communities highlight for us the centrality of ideological work as well as ideological entrepreneurship to the major social movements of the past. Moreover, they attest to the need for the creation of structured spaces within the existing order that enable critical thinking and the free exploration and exchange of ideas about alternatives.

Critical communities thus thrive in universities and other sites that foster intellectual creativity and free exchange of information. They are part of broader social movements, but they play a unique role within such movements as they help articulate and institutionalize ways of speaking about and understanding a problem. The democratic globalization network's congeries of critical communities consist of critical economists, social scientists, and other intellectuals working on questions of what policies might advance global equality and participation. Social movement organizations like the International Forum on Globalization, the Transnational Institute, and Focus on the Global South help bring together key critical communities and disseminate their ideas to broader publics. Ideas such as fair trade, taxing international financial transactions, programs for debt relief, or plans for environmentally sustainable technologies are just a few examples of the practical programs that have emerged from these kinds of communities. A challenge for these critical communities is to link their critiques of neoliberalism with proposals for alternatives in ways that resonate with an ever-wider public. By doing so, they chip away at the widely taken-for-granted nature of the culture of consumerism.

Network Relational Dynamics

While the idea of networks conveys a sense of loose coordination rather than a coherent and unified effort on the part of a collection of actors, as was discussed above, effective networks are those that have positive inter-organizational dynamics capable of generating sustained and consistent pressure on targets and opponents. Thus, the extent of communication and coordination efforts taking place within each rival network affects the prospects for the network to succeed in promoting its interests. As was noted above, negotiating common goals and strategies can be complicated, especially when the network involves a very diverse collection of actors and when power among these actors differs greatly (Bandy and Smith 2005; Keck and Sikkink 1998: 121). The more unified ideology of neoliberalism coupled with the higher degree of homogeneity within this network gives neoliberals a coordination advantage over their rivals.

As noted earlier, participants can move across different boundaries in the model. For instance, both rival networks seek to convince bystanders to either sympathize with their perspectives or to join their network. Looking at the transnational democratic globalization network, we find what we might call "defectors" from the neoliberal network such as financier and entrepreneur George Soros and former chief economist of the World Bank Joseph Stiglitz. By supporting democratization efforts and providing legitimacy to movement claims about neoliberalism's failures, these actors help advance movement messages in social circles that might otherwise remain closed to such messages. Network configurations can also shift when governments change through popular elections. Thus, the election of President Luiz Inacio Lula da Silva ("Lula") of Brazil's Worker Party helped bring movement allies into the halls of government. As we will see in many of the following chapters, movements often find allies within intergovernmental agencies such as those of the UN. These sorts of ties to official agencies help foster information flows and dialogues that both shape movement strategies and influence policy debates and enforcement.

In the neoliberal network, similar dynamics are at work. While we lack comparisons to the prominent defections of Stiglitz or Soros on that side, we do see attempts by proponents of neoliberalism to undermine the claims of their opponents by citing their participation in capitalist economies as evidence of defection—or at least of hypocrisy—by movement participants. For instance, countless mainstream media articles on protests against economic globalization try to challenge the seriousness of protesters' commitment to their cause by claiming that protesters visited Starbuck's coffee shops for double iced lattes or that they sported name brand apparel as they protested global capital.[8] More significant to the course of the globalization struggle is the circulation of actors between the neoliberal globalization network and government offices (e.g., Hertz 2001)— something that appears far more common than is movement between government and the democratic globalization network.

Examining the ranks of government offices, one tends to find strong ties to corporations and other actors that are part of the neoliberal globalization network. The reasons for this are numerous, but one important factor is that neoliberal globalization networks are supported by substantial corporate salaries and other sources of corporate funding that allow people to be consistently engaged in the work of promoting neoliberalism (Sklair 2001). Relationships to corporate interests represent the most cost-effective ways for politicians to raise the vast sums required to engage in today's expensive and media-driven political campaigns.

In contrast, challenger networks rely largely on voluntary labor and contributions, as well as some corporate and government grants.[9] Many proponents of democratic globalization must not only work for social change in the limited time that they are not working, but their very means of supporting themselves and their families can be threatened as a result of their activism. Union activists are routinely fired or even killed, and corporate employers frequently use more subtle means of discouraging their workers from participating in movement activities.

A second reason for close connections between neoliberal networks and governments is that the ideology of neoliberalism has demonized the public sector and organized labor while valorizing the private sector as the logical solution to the host of social problems faced by governments. As Sklair notes, "One of the most important ideological tasks of big business is to persuade the population at large that 'the business of society is business' and to create a climate of opinion in which trade unions and radical oppositions (especially consumer and environmental movements) are considered to be sectional interests while business groups are not" (1997: 526). The successful communication of this message has encouraged close working relationships between neoliberal proponents and government actors at the national and interstate levels (Robinson 2004; Sklair, 2001). A further boon to proponents of neoliberal globalization is that among the ranks of their rival network, comparatively few organizations or individuals actively work to cultivate ties to government officials. One reason for this is the strong aversion to hierarchy and a not unwarranted mistrust of government within the democratic globalization network.[10] Thus, while actors in the neoliberal network are fairly united in their goal of cultivating allies in government and international agencies, challengers remain divided over how to relate to these institutions.

There are also important hurdles to work with governments caused by the voluntary and less well-funded nature of activities by challenger networks. Many activists must do their advocacy work outside their regular work hours while government officials tend to work regular business hours and to schedule meetings and hearings during those hours. Also, corporate actors can support lobbying staff in the cities where government officials are located, while dispersed activist networks have a harder time maintaining such a presence. This is particularly true of people in the global South, who are increasingly influenced by the decisions of intergovernmental agencies based in global North cities such as Geneva and New York. Thus, even if the doors of officials were equally open to both networks, members of the neoliberal globalization network are more able to attend official meetings and to meet with public officials than are their opponents.

Further exacerbating this inequality is the fact that the countries most likely to favor neoliberal policies can afford to support more staff members at the headquarters of international trade organizations than can poor countries that may prefer to limit neoliberals' influence. The UN Development Programme reports that 15 African countries have no representatives at the World Trade Organization (WTO) headquarters, while another 16 have fewer than 3, and these delegates must cover their country's work at the more than 20 international organizations based in Geneva. In contrast, the U.S. delegation consists of 14 staff people devoted strictly to WTO work. Rich countries also tend to include corporate representatives on their trade delegations and advisory panels while excluding representation from organized labor and other sectors of civil society. For instance, a study of U.S. trade advisory committees found that of 111 members, 2 were from labor unions and none represented consumers or environmental groups.[11] Ninety-two members were from individual companies and 16 from industry associations (Ostry 2007; UNDP 2002: 68).

In their competition with challengers, actors in neoliberal networks in many contexts also have advantages in their abilities to use national courts to counter movement attacks. For instance, in Britain, the McDonald's corporation sued their critics, claiming that activist pamphlets detailing the harmful effects of the fast food industry on the global South, on the natural environment, and on human health constituted libel against the company (Meade 2005). Although the company ultimately lost the case, the financial costs of such trials to defendants can have a chilling effect on the decisions of other activists to make similar claims against corporate practices. The financial resources available to proponents of neoliberalism allow them far greater access to most courts than most social movements enjoy. Moreover, for businesses such costs are considered part of the operating costs of business and are included in operating budgets in the form of legal retainers and personnel. In some cases, these costs can even be deducted from a company's taxes. For activists, however, the costs of litigation are often paid for out of their personal bank accounts, and the litigation process can take enormous personal tolls on families and activist groups (Pring and Canan 1996).

Targets of these rival transnational networks are primarily government agencies at the national and international levels. Often the networks take aim at many governments at once, even as they seek to generate international standards such as global trade or environmental agreements that will help support uniform practices across many governments. Transnational corporations are also the focus of some groups within the democratic globalization network. A grassroots, or bottom-up, approach to social change leads popular groups to encourage individuals to adopt practices in their daily lives that mirror the broader social changes movements seek. Such "lifestyle politics" include boycotts of companies that engage in particularly undesirable practices, support for businesses that engage in fair labor or environmentally friendly practices, and investment strategies that reinforce these same pressures (Bennett 2004). Others in this network may target transnational corporations as part of a broader attempt to undermine the legitimacy and to disrupt the smooth operation and sustainability of neoliberalism.

Mass Media

An important piece of the story in figure 2.1 is the mass media. In the diagram, I have placed the mass media largely outside of both the alternative and neoliberal globalization networks, but there is in fact some overlap with both networks—although far more with the neoliberal one. We can consider the mass media to include any communications source that is accessible on a regular basis by a broad public. One most commonly thinks of newspapers and broadcast television and radio media, but increasingly important are Internet sources, including blogs and podcasts (Bennett 2003; Kielbowicz and Scherer 1986). While in most democratic societies the mass media are formally independent of governments, in practice governments maintain important influences over media content through regulatory functions such as establishing rules of fairness and regulating broadcast licensing, media content, and industry consolidation (Byerly 2006). Also, public monies are used to support public interest (noncommercial) broadcasting in many countries, even though neoliberal trends and competition from commercial media have reduced such public programming worldwide. In recent years the mass media have become more commercialized—that is, more geared toward generating profits than producing other benefits such as an informed public—at the same time as they are becoming more globalized and centralized. Today, just a handful of companies control the vast majority of the world market in news, entertainment, and telecommunications.[12]

A commercial or profit-seeking media establishment has vested interests in promoting the aims of the neoliberal globalization network. Thus, we would expect to find important overlaps between major media outlets and this network. On the other hand, we would expect hostility among commercial media outlets toward the ideas and actions of the democratic globalization network, given that the latter resists the consumerist culture upon which global capitalism depends.[13] At the same time, however, the commercial practices of media conglomerates may alienate professional journalists and lead some to bring skills and knowledge to the democratic globalization network. Indeed, the recent flourishing of blogs, alternative media sources, and published as well as online critical analyses of mainstream media reporting may at least partly reflect this.

As we will see in further detail in chapter 7, movements are not wholly dependent on the commercial media to communicate their ideas. They can also communicate to a wide audience through a variety of alternative media as well as through societal organizations. To the extent that they succeed in nurturing critical communities and other spaces of open, critical inquiry spreading their framings of social problems, they help give people a more critical perspective on the information conveyed through commercial media sources (see, e.g., Gamson 1992). Moreover, by working more consciously to mobilize a cultural fraction of civil society groups and individuals into critical communities or communities of discourse, change advocates can help spread to a broader public ideas about the unacknowledged costs of global capitalism and the existence of alternatives to it. This cultural and organizational work is key to the struggle between these rival networks.

Conclusion

Observers of the contemporary movement for a more just and equitable world have described this as a "movement of movements" (Mertes 2004). Others have used the metaphor of the rhizome to describe the ways ideas and tactics flow, like underground root systems, across spaces to unite this highly diverse and geographically scattered constellation of social change advocates. As Escobar explains, "the metaphor of rhizomes suggests networks of heterogeneous elements that grow in unplanned directions, following the real-life situations they encounter" (2003: 352). Khasnabish further elaborates on this metaphor:

> what the rhizome does is assert the profound and unfixed complexity of social realities, it reminds us that the world is not composed of discrete identities but rather is constituted by the connections between these elements. Thus, socio-political analysis ceases to be a process of interrogating identity, institutions, or any other fixed form and instead becomes a matter of understanding socio-political space as continually reproduced by connection and interaction. (2005: 250)

What these observers describe is a multifaceted and multicentered clustering of efforts to challenge predominant discourses and practices in the global economy. These efforts respond to the opportunities and challenges in their environments, offering the movements they advance the advantage of "distributed intelligence" (Escobar 2003: 355).

Linked through shared ideology, practices, organizations, and symbols, many groups operating through dense webs of horizontal ties can collectively challenge globalized capital in ways that no single effort alone could ever hope to do. These are the Lilliputians seeking to restrain Gulliver with millions of threads (Brecher et al. 2000).[14] The concept of networks helps capture the vast diversity among those seeking a more democratic world. The complexities of global interdependence and the vastness of the neoliberal project require challengers to respond quickly and adeptly if they are to succeed. A network, what Escobar (2003: 351) calls the "basic architecture of complexity," is how challengers to global neoliberalism organize and view themselves.

But opponents of the global "movement of movements," or the democratic globalization network as I am calling it here, also share the network form. This is likely due to the fact that they operate in similar environments and therefore must respond to similar pressures, opportunities, and constraints. Despite the vast differences in the organizational capacities of each network, we find some basic similarities in their forms and functions, and examining these more closely may lead to insights into how to better challenge global neoliberalism. I thus adopt in this book the concept of rival transnational networks to identify the collections of diverse actors working to promote each distinct vision of globalization, identifying some important differences in the capacities and mobilizing opportunities of each competing network. Each network can be seen to have organizational, political, technical, and cultural fractions, and these fractions create an informal division of labor within the network. Networks vary in the extent to which they can coordinate and control their participants.

While the economic resources and political influence of the neoliberal network give it distinct advantages over its rival, this network is far from united, and indeed it is populated by people for whom an appeal to basic values such as human rights and dignity may in the end become persuasive. Proponents of democratic globalization might learn ways to advance their interests by thinking about how each network's economic base, political organization, and culture-ideology is structured and reproduced. Can we think of ways to strengthen these important organizing foundations within the democratic globalization network? Moreover, are there ways to challenge the strength of the neoliberal globalization network? This requires thinking about how to create sustainable and substantial resources to support the ideals of democracy and multilateralism that are at the core of the democratic globalization network. It also demands that we learn more about how to reinforce solidarity, inclusiveness, participation, and sustainability within political organizations.

Finally, more deliberate cultural work is required to amplify the values of democracy, cooperation, and community over the neoliberal values of profit, competition, and individualism. By comparing proponents of a more just global order with their global capitalist rivals, it becomes clear that there are important differences in how each network's cultural component is integrated into its broader efforts. While the growth imperative and culture of consumerism permeates the neoliberal network and helps structure the activities of its diverse components, there is no such cultural cohesiveness in the work of the democratic globalization network. More explicit efforts to integrate an emphasis on human rights and core democratic values into the democratic globalization network's broader strategy would enhance its ability to challenge neoliberalism.

The following chapter describes the global political context in which these two rival networks operate, including the different institutional settings of the UN, the global financial institutions, the range of actors present, and the rules and strategies that shape global politics.

CHAPTER THREE

Politics in a Global System

The rival networks discussed in the previous chapter must compete on a global stage. This stage includes national governments that are enmeshed in an extensive and deepening network of ties to other governments and international institutions (Rothman and Oliver 2002; Slaughter 2004a). Any attempt to understand how proponents of competing global visions gain political influence must therefore account not only for political processes within countries, but also for the multiple links among governments and other actors in this broader global system. This chapter provides an overview of how the global institutional context structures opportunities for political action at local and national levels as well as transnationally. It also explores some of the tensions between economic and political forms of globalization and how these are manifest in global institutions. We begin with a brief look at how interactions between social movements and states have shaped the modern interstate system.

Social Movements and the Nation-State System

In *From Mobilization to Revolution,* Charles Tilly argues that social movements "grew up with national politics" (1978: 313). As modern nation-states emerged in Europe, he argues, they encouraged the formation of new groups demanding new rights or material advantages. And as political decisions of importance to citizens became the domain of increasingly remote political authorities, citizens' groups had to adapt their organizational strategies accordingly: "The distinctive contribution of the national state was to shift the political advantage to contenders who could mount a challenge on a very large scale . . . in a way that demonstrated, or even used, their ability to intervene seriously in regular national politics" (Tilly 1984: 310). This understanding holds that groups seeking to advance change have been influenced in fundamental ways by other forces in their political environments. So we cannot understand the modern national state without appreciating the ways it has been defined by struggles between diverse groups. This dynamic and reciprocal relationship between social movements, states, and other political actors is one that extends into contemporary global politics as well.

One important driver of social movement emergence was the need that newly emerging states had to mobilize armies to defend their territorial claims against potential intrusions from other emergent states. To raise armies, political authorities needed soldiers and gold. And over time, they needed more soldiers and more gold as technological advances increased the destructiveness of warfare. They also needed to build organizational structures to collect taxes and to provide the social services demanded by taxpayers. Thus, the emergence of the national state as we know it grew out of sometimes contentious interactions between elites who controlled military power and those with the economic and human resources to support their growing military and government bureaucracies (Markoff 1996; Tilly 1990).

The dependence that state authorities had upon the resources of people within their borders meant that these people could exert some influence over them through their decisions about whether or not to cooperate with state claims on their crops, money, and lives. And it is this tension that led to a process of give-and-take, whereby the state expanded its military capabilities while also providing a growing array of services and avenues for political representation to its citizens. This conflict also led to a shift from more hierarchical, aristocratic societies whose leaders governed by divine authority to more decentralized, egalitarian, and contractually based democratic societies. The authority of democratic governments derived not from a divine right of kings but from the consent of the governed (Markoff 1996: 1–5).

This understanding of state development emerges from analyses of European history, and the experiences of countries that were colonized by imperialist Western states differ from this in important ways. In countries of the West, states and social groups developed gradually, and there was some degree of balance between the relative strength of governments and other social groups. However, in later-emerging states—and particularly those that were former colonies—the competition between states, capitalists, and other social actors was strongly influenced by the self-interested intervention of Western governments and their capitalist allies. Such intervention generated strong, repressive militaries and weak states that were dependent for their survival on foreign aid. Thus, postcolonial states are far less autonomous than Western states, since many still depend upon Western military assistance and often lack strong civil societies and popular legitimacy. They are extremely vulnerable to pressures from richer countries and are therefore less able to determine policies within their borders and to shape international policies.

There are four key ideas one should take from this brief account of relations between social movements, national states, and the interstate system. First, states as we know them are a relatively recent form of social organization, and they have not always, nor will they necessarily continue to be, the principal way of organizing social life. Second, interactive, competitive processes surrounding the articulation, defense, and promotion of the interests of different social groups have shaped the evolution of both states and social movements. Third, states themselves differ dramatically in the amount and forms of power they can exert. And fourth, states are embedded in a competitive world system of actors that includes both other states and a growing array of non-state actors. This system affects relations between social movements and governments in important ways. The task of this book is to uncover these complex relationships between states, social movements, and the global system as we seek to understand the processes of social change and people's role in them.

National Politics in a Global System

Rather than privileging the state as the principal or necessarily primary arena in which social movements operate, this book emphasizes how multilateral institutional processes help to redefine the boundaries between national and international politics. While states remain important and even central in this model, greater attention is paid to the ways global institutions and processes simultaneously shape both states and other political actors, including social movements (and vice versa). Global institutions affect not only the political and legal contexts that define opportunities and constraints for states and all other actors, but they also influence how those actors view themselves and their interests (Campbell 2004; DiMaggio and Powell 1991; Meyer et al. 1997). Thus, the practices of states vis-à-vis their own citizens are increasingly constrained by transnational processes (see, e.g., Reimann 2002; Sassen 1998). Indeed, the notion of a state itself is irrelevant without an interstate context of other states able to recognize the rights and legitimacy of a given national authority. Collectivities define themselves in terms of broader sets of relationships, and an interstate system provides the context that encourages and facilitates the elaboration of transnational identities (Boli and Thomas 1999). As Buss and Hermann conclude,

To dismiss transnational activism as relevant only in terms of domestic politics overlooks the extent to which international law and policy are important realms in their own right. The "international" is more than just the space "outside" of the domestic. It has taken on a significance as, among other things, a site of struggle over the shape and meaning of social relations in the context of global change. (2003: 134)

Gay Seidman's analysis of antiapartheid and labor activism leads her to conclude that activists are capable of articulating multiple identities in the course of their struggles, or "shifting the ground" on which they work, moving quite easily across national borders. The fact that many conflicts are oriented around national political structures is merely an artifact of the institutional arrangements in which people are embedded: "the institutional fact that international bodies are generally composed of national representatives forces potentially global identities into national frames. But it need not blind us to the possibility that activists might under other circumstances frame their concerns more globally" (2000: 347). At the same time, we must avoid another conceptual pitfall of thinking that globally relevant politics occurs only in transnational contexts. For instance, looking at women's activism in India, Subramaniam and her colleagues found that analyses of the global downplay the extent to which local settings manifest global politics: "[Although] global processes are often viewed as taking place in a world context, above nation states, networks can be anchored between and across all borders (villages, districts, states, and nations) involving actors and groups at the grassroots" (Subramaniam et al. 2003: 335). Thus, Moghadam concludes that "the appropriate unit of analysis must combine global, regional and local" (2000: 80). These observations suggest that we must relax our traditional notions of borders and instead see states as just a bundle of comparatively dense networks of relations that have a variety of diverse ties to similar national networks and to other transnational actors around the world. This networked, multilayered political structure encourages many citizens and activists to develop what della Porta and colleagues (2006) refer to as "flexible identities" and "multiple belongings." As they do so, they are helping people to imagine themselves as part of diverse communities that transcend conventional political boundaries. They thereby contribute to the construction of new global visions and new possibilities for transnational politics.

Through their interactions with states and other global actors, social movements help shape the course of globalization. By cultivating transnational identities and alliances and by appealing to international norms, they strengthen transnational political institutions over time. They can press states to conform to international agreements, or they can resist new multilateral arrangements that infringe on democratic rights. Predominant, state-centered perspectives downplay the extent to which states are part of a broader social order, thereby making invisible the ways non-state actors influence world politics. In this study, I document some of the specific ways that social movement actors have helped shape both the content and structure of the global political order. But before doing so, I outline a framework for analyzing global politics as a system of interconnected political and institutional arrangements called "complex multilateralism."

Complex Multilateralism

The global political system is characterized by nearly two hundred national governments interacting in a variety of ways as they attempt to create a stable, predictable international environment that can benefit their "national interests." So governments might form bilateral, or one-on-one agreements with other countries, or they might join in multi-state regional arrangements that incorporate the concerns of states in a particular part of the world (such as Asia or Africa). More complex multilateral arrangements involving larger numbers of states include the UN and its complex of agencies and treaty bodies. All forms of international cooperation have expanded in recent decades to address a growing array of issues ranging from environmental protection to public health to scientific coordination. Multilateralism, then, is a response to global interdependence. And in turn, global institutions are encouraging the expansion of efforts to strengthen regional intergovernmental organizations (Farrell et al. 2005; Kim and Schmitter 2005; Malamud 2004; Massamba et al. 2004).

Recent decades have also brought greater strength and autonomy for multilateral institutions governing global economic relations, including the World Trade Organization (WTO), the World Bank, and the International Monetary Fund (IMF). While at least two of these organizations are considered part of the UN system, in practice they all operate independently and often in contradiction to the values of the UN Charter (see chapter 9). The expansion of intergovernmental organizations increases the possible venues for any group promoting a particular policy aim. Thus, we see that as global-level trade negotiations stalled in the late 1990s, the United States shifted its energies back to regional and bilateral contexts where it could maintain greater control. Thus it promoted the expansion of the North American Free Trade Agreement (NAFTA) to Central America (CAFTA) and South America (Free Trade Area of the Americas). Such venue-shopping possibilities are available to non-state actors as well, although it is the richest states and corporations that typically can take full advantage of such opportunities.

Robert O'Brien and his colleagues (2000) use the term *complex multilateralism* to describe the processes at work in shaping global affairs today. This concept expands traditional notions of multilateralism used by political scientists, and it accounts for how interactions among business actors, international organizations, and civil society groups shape national and global politics.[1] The concept highlights the limits of traditional approaches's emphasis on the primacy of the state, which tends to downplay the importance of economic and civil society actors in global politics. Complex multilateralism sees states' (and other actors') interests, preferences, and policy options as constructed in the course of interactions with other actors. While states are still important players, they are not the only important and influential ones.

The institutional context helps define the range of policy options and may privilege certain actors or outcomes. But a key idea here is that politics at both the national (domestic) and international levels influence the ultimate policy outcomes. It is not just national governments (or collections thereof) that determine the course of world affairs. National policy, moreover, cannot be understood independently of its transnational context. Examining politics in the European Union (EU), Marks and his colleagues observed that, in this situation of multilevel governance, states "no longer provide the sole interface between supra- and sub-national arenas, and they share, rather than monopolize, control over many activities that take place in their respective territories" (Marks et al. 1994: 6). Because of the interdependencies inherent in international politics, international institutions are not, according to Marks and his colleagues, "simple hierarchies," but consensus-seeking bodies. In other words, their authority relies not on their ability to force all members to comply but rather on the perception that particular policies are both consistent with the long-term interests of the larger community and result from a fair process that is respectful of individual members' basic needs. Thus, the need to generate consensus around multilateral responses to transnational problems creates openings for groups wielding more persuasive—as opposed to coercive—forms of power, including those working to shape public opinion and to mobilize popular groups (Boli 1999).

Of course, the consensus-seeking nature of international institutions does not mean that international politics is necessarily equitable, fair, and cooperative. Domestic-level politics in some countries—particularly those with the greatest economic, political, and/or military influence—have a more profound impact on global affairs than those of smaller, less influential countries. However, these powerful states are constrained by the fact that they operate in an interdependent system that requires cooperation on many diverse issues. By overusing coercive forms of power, these states can undermine their "soft power," or their ability to win the cooperation necessary to manage other global problems (Nye 2002; Sands 2005). Moreover, it invites other actors to challenge their military dominance, thereby destabilizing the entire system.

The international system effectively creates linkages among different, interdependent issues so that a country's use of coercive power to address a problem in one area can lead to a loss of trust and legitimacy that compromises its ability to win supporters for its goals in other areas. Friedman and colleagues refer to this as a "sovereignty bargain," whereby any government decision in a multilateral context involves a trade-off among four distinct elements of national sovereignty: autonomy, capacity, legitimacy vis-à-vis states, and legitimacy vis-à-vis civil society. Prioritizing autonomy through unilateral and often coercive action can mean a reduction in a state's capacity to muster support from other states for tasks that require collaboration, such as breaking up transnational criminal networks or protecting fisheries. Privileging autonomy can also cost legitimacy. What becomes clear is that, as global politics includes more issues and actors, and particularly as a broader public pays attention to these processes, the sovereignty bargain makes autonomous state action more costly and civil society actors more relevant in international decision processes (Friedman et al. 2005).

Another important component of complex multilateralism is that international institutions play key roles in defining the possibilities for different actors to articulate and advance their interests. Because they are transnational in scope, they encourage actors to build transnational alliances and envision their interests and goals in a broader, transnational if not global context (Bandy and Smith 2005; Buss and Herman 2003). By creating forums for states to interact with each other and articulate their particular concerns, they encourage greater awareness of different views of global problems, and they encourage a search for mutually beneficial solutions. Analyses such as those of Alger's study of delegations to one of the early UN General Assemblies (1963), Parsons's analysis of the gradual acceptance of an "idea of Europe" (2003), and Risse and his colleagues' analysis of a "norms spiral" in UN human rights institutions (1999) show how multilateral institutions can generate important changes in how actors perceive the world and their role in it.

Complex multilateralism produces five key features that affect global policy making (O'Brien et al. 2000). First, global institutions create diverse opportunities and limitations for particular policy aims. Specifically, the UN and its agencies are comparatively open and responsive to civil society groups and to social agendas. In contrast, the global financial institutions—the IMF, the WTO, and (to a lesser extent) the World Bank—have been far more restrictive. The International Labor Organization (ILO) offers some openings for civil society (notably organized labor) and more socially oriented agendas.

Second, complex multilateralism generates important differences among major participants over key interests and goals. This signals opportunities for challengers and authorities to mobilize new alliances that can take advantage of divisions among elites. Third, the conflicting interests among key powerholders tend to generate compromise positions that produce ambiguous results. This means that the enactment of policies and the emphasis of particular goals and values will depend upon the ability of proponents to mobilize sustained pressure on governments and international officials to enforce policy decisions and to otherwise follow through on public declarations.

A fourth feature of complex multilateralism is that states differ dramatically in their capacity to influence global policy processes, and analysts must account for these differences. This is in contrast to much conventional international relations literature, which implies a connection between the legal equality of states and their practical influence. Finally, complex multilateralism has expanded the global policy agenda to include more social issues. This latter result is most certainly from the growing participation by civil society groups in processes of global governance, but also from the need to establish the legitimacy of emerging institutional structures.

Global Capitalism and Economic Globalization

The institutional stage is shaped in fundamental ways by underlying economic relations, or what sociologists have called the "world-system." It is useful when thinking about global integration to distinguish between economic and other forms of globalization. Political globalization, for instance, involves the creation and expansion of international political institutions like the UN or the EU, and socio-cultural integration refers to expanding flows of ideas and culture across national boundaries, often through webs of interpersonal associations. Tarrow (2005) and Daly (2002) reserve the term *globalization* to refer to global economic integration, which is essentially the expansion of global capitalism. This is the form of global integration advanced by neoliberal globalizers. *Internationalization*, in contrast, is favored by democratic globalizers, and it refers to transnational political relationships and institutions. In practice, the two are happening simultaneously with mutual impacts (Munck 2002). Nevertheless, we must keep in mind the different logics and pressures at work in each framework so that we can identify better ways to structure relationships between economic and political globalization that might generate more equitable and sustainable outcomes than the current system.

While the interstate system emphasizes national political boundaries and identities, world-system perspectives see identities as primarily determined by the ability (or lack thereof) to control material resources. So rather than focus on countries as primary actors, these analysts emphasize economic classes and interests. In practice, world system analyses tend to link particular classes with specific groups of countries, and thus "core" countries are those that first experienced the industrial revolution and were able to use this to their advantage in obtaining access to the natural resources and markets of later-industrializing countries, known as the "periphery," or the intermediate "semi-periphery" (see, e.g., Chase-Dunn 1998; Wallerstein 2004).

Relations of global economic domination were most stark in the colonial era, when imperial powers established brutal and repressive colonial empires designed to most efficiently extract resources from the territories and peoples they conquered. World-system theorists explain imperial conquest and colonization as a logical consequence of the need for capitalist economies to constantly expand (Wallerstein 1976; Wolf 1982). As the availability of resources for production and markets for manufactured goods in core territories declined, capitalist producers needed to look outside national boundaries to maintain high levels of profit. They often worked directly with national governments to pursue their aims, and states seeking revenues to support armies provided institutional and material support to aid capital accumulation.

While colonialism has officially been denounced as an economic policy, world system theorists argue that colonialism has had lasting impacts on the structure of the global economic order, helping to sustain the inequities we see in the world today. Such neocolonialism may be less overtly violent, but it is reinforced by institutional arrangements that continue to allow the core countries—and in particular the wealthy classes within those countries—to dominate the periphery through a variety of mechanisms, most notably unequal trade relations and debt (Bello 1999; McMichael 2003; Stiglitz 2003).

The world-system perspective is important for its emphasis on questions about power and control of resources. While political institutions are designed to establish agreed-upon rules for making collective decisions and enacting policies, they typically reflect and reproduce inequalities present at their founding. Some groups—namely the elites in early-industrializing core states—had a stronger influence on shaping the rules of the interstate game than did later-industrializing states, many of which were colonies when major international agreements were established. Complex multilateralism, then, is a system of interdependent and unequal relationships among diverse political actors and institutions. We need to be sensitive to how some actors' disproportionate control over material resources affects the ongoing operations of political institutions. For instance, it is doubtful that peripheral states can freely exercise their rights to vote in international institutions when a vote against certain core countries might cost them valuable trade relationships or aid and investment finance.[2]

More recent work in this tradition has emphasized the role of a transnational capitalist class as a dominant actor in global politics (Robinson 2004; Sklair 2001). The transnational capitalist class is the main proponent of neoliberal globalization, and its access to resources and political leverage has grown markedly since the early 1970s. It has become a more self-conscious global actor in this era as it has cultivated alliances within governments and international agencies to expand its global agenda (Sklair 2001). Robinson attributes the emergence of what he calls a "transnational state" to the efforts of this class of actors. For Robinson, a transnational state is a network of integrated national states and international organizations, or "those institutions and practices in global society that maintain, defend, and advance the emergent hegemony of this global bourgeoisie and its project of constructing a new global capitalist historic bloc" (Robinson 2004: 100).

The addition of the notion of class to the study of global politics and economics helps us better understand how power serves to reinforce certain norms and relations while marginalizing others. Why, for instance, did the 1990s witness a global rise in neoliberal policies despite the presence of competing models for political and economic organization? How did globalizing capitalists win out over capitalists with more nationally oriented ambitions? An understanding of the transnational capitalist class and the sources of its influence over this time period can help us identify possibilities for advancing policies that advance social goals to which the transnational capitalist class is either indifferent or hostile, such as equity, sustainability, diversity, inclusion, and human rights. Drawing from the work of Sklair, Robinson, and others, we can conclude that the neoliberal shift of the 1990s is a result of efforts led by the transnational capitalist class to carry out what Robinson (2004) calls a "revolution from above," persuading or coercing members of national governments and international institutions to adopt its vision of globalization (more on this in chapter 4).

While the transnational capitalist class is clearly a dominant actor on the world stage, this class and the transnational state it advances is not monolithic, nor is it alone in promoting a vision for how the world should be governed. As the earlier discussion has made clear, there is much debate over what principles and structures should govern the world community and whether and how much to integrate national communities into a global economic and political order. And while there are clear connections between the interests of the transnational capitalist class and the actions of certain global institutions, most notably the IMF, the World Bank, and the WTO, these institutions are not the only ones through which governments work to coordinate policies and cooperate on global problems. As Tarrow observes (2005: 18), "combining Polanyi and Tilly's insights, we can say that the capitalist economy and the consolidated national state were interlocked institutional expressions of Polanyi's movement and counter movement." Other institutions such as the UN provide ideals and principles for organizing a transnational state that can challenge the neoliberal globalization project, providing a modern parallel to the double-movement envisioned by Polanyi (e.g., Korzeniewicz and Smith 2001; Munck 2002). The challenge for success of a counter-neoliberal movement will depend upon the capacities of democratic globalizers to mobilize international institutions and agendas around their own vision of a world whose economic life is embedded within a globalized society.

Diverse interstate organizations, national governments, and other global political actors help define the global system of complex multilateralism, which is shaped by interactions among these varied actors. Social movements are just one of these global actors, and they interact with states and other actors as they seek to promote changes such as human rights, peace, and a sustainable and healthy natural environment.[3] They build alliances with some actors in order to strengthen their hand against others. They may choose from a number of different institutional contexts in which they pursue their interests, and these choices, in turn, affect possibilities for advancing their aims. Understanding these various institutional arenas and global actors will help us uncover the range of possibilities and challenges that an increasingly global polity offers.

The Global Institutional Arena
Global Political Actors

Global political and economic institutions define who are considered appropriate actors, and they thereby affect the ways people organize themselves and portray their collective identities. For instance, the UN initially had just fifty-one members, and much of the world was still subjugated under colonial legacies. These former colonies had little choice but to form national governments resembling those of their conquerors, and this often meant that they had to imagine themselves as part of the geographically defined communities created by their occupiers. Because imperial powers wanted to exploit the resources of colonies, they often actively exacerbated conflicts among diverse ethnic groups in the territories they conquered in order to enhance their ability to control local populations. They did little to ensure that these places could one day become cohesive and effective national states, and in fact they fueled ethnic divisions that continue to plague nation-building efforts in former colonies (e.g., Chua 2003; Tilly 1990).

The rules of international politics also help reinforce the power of some global actors relative to others. For instance, the five permanent, veto-wielding members of the UN Security Council have far more influence in global affairs than the other 187 members of the UN. The rich countries that finance the World Bank and the IMF have far more influence on people in borrowing countries than do the governments of those countries themselves. And in international organizations, national governments—democratic or not—are privileged over other organizations as the only representatives of people living within particular boundaries. This section briefly describes the major (though certainly not all) political actors in the global system, identifying how global processes affect their operations and identities.

States are the principal organizational actors in global politics, and their authority derives largely from their control over political and economic activities within particularly recognized geographic boundaries. But the expansion of capitalism and technological innovation as well as changing environmental conditions have made it impossible for states to effectively control conditions within their borders without attempts to cooperate with other states. Thus, I spoke earlier of the "sovereignty bargain," which recognizes the multifaceted nature of national sovereignty. Legally, the concept of national sovereignty presumes that every state has the rights and ability to determine its policies independently. But in practice, the independence of states is largely a myth, with interdependencies creating very real constraints on autonomous policy making. Even at local levels, government actors are finding it necessary to cultivate links to international counterparts in order to govern effectively (Slaughter 2004b). As they do so, they challenge the primacy of national governments in global policy arenas.

Interdependencies affect states differently, and some states are more susceptible to international pressure than others. For instance, the previous section described how global South states are less autonomous than their Northern counterparts in terms of their internal economic policies. And countries sitting near sea level—such as small island states and countries like the Netherlands—are keenly aware of how their control over their very existence depends upon international environmental cooperation. The very existence of the international institutions described above attests to the needs governments have to manage interdependencies of all kinds. While I do not want to argue that the state is becoming less important because of these interdependencies, it is clear that the role of states is changing alongside global processes. States must increasingly subject policy choices to external influences, bargaining their autonomy in exchange for greater control and legitimacy. Thus, our analysis of political conflicts in a global context must account for the ways that states are being redefined through global political integration.

Intergovernmental organizations are created through formal international negotiations. The UN is a universal (global) example of this kind of organization, and its many related agencies help coordinate national policies around many issues, including public health, trade, environment, military policy, and social policy. These organizations are often very specialized (such as the International Postal Union or the World Health Organization [WHO]) although some are forums for the routine discussion of a variety of issues (such as the UN General Assembly). Regional organizations, such as the EU, the Organization of American States (OAS), or the African Union, help countries within a particular geographic territory respond to common interests and problems. These regional groups have been gaining in importance more recently (Wiest and Smith 2007). The EU has become more consolidated especially since the late 1980s, and perhaps in response to this, other regions such as Africa and Latin America have enhanced their own regional coordination efforts (Kim and Schmitter 2005; Massamba et al. 2004).

Transnational corporations are the core organizational base of the transnational capitalist class, and they are key players in the neoliberal globalization network. They are business organizations operating in multiple countries to produce or distribute goods or services for a profit. They can be privately held or publicly traded. While formally based in a single country (mostly in the North), their main operations take place in multiple locations, and often very little actual production takes place in the corporate headquarters. Increasingly, they encompass truly global production processes, as technology and international financial and legal developments have facilitated their efforts to move different aspects of production to the most cost-effective locales (Bonacich and Applebaum 2000; Moody 1997; Munck 2002). While globalization has encouraged a proliferation of transnational corporations, it also has promoted greater consolidation among corporations, and corporate mergers and acquisitions have grown exponentially from around a hundred in 1980 to more than thirty-five thousand in 1999 (Renner 2006).

Nongovernmental organizations (NGOs) is a term most commonly used in UN parlance to refer to nonprofit voluntary associations of citizens that are organized for some public purpose, including recreational, professional, religious, or advocacy aims. Some people also use the term *civil society groups* to refer to this subset of global actors. While many civil society groups remain uninvolved in politics and advocacy work, a subset of advocacy NGOs have long been active in global-level politics, and they are becoming increasingly so. NGOs are also increasingly organized across national borders, as new technologies facilitate international communication and travel. These groups have come to play important roles within global institutions, raising awareness of problems and providing information on government compliance with international agendas.

The UN System

Although the UN is a relatively young body—it arrived on the scene in 1945 following World War II—it inherited much older multilateral arrangements, such as the Geneva Convention on the Laws of War (which dates back to 1863) and the International Labor Organization (formed as part of the UN's predecessor, the League of Nations). The UN Charter is clear in identifying this body as the principal framework within which all other multilateral arrangements are governed. Thus, regional bodies, multilateral treaties negotiated outside the formal UN process, and global financial institutions are all (legally if not in practice) subsumed within the UN system (Urquhart and Childers 1996).

The United States was a leading force in the creation of the UN, as it sought to provide a more stable and predictable global political and economic order in the wake of two devastating world wars. Although the sentiments expressed in the UN Charter are quite noble, most analysts acknowledge that the United States promoted the UN organization mainly in an effort to ensure its own continued predominance in world affairs. This has hindered the effectiveness of the global body throughout its history. In particular, the structure of the UN Security Council is effectively a "dictatorship of the great powers" (Gowan 2004), with the victors of World War II (including the now nonexistent Union of Soviet Socialist Republics) retaining permanent membership status along with the exclusive rights to veto any Security Council resolution. Despite these persistent flaws, the UN has proved to be a crucial "global meeting place" (Anand 1999) where national leaders can work to identify common problems and to investigate and debate solutions. By bringing delegates from many countries together on a routine basis, the UN provides vital spaces for them to discuss emerging issues before they become more complicated conflicts. And beyond the formal negotiation sessions, the UN helps delegates to better understand the perspectives and interests of their counterparts elsewhere, creating an important basis for trust and cooperation.

The main deliberative body of the UN is the General Assembly. Here every member government has a single vote. The General Assembly meets annually in New York City during the fall, although it can schedule additional sessions as necessary. Its resolutions, while significant in that they reflect the majority of world opinion, do not carry legally binding force, and can only urge governments to take particular actions. But the General Assembly does have important influences on the UN organizational agenda and can refer issues to other UN bodies, including the Security Council. The Security Council is charged with addressing matters directly relevant to peace and security. It is the only body that can issue resolutions that are legally binding on all member governments. This is why the debate about Security Council membership is so crucial to the future of the global system. Since all governments are being forced to adhere to Security Council resolutions, they want to ensure that this body adequately represents the whole range of member country interests. The current Security Council, with just ten non-permanent members and five veto-wielding permanent members, hardly reflects the diversity of views in the UN's 192-country membership. Without efforts to remedy this, the UN risks alienating a majority of its members who may simply refuse to acknowledge the legitimacy of Security Council decisions. The Economic and Social Council houses the bulk of the operational work of the UN, and it is charged by the General Assembly with taking up debates on and coordinating responses to problems initially raised there.

As he worked with key allies to promote the organization of the UN, U.S.

President Franklin D. Roosevelt realized that he would need to win over a U.S. Congress that had derailed earlier U.S.-led attempts at multilateral institution building by refusing to join the League of Nations. Thus, he provided opportunities for citizens' associations to be part of early planning around the UN organization, and these groups were part of the U.S. delegation to the UN founding conference in San Francisco. The idea was that popular participation in the process of building the UN would create pressures on legislators to support the initiative. While this ultimately worked, it meant that citizens' groups were in a position to argue for a greater role in the international body. Analysts of the UN's founding have documented the important role that these groups played in establishing Article 71 of the UN Charter, which allows NGOs to establish "consultative" relationships with the UN (Willetts 1996). They also attribute the human rights language in the Charter to pressure from these groups (Chatfield 1997; Gaer 1996). These two provisions have helped legitimate civil society groups' participation in global politics, and they provide some (however limited) leverage and protection for social change advocates against states who oppose their aims.

Civil society groups can gain "consultative status" with the UN's Economic and Social Council (ECOSOC) through a process defined in Article 71 of the UN Charter. All international organizations whose work corresponds with the UN Charter mission may request consultative status, but a select committee of government representatives must approve their applications. Also, groups in consultative status are required to submit regular reports to demonstrate how they are working to support the UN's work. Paralleling growth in transnational associations in general, the numbers of groups in consultative status with ECOSOC more than quadrupled between 1970 and the mid-1990s to more than 1,600 organizations (Willetts 1996). Today more than 2,700 organizations have consultative status with ECOSOC.[4] This expansion in participation by civil society groups, coupled with their increased skills at using international negotiating processes to advance social change goals, has led some governments to call for limits on consultative arrangements and other measures to restrict civil society groups' involvement at the UN (Willetts 2000).

However, some governments support civil society involvement, in part because they recognize the legitimacy these groups bring to the work of that international body and because they have found these groups helpful in advancing some of their own agendas in the UN. In the mid-1990s the UN launched an initiative to review its consultative procedures with civil society groups, although to date few major changes have been enacted.[5] The review arose, as did previous ones, in response to rising numbers of groups seeking to participate in UN processes, observations that rules of access privileged groups from Western countries, and resistance from governments that were targets of NGO criticism (Charnovitz 1997; Otto 1996). While some governments continue to challenge the rights of their critics to be part of global political processes, governments have generally come to accept the appropriateness and legitimacy of civil society groups' participation at international meetings, and similar, though generally more restrictive, consultative arrangements have been established in the World Bank, the IMF, and the WTO as well as in the G8 richest countries (Charnovitz 1997: 279).

UN GLOBAL CONFERENCES

An important strategy used by the UN to address global problems is to host global conferences. At the suggestion of a member state or of the UN Secretariat, the main legislative body of the UN, the General Assembly, can call for these conferences as a way of focusing world attention on a problem and generating ideas, resources, and political will to address it. Government delegates meeting to discuss issues and to generate plans of action are subject to various kinds of public input and pressure through the conference process. This input can often be quite helpful, as delegates must negotiate on a wide array of topics, and they often lack the time or staff to adequately research all the details of the problem under discussion.

Civil society actors have provided concrete proposals for official declarations emerging from global conferences, and occasionally they are successful in getting a member state to introduce their draft language to the final document. In order to be effective at influencing global conferences, activists must familiarize themselves with the issues being discussed and the variety of state positions on the matter. They have learned over time that attending the conferences themselves is not enough. To have real influence, they must follow the preparatory meetings held well in advance of global conferences to draft the negotiating text and establish the parameters for debate. By attending preparatory conferences, activists have both gained important skills in multilateral negotiating processes and also earned the respect and trust of at least some delegates (Friedman et al. 2005; Joachim 2003; Riles 2001).

Global conferences are unique social spaces. Regardless of their national backgrounds, activists and delegates alike must learn how these spaces are organized and what norms and logics govern them. Of course, this is easier if one comes from privileged economic and educational circumstances and if one is familiar with Western cultural and linguistic traditions, but its global character makes it unlike any national political setting. Global conferences help reinforce multilateralism by fostering commitments to a peculiar set of transnational organizing forms, skills, and activities. They thereby help cultivate global identities. As Riles concluded from her work on transnational organizing for the 1995 UN Women's conference in Beijing, "more than any place or society, what the persons and institutions described here share is a set of informational practices [that include attending meetings, networking, coordinating, fundraising, organizing information, and drafting and redrafting international texts]" (Riles 2001: xv).

Activist groups have a long tradition of organizing conferences that parallel official intergovernmental ones, using these opportunities to expand public participation in transnational dialogues on the problem at hand, to network with other NGOs, and to gather information about government positions and decisions. Because the UN conference structure provides limited time and space for civil society actors to formally address government officials, civil society actors have been forced to develop routines for developing consensus statements. These common positions require extensive amounts of work before the conference itself to identify the shared goals and concerns of participants, but they are useful as methods of articulating civil society concerns to governments and for providing focal points for advocacy work in different countries. Accounts from observers and participants and from a survey of NGOs participating in global conferences document the importance of global conferences as spaces where activists develop their agendas and cultivate shared understandings and the collective identities that underlie them (Foster and Anand 1999; Krut 1997).

The significance of global conferences extends far beyond the groups that actually attend them. Many groups spend months working to develop positions on the conference agenda. They may sign petitions or other NGO joint statements regarding conference debates, often using these statements to shape their own advocacy agendas. In the absence of substantial mainstream media attention to many global conferences, civil society groups are often the only channels of information between global conference arenas and local communities. Activists attending global conferences return home from them energized and eager to report back to their colleagues about the outcomes of global meetings and the new networks that they cultivated at the conferences. Through this process, the strategic thinking and campaigns taken up by many local and national groups are infused with ideas from transnational dialogues taking place alongside global conferences. Such dialogues help identify variations in interests and the objections that people from different regions of the world bring to the topic, contributing to an ongoing process of building relationships and new identities among diverse activist groups.

Importantly, the transnational activities launched at global conferences have not ended when the delegations go home. In fact, for many groups, their work has only begun. The template of action that has become widely internalized by global activists is the conference follow-up and monitoring. As prominent activist and organizer Bella Abzug often stated about the conference processes, "We've had a lot of words on equality. Now we want the music, which is action."[6] What she meant is that, now that governments have reached a final declaration on how they intend to respond to a particular problem, it is up to their citizens to make sure that they actually follow through on these statements. This work requires rigorous attention to details of national governance, but it also encourages transnational connections to facilitate comparisons and for the sharing of strategies and insights into how best to pressure different national governments.

After a rapid sequence of global conferences in the post–Cold War 1990s, the UN—under budgetary and political pressures largely from the United States—moved away from the practice of holding frequent conferences. However, the 2004 report of the Eminent Persons Panel on UN–Civil Society Relations recommended more frequent, if sparing, use of these meetings to expand international understandings and enhance problem-solving efforts (UN 2004). At the same time, the treaties that have emerged out of the 1990s conference processes have generated their own meeting cycles, with many treaties providing for regular, five-year review conferences (often referred to as "+5" meetings). Additionally, the Commission on Sustainable Development was formed at the 1992 UN Conference on Environment and Development (UNCED) to provide a forum for annual consideration of the variety of global environmental concerns raised at that conference. These meetings bring treaty parties together to consider how a problem has evolved over time, to review their compliance with treaty commitments, and to consider new or stronger steps to address the problem. While these meetings are often somewhat specialized, they frequently attract large numbers of activist groups working on the issue. For instance, review conferences for the Nuclear Non-Proliferation Treaty, the World Conference of Women, and the Kyoto Climate Change Protocol have all generated substantial attention from activist groups.

In sum, the UN provides an important focal point for civil society groups of all sorts working to address issues that cross national boundaries. Social movement organizations have made extensive use of opportunities within the UN and have worked both to defend them from government challenges and to expand possibilities for public participation in this and other intergovernmental organizations. As a universal or global organization, the UN can command the attention of groups around the world, facilitating efforts to define transnational agendas.

It provides a common target for groups acting in a variety of national and local political contexts. Also, its consultative status arrangements help certify civil society actors as legitimate players on the international scene. Such credentials serve as an important source of power for groups lacking in more traditional kinds of power, namely money and political authority.

While the UN helps focus and validate popular participation in global politics, civil society groups also help legitimate and strengthen the UN and other international organizations. As we will explore in much greater detail in subsequent chapters, social movements and other civil society groups help to shape international agendas and bring new issues and groups to international attention while improving the effectiveness of international agreements. They do so by monitoring government compliance and enhancing global flows of information relevant to international negotiations and treaties.

The Global Financial System

The global financial institutions, namely the World Bank, the IMF, and the WTO, emerged from a meeting of economists and finance ministers in the summer of 1944 in Bretton Woods, New Hampshire. They were part of a plan to coordinate the world's economies in order to prevent another Great Depression. Unlike the San Francisco meeting that launched the UN, no civil society representatives were present at the Bretton Woods conference (Charnovitz 1997: 249). Firmly in the minds of the forty-four economic planners at this meeting were the devastating experiences of the Great Depression and World War II. The World Bank, officially known as the International Bank for Reconstruction and Development, was designed to help the war-torn countries of Europe by providing low-interest loans that would fill the gap in private lending for costly and high-risk projects such as road building and other infrastructure projects. Its work on development projects in low-income countries of the global South did not begin until the 1970s, when Robert McNamara became its president (Finnemore 1996; Rich 1994).

Unlike the World Bank, the IMF provides short-term loans not for specific development projects, but rather for the purpose of helping promote international trade by stabilizing currency exchange rates between countries. Countries finding that the value of their imported goods exceeds that of their exports can apply for loans from the IMF to meet their short-term cash-flow needs. The WTO grew out of the General Agreement on Tariffs and Trade (GATT), which was formed in lieu of the International Trade Organization envisioned by Bretton Woods planners. Its job is to provide a system of uniform rules to govern global trade, replacing a patchwork system of bilateral (two-state) and regional trade agreements that establish rates at which countries tax goods crossing their borders and otherwise manage trade relations between countries. A formal trade body serves many useful purposes, such as helping governments anticipate the values of what they export and import, stabilizing the economic environment so that producers can anticipate demand for their goods, and providing for the peaceful resolution of trade disputes, which can escalate into more violent conflagrations.[7]

In contrast to the UN, the global financial institutions are far less representative of the world's governments. Voting power in these bodies is determined by the size of each government's financial contribution. Thus, the United States enjoys a 17.5 percent voting power in the IMF, and European countries wield nearly 30 percent. The countries of the global South, which are most subject to the policies of these institutions due to the fact that they tend to be borrowing money from them, have virtually no voice in the governance of the institutions that have a major impact on their national policies (Stiglitz 2003).

The WTO differs from the World Bank and the IMF in that it is at least nominally more "democratic" with regard to governments (not their citizens). As in the UN General Assembly, in the WTO each member government has a single vote. And most decisions are taken by consensus or unanimous approval. However, in practice, a country's influence in the WTO is directly related to its economic power. Poor countries whose national incomes depend upon their ability to export to wealthier and more powerful states are unable to take positions that might threaten their trade relationships. And rich countries do not hesitate to use trade as a weapon to threaten any government that challenges its vital interests in global trade negotiations.

Operationally, too, rich countries have overwhelming advantages over poor ones. They can afford to support large diplomatic staffs at the WTO headquarters in Geneva, enabling them to carefully monitor and advance legislation that most suits their interests (or at least the interests of corporations and domestic producers of exports). Poor governments are woefully understaffed in global trade meetings, making them less able to ensure that trade laws are equitably enforced or to otherwise promote rules that can help them meet their development needs (Jawara and Kwa 2003; Malhotra et al. 2003).[8] Another important aspect of the WTO is its dispute resolution procedure, which makes this organization the only international institution with the ability to effectively and consistently enforce its rulings. The UN, in contrast, has been left without the teeth to enforce its varied and yet crucial agreements on disarmament, peace, and other matters that are important to the international community.

The rich countries exert influence on the global financial institutions not only through their individual economic strength, but also through their concerted efforts to coordinate and advance policies that favor the economic interests of their national elites. A number of formal and informal organizations exist to promote global capitalist interests among rich countries, including groups such as the Organization for Economic Cooperation and Development (OECD), the G8, and the privately organized World Economic Forum. What these groups have in common is that they are forums where government leaders and corporate officials meet on a routine basis to discuss how best to advance their common economic interests. As we will see throughout this book, these groups have been important in advancing the neoliberal globalization agenda.

Poor country governments have little capacity to influence the policies of international financial institutions, but they are far more subject to the influences of these institutions than are their richer counterparts. This reality is a direct consequence of the history of how these countries came to be integrated into an emerging global capitalist economy, namely through colonialism. Critical analyses of these institutions portray them as a form of neocolonialism, in that they perpetuate subordinate and exploitative relationships between former imperialist powers and the colonies they once controlled through more blatantly coercive means (Bello 1999, 2000; Khor 2000; Stiglitz 2003).

The rules that the global financial institutions impose on the countries of the global South are designed to promote international trade by requiring that these countries remove regulations that restrict international flows of goods and services into their domestic markets. While this ostensibly is meant to promote competition among producers, in practice it forces these countries' domestic producers to compete on a highly unequal playing field dominated by transnational corporations. Rapid liberalization in poor countries has obliterated domestic production in many sectors, leading to chronic unemployment and food insecurity in countries that were once self-sufficient in their ability to provide basic nutrition to their populations (UN Food and Agriculture Organization 2005; UNDP 2005). Wallach and Woodall note the hypocrisy of these rules, which say to the global South "do as we say not as we did" (2004). Had these same rules applied in an earlier era, the industrial revolution and economic growth of the global North would never have been possible. In fact, the economic growth of the West depended upon the protection of domestic markets, the absence of patent laws, and the promotion of wage laws that ensured that workers could afford to purchase the goods they produced. Under today's global economic rules, later-industrializing countries are denied the ability to follow the path that proved so successful in the West.

Global trade rules are enforced in a number of ways. A primary one is through the selective granting of access to rich country markets. Global South countries tend to produce what are called "primary commodities," agricultural or natural resource goods that tend to fetch lower prices on international markets than do manufactured goods. A country must produce a lot of coffee to import a single computer or car, and the terms of trade, or relative value of goods bought and sold, have long been stacked against the world's poorer countries (McMichael 2003; Wise and Gallagher 2006). The relative economic strength of Northern countries allows them to use the threat of withholding access to their own markets in order to force Southern countries to liberalize their markets. Although WTO rules forbid such double standards, the economic vulnerabilities of Southern countries effectively prevent them from using WTO dispute resolution procedures (Ostry 2007). These fundamentally unequal exchange relationships help profits accumulate in richer countries while perpetuating relative poverty in the global South.

In addition to using their market power, Northern country governments also work through the IMF and the World Bank to coerce global South governments to conform to neoliberal trade rules that privilege transnational corporations. The principal way this is done is through the use of what are called "conditionalities" that are attached to the loans made through these institutions. As part of their loan agreements, borrowing country governments are forced to adopt clearly specified policy changes known as structural adjustment programs, which help integrate national economies into global markets. They include, for instance, the removal of tariffs on imported goods; the loosening of restrictions on foreign investment; cuts in public spending; privatization of state-run enterprises, including public utilities and services; and state support for export industries.

Structural adjustment programs have come under harsh criticism for their disastrous effects in many countries, and in recent years this criticism has come from people who were once (and may still be) sympathetic to the neoliberal agenda (Soros 2002; Stiglitz, 2003). In the spring of 2000, the U.S. House of Representatives Meltzer Commission on international financial institutions concluded that the policies of the World Bank and the IMF contributed to economic stagnation in global South countries and were irrelevant to poverty reduction efforts. In addition, the report—which was produced by a panel of mostly conservative politicians—found that the policies of these institutions were driven by the interests of Western countries and their own bureaucratic imperatives rather than by the needs of poor countries (Bello 2003). Policies of global financial institutions have been linked to widespread and often militant protest in global South countries, and beginning in the 1970s social scientists have documented what they call "IMF riots" targeting the policy prescriptions of structural adjustment programs (Walton and Seddon 1994).

In contrast to the UN, the global financial institutions have much more restrictive policies regarding civil society participation. This is especially true of the IMF and the WTO, which remain quite closed to civil society participation, but it is also the case with regard to the relatively more open World Bank (Fox and Brown 1998; Nelson 1995). The well-established precedent of involving NGOs (other than business interest groups, who are often represented on government delegations) as observers at international meetings has been ignored or severely restricted in trade and financial forums, especially the IMF (Charnovitz 1997; Porter 2005). The WTO now allows limited access for NGOs, but a substantial number of those granted formal recognition are business interest organizations, and the accreditation process remains much more restricted than in the UN. For instance, WTO Guidelines for Arrangements on Relations with NGOs state: "it would not be possible for NGOs to be directly involved in the work of the WTO or its meetings, because of the politically sensitive nature of trade negotiations." The value of informal dialogue and information exchange with NGOs is recognized, but "primary responsibility for taking into account the different elements of public interest which are brought to bear on trade and policy making [lies at the national level]" (WTO guidelines cited in Krut [1997]).

This position grows in part from an ideology within these institutions that emphasizes rational, technocratic expertise in global economic policy making, thereby removing these crucial decisions from the messiness of public participation. The ideology assumes that the science of economics is neutral with regard to questions of power, and that disinterested, objective experts can provide better economic leadership than can political processes designed to integrate the views of various competing stakeholders (Daly 1996; Markoff and Montecinos 1993). This perspective fosters a culture of secrecy within the global financial institutions that inhibits efforts to cultivate more open and transparent ties to civil society groups (O'Brien et al. 2000). However, rising public pressure has brought some progress in expanding civil society's inroads into the World Bank and the WTO (Fox and Brown 1998; Nelson 2001; O'Brien et al. 2000).[9]

Following the models of civil society engagement at UN conferences, activists

have organized parallel conferences and protests at international financial meetings of the G8 and at the World Bank, the IMF, and the WTO. These protests date
back to the 1980s with a coalition of advocacy groups organizing "The Other Economic Summit" (TOES) to advocate for alternatives to neoliberal agendas. TOES
conferences were more parallel meetings of civil society than confrontational protests, and they generated analyses of the global economy that clearly inform contemporary debates. A substantial body of published material has resulted from
these meetings.[10] Until fairly recently, however, they have generated far less attention than the global conferences of the UN. In the mid-1990s, with the fiftieth
anniversary of the World Bank and the IMF, a large and diverse network of groups
came together to form "50 Years Is Enough" in order to coordinate more focused
protest against the World Bank's neoliberal agenda. These early streams of protest
contributed to the far more extensive protests at the Seattle World Trade Organization ministerial in 1999 and at subsequent global financial meetings.

As we will see in chapter 4, the neoliberal globalization network began a
more concerted effort to advance its global agenda in the late 1970s. This effort
came at least partly in response to the demands being made in the UN by the
growing ranks of the newly independent countries of the global South for a "new
international economic order" that would help create a more equitable and fair
trading system. Decolonization meant that newly independent poor countries
now outnumbered the rich ones, giving them a political majority in the General
Assembly. This generated a conservative backlash among Northern elites (particularly in the United States), who sought to undermine the UN and reduce its
influence (Bello 2000; Bennis 1997).[11] The United States, under pressure from
an emergent, more globally oriented transnational capitalist class, worked to systematically shift major policy decisions from the UN into the more exclusive
global financial arena, where its influence was strongest.

In practice, the global financial institutions have operated outside and independently of the UN, even though they are nominally contained within the UN
Charter. Indeed, a major goal of WTO negotiations has been to free trade from
laws that might restrict the flow of goods and services across borders, including
environmental, public health, and labor laws designed to protect and promote
public goods. This generates what I call institutional contradictions between
the UN Charter—whose aim is to "end the scourge of war" by addressing root
causes of conflicts and helping governments manage conflicts nonviolently—
and the global financial system, which promotes market governance and economic growth over other social aims. As we will see in chapter 9, many groups
seeking a more democratic form of globalization have sought to draw attention

to these contradictions in order to advance social agendas over market-dominated policies in global institutions.

Conclusion

To understand how global integration affects the ways people engage in politics, we must account for how local and national political institutions are embedded in broader sets of transnational relations. So our first analytical task was to reconceptualize state boundaries to account for the transnational influences on the content and conduct of domestic politics. Because globalization implies an expansion in the flows of information, people, and goods across borders, we must ask whether and how these flows affect a variety of conflicts that might once have been seen in strictly national or even local terms. National governments are nested within a system of relationships with other global actors. In addition to governments, transnational corporations and civil society groups cultivate interactive networks that can affect national and international political dynamics. This does not mean that the state no longer matters, but it does change how the state matters for the politics of social change. I introduced the concept of complex multilateralism to describe the character of this global system of multiple, embedded, and interdependent polities.

The twentieth century generated global institutions designed to help promote and manage a globalizing economy and polity. This chapter summarized the history of the UN and global financial institutions to illustrate how these institutions define opportunities and constraints for actors advocating different visions of global organization. UN conferences and processes for credentialing civil society groups help focus the attention of people in different parts of the world around a common agenda. They also provide contexts for coordinated action over time, enabling people to develop transnational relationships and collective identities. In recent years, the global financial institutions have become more powerful relative to the comparatively democratic and more broadly focused UN. This has contributed to rapid advances in expanding the global economy at the expense of other aspects of global governance. Global financial institutions now play a more central role in shaping the economic policies of governments (especially those in the global South), and these institutions have attracted growing opposition from civil society groups. A key objective for many critics of the global economy is not necessarily to abolish, but to subordinate the global economy to a system of norms that places greater value on human needs.

The rival global networks identified in the previous chapter operate within a global institutional context that can be characterized as complex multilateralism. While this multilayered global polity conditions the possibilities for action, it is also shaped in important ways by the actions of players on the global stage. Part II describes in greater detail the two rival networks that are the focus of this book. First, we examine how the neoliberal network has advanced a vision of globalization that promotes the interests of global capitalism. Chapter 5 shows how democratic globalizers have also been advancing their own vision of global integration by promoting multilateral cooperation through the UN. Chapter 6 outlines the organizational foundations of the democratic globalization network and how this has changed over time.

PART TWO

RIVAL NETWORKS EXAMINED

CHAPTER FOUR

Globalizing Capitalism

The Transnational Neoliberal Network in Action

Capitalism does not just happen . . . It is a social system that has to struggle to create and reproduce its hegemonic order globally.

(Sklair 1997: 514)

Because it seeks a world where all people and places are incorporated into a single globalized economy, neoliberalism threatens many, generating potential opposition everywhere it goes. Any group—including nationally oriented capitalists—that proposes some other model for meeting people's material and political needs can become a threat to the network. Although neoliberal globalizers control more structural power than their rivals, they must still actively promote and defend their vision. I argue in this chapter that the neoliberal globalization network pursued its interests by advancing a model of the state that favors capitalist interests, promoting multilateral institutions to enforce neoliberal policies, and propagating a culture-ideology of consumerism that lionizes global capitalism while demonizing its critics. Neoliberal efforts to counteract the democratic globalization network affect the political opportunities, strategies, and the configuration of allies and supporters available to those challenging neoliberal globalization (e.g., Davenport et al. 2005; Meyer and Staggenborg 1996). This chapter examines some of the key features of the neoliberal network and its strategy for advancing and defending its vision of globalized capitalism against pro-democracy rivals.

The Neoliberal Network and Its Strategies

Chapter 2 introduced the neoliberal network and its relationship to Sklair's notion of the transnational capitalist class (TCC). This network is transnational in the sense that its participants increasingly see their interests in global rather than local or national terms. Also, network activities as a whole aim to "exert economic control in the workplace, political control in domestic and international politics, and culture-ideology control in everyday life" (Sklair 2001: 18) around the world. Its members share an outward-oriented, global, rather than an inward-looking perspective on most issues dealing with economics, politics, and culture-ideology. They share similar lifestyles, education levels, and consumption patterns. And finally they seek to project images of themselves as citizens of the world as well as of their places of birth (Sklair 2001: 18–21).

The neoliberal network includes the corporate, state, technical, and cultural fractions (see table 2.1). Their activities tend to complement each other because of their overarching interest in advancing a globalized vision of capitalism. It does not take much reflection to recognize that these distinct fractions of the neoliberal network collectively command an immense amount of control over the world's economic, political, and cultural resources. And here the neoliberal network differs from its rival in that it is far more organized around a clearly specified, common aim. Without any effort to communicate or coordinate their efforts, members of the TCC know that they all share an interest in promoting laws and structures that protect rights to private property and that expand possibilities for maximizing profits from financial investments. Without routine meetings or even direct interpersonal ties, they know in advance that anything that increases possibilities for investment in new countries or sectors and that reduces public claims on privately held financial or physical assets will advance the aim of neoliberal globalization. This facilitates their "revolution from above" by reducing the need to coordinate or to actively mobilize broad support for their objectives (Robinson 2004).[1] Democratic globalization network participants, in contrast, are much more dispersed. Most do not draw salaries for their political work, and they must struggle to define their more nebulous and open vision of society. In the latter task, they must compete with and seek to use communications media that are strongly influenced if not controlled by their capitalist rivals. Coordinating joint action or even promoting complementary actions within the network is therefore a much more difficult task for challengers to global capitalism.

Nevertheless, as Sklair has argued, the dominance of this network is not automatic, and indeed members of the TCC might be seen to be operating from a "siege mentality" (1997), requiring constant work to defend and advance network aims. There are two fundamental assumptions in the capitalist logic that create ongoing tensions for the neoliberal network. First, the assumption that policies encouraging a steady accumulation of wealth by the owners of capital will improve the conditions for all of society has generated serious debate amid persistent and growing inequality (see, e.g., Babones and Turner 2003; Korzeniewicz and Moran 1997). The persistence of widespread poverty amid unprecedented wealth delegitimizes and destabilizes the system. Second, the assumption that the world's resources are infinite or at least that technology can overcome any resource limitations must contend with growing evidence to the contrary. Realities such as species extinctions, global warming, and shrinking reserves of natural resources such as energy and water have taken on greater urgency. These basic weaknesses in the capitalist logic require that neoliberal proponents constantly work to defend their preferred world order. Thus, Sklair (1997) argues that the advocacy activities of the transnational capitalist in some ways resemble those of conventional social movements.

Reviewing various analyses of neoliberal responses to global challenges, we might identify two major nodes in the transnational neoliberal network. Nodes represent centers of power or convergence of network members and they often play leading roles to help frame issues and coordinate actions of network participants. The primary neoliberal network node is the group of globalizing bureaucrats and politicians and their corporate advisors associated with the governments of the G8, the economically oriented association of the world's richest countries, and especially the U.S. government. The G8 includes the United States, Great Britain, Canada, Japan, Germany, Italy, France, and Russia.

The G8 governments not only gather routinely to coordinate policies and to explicitly advance the global economy, but they also control all decisions in the World Bank and the IMF, and they wield disproportionate influence in the World Trade Organization (WTO). It might be seen as the center of power of what Robinson calls the "transnational state" (2004). While the United States and other G8 governments have not always been consistent in supporting the interests of the neoliberal globalization network, they have certainly been its most reliable and most important allies. U.S. delegations to most international trade meetings are overwhelmingly filled with people employed by transnational corporations, and many bureaucrats in national trade and financial ministries (and increasingly others as well) have ties to the corporate sector (Domhoff 1998; Mills 1956). In any case, U.S. foreign policy—particularly with regard to the global economy—has tended to reflect the interests of the neoliberal network. This is particularly true since the 1980s, and often to the neglect of other social groups and viewpoints of other world leaders (Markoff 1996; Peet 2003; Robinson 1996).

A second important node in the neoliberal globalization network is the International Chamber of Commerce (ICC), which is based in Paris and serves as a global industry lobby. The single largest international organization of corporations, the ICC is made up of local and national sections, and it often functions as a liaison between transnational businesses and the UN and the multilateral economic organizations, organizing joint conferences and attending international conferences on behalf of its members (Charnovitz 1997). The ICC (not to be confused with the International Criminal Court or the Inuit Circumpolar Conference discussed in chapter 8) has worked consistently to advance the goals of globalizing capitalists in the international system, lobbying the UN and working to shape its relationships to business and to the multilateral economic institutions since the 1960s (Kelly 2001; O'Brien et al. 2000). And just as organizations in the democratic globalization network work to nurture transnational identities and commitment to global human rights values and principles, the ICC cultivates among its members—through conferences, publications, and exchanges of various kinds—its own global identity and organizational culture. The ICC is not alone in playing this kind of role, and in fact there is substantial overlap between its membership base and other corporate alliances such as the World Economic Forum, the Trans-Atlantic Business Dialogue, and other associations of private-sector business entities, all of which complement the work of the ICC and the neoliberal network more broadly.

The ICC works to generate common industry positions on international policy, to foster a globalizing agenda among its members, and to advance international policies that are consistent with the interests of the network (Sklair 2001). For instance, it helped draft and promote international legislation to protect intellectual property rights (McMichael 2003; Ostry 2007; Sell 2003), and it has also coordinated industry resistance to any international effort (in the various UN agencies or elsewhere) to monitor corporate practice (Robinson 2004: 126). The ICC sponsors workshops for members of the business community and politicians, helping develop greater understanding among members of how global political processes work, and generating consensus among elite policy makers about the most appropriate responses to major global problems. It led lobbying efforts on behalf of the Uruguay Round of the General Agreement on Tariffs and Trade (GATT), which led to the formation of the WTO, as well as for the North American Free Trade Agreement (NAFTA) (Karliner 1997: 144). And at the UN Conference on Environment and Development, it worked with a similar business lobby, the Business Council on Sustainable Development, to oppose any movement toward the international regulation of corporate environmental practices (Karliner 1997: 53).

There are four major political strategies that different elements of the neoliberal network have used to influence the world's political and economic life and to counteract its rival network. These strategies include: (1) redefining the functions of national governments; (2) marginalizing social welfare–oriented international organizations, especially the UN and its various agencies; (3) advancing international organizations that support neoliberal economic policies, particularly those most readily controlled by the G8 governments; and (4) promoting a culture-ideology that advances consumerist practices worldwide, justifies the activities of business, and delegitimizes opponents of neoliberalism.

Transforming the Welfare State into a Garrison State

The expansion of global capital has always been contested. Indigenous peoples fighting colonization and foreign occupation of their ancestral lands, farmers resisting government appropriation of their land, slaves struggling against their overseers, and workers pressing business owners for better wages and working conditions are all examples of such contests that have endured over many decades, if not centuries. In the course of these struggles, modern states have emerged to both promote the interests of capitalists through policies that encourage the accumulation and investment of wealth while also ensuring social tranquility through some regulation and redistribution of national resources (Markoff 1996; Tilly 1990). Such redistributive and regulatory policies, many argue, help remedy fundamental contradictions of capitalism by ensuring that workers can purchase the products they produce (thereby contributing to sustained economic growth) and by sustaining the material (ecological and human) base upon which capitalist production depends.

The ideology of neoliberalism, however, challenges the notion that the state should perform regulatory and redistributive tasks in society. Instead, it sees markets as the most efficient and effective mechanisms for allocating the resources of society. The regulatory state, then, is an enemy of markets. Left alone, the laws of supply and demand will address any emerging problem, be it one of social distribution or ecological scarcity. Government meddling is seen as a source of further problems rather than solutions. Where there is a demand for some new technology to solve unforeseen crises or curb a new disease, markets will provide for that demand so long as governments give them the freedom to do so. Economist John Maynard Keynes, in contrast, saw government regulation as crucial to ensuring the efficient operation of capitalist markets, providing corrective mechanisms to markets, which are unresponsive to many important social needs.

This portrayal of the neoliberal ideology differs from what most neoliberals actually advocate. In practice, few neoliberals hold rigidly to their ideal of minimalist government, and many welcome forms of market intervention by governments that suit their financial interests. For example, many support government policies that minimize financial risks for certain kinds of investments (through tax incentives, patent protections, and other subsidies); protect financial investments (through government insurance programs, bankruptcy laws, etc.); subsidize infrastructures such as roadways, water supply, and waste disposal; limit labor costs (generally by regulating borders); and provide a productive workforce (through public education, health care, etc.).

In addition to promoting a reduced role of governments in the regulation of national economies, neoliberals have also sought to limit public expenditures in order to open up new possibilities for private investment. Thus, services that were once largely controlled by governments—such as education, health care, utilities (water, electricity), and postal services—are increasingly being privatized. But government control of these services is generally seen as the only way to ensure that citizens have equitable access to basic services and to see that practices adhere to some national standards of quality and safety. For instance, telephone and postal services cost far more for people living in sparsely populated areas than they do for those in cities, and therefore turning these utilities over to market forces limits the effective access that rural people have to them. Privatization would mean that services such as education and health care would come to be seen as a commodity designed to maximize profits rather than to meet social needs. This logic threatens the quality and comprehensiveness of access to education and other vital services. Moreover, the market logic often encourages practices that run counter to broad public interests. For instance, health care providers earn profits from treating disease, and thus preventive care and other low-cost measures to limit and treat disease would not be priorities for privatized health care systems. As the 2002 North American blackout showed, the privatization of energy utilities leads to degraded infrastructure, since private companies seeking to maximize profits within short timeframes have little interest in taking steps to maintain and ensure the long-term functioning of utility infrastructures. And businesses that depend upon expanding quarterly earnings are unlikely to engage in long-term efforts to conserve limited natural resources.

Since the 1980s, neoliberal proponents have made significant headway in transforming the state from an entity concerned with ensuring some level of social welfare to one devoted to providing a secure and productive environment for global capital (Evans 1997; Robinson 2004). Multilateral economic institutions play an important part in this effort to transform the nation-state and its functions. Kim Moody summarizes this development:

> The national state is indispensable, but its ability to regulate the national economy had to be reduced and limited for the TNCs [transnational corporations] to operate freely on a world-wide level. Multilateralism has become the method of accomplishing this. To put this another way, the state is to retain its ability to protect property from internal conflicts, crime, or working-class rebellion at home. This protection is increased, both at home and abroad, by externally (multilaterally) removing the ability of the state to nationalize or otherwise expropriate or limit the property of the TNCs should the government fall into the hands of a radical or revolutionary working-class or nationalist party or movement. The ideology to provide the cover story for this maneuver lay at hand in the form of neoclassical economics. (Moody 1997: 138–139)

Neoliberal advocates want to transform the state, but to do so they must build a multilateral economic order that will support this goal. Their program also requires an ideological component to neutralize opponents and win over influential supporters. In addition to limiting the state's role in the market, neoliberalism seeks to strengthen the state's capacity to protect private property, which is essential for the continual accumulation of capital. As neoliberal advocate Thomas Friedman quipped, "the hidden hand of the market will never work without a hidden fist" (quoted in Robinson 2004: 139). Thus the withering of the social welfare state has been accompanied by a parallel growth of what we might call the garrison state. While a core idea in neoliberal ideology is that the state must be minimized to allow market forces to operate freely, in practice this has meant that governments have been pressed to reduce spending on social welfare while they increase spending on prisons and policing. Such cuts come at the same time as governments reduce their role in regulating domestic markets, thus increasing the vulnerability of their populations to global market forces. Maintaining stability in such a context requires what Peter Evans calls a "leaner, meaner state":

> In the most sinister version of this leaner, meaner stateness, politicians and state managers gain support for the state as an institution in return for restricting the state's role to activities essential for sustaining the profitability of transnational markets. The capacity to deliver services that the affluent can supply privately for themselves (for example, health and education) is sacrificed, while the more restricted institutional capacity necessary to deliver essential business services and security (domestic and global) is maintained. In turn, delivering security means devoting more resources to the repression of the more desperate and reckless among the excluded, both domestic and international. (Evans 1997: 85–86)

Global economic integration has indeed served to reduce state spending on social services in both the North and South (Kingfisher 2003), and this is especially
true in the South, where limits on state spending are dictated by the International
Monetary Fund (IMF) and World Bank (Rudra 2002). Reductions in state spending have, in the United States, been accompanied by rapidly growing prison populations, giving the leading neoliberal state the highest incarceration rate of all
advanced industrial countries. The garrison state is nothing new to many postcolonial societies, while it is new for most of the more established democracies (Tilly
1990). As we discussed in chapter 3, world-systems theory holds that colonial histories and subsequent economic relations among countries shape the character of
the state and of democracy in each region. Thus, the democratization of the global
North has come at the expense of the global South, on whose (inexpensive) labor
the North depends (Arrighi 1999; Chase-Dunn 1998; Markoff 1999). As workers
in the global North face growing downward pressures on wages and job security,
their situations increasingly resemble those of workers in the South.

One indicator of the rise of the garrison state is the militant and often brutal responses of governments to peaceful protesters at meetings of multilateral
economic institutions. The first very public confrontations between democratic
globalization proponents and police forces in the global North took place in Vancouver (1997) at the meeting on Asia-Pacific Economic Cooperation (APEC) and
at the Seattle meeting of the World Trade Organization (1999). In Vancouver,
more than 50 of the thousands of protesters were arrested, and more than $11
million was spent to pay for security at the event (Ericson and Doyle 1999). The
Seattle protests drew an estimated 60,000 to 80,000 people, leading to more
than 600 arrests at a cost of $18 million for security forces.[2] The meeting of the
G8 in Genoa in 2001 drew more than 300,000 protesters, who faced severe police brutality in what was later deemed a police riot. One demonstrator was killed
by police (della Porta and Reiter Forthcoming; Juris 2008).

These and subsequent protest events generated public inquiries that blamed
policing methods for the violence, and virtually all those arrested were released
without charges. Many filed lawsuits to protest their treatment by police (della
Porta and Reiter Forthcoming). These experiences raise questions about the protection of citizens' rights to political speech in a globalized economy. Analyses of
policing at global protests show that Northern states—what Couch (2004) calls
"post-democracies"—are more likely than they were in the past to emphasize the
protection of private property and maintenance of public order over the rights of
people to express publicly their political views.[3] Indeed, even before the attacks on
the World Trade Center in September 2001, police in the United States, Canada,

and the United Kingdom were using national counterterror legislation and other non-democratic methods against peaceful protesters at global economic meetings in Washington and elsewhere (Ericson and Doyle 1999). Police and neoliberal proponents alike do not tend to differentiate between fundamentalist militants and the deliberately nonviolent activists promoting a more tolerant and inclusive global system.[4] As O'Neill observed, from the point of view of authorities, transnational protest is just one of the threats to which they must respond, on par with terrorism, football hooliganism, and transnational organized crime (O'Neill 2004: 243). While police certainly face a challenge in managing the variety of threats to public safety and order that large protest gatherings pose, the more recent discourse in core democracies has tended to criminalize dissent and subordinate the protection of free speech to the maintenance of public order.

In the aftermath of these and subsequent protests at the sites of international meetings of the World Bank, the IMF, or the WTO, governments have opted to move their meetings to remote places that are more easily insulated from protesters. Protected by governments that limit political freedom and by settings that are far less accessible to cash-strapped activists, governments have opted for even greater secrecy in an effort to avoid opening economic decision making to greater public scrutiny. The need to insulate officials from the public so that they can hold such meetings demonstrates a lack of institutional legitimacy that cannot be remedied by refusing to expand opportunities for public participation in these institutions. Such secrecy is not new: David Rockefeller addressed a Trilateral Commission meeting in 1991 with these words:

> We are grateful to *The Washington Post*, *The New York Times*, *Time Magazine*, and other great publications, whose directors have attended our meetings and respected their promises of discretion *for almost forty years*. It would have been impossible for us to develop our plan for the world if we had been subject to the bright lights of publicity during those years. (Kent 2005: 66, emphasis added)

Marginalizing the UN

The globalization of capitalism requires that the garrison state model be replicated around the world. Investors want predictable and standardized guidelines when they move their operations across national borders. They are less inclined to invest internationally if they lack assurances that their property will be protected. This requires some form of multilateral institution to help standardize national policies that are conducive to a neoliberal global economy. But the emergent neoliberal network faced an important obstacle in the existing multi-national political order, which was defined by a UN Charter emphasizing peace, equality, and human rights over the promotion of global capitalism. They also were facing heightened calls in the 1970s from a large majority of UN member states for a "new international economic order" that challenged their continued dominance in the global economy. They therefore needed to downgrade the UN as a legitimate center of global political leadership as they encouraged neoliberal forms of multilateralism. They did this first by systematically attacking the UN and its agencies, mobilizing elite opposition to the organization in the United States. Second, they used U.S. influence over the UN to force major changes in the organization's agenda and staffing, significantly transforming the UN's orientation toward the private sector. Third, they exploited opportunities within this more pro-business UN for private economic gain.[5]

Members of the neoliberal network organized a systematic attack on the UN and its agencies aimed at delegitimizing the world body and undermining U.S. support for it. Beginning in the 1980s, elite social movement organizations[6] like the Heritage Foundation and the Cato Institute published hundreds of reports and other documents admonishing the world body. As Paine observes:

> Over the course of more than two decades, neo-liberal propagandists have defined the UN as an inefficient and unresponsive bureaucracy, threatening to impose itself on the world's people. Again and again, editorial writers and newscasters have repeated the term "vast, bloated bureaucracy," even though the UN staff is actually quite small. The mass media and the universities embraced these views, especially in the United States, and think-tanks sponsored by wealthy individuals and transnational corporations actively developed and disseminated them. (Paine 2000)

The extent of corporate mobilization against international agencies should not be underestimated. Much of this work has been secretive and explicitly aimed at misleading the public and policy makers.

For instance, in 2000, the World Health Organization (WHO) published a 260-page report that systematically analyzed the strategies used by industry to prevent global efforts to curb tobacco use. After reviewing millions of pages of industry documents, the expert panel outlined how corporations obstructed the work of the WHO. Because the strategies in this particular case illustrate tactics used by other industries against other UN agencies (e.g., Bruno and Karliner 2002; Sklair 2001), I reproduce the list in table 4.1. The WHO panel was clearly shocked by the lengths to which corporate actors went to undermine what they saw as legitimate and necessary public health work. The language of the document is quite strong for an official text:

3

TABLE 4.1
Corporate Strategies to Undermine International Public Agencies

1. Establishing inappropriate relations with WHO staff to influence policy
   a. Paying WHO consultants or advisors for information or services
   b. Maintaining other potentially inappropriate relationships with WHO employees or advisors
   c. Employing former WHO officials or promising employment to current WHO officials
2. Wielding financial and political power to influence policy
   a. Restricting or diverting WHO tobacco control budgets
   b. Using financial contributions to gain access and influence
3. Using other UN agencies to influence or resist WHO tobacco control efforts
   a. Food and Agriculture Organization (FAO), UNCTAD, World Bank, Economic and Social Council (ECOSOC), ILO, regional WHO offices
4. Discrediting WHO or WHO officials to undermine WHO effectiveness
5. Influencing WHO decision making through surrogates with tobacco companies' role concealed
   a. Front organizations
   b. Delegates of member states
   c. Food company affiliates
6. Distorting WHO research
   a. Secretly funding speakers at WHO conferences
   b. Holding scientific symposia to promote pro-industry positions, with tobacco companies' role concealed
   c. Misrepresenting tobacco company work as WHO-supported
   d. Using "independent" consultants with concealed tobacco company ties to lobby WHO scientists
   e. Contacting WHO study scientists to influence study results
      i. Presenting tobacco company arguments through "independent" scientists with concealed tobacco company ties
      ii. Compromising independence and credibility of WHO studies by involving investigators in tobacco company research or activities
      iii. Funding and promoting counter-research
      iv. Creating an ostensibly independent coalition of scientists
      v. Misrepresenting scientific studies to the media and regulators
7. Staging media events or other diversions to discredit or distract attention from WHO tobacco control initiatives
8. Systematic surveillance of WHO activities

SOURCE: World Health Organization (2000).

The evidence shows that tobacco companies have operated for many years with the deliberate purpose of subverting the efforts of WHO to address tobacco issues. The attempted subversion has been elaborate, well financed, sophisticated and usually invisible. That tobacco companies resist proposals for tobacco control comes as no surprise, but what is now clear is the scale, intensity and, importantly, the tactics, of their campaigns. *To many in the international community, tobacco prevention may be seen today as a struggle against chemical addiction, cancers, cardiovascular diseases and other health consequences of smoking. This inquiry adds to the mounting evidence that it is also a struggle against an active, organized and calculating industry . . .* This report details a pattern of influence and misconduct by tobacco companies aimed at thwarting global tobacco control initiatives. The committee of experts believes that

the harm caused by the tobacco companies' conduct was significant and far-reaching.
(World Health Organization 2000: 18–20, emphasis added)

The committee recommended that the international community take steps to monitor corporate practices and to counter corporate campaigns that undermine the activities of international public agencies. That this document stirred little in the way of a broader public discourse or government action, and that one is hard pressed to locate the document on the main UN or WHO Web pages, shows the influence corporations have on the everyday governance of these organizations.

Despite this systematic and well-financed campaign to discredit the UN, public opinion in the United States has remained consistently and very strongly supportive of the organization. However, it has affected U.S. politicians, whose votes on decisions related to the UN and various treaties differ markedly from those of voters (Chicago Council on Foreign Relations and Program on International Policy Attitudes 2004). Thus, despite strong public support for the UN, the globalizing bureaucrats and politicians who are part of the neoliberal network have been able to wage systematic war on the UN from Washington.

Neoliberal advocates in Congress successfully withheld U.S. dues payments from the UN, in violation of international law. Moreover, they have used the threat of further suspension of U.S. economic contributions to essentially blackmail the global body to bow to U.S. wishes. While U.S. contributions to the UN represent small change relative to the overall U.S. government budget (U.S. dues in 2005 were $440 million[7]), this contribution makes up 24 percent of the UN's regular budget, and thus withholding even part of this payment would cause serious difficulties for the organization's day-to-day operations. In addition to forcing the organization to audit its operations (using a U.S.-based firm), U.S. pressure led to the ousting of a popular and effective secretary-general, Boutros Boutros-Ghali, and his replacement with Kofi Annan, a graduate of MIT's Sloan School of Business who was far more sympathetic with Washington's neoliberal agenda. U.S. pressure also led to the curtailment of efforts in the UN to monitor corporate practices and to otherwise hold corporations accountable to international law. An important step in this direction was the 1992 elimination of the UN's Center on Transnational Corporations, which at the time of its disbanding was preparing an international code of conduct for transnational corporations (Bello 1999; Bennis 1997; Karliner 1997; Sklair 2001). Also under U.S. pressure, the post of director-general for international economic cooperation and development was abolished, and the UN Conference on Trade and Development

(UNCTAD) was severely constrained, denying it jurisdiction over matters being negotiated under the GATT (now the WTO). This effectively eliminated UN oversight over global trade matters (Bello 2000).

Under Kofi Annan, the climate in the UN became noticeably more hospitable to business. From his earliest days in office, Annan worked to cultivate his ties to the international business community by attending, in addition to private meetings with corporate leaders, meetings of the ICC and the World Economic Forum. He launched a plan to promote business "partnerships" with the UN body, and encouraged all UN agencies to cultivate partnerships with business.[8] The central locus of the partnership initiative is the Global Compact. The program seeks to sensitize corporate leaders to the values and norms of the UN system by encouraging them to sign on to its ten core principles.[9] Corporate partners are asked to submit case studies of how they have attempted to implement Global Compact principles, and "the hope and expectation is that good practices will help to drive out bad ones through the power of dialogue, transparency, advocacy and competition" (Ruggie 2002: 31). The idea that, by bringing corporations into the UN orbit and encouraging them to discuss the ways their operations affect human rights, the Global Compact might socialize corporations into UN norms and practices seems reasonable. In practice, however, there has been little in the way of dialogue or transparency, as few corporations have kept their commitment to file substantive reports, and the UN has bowed to industry pressure to keep the Global Compact from becoming a monitoring body. Thus, while businesses can gain some legitimacy by joining the Global Compact, they assume no costs, since compliance is voluntary and no effort is made to monitor practices to ensure that they are consistent with the Global Compact principles.[10] "Even [George] Soros noted that [the Global Compact] was nothing more than corporate image whitewash" (Robinson 2004: 171). Activists dubbed the program "blue wash," since it allows corporations to hide unscrupulous behaviors behind the UN's blue flag.

One serious consequence of the Global Compact, however, is that it obstructs other efforts in the UN to strengthen international oversight of corporate practices (Bendell 2004; Hobbs et al. 2003; Martens 2003). Another is that the Global Compact has contributed to the broader ideological campaign of the neoliberal network to delegitimize civil society groups while promoting the idea that "the business of business is government" (Hertz 2001: 166), that is, that corporations are legitimate representatives of broad public interest and therefore should be intimately involved in global decision making while "special interest" civil society actors should not.

U.S. pressure, Annan's leadership, and programs like the Global Compact have changed the UN in the eyes of many in the corporate world from a threat to an investment opportunity. Corporate advisors and lobbyists have profited immensely from the pro-business climate at the UN, and many have engaged in lucrative partnerships with the world body. Efforts to associate corporate brands with the UN aim to boost sales, especially by companies with poor environmental and human rights records. Also, the variety of UN agencies working on public health, education, development, and environmental initiatives around the world creates bountiful opportunities for product promotion as well as positive branding campaigns. Moreover, the partnership relationship between business and the UN allows corporations substantial influence over UN agendas, inhibiting a more comprehensive and democratic assessment of global priorities. Thus, Cisco Systems led an initiative to make global efforts to close the "digital divide" a priority. As Paine observed, "making computers available to all the world's citizens [is] absurd in light of the large number of the world's people without adequate food, shelter or drinking water" (Paine 2000).

Promoting Multilateral Institutions for Neoliberalism

As neoliberal proponents sought to weaken the UN and its various agencies, they simultaneously worked to enhance global institutions that would shape the global system in ways favorable to the interests of globalized capital. Robinson (2004) refers to this as a "revolution from above," whereby the neoliberal network creates a transnational state that can transform the global system into one more conducive to the profit-making aims of globalized capital. Not only did this transnational state need to be freed from the normative restrictions of the UN Charter, but it also needed to systematically expand global markets. The multilateral economic institutions proved to be a supportive venue for this project. Policies that advanced the neoliberal revolution from above included pressing governments to open their borders to the free flow of goods and services (but not people). This would allow transnational corporations to compete on "level" playing fields with local and national companies. They also advanced the replication of the neoliberal garrison state worldwide.

Analysts have documented systematic efforts by big business and its allies in government and international agencies to strengthen global economic organizations (McMichael 2003; O'Brien et al. 2000). National delegations at the WTO are frequently staffed by people on corporate payrolls (Malhotra et al. 2003; Wallach and Woodall 2004). And much of the staff of multilateral economic institutions is comprised of people whose credentials are based upon their professional socialization and adherence to neoliberal economic dogma rather than on their selection by or accountability to citizens (Goldman 2005; Markoff and Montecinos 1993; Pauly 1997; Rupert 2000; Stiglitz 2003). To the extent that these institutions exercise control over the economic policies of governments, they reinforce the interests of global capitalists both within and outside national borders (Robinson 2004: 50).

The global economic institutions effectively dictate the economic policies of most of the world's governments by making access to international financing contingent upon adherence to "structural adjustment" policies, or by threatening governments that violate international trade agreements or loan repayment terms with economic sanctions. They also serve as gatekeepers of global finance, providing (or not) the seal of approval required for countries to attract international lenders and investors. Obviously, it is the poorest and weakest countries that are most vulnerable to international pressure, but it is only the very richest countries that can resist such pressure for very long. Moreover, the neoliberal policy preferences of global capitalists are also reinforced in the bilateral relations of major world powers, so that trade arrangements, aid, and loans are all tied to demands for policy changes in line with neoliberal preferences (Peterson 2004). Thus, the practices of the global financial institutions parallel colonialism in both intent and effect (see, e.g., Bello 1999, 2000; Khor 2000). Scholars from the global South have lamented the irony in that, now that the end of the Cold War has allowed for greater democratization in much of the world, new democracies still have little freedom to choose their own economic paths (e.g., Hippler 1995).

Corporations and other neoliberal advocates must operate in national and local contexts that at least in theory provide for transparency in decision making, require constituent support and official accountability for policies, and involve citizens in deliberations about major policy changes. But public attention to many of the policies favored by the neoliberal network can effectively prevent them from coming to fruition. Thus, neoliberal advocates needed to cut off public debate and participation in the decisions governments took about whether and how to engage in multilateral economic cooperation. To do this, they engaged what we might call a "corporate boomerang effect" to use multilateral arrangements to press governments to adopt neoliberal policies without regard for domestic interests and pressures. By mobilizing allies among the G8 governments, the neoliberal network was able to shift economic policy making to international arenas, thereby freeing it from national democratic constraints. Keck and Sikkink use the notion of a boomerang effect to describe the strategy used by many public advocacy groups to appeal to international institutions when they find few domestic opportunities to press for changes in government practices (see chapter 8). The boomerang effect is at work when national actors engage international political processes—by forming transnational alliances and/or appealing to international norms or institutions—in order to bring international pressure to bear on their national governments. Typically, it is actors whose avenues of political influence are blocked domestically who turn to the international arena as a strategic alternative. The neoliberal network strategy of promoting multilateral economic institutions reflects a variation on this boomerang logic.

The corporate boomerang effect differs from Keck and Sikkink's effect in important ways. Corporate boomerangs seek greater secrecy rather than transparency. In contrast, human rights and environmental advocates operate in the open, and they use the boomerang effect to publicize issues and expand public participation in global affairs. Their domestic opportunities are typically closed because of antidemocratic forces operating within their country (such as systematic violations of human rights by military or police). They mobilize internationally to hold governments accountable to international laws that in many cases were adopted by democratically elected governments. This is a fundamentally pro-democratic and inclusive political strategy. Effectively, the boomerang used by democratic globalization advocates is one that enhances local-global connections and thereby strengthens the democratic underpinnings of the international institutional and legal order. The corporate boomerang, in contrast, has the exact opposite effect. It seeks to exclude large portions of the population from economic decision making and to insulate governments from the pressures of domestic groups of all kinds. Its aim is to create a stable and predictable policy environment for capitalists by limiting public scrutiny of government action and constraining public deliberation of global policy. This is a fundamentally antidemocratic agenda.

Corporate boomerang strategies seek to move outside of the domestic realm because of its very openness. Thus, some activists have referred to this kind of strategy as "policy laundering."[11] Like money launderers seeking to obscure the sources of illicit activity, policy launderers seek to hide the origins of global economic policy by moving these policy decisions overseas. Policies are then presented to sub-national authorities and citizens as fait accompli. The rationale for limiting public involvement in economic decisions is that economic policies are too complex to allow public input and that the globalized nature of the economy requires central coordination. Local authorities cannot be expected to understand global economics, much less to make prudent decisions regarding local economic matters, and therefore decisions should be left to the global managers who have the required expertise.

With the marginalization of the UN and its displacement by the multilateral economic institutions, advocates for alternatives to neoliberal globalization have been forced to shift their attention from a more hospitable and open UN forum to the far less amenable multilateral economic institutions. In other words, using a corporate boomerang, the neoliberal network has shifted the venue in which it operates to one that favors neoliberal over democratic models of globalization. A task for the democratic globalizers, then, is to throw more democratizing boomerangs that can shift the struggle back into a more hospitable venue. Because of the changes in the UN system wrought by the neoliberal network, however, democratic globalizers must also promote "deglobalization" by rolling back changes in that organization that have marginalized it and enabled corporate control over its agendas and actions (Bello 2003). Campaigns like that aimed at "reclaiming the UN" (see chapter 9) are moving in this direction.

McMichael describes the expansion of global economic institutions as "global managerialism" (2003). He argues that global managerialism creates a legitimacy crisis for national governments by eroding not only their legal sovereignty but also their capacity to make decisions that reflect the interests and needs of their societies. As governments are forced to cut public services and basic protections for their citizens, the democratic foundations upon which they are based are threatened in fundamental ways. Thus, while global managerialism and the global economic institutions that promote it have helped consolidate the neoliberal revolution from above in the short term, its longevity has never been certain. Proponents of neoliberal globalization have had to remain constantly vigilant to emergent threats to their preferred global order. An additional way the neoliberal network has worked to neutralize threats is to systematically delegitimize its opponents while promoting a culture-ideology of consumerism.

Delegitimizing Opponents and Promoting a Culture-Ideology of Consumerism

Neoliberal globalizers have long been advancing a culture-ideology of consumerism. This ideology is essential to promoting expanding consumption patterns, particularly among people whose basic needs are met and who have money to spend on high-profit luxury items. Thus, we see rapid expansions in the amounts of corporate spending devoted to the marketing of both products and corporate reputations or brands (Klein 1999).[12] The net result of this effort, however, is that modern societies are increasingly organized to promote consumption. Thus we see the global proliferation of shopping malls, and research shows that shopping has become a major component of many Americans' leisure time (Schor 1993, 2004). A consequence of this is rapidly rising consumer debt in the rich countries, and failures of both national and global markets to provide many basic needs for poor people.

As was mentioned briefly above, neoliberal globalizers have used their access to the new, corporate-friendly UN to influence the ideological work of the organization—such as the speeches given by UN officials, publications, briefing papers, meeting agendas, and the like. They have sought to discredit public initiatives to address major global problems (such as the WHO tobacco campaign discussed above) while promoting market-based solutions. By neutralizing the UN, one of the most prominent and vocal advocates of government action and accountability, neoliberals hoped to advance an ideology that is dismissive of all government as a solution to social problems and that celebrates corporations as concerned, helpful, and even necessary leaders in the search for a better world (Paine 2000).

Both within and outside of the UN, neoliberal advocates have worked hard to discredit their civil society rivals. At the same time, they have sought to convince the broader public that they are an essential part of the solution to the world's problems (Rupert 2000). As Sklair notes, "one of the most important ideological tasks of big business is to persuade the population at large that 'the business of society is business' and to create a climate of opinion in which trade unions and radical oppositions (especially consumer and environmental movements) are considered to be sectional interests while business groups are not" (1997:526). Thus, the ICC and other industry lobby groups have argued that industry deserves a special role in the UN, since, in the words of ICC president Helmut O. Maucher, "the ICC is 'different from the groups defending the number of butterflies in the world' because the ICC, in favoring free trade, is 'not driven by short-term interests'" (quoted in Charnovitz 1997: 280). This caricature of democratic globalization advocates is common among business elites and in the business-oriented media. The failure of many neoliberal advocates to take seriously any of the basic arguments being put forward by their opponents is pervasive, as this quote suggests. For instance, the very notion that species extinction is a frivolous and "short-term interest" is absurd.

Not only have neoliberal advocates challenged democratic globalization advocates' rights to have a voice in global settings, but they have also sought to delegitimize, ridicule, and demonize their rivals in the eyes of the public, using what Ferree calls "soft repression." Soft repression refers to "the nonviolent uses of power that are specifically directed against movement collective identities and movement ideas that support 'cognitive liberation' or 'oppositional conscious- ness'" (2005: 141). Soft repression occurs through micro-level ridicule, the creation of meso-level stigmas, and macro-level silencing—the exclusion of issues or voices from public policy and media discourses. One can find evidence of soft repression against democratic globalizers at all levels. Indeed, the surprise many felt in response to the anti-WTO protests in Seattle demonstrates the effective- ness of efforts to silence neoliberalism's critics—at least in the United States and other core countries. Given our concern here with meso-level dynamics, I focus on the use of stigma in the conflict between neoliberal and democratic globalizers.

By focusing media attention on militant forms of protest while ignoring the vast majority of protest actions that are explicitly nonviolent, the mass media help stigmatize all critics of neoliberalism, conveying the sense that protesters are violent, criminal (and therefore must be arrested or beaten by police), mis- guided or ignorant, and a minority. These messages seek to undermine demo- cratic globalizers' efforts to gain public support for the worthiness of their cause, and for the unity, numbers, and deep commitment of their supporters—what Tilly calls WUNC (Tilly 2004). The fact that police instigate most violence in pro- tests and that most nonviolent protests are ignored by mass media goes largely unnoticed by citizens who are dependent for information on a shrinking pool of large (and global) corporate media outlets. But its coverage of public protests is just a small part of the corporate media's effort to marginalize the voices of dis- sent against neoliberal globalizers. More routine matters such as the framing of media agendas and selection of spokespersons for different political viewpoints effectively shut out most skepticism about the neoliberal global agenda (Smith et al. 2001). This is why activists must use multiple strategies to try to gain attention to the issues they hope to address (see, e.g., chapters in Davenport et al. 2005).

The stigmatization or demonizing of protesters by neoliberal proponents goes well beyond actions in the mass media, however, and it pervades the or- ganizational cultures of many corporations and elite policy circles. This culture is evident in a mock police drill staged in New Jersey, which was framed as a struggle to liberate hostages taken at a Dow Chemical facility by three Justice for Bhopal activist-terrorists (McKenna 2005). Justice for Bhopal groups have never espoused hostage taking and/or violence to advance their cause. The fact that this particular conflict was selected also speaks of the extent to which the corporate culture and ideology is desensitized to massive human suffering, largely out of its interest in denying culpability for the social and environmental consequences of corporate practices. Justice for Bhopal groups seek restitution for victims of a chemical explosion in Bhopal, India, that caused more than fifteen thousand immediate deaths and an estimated eight hundred thousand birth defects and other enduring illnesses. Dow Chemical subsequently acquired the company that was at fault in the incident, and it claims that it bears no responsibility for its predecessor's actions and financial liabilities. Such use of misleading caricatures of activist groups both stigmatizes dissent and feeds into a broader culture of disdain for critical democratic dialogue. At the same time it reinforces the mythic image of corporations as irreplaceable providers of social needs and benefits.

Another way that neoliberal globalization network members work to undermine their rivals is by cultivating their own movement against NGOs and other civil society groups (Bob 2004). This seems to be a fairly new development, and it appears to be centered in right-wing think tanks based in the United States that are responding to perceived successes of civil society in international forums. The American Enterprise Institute (AEI) hosted a conference in 2003 entitled "Nongovernmental Organizations—The Growing Power of an Unelected Few." The conference featured numerous presentations lambasting the supposedly undemocratic and unaccountable organizations that populate civil society, and it helped launch a new Web site sponsored by the AEI and the Federalist Society called NGO-Watch.[13] The conference organizers summarized their rationale as follows:

In recent years, nongovernmental organizations (NGOs) have proliferated, their rise facilitated by governments and corporations desperate to subcontract development projects. While many NGOs have made significant contributions to human rights, the environment, and economic and social development, a lack of international standards for NGO accountability also allows far less credible organizations to have a significant influence on policymaking. The growing power of supranational organizations and a loose set of rules governing the accreditation of NGOs has meant that an unelected few have access to growing and unregulated power. NGOs have created their own rules and regulations and demanded that governments and corporations abide by those rules. Many nations' legal systems encourage NGOs to use the courts—or the specter of the courts—to compel compliance. Politicians and corporate leaders are often forced to respond to the NGO media machine, and the resources of taxpayers and shareholders are used in support of ends they did not intend to sanction. The extraordinary growth of advocacy NGOs in liberal democracies has the potential to undermine the sovereignty of constitutional democracies, as well as the effectiveness of credible NGOs.[14]

Although there may be some validity to these charges, the papers presented at the AEI conference suggested that "credible" NGOs are ones that accept market ideologies and view corporations as legitimate and rightful players in the policy-making process. "Advocacy" NGOs, on the other hand, are those questioning the role of corporations and free market policies in policy making.[15]

A major theme in many of the papers is that advocacy groups are undemocratic because they discriminate against the unorganized people who do not want to spend their time being active in politics. In the view promoted here, representative democracy adequately incorporates the views of the unorganized masses of the population. The fact that corporations might themselves be considered organized political interests is dismissed by their implicit assumption that corporations are not special interests and that they play some special role in the maintenance and well-being of society. Their success in the marketplace is seen to entitle corporations to a privileged position in policy circles. Thus the fact that, contrary to the claim quoted above, the UN has a rather elaborate system of NGO accreditation that subjects groups to regular scrutiny by member governments while it lacks any effective oversight even for its corporate partners is unproblematic (Bendell 2004; Wapner 2002).

Another example of neoliberal network efforts to stigmatize critics of neoliberal policies appears in a study of NGO accountability that was co-sponsored by a business lobby, Sustainability, the UN Global Compact, and UN Environment Programme, along with business partners such as Dow Chemical. The study, "The 21st Century NGO: In the Market for Change," essentially argues that civil society should conform to market principles in order to be seen as a responsible social actor and to free up billions of dollars of financial potential. It outlines a typology of NGOs that compares them to marine mammals, highlighting the extent to which each category of NGO is a "polarizer" and is "discriminating" in its choice of allies. Groups like Greenpeace and Global Exchange (Orcas) are considered polarizers (along with less discriminating groups using less discriminating, terrorist tactics—the "sharks"). "Dolphins" are the heroes of this analogy, and these include socially responsible investment groups. The lesson: if you want to be a legitimate, credible NGO, do not question basic market principles.

Although many of the arguments made by groups seeking to undermine civil society participation in politics are weak and susceptible to serious challenges by any advocate of democratic values, neoliberal influence over mass media and other mechanisms of ideology production gives these arguments more force than they might otherwise have. While corporations resist efforts to promote their own accountability to social norms, they demand greater accountability for civil society groups. And because of their relative powerlessness as well as their sincere commitment to democracy, civil society has taken action to enhance its own accountability and transparency,[16] even though its power to influence the conditions of most people's lives is dwarfed many times over by the overwhelming power of corporations. The relatively greater access corporate actors have to politicians and public officials means that their criticisms of civil society have become internalized in much official and academic discourse. At the very least, this has meant that neoliberal opponents have had to divert time and energy from their struggle against neoliberalism to answer to these challenges from their rivals. Few elites operating in governments or international forums have seriously questioned whether in fact civil society groups are unaccountable as charged. However, Wapner (2002) argues that by virtually any concrete measure, they are more accountable than either governments or corporations. What policy makers tend to ignore—and what neoliberal ideology seeks to obfuscate—is how the vast power discrepancies between corporations and citizens' groups distort attempts to govern global affairs along democratic principles.

In addition to their efforts at soft repression against their critics, neoliberal network members engage in another form of ideology-production that might be called "if you can't beat 'em, join 'em." While they work to discredit progressive civil society groups and otherwise marginalize them in the eyes of the public, neoliberals are also working to adopt strategies similar to those of their opponents by mobilizing their own grassroots support structures.[17] Much of this is consistent, however, with the revolution from above strategy discussed earlier. Support for neoliberalism, in other words, does not get large numbers of people out in the streets to show solidarity. But corporate players have sought to demonstrate that the policy preferences they espouse have widespread grassroots support. They have done so by creating their own NGOs, such as the now defunct Global Climate Coalition, an oil industry lobby that formed to oppose the Kyoto Protocol (Bruno and Karliner 2002). While that group disbanded after it was discredited as an industry front, another group, the Cooler Heads Coalition, seeks to fill its shoes while also ridiculing environmentalists as extremists who, it claims, exaggerate environmental problems and demand excessive and unnecessary policy responses. The U.S. government has also gotten into the act. For instance, it supports the nominally nonpartisan National Endowment for Democracy (NED), which has funded groups in a variety of countries (such as Haiti and Venezuela) that support neoliberalism and other U.S. foreign policy aims. The NED performs, in the words of a former director, some of the very same tasks the CIA used to carry out to promote regimes that were favorable to the United States (Schell 2005). Schell describes this strategy as "faking civil society," noting that this has long been practiced by agents of the U.S. government acting in other countries, but that more recently its use has grown within the United States.

Conclusion

Neoliberal globalizers have promoted global integration that advances the interests of global capitalism. Because the policies neoliberals espouse generate possibilities for resistance from many different groups while also contributing to social and ecological crises that could ultimately destroy the entire system, advocates for this system must constantly work to reinforce their position strategically and ideologically. As we saw in this chapter, actors in the neoliberal network have promoted a global order that has transformed the state in ways that favor the interests of global capital, marginalized the UN in favor of the multilateral economic institutions as the key arena of multilateral institution building, and supported a culture-ideology favorable to capitalist interests. In other words, although neoliberals have sought to portray it as such, the economic globalization we have today is not inevitable. It has been systematically advanced and supported by a very powerful network of business and political elites.

Understanding how this network operates is an important step in determining how a more democratic vision of globalization might be more effectively advanced. This analysis suggests that more concerted efforts to unify democratic globalizers around a plan to strengthen the UN and to subordinate the multilateral economic institutions to the UN Charter are important parts of any strategy for global democracy. This discussion also shows that a major part of this pro-democracy struggle is ideological. Democratic globalizers must seek to limit the power of neoliberal advocates to control public policy debates at national and international levels. Governments and the broader public must be allowed to scrutinize the widespread assumption that business interests necessarily coincide with those of the broader society and that special interests such as labor, human rights, and environmental groups are dubious if not devious. This is likely to require serious efforts to restructure transnational corporations and states so that the latter can effectively govern the former.

The anti-democratic nature of the neoliberal revolution is apparent in this analysis. If democracy is the source of political authority in modern society, then this neoliberal system is illegitimate and therefore vulnerable. By promoting a culture-ideology of human rights, the democratic globalization network can both reinforce more socially cohesive forms of multilateralism while posing a fundamental challenge for the neoliberal network and the culture-ideology of consumerism upon which it depends (Sklair 2002). Although it seems a daunting task given the capacities of the neoliberal network discussed here, we might remember the words of Genoa protesters: "You G8, we six billion" (quoted in della Porta et al. 2006).

The following chapter presents a historic overview of how the democratic globalization network has been promoting multilateral institution building that is consistent with its vision of how the world should be organized. It also highlights some important contrasts and new developments among more recent transnational popular mobilizations on questions of globalization. Although much of this history is not well known, it demonstrates the central role of citizens' groups in changing the world.

CHAPTER FIVE

Promoting Multilateralism

Social Movements and the UN System

Human rights NGOs [nongovernmental organizations] are the engine for virtually every advance made by the United Nations in the field of human rights since its founding.

(Gaer 1996: 51)

Historical accounts privilege the powerful, and thus our understandings of international institutions tend to overstate the roles of governments and major economic actors relative to other, less powerful actors. It is only very recently that international relations scholars have devoted much attention to NGOs, although a rich body of research now attests to their influence in global affairs. The previous chapter conveys a sense that the neoliberal globalization network has largely been able to dictate the course of global integration, but I want to show in the remainder of this book that popular groups have long been laying foundations for a different sort of world from that offered by neoliberalism. Democratic globalizers must claim and learn from this history if they are to effectively challenge global neoliberalism.

Robinson's notion of the neoliberal "revolution from above," described in the previous chapter, reflects the efforts of the transnational capitalist class (TCC) to capture national states and bring their influence to the cause of implementing neoliberalism. A key part of this revolution has been the creation of what Robinson calls a "transnational state," or the collection of transnational institutions and practices that "maintain, defend, and advance the emergent hegemony" of the TCC (2004: 100). He concludes that this transnational state "must *become* a contested site" (2004: 177, emphasis added) if there is to be any progress in reducing global inequalities and ensuring environmental sustainability.

But the transnational state has *always been* contested territory. In fact, emerging only in recent decades, the TCC, as a class, should be seen as a relative newcomer in this regard (Sklair 2001). Although it helps explain how a transnational capitalist elite amassed such tremendous influence, Robinson's analysis neglects the important work of ordinary people, who have long been involved in efforts to change the world. This chapter explores specific ways social movement actors have helped foster international cooperation to address global problems. I use the term *multilateralism* to refer to such relationships, which can be ad hoc and informal or long-term and formalized through intergovernmental organizations and treaties. Multilateral institutions cover a range of different cross-border issues, and some issue areas attract more movement mobilization than others. For instance, as we will see in chapter 6, human rights are a major emphasis of many activist groups active in promoting international law and institutions. Indeed, throughout its history (and at its founding), the UN attracted consistent attention from a range of different advocacy groups.[1]

People acting outside of governments or commercial settings have had important influences on the structures that govern the world. In particular, when we look at the ways citizens have been involved in efforts to shape transnational governance, we can see that they perform some key functions relevant to the development of multilateral cooperation and governance. First, they help *cultivate constituencies for multilateral institutions* in a context where there are no political parties, elections, or bureaucratic agencies to promote the legitimacy or to justify the existence of such institutions.[2] National political institutions depend upon the active support of popular constituencies for their very survival, and people in those offices consciously cultivate these ties between government and popular groups (O'Brien 2002; Wolfson 2001). But looking across the global landscape, we see very few formally organized actors who are both interested in and capable of performing this crucial role in a multilateral context. Social movements are one—and perhaps the most important—such actor.

Second, social movements and their broader alliance networks help *generate new ideas and proposals for cooperative multilateral initiatives*. While states are unlikely to voluntarily accept policies constraining their freedom of action, and while the transnational capitalist class is single-mindedly focused on the goal of increasing profits, social movement actors are seeking to generate new ideas for confronting a growing array of problems that require transnational attention. Their focused attention to problems such as human rights violations, poverty and social exclusion, or environmental degradation generates intensive efforts by social movement activists to come up with new ideas about how to improve these conditions. Moreover, when states seek to block progress on multilateral cooperative initiatives, we often find social movement actors working to overcome these state-imposed obstacles and advance multilateral programs. For instance, the efforts of the international civil society campaign to promote the International Criminal Court (Glasius 2002; Johansen 2006), the Land Mine Ban (Price 1998), and the nuclear test ban treaty (J. Smith 2000) all reflect successful efforts led by social movement actors to promote major multilateral initiatives in spite of objections of powerful states.

Third, social movements help promote multilateralism by *strengthening the correspondence between international norms and national and local practices.* They help generate the connective tissues between local and global that are needed to help build global structures that can address transnational problems in an effective and democratic manner. They do this when they work to domesticate international laws by monitoring state behaviors and calling upon local or national authorities to adapt their policies and practices. In addition to monitoring government action and drawing attention to failures, many groups also work in more proactive ways to help governments conform to international standards by, for instance, helping educate police and other public officials on how to incorporate international norms into their everyday routines. Some argue that enhancing the capacity of states to conform to international law is a more effective way to shape behavior than is the negative sanction of public shaming (Tharoor 2001).

Either way, by appealing to international norms, activists lay claim to recognized rights and expectations, calling on local and national authorities to respect those rights. They help bring complementary pressure on local and national authorities to harmonize state practices with international expectations. This is essential to strengthening international institutions, not only because it contributes (over time at least) to greater correspondence between international norms and practice, but also because it enhances the legitimacy, or popular acceptance, of global institutions (A. Clark 2003; Risse et al. 1999). Moreover, when they make such appeals, they expand the frame of their struggle from one that is locally defined to one that seeks input from a global court of appeals. They are saying, in other words, that national governments are not the final arbiter of some conflicts and that more universal rules or identities apply. This also helps create new possibilities for groups to form alliances with other elements of this emergent and increasingly organized transnational network of "global citizens" and international officials.

Here we look at how transnational social movement activism has promoted a democratic vision of a transnational state that is not simply a tool of global capitalism but instead promotes a more inclusive and democratic vision of global governance. I begin with a very brief discussion of some of the history of transnational activism that—while failing to do justice to these important and pathbreaking struggles—provides some historical background to the analysis of contemporary global activism that follows. Examining shifts in how social movement actors have related to multilateral institutions over time, we see that today's struggles seem less devoted to the aim of strengthening multilateralism than were their predecessors. Nevertheless, we do find groups within the democratic globalization network working to support multilateral institutions in various ways. I summarize some of the major campaigns in the contemporary global justice movement, which in this book I treat as an important part of a temporally and sectorally broader democratic globalization network. Subsequent chapters explore in more detail efforts of some groups that are part of contemporary global justice activism most directly linked to the aim of strengthening multilateral institutions. While the neoliberal network's revolution from above may lead many global activists to give up on multilateralism as a solution to the world's crises, I believe that only the transformation of multilateral institutions will allow us to manage global problems in a way that is equitable, inclusive, and sustainable.

A Short History of Transnational Mobilization for Human-Oriented Globalization

Like other aspects of globalization, political activism has a long history of transcending national borders (see, e.g., Boswell and Chase-Dunn 2000; Chatfield 1997; Hanagan 2002; Keck and Sikkink 1998; Nimtz 2002). Throughout modern times, the world has seen a variety of attempts by people working across national borders to effect change at the national and interstate levels. They have shared ideas and analyses, cultivated networks to support and advance their respective struggles, and increasingly have built more formal and sustained structures for transnational exchange and cooperation. They have promoted goals such as the abolition of slavery, the expansion of worker rights and other international human rights, the elimination of war and colonialism, and the promotion of socialism and political democracy.

In a variety of ways, transnational activists have sought to challenge the influence of capitalists on the evolving global order, aiming to reorient the distribution of economic and political power in the global system. While the issues on which they focus have varied, there is a common theme in that they all have somehow sought to define limits to states' authority. For instance, they work to constrain states' abilities to wage war, to promote human rights as a protection against the arbitrary use of state power, or to expand access to political and economic resources by marginalized groups. Occasionally they have sought to build formal interstate institutions that could check the militaristic activities of individual governments. And at times capitalists themselves have joined these struggles to advance multilateralism, seeing their own financial interests (if not their human interests) advanced through the cultivation of a system that could ensure greater international security and limit the scope and intensity of wars. Over time, the major emphases of transnational activism shifted, building upon the lessons of prior activism. Table 5.1 summarizes four major streams of activism for multilateralism during the twentieth and early twenty-first centuries.[3]

Socialism and Liberal Internationalism

The earliest forms of transnational activism centered on building an international socialist movement, opposing slavery and war, and promoting international law and institutions.[4] In this era, transnational ties were being mobilized to help define relationships between states, capitalists, and citizens, and by going outside the state, activists could find ideas, legitimacy, and leverage to advance their causes. They also aimed to define an interstate system that would help protect people from war and its consequences. This era saw the achievement of major advances for workers. Movements such as women's suffrage grew out of international labor, antislavery, and pacifist efforts (Ferree and Mueller 2004; Rosenthal et al. 1985; Rupp 1997). Some of the organizations of this period—such as the International Anti-Slavery Society, the War Resisters League, and the Women's International League for Peace and Freedom—remain active today.

From Altruism to Interdependence

A second era of transnational activism was marked by the rise of national independence movements and corresponding third world solidarity movements. Transnational ties helped mobilize opposition to colonial practices (e.g., Hochschild 1998), convey messages about revolutionary and anti-colonial struggles (McAdam et al. 2001), and cultivate transnational networks for financial and other support (Rucht 2000). The era was marked by transnational efforts to keep opposition to apartheid on the international agenda, even as Cold War rivalries dampened much hope for multilateral cooperation in the UN.

TABLE 5.1
Historical Shifts in Transnational Activism

Period	Key Themes	Central Emphases/Developments
Pre-1945–1950s	Socialism and liberal internationalism	* Antislavery * Anti-capitalist-socialist * Pacifist * World federalist/multilateralist
1960s–1970s	Altruism to interdependence	* National independence movements * Third world solidarity * Human rights * Rise of Amnesty International, Greenpeace
1980s–1990s	Exploring interdependence and seeking solutions	* Peace movements * IMF/World Bank protests * UN global conference organizing * Emphasis on alliances/ networking
2000s	Global justice	* Greater militancy (esp. in the North) * More explicit opposition to capitalism/corporate globalization * Reduced focus on/confidence in UN * World Social Forums and proactive organizing

The spread of information about conflicts and suffering in different parts of the world, and the connections these had to colonialism or superpower intervention helped foster greater understandings of global interdependence. The experiences of activists working to change the policies of governments, promote national liberation, or mitigate the suffering of people in the global South helped lay the intellectual groundwork for future activism. The contacts between Northern and Southern activists helped transform (though they could not eliminate) paternalistic visions of some Northern activists into more complex understandings of how the policies of Western states were implicated in wars and human rights violations around the world (Livezey 1989). Amnesty International was formed in this era, followed a decade later by Greenpeace, marking the beginning of a new phase of rapidly expanding transnational mobilization.

Exploring Interdependence and Seeking Solutions

The 1980s and 1990s saw a quickening pace of transnational communications, as peace movements expanded transnational ties and as opposition to global economic policies mounted around the world, especially in the global South. While there was not necessarily much transnational collective action, the mobilization of similar movements around common issues generated transnational contacts and analyses that further enhanced understandings of global interdependence and helped sharpen analyses of problems and their solutions (Cortright and Pagnucco 1997; McAdam and Rucht 1993; Rothman and Oliver 2002). Struggles in national contexts were more likely to be framed in transnational terms, and they more frequently focused on international targets. Popular protests in the global South against the International Monetary Fund (IMF) (Walton and Seddon 1994) coincided with environmental and human rights mobilizations against the World Bank in Europe and North America (Gerhards and Rucht 1992; Rucht 2003). At the same time, more people were focusing on the UN as a potential target for social change activism.

As we discussed in chapter 3, the UN hosted a series of global conferences during the 1990s addressing major global problems. The conferences proved fruitful settings for transnational exchanges of all kinds, aiding in the development of new understandings of global problems and encouraging transnational networking among those seeking to address them (Friedman et al. 2005; Willetts 1989). They also encouraged citizens' groups to promote multilateral institutions as tools for addressing a variety of problems such as poverty, environmental degradation, and human rights violations. This paralleled early efforts of peace activists to promote international law and organization as a means of curbing state violence (Chatfield 1997). Addressing themes such as environment and development (1992), human rights (1993), population (1994), social development (1995), women's issues (1995), and housing (1997), UN conferences created spaces for individual activists and public officials to discuss shared problems and possible solutions. The rather short timeframes between conferences, coupled with the preparatory and follow-up meetings associated with each conference, allowed sustained discussions of the issues and provided spaces for activists to learn from each other and adapt their views as they gained new information. Moreover, the conferences institutionalized routine review meetings that encouraged activists to monitor government compliance with their promises—thereby both providing a focal point for geographically dispersed activists and stimulating more systematic efforts to enhance transparency and accountability in global policy matters, thereby increasing governments' willingness and capacity to uphold international agreements.

As we saw in chapter 3, governments initially encouraged citizens' participation at the UN in part because they recognized that the organization would not succeed without the popular support and legitimacy that social groups bring to it. Broad popular support was lacking in the case of the League of Nations, leading to the failure of the Wilson administration in the United States to win congressional support for its decision to join the organization it helped to establish. A similar logic drove UN officials such as Maurice Strong, the secretary-general of the 1992 UN Conference on Environment and Development, to press for broad recognition of citizens' associations at global conferences sponsored by the UN. From the perspective of international officials, the most powerful governments are unlikely to take dramatic actions to promote environmental or social goals without public pressure and support. Encouraging ties between civil society and UN conferences was therefore a way to cultivate the political will to support multilateralism in the UN.

Global Justice

The end of the Cold War paved the way for the most recent period of transnational activism, the global justice era. It did so by, among other things, opening up space on the international agenda for debates on economic development issues and other concerns that had been caught up in the standoff between the two global superpowers (Kriesberg 1997). This period is characterized by heightened confrontation between civil society actors and international institutions, as more militant popular protests at meetings of the global financial institutions emerged in the 1990s. The aims of protesters also have become more explicitly anti-capitalist than they have been in the past, and more diverse groups are focusing on transnational corporations as a major source of their grievances. The framing of issues in more systemic and inter-related ways can most certainly be linked to the years of sustained transnational dialogue enabled by the UN conference process (e.g., Friedman et al. 2005; Krut 1997; Snyder 2003).

This era also reflects a much greater diversity in the structures and tactics used by activists in transnational campaigns. Advancements in technology have allowed more decentralized organizing structures, and it is now more possible than ever for local individuals and groups to have direct contact with activist counterparts around the world. Table 5.2 identifies generations of transnational activism, highlighting how the latest phase of activism compares with earlier ones in terms of its relationships to multilateralism.

Among other changes, many organizers in the most recent period have made the Internet more central to transnational organizing work. By communicating details of protests instantaneously to supporters around the world, transnational

TABLE 5.2
"Generational" Shifts in Movement–UN System Relations

Generation	(1) Multilateralist	(2) Transitional Advocacy Networks	(3) Direct Action
Timeframe	Pre-1980	1990s—UN conference era	Late 1990s—Seattle/ post-Seattle era
Relation to UN System	Requesting access Expanding agenda	"Loyal opposition" and creative multilateralism	Ambivalent
Focus	Institutions and policy	Policy/issue advocacy; institutions	Diverse social justice agenda Policy/issue advocacy and culture
Targets	Intergovernmental bodies and government delegations	Government (all levels), UN system, some corporations	Financial institutions—TNCs, World Bank, WTO, etc.; less focus on UN Social/cultural— creating alternatives to formal politics*
Goals	Establish civil society access to intergovernmental organizations Expand multilateral agendas to include social concerns Legitimize civil society role in global arenas	Strengthen multilateral agreements, enhance enforcement and regulatory mechanisms and expand their attention to social concerns Establish information regimes/policy networks Defend and expand access and legitimacy for civil society in global arenas	Participatory politics Changing values of predominant sociopolitical order Communications and solidarity networks to empower individuals, maximize information flows Alternative venues for global problem-solving

SOURCE: Adapted from Bennett (2005: 214).
  * Activities to shape cultural and social spaces are common to all three "generations" and to most social movement activism generally, but they are more pronounced in the latest period.

activists help amplify the voices of those marginalized by mainstream political processes and heighten awareness among activists of the many similarities they share with people in very different parts of the world. Whereas prior to the late 1990s most transnational activism was limited to lobbying and symbolic protests at formal international meetings, large public demonstrations are more frequently used to target global institutions.

The other shift between this period and the previous one is that, on the whole, activists seem to be devoting less energy and attention to the UN. In part this change is related to the absence of large-scale UN conferences and the mobilizations that surrounded them. Whereas during the 1990s activists were being asked by governments and the UN to actively participate in international discussions about how to address the most pressing global problems, these invitations have become far fewer and more conditional and contested in recent years (Charnovitz 1997).

Another reason for the shift is the sense that the global financial institutions have in many ways eclipsed the UN and undermined its importance, and activists recognize a need to shift their attention to those powerful institutions. Many found that the treaties on which they focused their energies during the 1980s and 1990s were essentially trumped by international trade agreements that allow trade law to supersede other international agreements. Some in the activist community had also grown wary of a growing corporate influence in the UN, which became evident during the mid-1990s (see chapter 4). The International Forum on Globalization articulated this fear most directly when it hosted a meeting to parallel the UN Millennium Forum entitled, "Can the UN be Salvaged?" David Korten, a leading activist and intellectual, expressed his own disappointment at this realization:

> Those of us who have been studying these issues have long known of the strong alignment of the World Trade Organization (WTO), the World Bank, and the IMF to the corporate agenda. By contrast the United Nations has seemed a more open, democratic and people friendly institution. What I found so shattering was the strong evidence that the differences I have been attributing to the United Nations are largely cosmetic. (Korten 1997)

Few groups have actively mobilized against the UN, and those that do tend to advocate the anti-globalist positions (see, e.g., Buss and Herman 2003). Nevertheless, there has been a noticeable decline in attention to the institution within major civil society forums such as the World Social Forum (WSF). Surveys of activists showed that many felt that UN negotiating processes are too slow and narrowly focused to address urgent global crises (Krut 1997). Others grew tired of condescending attitudes of officials, a sense that governments do not listen to their input, and reduced access to UN forums.[5] At the same time, however, activists I have spoken with and listened to generally acknowledge that, despite its many flaws, the UN is essential to addressing major global problems.

Amid this ambivalence about the UN, many organizers are responding to democratic deficits in global institutions by exploring more popularly based approaches to advancing a different global political and economic order. The cases examined in the following chapters illustrate how some groups have drawn from past experience in international institutions to develop new approaches to influencing global political processes. Using skills learned at UN conferences and in other transnational settings, these groups have helped create new forms of global political action. These may one day become routinized in a more democratic global polity.

A final important characteristic of this latest phase of transnational activism is that instead of mobilizing according to the conference schedules of global institutions, activists have advocated a proactive approach that is more decentralized and grassroots-oriented than those in previous eras. Following criticisms that protests at the WTO and other global financial meetings were only against something but lacked a coherent vision of an alternative to economic globalization, activists in Brazil and France came together to launch the WSF process in 2001 (see chapter 10). Under the slogan "another world is possible," activists gather to exchange experiences, support each other's struggles, build transnational alliances, and plan coordinated strategies and actions. In many ways, its form reflects the NGO conferences that ran parallel to UN global conferences, but the WSF represents an autonomous civil society approach to shaping a global agenda in a space that is not defined by existing institutional frameworks.

Evidence of this shift away from multilateralism was emerging well before the massive protests against the WTO. For instance, a 1995 survey of participants in UN conferences[6] concluded that "NGOs are more interested in creating direct citizen to citizen links at and around international events than in attempting to alter what apparently is perceived to be the relatively weak or weakening existing intergovernmental machinery" (Benchmark Environmental Consulting 1996: 54). The survey found that many participants were beginning to recognize a role for themselves in shaping the global system, since

> the nation state has failed to adequately "represent" its citizens on a range of global issues. The nation state has been eclipsed by the development of a global consciousness, a consciousness of nature, a women's consciousness, along with the collapse of the ideological cohesiveness fostered by the Cold War . . . In this situation, the international NGO community sees itself—and is increasingly seen by governments—as part of embryonic institutional structures that will define a different form of global governance, a model in which citizen action occurs at a global level. (Benchmark Environmental Consulting 1996: 4)

Thus, in contrast to earlier eras of transnational activism, today's transnational struggles lack the same focus on and commitment to supporting multilateral institutions (see, e.g., Bennett 2005; Hill 2004). In fact, Friedman and her colleagues report that some groups found that their national-level work could be "jeopardized, 'tainted' by association with conference declarations that domestic actors find illegitimate" (2005: 171). It is not a coincidence that this trend corresponds with neoliberal globalizers' efforts (described in the previous chapter) to cultivate their own vision of a neoliberal, globally integrated economy. By co-opting national and international institutions for the cause of neoliberal globalization, they have led those who feel excluded by the global capitalist order to seek solutions outside these existing structures. Our focus in this book is on the nonviolent and pro-democratic responses to the social exclusion caused by economic globalization. But the loss of popular legitimacy in global institutions also motivates growing networks of people advocating violent and fundamentally antidemocratic resistance to social exclusion, and their popularity will only increase if democratizing forces are ignored or repressed.

NODES OF THE DEMOCRATIC GLOBALIZATION NETWORK

The notion of the democratic globalization network as I use it in this book combines a wide variety of diverse streams of activism into a single, broadly conceived network. Certainly many, if not most, participants in these groups would not necessarily see themselves in these terms. Nevertheless, in the course of their struggles, all campaigns to promote some sort of progressive change in the global system tend to generate democratizing pressures on global institutions.[7] The cases discussed in the following chapters represent just a small part of the broader democratic globalization network, which, like the neoliberal network, is multifaceted and expansive. To provide a more complete picture of the whole, I briefly describe some of the more prominent streams of contemporary activism for global democracy and social justice.[8]

Early anti–free trade activism has attacked neoliberal policies most directly at the sites of international negotiations over regional economic integration (Peet 2003). Activists in Europe and North America have long been resisting efforts to open borders to the free flow of goods and services without maintaining measures of social protection. Ayres (1998) describes the campaigns against North American economic integration, tracing the progression in activists' discourse from more nationalist-oriented frames to more transnational, pro-democracy frames. This happened especially as the initial plan for a bilateral agreement between the United States and Canada expanded into the trilateral North American Free Trade Agreement (NAFTA). Foster (2005) demonstrates how anti–free trade networks in North America gradually flowed into (and helped build) the WSF process. Similar transformations in framings of conflicts occurred in other parts of the world (Coleman and Wayland 2004; Imig and Tarrow 2001). Perhaps the most visible counterpart to the anti-NAFTA alliance is the European farmers' coalition (Confédération Paysanne), whose fiery spokesperson, José Bové, has drawn widespread attention to their concerns. Many of the intellectual leaders who emerged from national anti–free trade initiatives around the world came together in 1994 to form the International Forum on Globalization (IFG), an organization that helped disseminate analyses and critiques of the global economy through its teach-ins and publications. IFG was especially important in bringing Southern perspectives to Northern debates, and this network of leading international thinkers published *Alternatives to Economic Globalization: A Better World Is Possible* (Cavanagh and Mander 2004) to publicize an integrated set of analyses and prescriptions for global change.

Jubilee 2000, the campaign to press rich country governments to drop the debt of poor countries, emerged largely from faith-based networks of activists, many of whom had been active in development and other social justice work that brought together activists from the global North and South. The long-term work of faith-based and development organizations in poor countries gave them an important perspective on how international debt impacts countries' prospects for development. Many of these groups were therefore also active in the events surrounding the World Bank/IMF fiftieth-anniversary celebration, which inspired the creation of the Fifty Years Is Enough network (Khagram 2004; Peet 2003). As activists looked forward to the turn of the twenty-first century, they called upon the biblical notion of jubilee, which by tradition meant that debts were wiped clean, to press governments to use the occasion of the new millennium to give poor countries a fresh economic start. The religiously inspired theme of jubilee extended its appeal to a much wider range of activists than might typically have been reached, and certainly this campaign was central to helping frame the agendas of activists and building the momentum for the widespread global justice protests that emerged in the late 1990s. Jubilee 2000 activists pursued government officials to their meetings of the G8, World Bank, and other venues, bringing ever-larger numbers with them as they did so. The seventy thousand anti-debt protesters who turned up at the 1998 meeting of the G8 in Birmingham, for instance, should have given the Seattle police plenty of advance warning to prepare for the WTO ministerial there.

Other important activist streams include transnational labor, which over the late 1990s in particular had been transforming its approach away from the business-unionism that had characterized many Northern unions in the past toward more social movement unionism. As unions faced growing pressures from employers and declining memberships, they sought to expand their leverage by seeking alliances with other social groups. Efforts continue to expand cooperation between labor and other social movements (Munck 2002; O'Brien Forthcoming; Waterman 2005).

Transnational environmentalism has been challenged by the often very localized focus of some conservation campaigns, and this issue in particular has proved to be an important stumbling block between activists in the North and South (Faber 2005; Rootes 2005). Nevertheless, some environmental groups have made some important breakthroughs in overcoming the North-South divide, and this has happened when environmentalists have expanded their analyses to adopt a political ecology frame, which accounts for the human rights implications of environmental destruction (Rothman and Oliver 2002). Another important environmental-based conflict is the debate over the use of genetically altered seed and the related intellectual property/bio-piracy implications. These concerns have generated massive resistance from farmers around the world (Shiva 2005).

Women's rights and gender questions have also contributed important streams of activism, as many analyses show that women and children are most harshly affected by neoliberalism. A group of women intellectual/organizers from global South countries launched an organization called Development Alternatives for Women in a New Era (DAWN) in the 1980s. The group formed in the course of preparations for the UN women's conference in Nairobi (1985). DAWN's network of activists helped articulate and publicize for activists in both the North and South a critique of globalized capitalism that took into account the particular perspective of women. Their solution to the ills caused by globalized capitalism was women's empowerment. DAWN remains a prominent organization in the democratic globalization network, and its analyses have been crucial to helping inform a broader public about the effects of neoliberalism, inspiring many to action (Mayo 2005; Moghadam 2000, 2005). But even as gendered analyses offer much to the broader critique of neoliberalism, women have generally faced an uphill struggle to keep gender issues on the agenda of the global network (Macdonald 2005).

Another prominent transnational organization that deserves mention here is the Association pour la Taxe Tobin pour l'Aide aux Citoyens (ATTAC). ATTAC was formed in France, at the initiative of organizers with *Le Monde diplomatique* as an effort to initiate a small international tax on international financial transactions that would help prevent destabilizing forms of international currency speculation while also raising money for development assistance. The idea for the tax came from Nobel-laureate economist James Tobin, who along with many economists believe that speculative international currency transactions are fundamentally destabilizing and must be discouraged (although Tobin himself is not associated with ATTAC). ATTAC expanded quickly and, like Jubilee 2000, helped bring critiques of neoliberalism to a wider public. As we will see later in the book, ATTAC has also become an important player in the WSF process (Kolb 2005).

Finally, although I cannot devote much space to it here, the international peace movement is also an important stream of activism feeding contemporary social justice activism. Indeed, as the U.S. occupation of Iraq continues, many groups that were once primarily focused on opposing neoliberalism have had to alter their frames to demonstrate how militarism and imperialism are connected with other features of global economic integration (Bennis 2006). Nevertheless, many activists involved in the groups discussed above have also been involved in peace movement campaigns, and for many their critiques of globalization emerge from anti-U.S. intervention activism that familiarized them with the ways U.S. military intervention was used to support neoliberal economic policies (Marullo et al. 1996; C. Smith 1996). As we will see in chapter 8, a precursor and perhaps a warm-up to the 1999 Seattle protests happened in May 1999 at a conference declaring that "peace is a human right." That meeting gave evidence that many groups framing their concerns around peace were preoccupied with efforts to restructure the global economy and to strengthen international law. Antiwar mobilizations surrounding the U.S. invasion of Iraq built upon the base of activism generated by global economic justice campaigns. Activists whose introduction to the democratic globalization network came through their antiwar sentiments will likely gain new insights into the connections between militarism and the global economy.

While these may seem to be diverse and meandering streams that do not fit neatly into one's conception of what contemporary global activism is about, what unifies them is that *each of them raises claims that demand new ways of organizing the world*. Whether or not they begin with this clearly articulated idea, many activists find in the course of struggle that many different causes can benefit from new and more democratic architecture of global governance (see, e.g. Economy 2004). Ideas for such an institutional reordering are becoming more apparent as more groups have opportunities to interact and work together—in the words of the Zapatistas, "against neoliberalism and for humanity."

This broad historical overview demonstrates several key points. First, the movement for global democracy and economic justice has a long history. In fact, its organizational and intellectual origins can be traced back much farther than most people think, and many of the critiques found in contemporary activist discourse have evolved over years, if not decades. Themes such as human dignity, a prioritization of human rights, and sustainability can be found in many of the historic streams of activism that have fed the contemporary river of activism that is forming to demand a more democratic world order.

Also, global South activists have been more central to setting the stage for contemporary global justice activism than is often recognized. The "battle of Seattle" really began with the IMF riots in the global South, if not earlier. Southern struggles against colonialism, apartheid, and the neocolonialism of the global financial system both fostered transnational linkages and helped sensitize Northern activists to issues of interdependence and the structural sources of economic inequality. Contacts between activists in the global North and South, while at times tension-filled, helped sensitize activists to issues of power and to the ways contemporary globalization parallels earlier forms of imperialism. The practical need to build broad transnational alliances in order to establish the worthiness, unity, numbers, and commitment of their cause helped sustain efforts at transnational dialogue and compromise even when the going got tough (e.g., Doherty and Doyle 2006; Rothman and Oliver 2002; Snyder 2003; Wood 2005). In the current era, it is the Southern unions, political parties, and movements that are playing central roles as drivers of innovation (Baiocchi 2004; Chase-Dunn 2002; Kitchelt 2003; Moody 1997).

A third conclusion is that the experience of struggle has informed and nurtured new skills, ideas, and structures for transnational organizing, and these lessons have developed over time (see, e.g., Polletta 2002; Starhawk, 2001). Activists have learned new ways of doing politics within a global context, and they have disseminated these skills through training sessions, Internet sites, and ongoing organizing efforts. They have learned ways to nurture transnational "imagined communities" and foster collective identities emphasizing transcendent values and goals. They have refined organizing techniques and leadership skills to bridge the differences between different cultural and sectoral groups. Such work has been essential to the various efforts throughout history to promote and support multilateral forms of global governance.

Conclusion

Recent history might lead analysts to conclude that it is global corporations and their supporters in governments and international agencies who rule the world (Robinson 2004). Indeed, the neoliberal globalization network has, as I showed in chapter 4, worked to marginalize the UN system and to strengthen the influence of global institutions governing international trade and finance. These developments have encouraged the global expansion of capitalism while exacerbating economic and political inequalities. However, a closer look shows that transnational alliances of civil society actors have long been at work trying to shape a vision of world order that is not defined by the needs of capital, but rather that responds to broader concerns for human well-being. Transnational campaigns to end slavery, promote the rights of women, and limit the destructiveness of wars are but a few examples of these multilateralist campaigns by early transnational networks of activists that have most definitely helped change the world. This history should inform and guide today's struggles, and indeed the remaining chapters show how some contemporary groups carry forth the pro-multilateralist legacy of transnational activism.

Over time, transnational organizers learned new ways of acting in the world, discovering more inclusive ways to frame their struggles as they incorporated new and diverse groups from different parts of the world. They also learned new strategies for engaging with international political processes, and they cultivated important allies within developing international institutions, particularly in the UN. They have helped draft the blueprints and build the structures of the global institutions that govern our world today. While these institutions have not lived up to the expectations of most activists, they still bear the imprints of those seeking alternatives to capitalist globalization. I argue with great certainty that without the democratic globalization network, the world would be a much different and much less desirable place to live. Many national and international officials would see their work as impossible without the contributions of civil society groups who monitor government compliance with international agreements, educate the public about international institutions and norms, and help develop ways of overcoming obstacles to multilateral cooperation.

Despite this rich and long-standing tradition of transnational activism to support multilateralism, many in the contemporary transnational network promoting alternatives to neoliberal globalization express ambivalence toward multilateral institutions. This comes at a time when the organizations and networks supporting transnational activism are far stronger, denser, and deeper than they have ever been. While it is often true that formal institutions can inhibit attempts to address fundamental inequalities, it is also the case that we know of no other mechanisms for resolving conflicts nonviolently. Multilateral *political* institutions are essential to any attempt to subordinate economic institutions to democratic practices and promote a more peaceful and humane global order.

The important question for those wishing for something other than the neo-liberal vision of globalization is how to reclaim the UN and other global institutions for all the world's people. A first step is to reclaim the history of social movements as important players in the process of constructing multilateral institutions. Early global institutions were indeed radical initiatives to socialize states, reining in their more destructive activities and defining new rights for citizens (Finnemore 1996). They are also potential tools for prioritizing the role of national governments as legal guarantors of human rights rather than as commanders of armies and managers of national economies. Certainly an aim of the neoliberal network is to prioritize the economic managerial role of states, and some portions of the transnational capitalist class benefit from, and therefore encourage, the militarized states that spend more than a trillion dollars on their militaries every year. But the modern "transnational state" (in Robinson's definition) still must rely for its long-term survival on the continued support of those it governs. The failures of neoliberal economics to provide the basic needs of much of the world's population, environmental destruction, the self-destructive tendencies of modern warfare, and the growing threats militarization poses for civilian populations undermine this essential foundation of legitimacy. Thus, there is hope that advocates of a different world order can reclaim the transnational state to serve the interests of more of the world's people.

A lesson from this analysis is that social movements should work more closely with international, national, and local officials in their efforts to promote an alternative to the neoliberal vision of globalization. Governments are not unitary actors with a single vision for the common good, and movements can often find allies in these institutions. While they will have to work harder than their rival network counterparts do to win the ears of those in powerful offices, the correspondence of many of their aims with those of local and national governments and international agencies can create opportunities for alliances that might be used to greater effect than they have been thus far. Even when they are sympathetic to the aims of movements, public officials often lack the access to information and opportunities to organize the analyses they need to affect policy changes. But the democratic globalization network can bring important skills and resources to efforts at remedying such information gaps, if only they can work to build ties to relevant public offices and find ways to convey such information and ideas effectively. Moreover, they must assert their rights to have a voice in these settings. Despite claims by their neoliberal rivals that civil society groups are not elected and are not democratic in a formal sense, in practice these groups are more accountable and responsive to citizens than are corporations and most government officials. Furthermore, as a collection of voluntary actors committed to public deliberation and "cooperative inquiry," they operate in ways that are far more democratic than those of most formally democratic institutions (Nanz and Steffek 2004; Wapner 2002).

A point I emphasize throughout this book is that social movement actors should be more self-conscious of their historic role as forces for democratizing both national and international political institutions, and they should be more purposeful in their efforts to come together around the cause of global democracy. A more mindful commitment to the promotion of democracy would strengthen possibilities for multilateralism (and vice versa: see Kaldor 2003: 138). More deliberate work to develop proposals for institutional reforms that make these bodies more representative of and responsive to human needs is sorely needed. For many civil society groups, advocating for more democratic institutions is at best seen as secondary to their work on particular issues. But more coordinated and self-conscious efforts by social movement groups to promote global democracy would enhance the effectiveness of a wide variety of social change campaigns. Moreover, by cultivating deeper appreciation within countries as well as in global discourse for the basic principles that constitute democracy, social movements can help nurture a human rights culture that can overcome the dangerous divisions the world now faces.

This chapter has sought to challenge assumptions that neoliberal globalizers are the only actors offering a vision of how the world might be organized. Looking at the ways citizens' groups have engaged international processes over centuries we can see traces of an emergent democratic globalization network articulating and promoting a vision of a democratic, human rights, and dignity-based global order. In the following chapter I explore the social and organizational infrastructures that help support this transnational network and its efforts to change the world.

CHAPTER SIX

Mobilizing a Transnational Network for Democratic Globalization

Previous chapters have outlined the neoliberal and democratic visions of globalization and the rival transnational networks that advance each one. They also considered some of the different capacities and relative advantages of these two rival networks and the broader political arena in which these networks compete. This chapter looks at the social infrastructures, the "preexisting structures of organization and communication" (Zald and McCarthy 1987: 71) that make up the democratic globalization network. It considers more specifically *how* people bring together the resources and skills needed to do transnational political work, and what organizational forms have been developed for this purpose. We explore organizational patterns over time to gain insights into how changes in the broader political environment have affected the network. Specifically, do we find evidence that this network has been successful at overcoming important differences in cultures and experiences to forge durable transnational alliances? And how is the network's evolution related to the broader context of mobilization and contestation?

Concepts of Social Movements

Most recent work in the field of social movements emphasizes the need for greater efforts to understand movements in terms of their interactions with opponents and for a greater appreciation of the network-like structure that characterizes both social movements and their adversaries (Diani 2003; Maney 2001). Social movements are increasingly described as "networks of informal interactions between a plurality of individuals, groups, or associations, engaged in political or cultural conflict" (Diani and Bison 2004: 282). Analysts of contemporary global activism argue that, to understand contemporary social movements, we need to focus less on organizations and actors and more on processes and interactions among actors (Anheier and Katz 2005; Chesters 2004; Juris 2008). By discussing the contemporary movement for global justice as part of a much broader transnational network mobilizing in opposition to a rival neoliberal network, this book responds to these two challenges. I begin by unpacking the concept of social movement to reveal its various components.

Social movements differ from more conventional political actors such as interest groups in that they lack regular access to political institutions and the elites operating within those institutions. In contrast to interest groups, which are principally involved in promoting the material concerns of particular (and usually relatively privileged) groups within the existing political arrangement, social movements pursue more "transformational" goals that alter power relations in society. To borrow a metaphor, movements are less concerned with the division of the pie than with the recipe for making it (Foster 1999: 135). This places them at odds with more powerful established interests within governments and transnational corporations.

While we might agree on the rough ideas about what constitutes a social movement, what can become difficult is how to analyze them. For instance, while most people agree that social movements engage in contentious collective action, we know from studies of social movement organizations that very few of them spend very much of their time actually engaging in protest. Most social change groups spend far more time doing public education, attending meetings, and building their organizations than they do on the streets. Many movement actors engage in conventional political actions such as voter registration or lobbying in addition to other non-conventional or "transgressive" activities (McAdam et al. 2001). Analysts are increasingly attentive to the cultural work of social movements, stressing the ways movements cultivate identities and cultural norms that challenge predominant social discourses and logics through actions that go well beyond public protests (Escobar and Alvarez 1992; Rochon 1998). If analyses of social movements refer only to evidence of actual protest activities, they miss the bulk of the collective action in which social movement actors are engaged.

Another important question is what constitutes *transnational* collective action. While we have observed large increases in the number of transnational organizations promoting social movement aims, analyses of protest episodes have found only small numbers of protests that specifically target transnational institutions and goals (Imig and Tarrow 2001; Rootes 2002). At the same time, many groups promote campaigns that urge their members to organize parallel pressures on their respective national governments. For instance, after having helped achieve the passage of a treaty to establish the International Criminal Court, supporters of that campaign are now working to put simultaneous pressure on multiple governments to ratify and begin implementing this international convention. Such campaigns represent transnational collective action in the sense that they are coordinated transnationally and that they are all focused on a particular, transnational target or agenda. But they do not require that people from different countries converge on a common site to put pressure on a representative of transnational authority.

Both of these conceptual challenges are related to a third challenge for those studying transnational social movements. Specifically, most conventional understandings of social movements cast these actors in opposition to state authorities. However, when we consider a setting of complex multilateralism, the relationships of movements and states and intergovernmental organizations can often be complementary rather than competitive.[1] As we saw in chapter 5, movements have been important advocates for multilateral governance as a means of reining in the more destructive tendencies of state power. This is most evident in the area of human rights law and conventions on the laws of war. Advocates of human rights and of greater economic equality are finding themselves in the position of advocating for stronger state authority relative to, for instance, transnational corporations or international financial agencies that are seen as contributing to human rights violations and economic inequalities (e.g., Guidry 2000; Seidman 2004; Wainwright 2003).

When social movement actors promote specific changes in international law, they frequently must build alliances with and otherwise strengthen the political leverage of sympathetic governments (Bennis 2006). So states and movements are not necessarily adversaries; and in fact, as our rival transnational networks model suggests, the role of the state itself is an object of contention between neoliberal and democratic globalization networks. For instance, while some transnational corporations desire a state that has minimal regulatory capacity but that can enforce property rights and social order, other actors prefer (and need) a state that governs corporate actions in a way that ensures a healthy environment and a decent standard of living for all people. Officials within any given state will differ themselves over this matter, with environmental and health officials likely seeking greater state regulation and financial officials wanting less. Indeed, given that a major aim of neoliberal globalizers is to privatize many aspects of the state, a key aim for some opponents of neoliberalism should be to defend the public sector from efforts to turn it into a means of private profit making (e.g., Evans 1997; Korzeniewicz and Smith 2000).

Mobilizing Structures

The network concept integrates the understanding that a wide variety of actors participate in social movements at various times and places. Analysts have used the concept of mobilizing structures to refer to the many different formal and informal entities that tend to be involved in a wide variety of different movements. A key idea here is that, as modern societies become increasingly bureaucratic, or formally and professionally organized, they generate many different spaces that have the potential to be appropriated for social change efforts. Indeed, by increasing demands on people's time and generating built environments that hinder regular face-to-face communication with friends and neighbors, modern societies may require that those promoting social change work to bring political messages into these diverse spaces (Wuthnow 1998). Churches, social justice committees of professional associations, and even softball leagues linked to communities can become involved in collective efforts to promote change (Zald and McCarthy 1987).

At the same time, most broad-based and long-term movements contain a number of formal organizations whose primary goal is to advance movement-specific aims. But movements are not only made up of formal organizations, and some would argue that they are becoming increasingly decentralized and informal in their structure, as individuals and loosely defined networks become more common (Bennett 2005; Diani and Bison 2004). McCarthy (1996) uses the concept of mobilizing structures to describe the variation in who participates in typical social movements. Table 6.1 draws from this work to describe the mobilizing structures that characterize transnational social movement networks.

The top, left-hand cell of table 6.1 displays some of the *informal, non-movement structures* through which transnational movements can mobilize influence. National mobilizing structures are likely to include friendship and professional networks, or informal collections of individuals and/or organizations that because of social or work routines have either incidental or deliberate contact on a regular basis. However, their transnational importance has expanded with the greater ease of travel and communication. In addition, officials in international agencies and delegates on national missions to international governmental organizations can be important channels of transnational mobilization. There are also distinctly transnational networks of people likely to be responsive to movement goals, such as refugees, immigrant workers, or international students, who might bring pressure on their state of occupancy (or of their birth) to modify policies vis-à-vis their home (or host) states.

TABLE 6.1
Transnational Mobilizing Structures

	Non-movement	Movement
Informal	Friendship networks Professional networks Expatriate networks Individuals in intergovernmental bureaucracies or national delegations	Activist networks Affinity groups Refugee/exile networks
Formal	Churches Unions* Professional associations Regional cooperative associations Service organizations Intergovernmental and state bureaucracies National delegations Foundations	TSMOs Unions* SMOs (national and local) Protest committees (of other NGOs) Transnational NGO coalitions Movement research institutes

SOURCES: Adapted from McCarthy (1996: 145); Smith et al. (1997: 62).

* In some national contexts, unions may be more appropriately considered movement structures because their key operations challenge fundamental power structures. But in most Western societies their principal strategies and formal organizational missions do not include broad social change goals, and in other countries they are controlled by governments. Thus they are included in the non-movement column.

The *formal, non-movement* cell lists societal organizations that often support nascent movements or join broader social change campaigns. Some of these groups—including some labor unions and many service-providing organizations—may have grown out of earlier social movements. In transnational settings, this category may include large organizations working on development projects, resettling refugees, and undertaking other humanitarian initiatives. In some countries, unions are more likely to be considered movement than non-movement actors, given their more confrontational approach to governments and capitalists. Such formal organizations may be seen as sites for what Oberschall calls "bloc recruitment" for movements (Oberschall 1980). When they support or join broader movement campaigns, they can bring large constituencies whose activism may enhance a movement's political impact. Moreover, churches, unions, and professional associations may at times provide protection from government repression or lend legitimacy to the movement.

The important role of religious institutions is worth emphasizing here. Zald and McCarthy (1987) identify ways that religious institutions have supported various social movements by providing essential resources, personnel, and ideological support to movements. Religious institutions also serve as organizational settings where transnational identities and solidarities can emerge (Nepstad 2002). This greatly facilitates transnational mobilization and diffusion of movement ideas (see, e.g., Livezey 1989).

The aims of some governmental and intergovernmental organizations frequently overlap with those of social movements, and thus these structures may also assist movement mobilization (McCarthy and Wolfson 1992; Stearns and Almeida 2004; Swarts 2003). The UN Human Rights Commission, for instance, relies heavily on the work of human rights organizations. As we saw from the previous chapter, international officials often seek to work with civil society groups not only to gain access to the knowledge and skills that these groups have but also to expand their support base, enhance their capacities to monitor government practices and to address problems, and foster constituencies to support multilateralism.

The *informal movement* dimension of mobilizing structures may be the most dynamic and important one for contemporary global change. This category consists of networks of activists or like-minded individuals. Sometimes these networks take the form of affinity groups, which are informal structures characterized by clearly defined norms and shared expectations that emerged from early anarchist and direct action protests in the West (Epstein 1991). These were also important in the protests of the late 1990s and early twenty-first century against global financial institutions. These more informal networks might be even more important for transnational movements than they are for national ones. As was discussed in earlier chapters, networking among individuals and groups is facilitated by the same transportation and communication technologies that help to break down the boundaries between states and encourage global trade and other forms of integration (Giddens 1990). Analysts cite the expanding role of information in contemporary societies as a major factor enhancing the role of networks relative to more hierarchical and formal organizing structures (e.g., Castells 1996). Perhaps because social movements are most clearly engaged in "information politics" and communication-based political work, scholars have emphasized the importance of informal and fluid networks of actors to global social change processes.

Finally, the *formal movement* actors in transnational movements include transnational social movement organizations as well as increasing numbers of national and locally organized social movement organizations. They can also include protest committees of other formal organizations such as professional associations or unions. Increasingly, movement activity generates formal transnational organizations that help coordinate action on particular issues or campaigns over time. And because modern politics involves extensive amounts of information and deliberation of a variety of scientific evidence and political viewpoints, think tanks and research institutes established to promote the aims of particular social movements are increasingly common and important.

Movement networks will vary over time in terms of which actors they integrate and how extensively different types of actors are involved in network activity. But an analysis of the mobilizing structures available in a given context helps us identify the possibilities for broadening support for the more particular goals of global justice activists as well as for the more encompassing aim of enhancing global democracy in a given social setting. Also, it can help us assess the organizational, political, cultural, and technical capacities of the network.

Organizations and Episodes

Mobilizing structures help link people, ideas, and resources, but the essence of social movements is collective action in public spaces. Such actions might be called "episodes of contention," or instances where opponents mobilize public, collective challenges to authorities (McAdam et al. 2001: 85). Often these episodes involve mass demonstrations, civil disobedience, and even violence against property or (far less frequently) persons. Typical protest episodes today are shaped in important ways by social movement organizations, which devote extensive efforts to spreading particular understandings of problems and encouraging public support for social change ideas.

Social movement organizations facilitate demonstrations by specifying and publicizing the date and location of action, arranging with public authorities for permission to use public spaces, providing marshals and other facilities to accommodate protesters, and building alliances with social networks outside the movement in order to generate large numbers of demonstrators. For instance, in the 1999 protests against the World Trade Organization (WTO) meeting in Seattle, the consumer rights organization Public Citizen devoted a staff member and opened an office in Seattle specifically to help mobilize widespread support for the protests among Seattle's labor groups, churches, and other social movement groups (Gillham 2003; Murphy and Levi 2004).

Contemporary transnational activism tends to involve a more diverse array of actors and a more complex and multilayered analysis of political issues than most local or national protests. Thus, we would expect that episodes of transnational contention would involve a different constellation of mobilizing structures than we are likely to see in more localized contexts. Table 6.2 illustrates some of the key organizations mobilizing around the 1999 WTO protests in Seattle. It examines how different mobilizing structures contributed to that particular protest episode.

Table 6.2 illustrates the varying roles different movement actors played in one of the more prominent confrontations in the contemporary movement for

TABLE 6.2
Mobilizing Structures and Divisions of Labor in the "Battle of Seattle"

Intensity of Transnational Tie	Movement of Mobilizing Structures*	Major Roles
No formal transnational ties	Local chapters of national SMOs (e.g., NOW) Neighborhood committees United for a Fair Economy	Public education Mobilizing participation in protest Localizing global frames
Diffuse transnational ties	Direct Action Network Reclaim the Streets Ruckus Society Coalition for Campus Organizing	Public education Mobilizing participation in protest Localizing global frames Tactical innovations and diffusion
Routine transnational ties	Public Citizen Global Exchange Rainforest Action Network United Students Against Sweatshops Council of Canadians Sierra Club	Public education Facilitating local mobilization by others Tactical innovations and diffusion Articulating and disseminating global strategic frames Research/publication of organizing materials Facilitating transnational exchanges Monitoring international institutions
Formal transnational ties	Greenpeace Friends of the Earth International Forum on Globalization Third World Network Peoples' Global Action 50 Years Is Enough Network Women's Environment and Development Organization	Public education Facilitating local mobilization by others Articulating and disseminating global strategic frames Research/publication of organizing materials Monitoring of international institutions Coordinating transnational cooperation Cultivating and maintaining global constituency Global symbolic actions

SOURCE: From Smith (2005b).
NOTE: The list of structures and divisions of labor in this table is illustrative, not comprehensive.
*Organizations vary a great deal in their levels of formalization and hierarchy. For instance, Friends of the Earth and Greenpeace have well-defined organizational structures and institutional presences while groups like Peoples' Global Action resist forming an organizational headquarters, and Reclaim the Streets seeks to sustain a loose, network-like structure relying heavily on electronic communications.

global economic justice. A key idea this map reveals is that the groups with the least formal and routine transnational ties were more likely to be engaged in the important work of grassroots-level education and mobilization. While they may be using educational materials produced by groups that have more formal transnational structures or ties, they were better able to reach the actual people who lived near the site of the Seattle WTO meeting and who therefore were most able to attend the protest site (Fisher et al. 2005; Gillham 2003; Lichbach and Almeida 2001).

In contrast, groups with more routine transnational ties and formal transnational structures were better able to monitor developments in international policy and to help people make connections between locally experienced grievances and global processes.[2] Starhawk, a U.S.-based feminist/ecology/peace activist, defended the importance of this division of labor in her response to a "Manifest of Anti-capitalist Youth against the World Social Forum":

> I do think the NGOs serve a useful and necessary purpose—they're like a different part of an ecosystem, that simply does a different job. But they wouldn't have much impact without people in the streets. We know that—they do too even if they don't always admit it publicly. They also have resources and information that can help our work, as long as we don't let them dictate our politics or our strategies. (Starhawk 2001)

Fisher and her colleagues (2005) also found evidence of this division of labor, reporting that transnational and formal organizations were responsible for generating non-local participation in transnational protests. In short, we see an important division of labor among social movement organizations, and the complementary activities help sustain transnational movement identities and actions.

The key point of this discussion of mobilizing structures is to demonstrate the range of different social actors that can become involved in social movement activities and to identify some of the actors that can be important to global movements or to global civic engagement more broadly. The strength of any movement will depend largely upon the extensiveness and range of different mobilizing structures it includes. Strong movements are those that can reach people in the *spaces of their everyday lives*, namely in the more informal and non-movement spaces where people socialize, recreate, worship, and nurture their families and communities.

The strongest democracies are ones where political spaces articulate with those of people's everyday routines. Where government policies and employers' practices help enable people to learn about and remain attentive to political issues and to participate in politics, we can expect to find strong democracies. Providing effective political education in public schools, promoting the emergence of spaces for public discourse about politics (such as labor unions or more participatory political parties), and scheduling elections at times and places that do not conflict with voters' life and work routines are examples of pro-democracy policies (Radcliff and Davis 2000). Such policies are especially important in today's societies where we find that more people spend more of their time earning a living, leaving limited time and energy for them to invest in political work (Bennett 2004; Edwards and Foley 1997).

Many governments and economic elites do not have much direct interest in seeing broader public participation in the political life of society. In fact, they may see their interests as directly threatened by a more participatory system of governance. Thus, those actors with the most power tend to see their interests as preserving the status quo rather than the democratic ideals of contemporary political institutions. Herein lies the challenge for social movements and their pro-democracy alliance networks. Efforts to bring political education, discussion, and action into the places where people engage in their everyday routines of reproducing social life will expand the possibilities for people with fewer resources and less leisure time to be active participants in politics. Without such connections, only those individuals with the most resources, free time, and skills can enjoy full rights of participation in political life. By default, then, it is those already privileged by the existing order that will be best served by policy decisions. If we want a more democratic political order that responds to the needs of less privileged groups, it is important to strengthen the various mobilizing structures that encourage civic engagement at local, national, *and* global levels.

Transnational Connections

Episodes of contention, such as the UN global conferences or the "battle of Seattle," have been important for generating new relationships and action by the transnational democratic globalization network. These episodes can also trigger the spread of new collective identities and relational forms. They help introduce activists from different countries who would otherwise never meet, and they challenge activists to conceptualize their concerns in broader terms. They also create spaces that encourage the formation of new interpersonal and inter-organizational relationships that can generate new transnational alliances. For instance, many new transnational organizations were formed in the years surrounding UN global conferences, and major transnational networks such as Peoples' Global Action emerged from specific international activist gatherings (Adamovsky 2005; J. Smith 2004).

As should be clear in this discussion, transnational connections among activists take a range of different forms, networks, campaigns, and organizations that reflect varying degrees of coordination and shared ways of thinking. Communication may be more or less frequent and more or less defined by explicit rules and procedures. Table 6.3 reproduces Jonathan Fox's useful scheme for analyzing variation in the density and content of transnational ties.

Table 6.3 introduces three interconnected forms of transnational association:

networks, coalitions, and formal transnational organizations. At one end of the spectrum are networks, which involve the lowest density, fewest connections, and least commitment to transnational alliances. Networks themselves vary considerably in the extent to which they reflect a coherent and unified collection of actors. The rival transnational networks described in chapter 2, for instance, represent the loosest form of association, containing very diverse collections of actors (including coalitions and organizations), many of whom never have any direct or indirect contact. What makes them part of the network is their commitment to the promotion of a certain vision of how the world should be organized.[3] We can speak of them as a network because this commitment to shared principles or ideas makes them likely to engage in particular practices and come in contact with certain ideas and institutions that contribute to the maintenance or promotion of the network's vision. Embedded within these very broad networks, we can find some more coherent and denser networks. Such networks are described by Keck and Sikkink as "transnational advocacy networks" (1998).

Compared to networks, coalitions involve more routine communications, more clearly defined expectations and efforts at mutual support, and more explicit commitment to specific campaigns, such as the abolition of third world debt (as is the case of the coalition called Jubilee 2000). However, many of these tend to be defined around short-term goals, with few long-term commitments to *sustained* transnational cooperation. To minimize the need to engage in difficult discussions about collective decision making or otherwise to devote time to coordinate action and thinking, many coalitions tend to adopt very specific and limited objectives. They agree to promote only those specific aims as a collective, and they have varying levels of organization that can integrate coalition participants into decision making. The limited scope of coalitions makes it less necessary that the group have formal mechanisms for participation by members and for the resolution of conflicting interests within the coalition (Wood 2005).

The most intense and integrated forms of transnational cooperation are formal transnational organizations, which reflect more frequent communication and cooperation across different political campaigns and a commitment to shared ideologies and cultures. A key difference here is that relations in transnational organizations are more explicitly or formally defined, meaning that structures for regular communication and cooperation are clearly established and actors can operate around shared sets of expectations and commitments. There are explicit guidelines for resolving disputes within the organization and most groups have mechanisms to incorporate input and participation from members. This helps generate trust among participants and helps sustain long-term trans-

TABLE 6.3
Transnational Networks, Coalitions, and Movements

Shared Characteristics	Transnational Networks	Transnational Coalitions	Transnational Movement Organizations
Exchange of information and experiences	Yes	Yes	Yes
Organized social base	Sometimes more, sometimes less or none	Sometimes more, sometimes less or none	Yes
Mutual support	Sometimes, from afar and possibly strictly discursive	Yes	Yes
Joint actions and campaigns	Sometimes loose coordination	Yes, based on mutually agreed minimum goals, often short-term tactical	Yes, based on shared long-term strategy
Shared ideologies	Not necessarily	Not necessarily	Generally yes
Shared political cultures	Often not	Often not	Shared political values, styles and identities

SOURCE: Fox (2002: 352).

national relationships that are needed to support multifaceted political actions that go beyond single-issue campaigns. Because behaviors are routinized within the organization, there is space for the emergence of a shared organizational culture marked by common political understandings, collective identities, and styles of communicating and engaging in political action.[4]

As is true of most typologies, this table may overstate the differences between networks, coalitions, and organizations. But the essence of these conceptual distinctions is that the extent to which transnational relations are routinized or defined as part of the regular practices of activists will affect the character of transnational alliances and their possibilities for generating collective action over the long term. Enduring and dense transnational alliances depend upon the cultivation of shared understandings of political realities and of mutual trust and respect. Not all transnational efforts seek or demand that quality of tie. For instance, some coalitions may simply come together to promote a particular aim, after which they find it most advantageous to return to their other priorities. In the short run, they may or may not generate more formalized transnational ties. However, they do generate interpersonal and inter-organizational connections that can, over the long term, stimulate future transnational networking, campaigning, or organizing efforts. And there is evidence that many of the more densely connected forms evolved from the bonds of connection and trust that grew out of earlier and more loosely connected ones (Cullen 2005; Foster 2005; Rothman and Oliver 2002).

Another important point to note is that transnational ties do not necessarily displace local and national ones, and in fact they may even complement them. Stark and his colleagues, for instance, examined the inter-organizational networks of voluntary groups in Hungary. They found that groups with transnational ties were more likely to maintain ties to other local and national groups than were groups lacking transnational connections. Moreover, transnational connections were associated with more active forms of member participation. They conclude that "the richest and most encompassing patterns of [national] integration go hand in hand with the deepest and most encompassing patterns of transnationalization" (Stark et al. 2005). Whether this case reflects realities elsewhere deserves further investigation, but there is no a priori reason to believe that when activists look across national borders, they neglect their colleagues at home. Indeed, participation in a transnational network can generate new strategic insights and skills relevant to local-level organizing work.

There is an uneasy relationship between social movements and formal organizations that surfaces frequently in social science analyses and in discussions among activists themselves. Key features of social movements are their fluidity, adaptability, and decentralization, while formal organizations require structure, stability, predictability, and some degree of centralization. Thus, activists face a constant tension between the need for more formalized and predictable decision-making processes and structures and the demand for flexibility and openness to participatory politics. More informal structures can also make movements more resistant to efforts by their adversaries to repress them. Although these conflicting demands for some level of formal organization and for flexibility are not unique to transnational movements, they seem especially daunting in struggles that bring together activists of widely varying cultural, political, and economic backgrounds to confront a complex and uncertain global political environment. An important response to this tension in the democratic globalization network is to encourage hybrid, network-like organizational structures that seek (with varying degrees of success) to allow coordination while maintaining decentralized and participatory relations within the organization (Chesters 2004).

Formal organizations provide predictability and stability needed for long-term campaigns, and they help secure steady flows of resources, ideas, and skills for movements. They also provide opportunities for organizers to make a living by doing the work of the movement, thereby supporting and cultivating personnel who help with mobilizing and supporting popular participation in movements as well as with the more detail-oriented tasks of monitoring political developments and "translating" international legal documents for the activist community. They also have been at the heart of heated debates among activists, some of whom decry the influence of nongovernmental organizations (NGOs)—a catch-all term used in the UN to include all civil society groups, including those created by business interests as well as the vast majority of organizations doing work outside the realm of political advocacy—in transnational movements. Some critics see these groups as preferring reformist to more transformative goals, reflecting the interests of more privileged activists, as largely based in the global North, and as placing the needs of organizational maintenance over the promotion of the movement's aims.[5]

In the following section I summarize the broad outlines of what we might call the "organizational fraction" of the democratic globalization network, or the population of more-or-less formally organized transnational social movement organizations (TSMOs). While some may see a fundamental incompatibility between organization and movement, most people with experience in activism recognize that movements need to adopt some structure to allow for predictable and regular communication and joint decision making. They must do so even as they resist organizational forms that promote hierarchy and reduce flexibility and spontaneity. Movements are made up of networks of formal organizations, individuals, and many informal associations and alliances that interact in a variety of ways. As table 6.2 shows, formal transnational organizations play a particular role in a global division of labor within the network. Understanding this subset of network actors can help us better understand the makeup and capacities of the broader collection of actors.

The Transnational Social Movement Sector

Using data from the *Yearbook of International Organizations*,[6] I have mapped the population of TMSOs working to promote social change. This will help us assess how social movement actors have responded to broad global political and economic changes and to assess some of the strengths and weaknesses of transnational movements. While these organizations often rely on the popular mobilizing potential of both formal and informal associations working at local and national levels, they help activists relate global forces to local conditions, and they help broker connections between local actors and transnational settings.

The predominant trend in this analysis is that we see rapid and dramatic growth in the population of TSMOs. Figure 6.1 charts this growth, from just around a hundred groups in the early 1950s to over a thousand by 2003. The

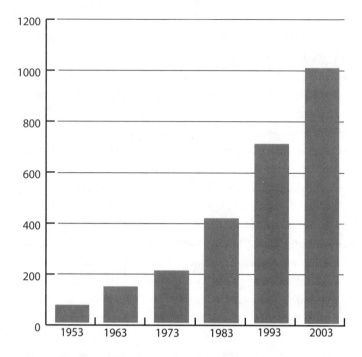

Figure 6.1. Growth of Transnational Social Movement Organizations
Source: Yearbook of International Organizations.

most rapid growth occurred during the decade of the 1980s, probably in response to new openings created by the ending of the Cold War and the renewed
hopes for multilateral problem solving this generated, hopes that helped launch
a series of global conferences on issues ranging from the environment to development to human rights. Figure 6.1 shows that the last few decades of the twentieth century were marked by the expansion of an organizational infrastructure
for transnational social change activism. This growth appears to mirror that of
other forms of transnational association, and may both support and respond to
expansions in the numbers and intensity of intergovernmental organizations
(Chatfield 1997; Kriesberg 1997; Willetts 1996).

What issues have generated this kind of transnational organizational response? Certainly we would not expect people to organize transnationally
around all possible issues, but we do anticipate that they would organize around
problems that require international responses for their solution. The top issues
attracting the attention of transnational social movement organizations were

TABLE 6.4
Issue Focus of TSMOs, 1963, 1983, 2003:
Percent of all Groups with Primary Focus on Issue

	1963 Total No. TSMOs = 179	1983 Total No. TSMOs = 429	2003 Total No. TSMOs = 1031
Human rights	34%	32%	33%
Environment	2	8	18
Peace	27	18	16
Women's rights	11	8	10
Development	4	5	8
Global economic justice	3	5	11
Multi-issue	18	18	28

SOURCE: *Yearbook of International Organizations*
   NOTES: These figures exclude labor unions. Figures do not total 100% because categories are not mutually exclusive (e.g., groups working on "human rights and peace" or "women and development" are counted in each of those issue categories as well as the multi-issue category).

human rights, the environment, women's rights, peace, and economic justice. Table 6.4 displays these changes.

   Throughout the late twentieth century, roughly a third of all TSMOs focused on human rights. About 10 percent focused on peace and another 10 percent addressed women's rights issues. Environmental issues attracted growing attention from TSMOs, with the percentage of groups rising from just 2 percent in the early 1960s (before the first major global environmental conference) to nearly 20 percent of all TSMOs in 2003. Economic justice also attracted growing support, rising from 3 percent to 11 percent of all TSMOs between the 1960s and 2000. Finally, groups adopting complex, multi-issue frames—often ones explicitly advocating for international law and multilateralism—expanded from around 17 percent of all groups in the 1960s to 28 percent in 2000.

   Reviewing the TSMO population in the latter part of the twentieth century, we notice two important and consistent trends. First, there is a shift toward more decentralized organizational structures. Second, TSMOs are expanding their networks of ties to other groups in their environment, including both international nongovernmental and governmental organizations. Table 6.5 summarizes the data on these trends.

   In the earliest decades of this study, TSMOs tended to adopt what I have called the "federated organizational structure." This structure has an international secretariat that retains the authority to grant or withhold affiliates' rights to use the organization's name, and that otherwise regulates the activities of member groups, which tend to be organized into national sections. Amnesty International is a prominent example of this more centralized structure. While this sort

TABLE 6.5
Changes in TSMO Network Ties, 1973–2003

	1973	1983	1993	2003
Number of TSMOs	236	429	735	1031
Ratio coalition/federation structure	.62	.93	1.38	1.82
% TSMO headquarters in global South	11%	18%	24%	23%
% with UN consultative status	56%	49%	38%	42%
Average # NGO ties (st. dev)	1.00	1.62	4.26	3.54
	(1.36)	(2.69)	(5.06)	(4.53)
Average # IGO ties (st. dev)	1.43	1.42	2.19	2.30
	(1.81)	(1.97)	(3.32)	(3.07)

SOURCE: *Yearbook of International Organizations.*

NOTES: Counts exclude labor organizations. The reported average numbers of ties to IGOs and NGOs have been calculated using a maximum value of 10 for IGOs and 20 for NGOs, since a very small percentage of groups report unusually large numbers of contacts.

of federated structure might have proved effective in earlier times, technological change has reduced the need for such centralized and hierarchical structures. To sustain the voluntary participation of members, activist groups needed to find ways to satisfy a desire for more local autonomy. Moreover, a changing political environment demands new ideas and flexible responses, and more decentralized structures better accommodate such needs. Not surprisingly, we find an almost directly parallel rise in the percentages of TSMOs adopting a more decentralized, coalitional structure alongside a precipitous decline in the percentage of groups maintaining more centralized, federated structures. Whereas about half of all TSMOs were coalitions in the 1970s, by the 2000s, there were twice as many coalitions as federations in the population of TSMOs. A related pattern of decentralization is reflected in the fact that, starting in the 1980s, we find more TSMOs forming *within* either the region of the global North or South than was true in the past, when most groups crossed this regional divide. This pattern seems to reflect the desire to cultivate more intermediate spaces for developing connections between local- and global-level politics (J. Smith 2005a; Wiest and Smith 2007).

The second pattern we find in this analysis is a distinct tendency for TSMOs to be active networkers, forming ties to both nongovernmental and intergovernmental organizations as they pursue their social change activities. The average number of ties transnational social change groups reported to other organizations increased during the past two decades. Whereas in the early 1980s TSMOs reported an average of fewer than two ties to either other international NGOs or to intergovernmental organizations, by 2000 these organizations reported an average of 2.3 ties to intergovernmental bodies and about 3.5 ties to other international NGOs.[7] These figures, moreover, do not reflect what are likely to be substantial increases in ties to national and local organizations.

In sum, the evidence available here shows a distinctive shift in the late twentieth century toward higher levels of transnational association by citizens advocating social and political change. Over time, the organizational structures of TSMOs have become both more decentralized and more densely connected to other organizations in the political environment. This evidence supports my contention that the network concept is useful for analyzing the collections of actors involved in social change efforts. Below I explore the implications of the trends discussed in this chapter for our understandings of how transnational networks for global democracy operate in the contemporary global system.

Toward a "New Global Politics"?

The discussion thus far has demonstrated relationships between social movements, organizations, and broader institutions and processes. Social movements, while attempting to alter relations of power, are shaped in important ways by the political and economic institutions that reflect and seek to preserve existing power relations. At the same time, social movements are seeking to bring new actors and claims into the political arena in order to generate changes in those institutional rules and relationships. Over time, they help democratize these spaces by bringing new actors and issues to political agendas and by helping to give political voice to groups that are excluded by existing institutional arrangements.

Social movement actors have adopted the technologies used by states and private-sector actors and applied these technologies in new ways as they sought to mobilize new groups of people. Governments and corporations have often appropriated these innovations for their own purposes (e.g., Greenberg and Knight 2004). As Markoff notes, "Just as literacy was as much an instrument of bureaucratic power as of social movement challenge, the new electronic technology seemed as likely to expand the toolkits of the powerful as to undermine them" (2001:393). Few activists in recent (and not-so-recent) protests would deny the importance of new information technologies to their work. Over the last decade especially, these technologies have dramatically transformed possibilities for transnational political organization and action in an increasingly global polity. Moreover, innovations in the subversive use of technologies are being met with new challenges as political and corporate elites seek to control and to better exploit their commercial potential.

Transnational social movement networks have clearly become more decentralized and more closely connected with the everyday routines of greater numbers of people. Local and national groups can more readily relate to transnational organizations and campaigns and can participate more directly in transnational political processes than they could in the past. Advances in information technologies as well as the professionalization and global integration of the global workforce have facilitated this decentralization (Smith and Fetner 2007). While the former process facilitates rapid and extensive information flows, the latter facilitates the ready interpretation and mobilization of information by diverse groups working at local levels. These changes have led growing numbers of activists to speak of a new global politics that is more participatory and innovative than that of earlier decades. A key feature of this new politics is its reliance on electronic forms of communication and its decentralized network structure, which contrasts with the more hierarchical forms of "old-left" social movement organizing (Juris 2008; Keraghel and Sen 2004; Whitaker 2005).

Because social movements are most clearly engaged in information politics and communication-based political work, scholars have emphasized the importance of informal and fluid networks of actors to global social change processes. Our notion emphasizes a complex multilateralism, global politics as increasingly made up of interactive networks of state, non-state, and intergovernmental actors. By facilitating communication and translation across different political spaces and levels of action, transnational networks help relate the practices and ideas in local contexts to global-level institutions and processes.

Bennett associates the adoption of network structures with the emergence of what he calls "lifestyle politics."[8] Fluid communications networks, especially among younger activists, are displacing more formal and centralized organizational forms. Because of their relations to communication technology, these new forms of activism more readily permeate multiple aspects of activists' lives. According to Bennett,

> Lifestyle politics are characterized by emotional attachments to issues based on their meaningful associations with social identity claims, personal and professional networks, neighborhood relations, social trends, work and family schedules, health care needs, sexual preferences, fashion statements, travel venues, entertainment, celebrity cues, and other connections to lifestyle concerns. Such connections transcend easy ideological categorization, such as the linkage of songbirds to fair trade coffee, or buying products that display eco-labels as a direct personal contribution

to environmental protection. Personal political choices in fashion, food, travel, investments, and social memberships permit relatively fluid movement in and out of issue networks as they touch on dynamic lifestyle values. (2003: 4)

Table 6.6 describes changes in the forms of transnational organization characteristic of the different "generations" of activism introduced in the previous chapter.

The table shows several important shifts in transnational activism. First, the scope of transnational activism has expanded, including growing numbers of actors from the global South. Economic disadvantages and higher levels of political repression in the South are no longer preventing people in those countries from cultivating transnational activist networks that aim to remedy the problems they face. A second change is in the structure of transnational organizations, which has become less centralized and more connected to local and national activist networks. Third, the scale of transnational action has changed as well, moving from global to more locally oriented sites. In other words, transnational organizing efforts are becoming more connected to the daily routines of larger numbers of people. Fourth, strategies have shifted from a focus on global institutions in the earliest generation of activism toward the cultivation of issue-based campaigns led by key organizations to more permanent and Internet-based forms of mobilization with more decentralized leadership and individualized identities. Transnational campaigns—sometimes labeled "dot-causes"—are more likely to involve actions that people can readily take in the course of their daily routines (J. Clark 2003).

A final conclusion from table 6.6 is that the capacities of transnational collections of activists have changed from more limited, elite-level lobbying toward increasingly mass-based political action. This has fundamentally altered the organizational demands of transnational movements, and more established organizations like Greenpeace are finding that they risk being "outflanked" by new movement actors, and they have adopted new strategies to respond to these developments (Chesters 2004). Chesters argues that the kinds of shifts documented here signal a need for analysts to adopt an approach that focuses less on specific organizations and more on the *processes* and *relations* among diverse actors. While some of these may indeed be captured within our more traditional understandings of organizations, many may be taking on new forms. The increasingly common reference to the idea of a "new politics" by transnational activists suggests that many are noticing important changes in the character of global political organization and action.

TABLE 6.6
Changing Structures and "Generations" of Transnational Activism

Generation	(1) Multilateralist	(2) Transitional Advocacy Networks	(3) Direct Action
Timeframe	Pre-1980	Late 1980s–1990s—UN Conference Era	Late 1990s–Seattle/Post-Seattle Era
Geographic Scope	Mostly Northern	Mostly Northern—growing participation from South	Rapidly growing Southern participation
Organizational Structure	Small networks, strong role for individual leaders, transnational organizations central	NGO-centered issue networks, transnational organizations central but more national groups	More informal and polycentric; multi-issue/multi-sectors; More national and sub-national organizations in addition to trans-national
Scale of Action	Mostly in global forums—limited mass mobilizing efforts	Mostly in global forums or focused on UN conferences or summits	More autonomous from inter-governmental agenda Connecting local problems/actions to global conditions—domestication of issues
Major Strategies	Elite lobbying Formal lobbying	Strategic campaigns: Limited political goals Turned on and off by lead organizations Maintained organizational identities	Permanent campaigns: Diverse political goals Decentralized control and leadership Organizational and tactical innovation Foster movement identities
Capacity		Problem- and campaign-focused networking, some popular mobilization	Mass protest, value change Technological adaptations/innovation

SOURCE: Adapted from Bennett (2005: 214).

NOTE: Activities to shape cultural and social spaces are common to all three "generations," and to most social movement activism generally, but they are more pronounced in the latest period.

The shift toward more personalist-oriented lifestyle politics can enhance political activism by breaking down the boundaries between politics and other aspects of social life. Also, Lichterman's analysis of how personalist politics was employed in U.S. Green Party activism suggests that by encouraging an ideology that empowers individuals to act on behalf of broadly shared principles, personalism can provide a foundation for the emergence of broad coalitions (1995: 529; see also Wuthnow 1998). Research in transnational settings, moreover, supports the contention that the emergence of personalist politics is not unique to the global North (della Porta et al. 2006; Doherty and Doyle 2006).

Conclusion

This chapter presents evidence of the social infrastructure for an evolving democratic globalization network that is expanding possibilities for people to act collectively beyond their immediate local and national settings. We see some significant trends that are likely to generate more participation in the democratic globalization network over time, as expanding global institutions and interdependence strengthen demands for transnational cooperation. First, transnational social movement organizations have expanded in recent decades, adopting more decentralized organizational structures. They also increasingly cultivate more ties to both nongovernmental and intergovernmental actors. Information technologies have allowed more local and national groups to connect to transnational networks, limiting the need for formally structured transnational movement organizations. These trends help explain the expanding representation of people from outside the global North. We also find that more leadership and innovation in transnational campaigns has been coming from national and local levels of action rather than from transnational sites, and at the same time we have seen more mass mobilizations around global issues. This decentralized, network pattern, moreover, mirrors a trend in governmental and corporate sectors, which have also seen a trend toward decentralization in the face of globalization forces. The network form, then, is an important feature of contemporary political and social organization, and we will consider the implications of this development in later chapters.

The expansion of a more formally organized and more densely networked global civil society might contribute to the democratization of the global political system. Referring to the criteria for assessing these contributions that I outlined in chapter 1, the strengthening of global civil society contributes to all of these. First, it helps increase flows of information between global and local contexts,

thereby enhancing public awareness and debate on global problems and policies. Second, by helping empower groups that are marginalized by formal political processes and by structuring opportunities for them to participate in global
politics, it increases the openness and representativeness of international institutions. Third, by expanding capacities for rapid transnational communication
and public participation, it can enhance the transparency and accountability of
governments to both their citizens and to other governments. Fourth, by cultivating transnational identities and shared organizational bonds, it can generate
global notions of fairness that become a yardstick against which various proposals and policies can be evaluated. And finally, by providing for the sustained public attention to global problems, transnational organizations and networks can
increase the effectiveness of global institutions through ongoing efforts to monitor and to mobilize pressure for compliance with international agreements.

Part III that follows provides examples of how transnational collections of activists have sought to advance global democracy through particular campaigns. The
aim of these analyses is to demonstrate how citizen participation in global politics contributes to strengthening and building multilateral institutions as it de-
mocratizes global politics. While many activists are understandably wary of being co-opted by formal political institutions, by abandoning this sphere of action
they cede these important political spaces to neoliberal opponents, who have
used their many advantages to conduct a revolution from above. Democratic
globalizers must lay claim to their history of successes in global forums. By focusing on efforts to promote multilateral cooperation within more democratic
global institutions, transnational groups whose energies are now stretched thin
across many issues might find new possibilities to forge a united struggle for a
world governed by principles of international human rights and social justice.
We begin this exploration of transnational struggles to shape multilateral institutions by considering how transnational challengers have tried to shape global
policy agendas.

STRUGGLES FOR MULTILATERALISM AND GLOBAL DEMOCRACY

CHAPTER SEVEN

Agenda Setting in a Global Polity

If it is to compete effectively against those advocating a neoliberal vision for the world, the democratic globalization network must consciously strive to articulate its own alternative vision in an emerging "global public sphere." John Guidry and his collaborators define the global public sphere as the "space in which both residents of distant places (states or localities) and members of transnational entities (organizations or firms) elaborate discourses and practices whose consumption moves beyond national boundaries" (Guidry et al. 2000: 6–7). Capitalists have done this well, and they have not been challenged as effectively as they might be. Those advocating for more democratic forms of globalization must find ways to better communicate their visions of how the world might be organized to compete with the far more influential advocates of neoliberalism. Numerous analysts have begun to emphasize the importance of "discursive repertoires" to social movement challenges, showing how discourses can reinforce or constrain the possibilities for movement impact (Ferree et al. 2002; Koopmans 2005; Steinberg 1995; Wuthnow 1989).

This struggle is not only about how to express ideas of resistance, but it is also about how to get one's message heard. The competition among different visions or models for organizing the world's economic and political life does not take place only in remote sites where international diplomats meet. It is waged in a variety of spaces, ranging from neighborhoods to local town councils to national parliaments and global meetings of citizens or government officials. It is waged through newspapers and increasingly online. This chapter discusses two examples of how actors in the democratic globalization network—the Independent Media Center and Kyoto Now!—are advancing multilateral agenda-setting initiatives. We consider the various arenas where the meaning-making of societies takes place, and explore how the system of complex multilateralism discussed in chapter 2 affects public agenda setting in local, national, and global contexts.

Creating an Alternative Media

The Independent Media Center (Indymedia, or IMC) emerged during the mobilization against the World Trade Organization (WTO) at its Seattle ministerial meeting in 1999.[1] Their organizing rationale states: "The Independent Media Center is a network of collectively run media outlets for the creation of radical, accurate, and passionate tellings of the truth. We work out of a love and inspiration for people who continue to work for a better world, despite corporate media's distortions and unwillingness to cover the efforts to free humanity."[2] Indymedia organizers knew from experience that their campaigns to challenge neoliberal globalization were unlikely to be reported in media outlets that are controlled by transnational corporations. And any media attention they might gain was unlikely to portray their claims in a fair or comprehensive way. Thus, they encouraged activists to "be the media" by forming a network that would enable activists themselves to become reporters, photographers, and videographers on behalf of the democratic globalization network. They set up a Web site and arranged for computer facilities in downtown Seattle where activists could upload their stories about anti-WTO protests so that those who could not attend could have a non-corporate source of information about the protests and the issues surrounding them. The IMC issued press passes to volunteer staff and held regular meetings during the days of the WTO ministerial to coordinate their efforts to cover the event. Not only would the source differ from traditional news accounts in its motivations, but it also would enable more democratic forms of newsmaking by allowing users to submit their own commentaries on IMC material and on the commentaries of other users, using a model that is known as "open publishing" (Morris 2004).

Following the Seattle protest, Indymedia Centers (IMCs) spread rapidly, and there are now more than 160 IMC affiliates organized at national, state/provincial, and municipal levels. At national and local levels, IMCs report on locally relevant events and provide spaces for analysis and commentary on global events. While most IMCs operate only online, many hold regular face-to-face or online meetings and engage in collective decision making. Other local IMCs publish occasional print versions of their reports, often in conjunction with movement-related gatherings. The IMC has become an important referent for movement activists wanting analyses and information on the diversity and extensiveness of movement activities in different parts of the world. While the decentralized structure means that the quality of reporting is quite varied, Indymedia is an important example of how people can create new spaces on the global mass media agenda that can challenge neoliberal globalization. And the network of activists the IMC nurtures helps support values of solidarity, nonviolence, and commitment to democratic globalization. Indeed, the participatory nature of Indymedia challenges the authority of mainstream commercial news media as well as its information monopoly. By empowering individual activists as news gatherers and analysts, it both critiques and challenges the power of corporate media. Perhaps more important, however, it creates opportunities for individual activists to learn skills in media production, empowering them as critical media producers while reinforcing critical perspectives on the corporate mass media.

Direct Action on Climate Change

The Kyoto Protocol is a legally binding addendum to the International Convention on Climate Change that sets specific targets for cuts to national levels of greenhouse gas emissions. The Climate Change Convention resulted from the UN Conference on Environment and Development (UNCED) in 1992, and it aims to curb global warming associated with these emissions. A key obstacle to progress on this agreement, however, has been fierce resistance from the United States, whose policies have been influenced by large oil companies, automobile producers, and other powerful interests (Bruno and Karliner 2002; McCright and Dunlap 2003).[3] Not only has the United States not signed the Kyoto agreement, but it also has actively worked to undermine the growing scientific consensus that global warming is indeed occurring and that human activities are a major cause (Karliner 1997; Vasi Forthcoming).

Responding to the stubborn refusal of the world's largest polluter, the United States, to sign the Kyoto Protocol, students at Cornell University and Lewis and Clark College independently launched the Kyoto Now! campaign.[4] The campaign encourages universities and other local institutions to cut their emissions of greenhouse gases in accordance with Kyoto targets, even in the absence of national-level commitments. This, activists argue, will not only encourage public understanding of the issues, but it will also demonstrate the feasibility of reducing greenhouse gas emissions, creating momentum for changes in national policy. The Kyoto Now! Web site now has links to forty-three other campus Kyoto Now! chapters.[5] The campaign reflects a bottom-up strategy of promoting local compliance with international conventions in order to generate pressure for more nationally consistent policies.

A similar initiative—Cities for Climate Protection (CCP)—is promoted by the

International Council for Local Environmental Initiatives (ICLEI). This campaign works with local activists and public officials to pass local resolutions to limit emissions of greenhouse gases. The CCP program seeks to promote public awareness of environmental issues and the Kyoto Protocol, but it also tries to demonstrate to industry and government officials the benefits of adopting proactive environmental policies. For instance, in 2000, the ICLEI reported that sixty of its local CCP programs generated $94 million in energy cost savings (Ellison 2002).[6] Such evidence helps undermine arguments by the U.S. government arguments that Kyoto Protocol requirements are too costly to implement. The campaign drew this editorial from the prominent U.K. newspaper *The Guardian:*

> The White House is not America, and over the past few years concerned local authorities, institutions and groups of all political persuasions have quietly cocked a snook at the president by committing their communities to the same targets and timetables that the US would have been legally obliged to meet had it signed up to Kyoto. As of yesterday, 154 US local governments—representing more than 50 million people and responsible for 20% of all US greenhouse emissions—are part of a coalition that has pledged to reduce emissions by 7% below 1990 levels by 2012: more than Europe has committed to. Rather than fall for the White House line that meeting Kyoto targets means higher petrol prices and millions of lost jobs, they are taking industry and voters with them, dramatically cutting energy costs. (*The Guardian* 2005)

In addition, by "cocking a snook" at the U.S. government, climate activists help harmonize local environmental standards, and this might eventually find support even in the neoliberal network. Although they tend to resist government regulation and any policies that impose short-term costs (such as fuel-efficiency regulations), companies also want to prevent unfair competition among businesses that results from differences in local regulations. On a practical level, this campaign can help generate innovations in energy conservation that could prove lucrative to responsive corporations and/or that can serve as models in other communities (Vasi Forthcoming).

A key goal of the CCP and Kyoto Now! campaigns is to expand public attention to the problem of climate change and to international efforts to address the problem. In the absence of impartial mass media coverage of the treaty in the United States,[7] these localized efforts can help generate attention to climate change within more localized public arenas where face-to-face contacts rather than mass media are crucial. This helps people learn about issues not addressed well in the mass media while providing them with concrete actions they can take to address the problem. Campaigns like this can also generate more favorable local media attention to the problem, since the institutions targeted and the activists involved are often prominent in local communities. Also, international media coverage can bolster work in other countries to press different governments to act on climate change. Local Kyoto Now! and CCP campaigns can also affect formal policy agendas, generating candidates for electoral office who might gain public recognition for their environmental positions or even run on platforms for reducing local pollution levels.

How can efforts like the IMC and Kyoto Now! influence local and global agendas? The following section examines research on agenda-setting and policy-making processes to identify how global changes create both opportunities and challenges for democratic globalizers.

Agenda-Setting Processes and the Global Public Sphere

Michael Lipsky (1968) emphasizes the importance of recognizing the diverse audiences movements must target in order to change public policy. Because they lack direct access to officials, movements must appeal to the mass media to help convey their messages to publics with which they lack channels for direct interpersonal communication. However, mass media actors have interests that will affect whether and how this is done (Gamson 2004; Ryan 1991; Smith et al. 2001).

Effective change strategies must account for how different agendas are shaped. For instance, we might think about how the democratic globalization network may have more direct influences on different agendas, reducing the network's reliance on mass media strategies. And we might also think of ways that movements can make more effective use of the direct interpersonal connections they mobilize or generate new forms of access to mass media agendas. Ultimately, unless people have opportunities to question dominant paradigms and to envision alternatives to neoliberalism, struggles for global democracy will fail to gain a wide reception.

McCarthy and his colleagues discuss movement framing struggles as structured around four distinct and somewhat overlapping arenas, namely the public, media, electoral, and governmental (1996a). They argue that each arena has a distinct process for generating its respective agenda or set of issues and ideas emphasized in the discourse among those in the arena. Each arena has its own logic, language, gatekeepers, and rules of engagement, which movements must consider if they are to affect public policy. The public agenda is the most open and has the broadest "set of issues that are accorded importance by mass and narrower publics." The media agenda is made up of the selection of issues receiving attention in the mass and largely commercialized media. This is, according to Gamson (2004), the "master agenda," since all people seeking to influence public policy debates must relate to it in some way. Electoral agendas constitute the set of issues that receive attention from candidates for public office, and are strongly influenced by political parties, while governmental agendas are made up of the issues taken up in legislatures and by governments (McCarthy et al. 1996a: 293). There are obvious relationships among these arenas, as the public agenda should shape the agendas of at least democratic governments, and government agendas often influence media and public agendas to a greater or lesser degree.

As Figure 7.1 shows, there is partial overlap among these arenas, and each becomes more restrictive, centralized, and selective in the issues it raises when we move from the public to the governmental arena. More democratic systems will have more inclusive rules and processes defining each agenda, thereby allowing less powerful groups to have a voice in shaping *what* the public, the media, politicians, and government officials talk about as well as *how* they do so. Systems with more limited or closed processes for defining public agenda setting are less democratic and are less likely to be responsive to the interests and needs of less powerful members of society. Thus, an important consideration is how each arena creates a variety of constraints that expand or limit the possibilities for different actors to communicate their interests and preferences.

This perspective on the variety of arenas and agendas through which policy debates are processed also sensitizes us to the fact that messages are always mediated through some social context (Gamson 1992). In the case of the democratic globalization network, we see that the rival neoliberal network has distinct agenda-setting advantages in each arena, but there are still opportunities for challengers. For instance, the democratic globalization network can work in the public and other accessible arenas to try to affect how neoliberal messages are heard and interpreted by various target audiences. The point of this conceptual scheme, then, is to help us understand the logics and structures that shape each distinct arena so that we can identify opportunities less powerful actors have to influence policy agendas.

The challenge for us here is to think about how these different arenas should be considered within the context of complex multilateralism. What are the relationships among different arenas and agenda-setting processes at local, national, and international levels? How do ideas and agendas formed in global contexts,

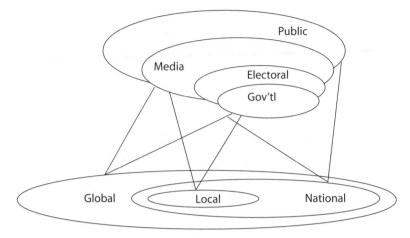

Figure 7.1. Overlapping Agendas

for instance, affect those at more local levels, and vice versa? Social movements are some of the *few* players trying to build connections across these different arenas as well as across the levels of political organization. They work to enhance public awareness of issues as a means of building pressure on politicians and government officials to attribute importance to these issues. Ultimately, they aim to translate public pressure into policy outcomes, but they must often work consciously to advance their issues to the different agendas. This requires that they consider the various opportunities and constraints each arena defines for doing so.

Public Arenas

Public arenas are made up of the broadest collection of civil society groups and individuals, and they vary cross-nationally in how structured and open they are. In most contemporary societies, organizations tend to serve as important gatekeepers or agenda setters in this arena, since they help structure ties among large collections of individuals. The success of various movement initiatives depends on the extent to which major organizations like churches, school boards, parties, labor unions, or recreational clubs pay attention to them and support their ideals. Of course, different political and cultural contexts produce different gatekeepers, and strategists and analysts must be sensitive to these differences.

While the spread of Internet and other technologies may be reducing the influence of formal organizations in agenda-setting processes by enabling and empowering more loosely defined networks to generate mass pressure, the capacities of traditional organizational structures should not be overlooked. For instance, McCarthy attributes the successes of the pro-life movement in the United States more to mobilizing efforts by religious institutions than to its level of popular support (McCarthy 1987). In particular, we should remain sensitive to how different organizational structures relate to different classes and categories of people. While middle-class and younger audiences may be more attracted to the individualized and personalist politics of the new communications technologies (Bennett 2003), older people and less economically privileged groups may feel more comfortable in formal and hierarchical organizations (Lichterman 1995; Polletta 2002). And people familiar with labor union organizing will have very different expectations about how organizations should work than will those emerging from social movements (Rose 2000; Waterman 2005). Finally, while Internet-based organizing offers important new capabilities for large-scale international mobilization by social movements, the new technologies may not by themselves overtake traditional ones.

Working in public arenas, movements can most readily seek to mediate messages coming from other arenas such as the media or governments. Interpersonal networks are important filters for the information people receive from television and other sources (Gamson 1992). In a similar way, while people might initially resist a movement's message, if it is delivered directly by a person whom they know and respect, they will likely be more receptive to the message. Or perhaps they have vague ideas about an issue they have heard about in the mass media, but by meeting people who are active on that issue they might find reason to invest the time and energy into learning about the issue and taking a position on it.

The networking ideology of the contemporary global justice movement is probably a response to this recognition as much as it is to changing technologies, and more groups that got their start on the Internet are working to cultivate direct ties with the communities in which they live and work (Juris 2008; Wood 2004). Internet-based groups such as Moveon.org—which were seen as revolutionary in their ability to quickly mobilize vast numbers of people—have sought to expand their real-time presence by encouraging participants to organize local gatherings of people to reinforce their online work. Most research on participation in social movements shows that direct interpersonal networks are the single most important factor in shaping people's decisions about whether to participate in social movement activities (McAdam 1988; Snow et al. 1980). Thus, the public arena is a very important, and certainly the most open, space in which social movements operate.

NEOLIBERAL GLOBALIZATION AND THE PUBLIC ARENA

Neoliberal globalization has had significant effects on the public arena as a space where social movements can flourish. As capitalism becomes more global, and the role of governments as regulators of capital is diminished, the power of corporations relative to other social actors has increased dramatically. This creates a highly unequal playing field that disadvantages those critical of corporate power in important ways. First, it has enabled the neoliberal globalization network to advance the notion that private, capitalist interests represent legitimate social interests in a way that voluntary civil society groups do not. This has legitimized and encouraged the creation of relationships between government actors and the private sector that at other points in time would be considered highly corrupt and anti-democratic (see chapter 4).

Probably the most important effect of the globalization of capitalism is that it generates competitive pressures on producers that lead them to shift more and more of their costs onto workers, who, because of these kinds of pressures, are less likely to be unionized than they were in the past. Even where workers have unions, they are often forced to accept reduced wages and benefits (Munck 2002). Real wages for workers in most countries have declined with globalization, and workers must put in more hours to simply maintain their standard of living. Increasing numbers of families worldwide have at least two wage-earners, leaving less leisure time for the entire family (Frank 2000; Schor 1993). This weakens the public arena.

Another trend that is related to increased global economic integration is that, as governments focus resources on export-oriented development, workers must travel ever farther to find work. Increasing numbers of people leave their homes and families to find work in nearby (or not so nearby) cities, and often these migrants eventually move overseas when they find their prospects limited there (Sassen 1998). Migrant workers live in conditions lacking in the supportive social networks of family and friends considered essential to human well-being, and they are often victims of discrimination and abuse in the places where they work. They typically are forced to take the most dangerous and least appealing jobs in an economy, and often they lack legal status that allows them to claim basic rights and protections. Even where people do not actually leave their homes, many find that they must spend more of their day traveling to and from their jobs.

At the same time as it increases pressures on workers, neoliberal globalization also reduces public spending on services such as health care, education, and public utilities, leading to rising costs and less availability of these services for many people around the world (Kingfisher 2003). This further compounds the need for people to spend more time working, thereby limiting the amount of time and energy they have to engage in political life. Also, the increasing sprawl that characterizes the geographic spaces of many people's lives makes it difficult for people to routinely interact with neighbors or to form local associations, isolating people in dispersed single-family homes from which they travel only by car (Kunstler 1996). By inhibiting people's ability to participate in civic groups of any kind, neoliberal globalization serves to decrease their access to information that is mediated through local and trusted groups and individuals that, in a healthy polity, serve as interpreters and filters of outside information. They also make people more dependent for information upon more centralized information sources over which neoliberal proponents have greater control.

Media Arenas

Media arenas have important impacts on public discourse, and they occupy a privileged position between formal policy arenas (electoral and governmental) and the public one. Because they are more centralized and reach large numbers of people, they help cultivate discourses that bridge policy arenas and localized social networks. They are defined largely by the rules that govern the operation of the mass media as well as by the ownership structure of news media outlets. The front-line gatekeepers are media editors and reporters, but these professionals are increasingly limited by a further set of corporate gatekeepers who own and control the mass media industry. Neoliberal policies have contributed to a concentration in the media industry, and now just a handful of companies control a vast majority of news, entertainment, publishing, and other information-related industries.[8] In describing how media gatekeepers determine what issues will gain attention on the more selective media agendas, analysts point to news-gathering routines, the need for "news pegs," and media issue cycles, in addition to the broad corporate interests of media owners (Clayman and Reisner 1998; Gamson et al. 1992; Gamson and Modigliani 1989; Ryan 1991; Smith et al. 2001).

Issues selected for coverage in the mass media are ones that fit best within media news-gathering routines. In other words, if an event takes place during a time convenient to reporters' schedules and story lead-times, if its location allows ready access to newspaper photographers or television video crews, if organizers have prepared clear, informative, and persuasive background materials for media staff making decisions about what stories to cover, then it will be more likely to win a spot on the media agenda. The news-peg hypothesis holds that stories with a compelling hook or innate attractiveness to media audiences are more likely to be included on agendas than are those with less ability to hold media audiences' attention. And finally, analysts have identified distinct media attention cycles that show how reporting practices that tend to cluster stories on particular themes make it more likely for particular issues to gain a spot on media agendas at some times than others. Few issues gain long-term media attention, even if such attention is required to inform the public about relevant developments in legislative and government arenas (Smith et al. 2001).

One important point to this discussion is to show that the key drivers of the media agenda are only indirectly related to the objective importance of an issue. Many analysts point out the discrepancies between the substance of media attention to a particular issue and the actual informational needs of citizens. Thus, while extensive media attention is devoted to plane crashes and other dramatic but relatively uncommon tragedies, very little attention is given to more substantial and widespread risks such as automobile fatalities and environmental-related disease and threats (Greenberg et al. 1989; Mooney 2004). Commercial media are also not necessarily concerned with providing information relevant to citizens, such as detailed coverage of the issues surrounding electoral campaigns. For instance, a 2005 study of U.S. media broadcasts showed that local news stations devoted twelve times as much coverage to sports and weather, and eight times more to stories about accidental injuries, than they did to *all local political races combined*. And most of the coverage of political races was framed in terms of what is called the "horserace" among contenders than around the actual substantive issues.[9]

Since social movements are more likely to be focused upon the real but often mundane risks people face, they must find ways to make these risks somehow newsworthy if they are to win a spot on mass media agendas. As Rochon notes (1998), movements face the challenge of turning what are chronic problems into urgent or acute issues that demand timely media attention. But these strategies involve important trade-offs. Essentially, what movements must do is work to frame issues in ways that make them more compatible with mass media agenda-setting processes. The most obvious and frequent way movements do this is by staging a protest event—a demonstration, rally, or direct action of some sort—that attracts attention by causing a public spectacle. The protest event itself becomes news, particularly if it disrupts traffic or otherwise interferes with everyday routines. Protests involving property destruction or arrests are more likely to attract media attention than those without such disruptive elements (McCarthy et al. 1996b). The problem with this strategy, however, is that in the few cases where protest attracts media attention, the reporting tends to focus on the protest event itself rather than on the issues that inspired it. This is particularly true for issues that most directly challenge the interests of economic elites (Smith et al. 2001).

Other movement strategies for turning chronic problems into acute ones that will draw media attention include highlighting individual victims of a particular problem. This strategy might gain more in-depth attention to the underlying issues than public protests do, but it has limitations. First, it can serve to foster what Iyengar calls "episodic" framing of a problem, or the portrayal of a problem as isolated and resulting from an accident or the actions of an individual rather than some systemic failure. In other words it "obscure[s] the connections between social problems and the actions or inactions of political leaders . . . [thereby impeding] electoral leadership" (Iyengar 1991: 141). Iyengar's research,[10] moreover, leads him to argue that television news distorts information about public affairs and "contributes to the trivialization of public discourse and the erosion of electoral accountability" (1991: 143).

This problem parallels that described by Oliver and Johnston (2000) as the inherent tensions between movement efforts to frame their issues in ways that resonate with a broad public and their need to cultivate deeper understandings and insights that are part of a more systemic interpretation of problems. As these authors noted, while one task involves what is essentially marketing and resonating, the other involves education and thinking:

> Ideologies are complex systems of thought that cannot be communicated accurately in stock phrases or sound bites . . . Persuading other people to take on an ideology is an education or socialization process: it takes time, involves repeated contact between the educator/socializer and the learner, and requires substantial effort on both their parts. These processes are reinforced by social group membership and networks in which other people share the same meanings and learn new ideas together. (2000: 48)

Thus, while the mass media can help provide a window through which members of a broader public might get a glimpse of a movement's ideas and critique, more extensive social networks are necessary to translate media-generated interest in an issue into meaningful political action.

One important aspect of the media agenda is that it is not wholly dominated by corporate media organizations. Although the corporate media in many countries have a considerable influence on what news much of the public receives, a variety of other information sources are available to individuals through publicly funded mass media services, special-interest publications, and newsletters, magazines, and online sources published by movement-based organizations such as the IMC. Radio and cable stations also represent more accessible venues where nonprofit actors can seek to gain a foothold on the media agenda. And the Internet is an increasingly important space where a variety of groups work to promote alternative news programming to general audiences.

NEOLIBERAL GLOBALIZATION AND MEDIA ARENAS

Neoliberal globalization has substantially transformed the media arena by making this industry increasingly subject to commercial pressure. Also, it has led to the creation of rules that allow and encourage trade in media content, contributing to the globalization of culture. Because information and knowledge of current affairs is so central to democratic governance, many believe that the provision of free public media is an important function of democratic governments. If they are to be active and engaged in political life, every citizen requires equitable access to information, and only non-commercialized media sources can reliably provide such access. Thus, many governments devote substantial public monies to support independent public television and radio news programming. However, with the expansion of neoliberalization and international trade agreements aimed at expanding international investment in public services,[11] governments are finding it increasingly difficult to maintain public programming in an increasingly concentrated and competitive media market. For instance, the UN Development Programme reported dramatic increases in the entertainment-related programming of public broadcasters in several countries alongside substantial cuts in news and current affairs programming as public broadcasters are forced to compete with commercial ones (UNDP 2001: 79). This commercialization of the mainstream media limits the space for any serious consideration of challenges to capitalist ideology. As one activist newsletter put it, "the global enemy is relatively well known, but the global resistance that it meets rarely passes through the filter of the media" (Peoples' Global Action 2000: 7).

As a result of the increased globalization and commercialization of the mass media, and although editors and other news professionals are given some freedom to select the news on which they report, their choices are increasingly dictated by the interests of the corporations that own the news media outlets. Moreover, because within the corporate logic it is more important for news programs to be profitable than informative, the content of news is shaped by concerns about attracting large audiences and maintaining programming that compares favorably to that of competing media companies. Thus, we find increasing trends in numerous countries toward sensationalism and "infotainment" over hard news programming as well as widespread practices of "pack journalism," where different broadcasters report on the same stories regardless of their level of importance (Herman 1995; Herman and Chomsky 1988; McChesney 1999).

Electoral Arenas

The next two arenas move us into what analysts have called the "formal" agenda, or the list of issues that attract serious attention from decision makers (Cobb et al. 1976). Kingdon (1984) argues that the movement of issues from problem-related (i.e., public and media) to policy (i.e., electoral and governmental) agendas requires the presence of "policy entrepreneurs" who help bring together the processes of articulating a problem and its possible solution with that of developing, passing, and implementing legislation to address the problem. Social movements actors are such "policy entrepreneurs." By mobilizing public attention and pressure around particular problems, movements seek to affect what politicians talk about and what they do once they get into political office. By definition, movements have less direct access to electoral and governmental arenas, but effective movements are those that can mobilize allies and sympathizers in these spaces.

Electoral arenas are again more centralized and restrictive than public and media arenas, and they are defined by the system of rules that organize competition for political office. This limited set of issues becomes central to public discourse and debates over the selection of candidates for political office. For many democracies, political parties control much of this arena, and the electoral rules and party strategies will largely determine how open or closed the related agenda-setting processes are. In general, systems with larger numbers of effective parties (i.e., ones with proportional representation or single-transferable voting procedures) should have more open agenda-setting processes than those with fewer parties (majoritarian or first-past-the-post systems). Also, compared to presidential systems, parliamentary systems tend to create more space for electoral competition.

Party histories and organizing strategies also affect electoral arenas and agenda-setting processes (e.g., Putnam 1992). Some parties are highly democratic and offer ready opportunities for citizens to become active and influential in them. A number of analysts suggest that political parties based in countries of the global South may be more responsive and open to democratic participation from their members. In part this results from the ability of these less consolidated and ossified parties to experiment with different strategies of citizen participation, as Baiocchi found in his analysis of Brazil's Worker's Party (Baiocchi 2004; see also Kitchelt 2003). But Norris (2002) makes another argument for why this is the case. She found that countries where broadcast television has not become widespread had higher levels of grassroots party activism. She argues that where television broadcasting is widely available, parties develop television-based electoral campaigns that limit opportunities for grassroots mobilization and participation.

As the above example suggests, electoral agendas are strongly influenced by the media as well as public arenas. Candidates, like movements, must find ways to bring the issues they care about into broader public discussion, and in most Western democracies they do this primarily through the mass media rather than through more direct contact with voters. The above-cited study of U.S. local broadcasts, however, shows the difficulty candidates have in gaining news media attention to their campaigns—much less the issues that motivate their runs for political office. Movements hoping to influence the electoral agenda must consider the system of rules and party structures that affect this agenda as they seek to bring new issues onto the more restricted agendas that characterize electoral arenas.

NEOLIBERAL GLOBALIZATION AND ELECTORAL ARENAS

Neoliberal globalization's impacts on public and media arenas have ripple effects on the electoral arena. By affecting the structure of the mass media and the amount of free time and the availability of opportunities people have in their communities to engage in all forms of public life, it shapes the ways political parties and candidates can communicate with their constituents. As we saw above, more political parties are relying upon television broadcasts to communicate their messages to citizens, and this is associated with a decline in grassroots participation in party organizations. It also suggests that political discourse has become less diverse and responsive as centralized party structures can more readily control the messages conveyed through mass media than through more decentralized and participatory structures.

Declining opportunities for people to participate in the process of building public support for particular political platforms and candidates (by means other than giving money to party organizations) has led to sharp reductions in party memberships in many countries, particularly those with the most established democratic systems (Norris 2002). At the same time, surveys in the newer democracies of Central and Eastern Europe and in Latin America show that political parties have earned little public confidence, ranking among the lowest of public institutions such as the president, television, police, national legislature, and armed forces (UNDP 2002: 69). These two patterns are clearly related. To the extent that people have opportunities to be active in the work of political parties, they are more likely to see these organizations as open and transparent entities. But without opportunities to connect on a personal level with party organizations, rather than through mailed fundraising campaigns or through television advertising, people will understandably become disengaged from and even suspicious of party leadership.

The neoliberal globalization network is, however, likely to be supportive of the trend toward greater party reliance on mass media campaigning and toward a demobilization of voters. Not only are media profits increased by the massive and often unprecedented party advertising expenditures, but a demobilized electorate gives members of the neoliberal network more space to shape the policy agenda without much public oversight or scrutiny. Indeed, because they need to raise ever-greater amounts of money to fund their media advertising campaigns, politicians are increasingly dependent upon large corporate donations for their electoral success. Lacking the grassroots organizational capacities to raise money from individual voters, politicians find that they must appeal to corporations if they are to win elections (Hertz 2001).

Governmental Arenas

Finally, government agendas are the most limited and centralized of those we consider here. They are shaped by the structure of a political system's government, so they would include both the legislative branch as well as executive and judicial ones. Different national laws determine how people can appeal to elected officials and the courts to bring new issues to their attention or to shape decisions about how regulations are enforced. Different movements will have different levels of access to governmental agendas, and McCarthy and his colleagues found that environmental movement organizations and consensus movement groups such as those opposing drunk driving were far more active in this arena than were peace movement and poor empowerment groups (McCarthy et al. 1996a: 303).

Access to governmental arenas will also vary according to which party(ies) occupy political offices. Some parties will be very responsive to certain movement aims, while others leave little hope that a movement's concerns will gain a hearing. In any case, by forming alliances or otherwise engaging with actors within governmental arenas, movements can gain access to important information about the policy-making process and about the implementation of policy. They can improve their capacities for monitoring the practices of governments that are indifferent or even hostile to movement agendas, helping to ensure that elected officials adequately implement legislation that has passed. An important lesson from the history of social movement activities is that movements without the ability to track whether politicians and governments make good on their promises are likely to find that their policy victories are inconsequential.

NEOLIBERAL GLOBALIZATION AND GOVERNMENTAL ARENAS

Government agendas are shaped by the agenda-setting processes within other, more expansive arenas, and thus, neoliberal globalization has already served to limit the possible range of issues and policy choices that define governmental agendas. Also, the reliance of political candidates on corporate funding leads them to establish relationships with corporate actors that continue after they move from the role of candidate to that of public official. Indeed, that is what inspires large campaign contributions. With regard to climate policy, the fact that thirteen of the world's fifty largest economies (including both governments and corporations) are corporations dealing in fossil fuel energies and automobiles helps explain the stubborn U.S. refusal to act on the threats caused by climate change.[12]

Moving beyond these effects, the neoliberal globalization network influences governmental arenas more broadly by shaping the rules of the global system in which governments must operate. They do this most directly by shaping the policies of global financial institutions like the World Bank and the International Monetary Fund (IMF), which exert important influences over the practices of governments in borrowing countries. They also shape the possibilities for government action by working to define the global trade rules and to advocate for stronger international trade agreements (see chapter 4). These agreements limit the possibilities for governments to determine what policies are most appropriate to their needs, requiring that they progressively open their borders to international trade and investment regardless of the effects of such policies on their domestic economies. Indeed, even government purchases are now subject to international trade agreements, and local and national governments are thus denied the ability to freely choose their own procurement policies.

A further way that the neoliberal globalization network affects government arenas is by promoting and using international trade dispute mechanisms to advance their corporate interests. While governments must bring these cases to the dispute panels, they often do so at the behest of corporate actors, many of whom are contributors to officials' political campaigns. For instance, Chiquita Brands International instigated the famous dispute against the European Union (EU) over the EU's policy of providing preferential access to its markets by Caribbean banana producers. The United States brought this case to the WTO even though no bananas are grown on its territory for export. However, Chiquita company officials have long had close ties with U.S. government officials (Wallach and Woodall 2004). In another case (again led by the United States), the Gerber baby food manufactcurers threatened Honduras over its policy of restricting the company's ability to use its official logo (a chubby, healthy infant) to market its products in that country. What makes this case most egregious is that Honduran policy followed UNICEF guidelines established to prevent misleading and dangerous forms of baby food marketing in poor countries (Sikkink 1986).

These kinds of cases have two important consequences for shaping government arenas. First, they have a chilling effect, leading governments to avoid making any policy that might trigger a trade dispute, regardless of how much a policy might reflect their own people's preferences. This is especially likely among poor countries, which are most vulnerable to economic and trade sanctions and least able to fund the legal teams necessary to either prosecute or defend trade disputes. Second, they serve to undermine international norms and practices that have emerged through the UN and other treaty bodies that are more open and responsive to demands that lie outside of purely economic debates. In other words, they contribute to normative and legal contradictions in the global policy arena (see chapter 9).

This section has described the four main arenas where agenda setting takes place, identifying important factors that shape how social groups identify important issues that might generate new proposals for policy changes. Because they generally have less direct access to formal policy arenas, social movements hoping to bring about social and political change must first bring their issues to the attention of a large and/or influential public. This means that they must try to influence public and media agendas while also working to move issues to the more formal policy agendas.

Challenging Neoliberal Agendas in a Global Arena

Within the neoliberal globalization network we find a specialized fraction of actors devoted specifically to the goal of promoting and extending the culture of consumerism, which guarantees ideological support for the continued expansion of capitalism. This ideological work helps ensure that the activities of the different fractions of the neoliberal network are mutually reinforcing, even without extensive efforts to coordinate them. The cultural cohesiveness and vast resources of the network have helped it attract large numbers of influential politicians and knowledge workers to promote its interests. As the above discussion shows, this has contributed to its ability to shape public, media, electoral, and government agendas, thereby helping the network expand its control over the world's material and human resources.

While this may lead to a sense that nothing can be done to fundamentally alter the relations of power in the global system, the framework I propose here allows us to unpack the ways that public discourse is shaped through broader structures and institutions. We can see, for instance, that the logic of consumerism helps unify the neoliberal network and generate, without explicit coordination, complementary pressures by different actors. It also reinforces the power of the neoliberal globalization network by providing the "invisible hand" that leads people to continue to act in ways that support neoliberal network interests without questioning whether such actions serve their or society's larger needs and interests. This approach also sensitizes us to the ways the organization of the economy impacts possibilities for democratic politics.

What sort of culture or logic can be seen as a unifying framework for the democratic globalization network? Examining the discourse of analysts and activists, it seems that the democratic globalization network might find unity around the aim of promoting a human rights culture against their rival network's culture of consumerism. A human rights culture emphasizes the fundamentally social aspect of humanity, while recognizing the individual as a site for human rights. Unlike the culture of consumerism, which relies upon the unquestioned assumption that there are unlimited resources on the planet, the human rights culture recognizes the very real constraints of our planetary ecosystem. It sees the economy as a means to enhancing human life rather than an end in itself. It acknowledges the realities of global interdependence. The human rights culture does not privilege any particular gender, race, or religious or cultural tradition but rather celebrates all as legitimate expressions of human diversity.

The global public sphere is realized in a variety of spaces outside of those that are explicitly transnational, and a challenge for those seeking to promote global change is to connect local sites of public discourse with transnational ones (Guidry et al. 2000). For social movement networks like those considered here, this might be done by finding ways to bring globally oriented frames, identities, and ideologies into the public, media, electoral, and governmental arenas in local and national settings. This can encourage people to view themselves more as members of a global human community than as individual consumers. The two examples of transnational activism I highlight in this chapter illustrate ways that participants in the democratic globalization network have sought to expand opportunities for citizens to engage in global policy processes and debates. More systematic attention to the different arenas and the possibilities and limitations they pose for those seeking to shape policy agendas can help enhance global work to democratize globalization.

Agenda Setting and Network Politics

Examining the two initiatives introduced in this chapter, we can see evidence that attempts by activists to shape political agendas can challenge the legitimacy of rival networks while also impacting multilateral political processes. In particular, by serving as alternative sources of information that expand local understandings of global issues, these initiatives deny neoliberal proponents a monopoly over public, media, and policy agendas. They expand possibilities for policy solutions to emerge from outside the neoliberal network. By maintaining critical attention to the activities and claims of neoliberal proponents, activists can promote greater transparency and accountability in global politics, even without the formal institutions of democracy (e.g., Falk and Strauss 2001; Florini 2003; Monbiot 2003). Finally, by helping create more open and transparent flows of information about global agreements, they expand public participation in global politics, opening further possibilities to challenge neoliberals' influence on policy.

CHALLENGING THE LEGITIMACY OF THE NEOLIBERAL NETWORK

The IMCs challenge the agenda-dominance of the neoliberal network by generating and disseminating reports on events that mainstream commercial media tend to ignore. They enable individuals to remain informed about democratic activism around the world. Indeed, before the IMC, it was difficult to find a single Web site that could provide a global picture of activism challenging global capitalism. And the open and participatory nature of the IMC makes it one of the more comprehensive sources of information about global campaigns of all kinds. But beyond this more immediate impact, the IMCs help cultivate critical media activists while providing spaces for activists to learn skills in media production. This offers a more long-term resource for the democratic globalization network.

By serving as a non-commercial and anti-capitalist source of information on global issues and events, the IMC also challenges neoliberal dominance over policy agendas. Cases such as the mass mobilization against the Multilateral Agreement on Investment, a highly unpopular proposal to limit the abilities of governments to regulate international investors, and the Seattle protests show how public scrutiny can bring neoliberal initiatives to an abrupt halt. As Laurie Wallach has remarked in speeches to activists, "sunshine is the best disinfectant." If governments know constituents are watching (and therefore expect that votes may be won or lost on an issue), they are unlikely to pursue policies that clearly benefit a small minority while neglecting and often adversely affecting a majority. The fact that police at various global meeting places (including Seattle, London, and Genoa) have targeted IMCs demonstrates the extent to which neoliberal proponents perceive these activities as a threat (Morris 2004).

The Kyoto Now! and Cities for Climate Protection campaigns help challenge the legitimacy of neoliberal claims by encouraging public suspicion of leaders' assertions, such as that by U.S. administration officials that implementing the Kyoto Protocol would harm the U.S. economy. Activists in these campaigns are very conscious in their efforts to demonstrate not only how Kyoto can be implemented locally but how it can actually help save money and enhance economic efficiency. Kyoto Now! activists, for instance, claim to have helped the State University of New York at Buffalo save $9 million in annual energy costs. Students on campuses such as Lewis and Clark and Oberlin College have pressed their campus administrations to adopt carbon assessment policies to monitor and reduce emissions from campus facilities (Smithson 2002). Confronted with local evidence of how global policies can work, continued claims by politicians and industry leaders that contradict local experiences begin to cost credibility. Student activists have also challenged the legitimacy of governments and industry by stressing intergenerational responsibilities of environmental policies. For instance, at the 2005 Convention of the Parties to the Climate Change Convention, student activists donned T-shirts proclaiming "Stop asking how much it will cost you and start asking how much it will cost us." And one youth campaigner with the Environmental Justice and Climate Change Initiative was arrested for entering a meeting hall to deliver a "climate change survival pack" to a U.S. delegate that contained a face mask, a life jacket, and a can of Spam (Revkin 2005).[13]

SHAPING GLOBAL PROCESSES

The agenda-setting activities of transnational groups of activists have had significant impacts on global policy processes. The cases of IMC and Kyoto Now! demonstrate ways that democratic globalization activists have sought to shape global agendas by expanding public participation in global-level politics. In doing so, they both create new avenues for political participation and allow people to see the connections between their local experiences and global politics, thereby strengthening popular support for multilateral institutions.

One procedural consequence of the long history of citizen participation in UN global conferences has been the inclusion in many international agreements of requirements that governments and international agencies consult with or otherwise solicit input from local communities. Despite wide variation in the extent to which authorities make good faith efforts to carry out these requirements, their existence has created new spaces for deliberation about global policy where none existed. And the enhanced networking among civil society groups and local government officials means that information about these consultations (or the lack thereof) will quickly spread to groups concerned with making sure that governments carry out their agreements. The work of groups like IMC and Kyoto Now! is a crucial element of efforts to expand the spaces for deliberation about how societies should respond to the problems they face (see, e.g., Riles 2001; Subramaniam et al. 2003).

Multilaterally mandated consultations can affect not only public agendas but also media, electoral, and governmental ones. The public agenda is most directly shaped by them, as groups are likely to organize preparatory meetings to help them come to joint positions and otherwise consider how best to present their understandings of the issues that need to be addressed. These kinds of dialogues can also help broker new relationships among local groups, shaping subsequent collaborative efforts and discussions on the issue. And civil society groups might organize follow-up meetings with officials to find out how their input was used. Depending upon local media contexts, these meetings themselves might win places on media agendas, or the participants in these sessions might organize press conferences or write press releases to help expand media attention to the connections between global agreements and local conditions and actions. For instance, Kolb (2005) found that media coverage of international protests helped spur the formation of new local chapters of the international advocacy group, Association pour la Taxe Tobin pour l'Aide aux Citoyens (ATTAC). Also, public officials might find that ties to activist constituents are good ways of advancing their own political careers while expanding their knowledge of and attention to global issues. And finally, by requiring government officials to communicate with citizens on particular problems, these international agreements help open spaces on governmental agendas for greater citizen influence.

Activist strategies for following up international agreements also generate more bottom-up kinds of pressures that help expand public deliberation and contribute to local and national processes that help legitimate international policies and institutions. Organizations targeting global conferences have adopted the strategy of mobilizing local activists around the aim of monitoring their own governments' compliance with international agreements. The popular outreach activities of Kyoto Now!, such as Tufts University's "Do It in the Dark" event, help raise youth awareness of energy use, reach new audiences, and bring global issues to people otherwise left out of global policy debates. Thus, Revkin reports that youth participation in global climate meetings has flourished since 2000, when Greenpeace began more youth-specific organizing work. Whereas in the early 2000s most youth delegates were recruited from the major environmental groups, the more recent meetings were characterized by more homegrown groups such as a Montreal group called Apathy is Boring, which hosted a party for youth attending the 2005 Conference of Parties to the Kyoto Protocol (Revkin 2005).

One can find many other examples of democratic globalizers helping to hold governments accountable to international commitments. Groups like the Women's Environment and Development Organization (WEDO), for instance, have created checklists for organizers to use as they rate their national and local governments' performance with regard to international agreements. And Social Watch is one of a number of transnational social movement groups that publishes annual updates on countries' performance with regard to their commitments on social development and aid policies, providing local and national organizers with effective tools that can be used to shame governments that fall short of their goals or to praise those that do well. If activists considered these efforts as part of a broader strategy of building a multilateral system that prioritizes human dignity and environmental sustainability over wealth production, governments may find themselves facing far greater pressure to change their policies.

Efforts to ensure that governments at all levels are doing all that they can to uphold their commitments can strengthen the global polity in important ways. By expanding public deliberation on important global issues, agenda-shaping activities like Kyoto Now! and the IMC reinforce global-level standards and accountability. They also prompt people to think of themselves as part of a transnational community of human beings with problems that are not confined within national boundaries. While this does not negate national identities, it does generate different standards against which to evaluate national government practices, providing different criteria for government legitimacy in the eyes of both their own constituents as well as other nations' peoples and governments. Campaigns to monitor government compliance with international agreements can help make the local-global connections needed to effectively bring global issues

and concerns onto more localized public agendas. They also help provide the local "hook" that can draw media attention to issues that might otherwise appear
too remote or complex. Effective use of public pressure or political leadership
can help bring global issues onto national and local electoral and governmental
agendas.

What these different agenda-setting strategies have in common is that they help
make vivid the connections between global policies and local conditions. Given
that people live in local political settings and that most have little firsthand knowledge of global-level problems or processes, those seeking to challenge neoliberal
globalization must find ways to demonstrate the relationships between the global
political and economic system and people's everyday experiences. Considering
the various arenas in which people discuss policy global issues allows us to identify the factors that determine both how issues are selected for various agendas
as well as the conditions that shape the portrayal of these issues.

Conclusion

The neoliberal globalization network has been successful in getting many
people around the world to think that its vision for world order is the best, the
most logical, inevitable, and natural. One way it has done this is by making more
and more people dependent upon capitalism for their livelihoods. The culture of
consumerism that supports the operations and ideologies of capitalism is largely
unquestioned, and powerful actors routinely reinforce it through their regular
public statements and policy decisions. Any attempt to challenge the neoliberal
version of globalization must identify how the neoliberal ideology has become
and how it remains so pervasive. By analyzing how public issues are discussed
and how they enter the formal policy process, this chapter sought to identify
strategies through which groups challenging neoliberalism might advance alternative visions.

Public deliberation is an essential element of democratic governance. And
public deliberation can only take place where there is a public sphere where
large numbers of well-informed citizens can discuss problems and the variety
of possible solutions to them. Analysts have long pointed to the importance of
social movements and other civil society groups to cultivating and sustaining
vibrant public spheres (Edwards et al. 2001; Evans and Boyt 1986; Guidry et al.
2000; Nanz and Steffek 2004; Polletta 2002). If global policy processes are to be
democratized, people must find ways to bring global issues onto locally defined
agendas.

This chapter has argued that we can think of the global public sphere as shaped by distinctive national and international public, media, electoral, and governmental arenas that each have their own agenda-setting processes. Public deliberation serves a number of democratic purposes. For instance, Polletta's (2002) study of participatory democracy in U.S. social movements led her to conclude that participatory forms of democracy helped people expand their notions of self- and collective interests. In other words, it led people to alter their understandings of their interests as they integrated new understandings of the perspectives and needs of others. The two campaigns explored here illustrate just this dynamic. By expanding public discourse on global issues and policies, social change advocates can help people imagine themselves as part of a wider, global community and thereby enhance the prospects for a more democratic global order. They do so, according to the criteria outlined earlier in this book, by expanding public awareness and engagement in policy debates, by enhancing the transparency and accountability of national and international policy processes, by putting pressure on governments to make international institutions more open and fair, and by mobilizing constituencies supportive of multilateral law and policy.

Thus far we have explored how the democratic globalization network has helped generate new organizational capacities for transnational political engagement and how it has reinforced multilateralism by mobilizing around global political agendas. The following chapters identify how specific campaigns contribute to the expansion and strengthening of multilateral institutions. We begin by looking at efforts to domesticate international human rights norms.

CHAPTER EIGHT

Domesticating International Human Rights Norms

Well I went down to the rich man's house and I
Took back what he stole from me
Took back my dignity
Took back my humanity . . .
Ain't no system gonna walk all over me.
—*The Economic Human Rights Choir,*
Poor People's Economic Human Rights Campaign

Protecting human rights is the most fundamental responsibility
of civilized nations. Because climate change is threatening the lives,
health, culture and livelihoods of the Inuit, it is the responsibility of
the United States, as the largest source of greenhouse gases, to take
immediate and effective action to protect the rights of the Inuit.
Petition to the Inter-American Commission on Human Rights

In their important work on transnational activism, Margaret Keck and Kathryn Sikkink document the ways activists used transnational connections to generate a "boomerang effect," which engaged international legal institutions or other forms of pressure that would alter the balance of power between challengers and powerful government and corporate actors in particular domestic contexts. In chapter 4, I discussed how the neoliberal network uses a different version of this boomerang to *limit* the power of local and national groups relative to governments and other powerful actors. But in this chapter we explore how groups in the democratic globalization network have used the boomerang effect to integrate international law into government practices. In the process, they are engaging a "double-boomerang" (Kaldor 2003: 96) that not only seeks protection for victims, but also enhances the coherence of international law by demonstrating how established human rights are violated by governments' economic and environmental policies.

The cases we explore in this chapter, the Poor People's Economic Human Rights Campaign and the Inuit people's petition to the Inter-American Human Rights Commission protesting U.S. environmental policies, demonstrate how, as more and more people become aware of international laws, they seek opportunities to apply those laws to particular local contexts. We find here that poor people and indigenous groups have become important catalysts, or "norm entrepreneurs" (Finnemore and Sikkink 1998), in the development of international law as they begin to know and claim their internationally defined human rights.

An important element of the boomerang strategy is to expose the hypocrisy of governments, which often sign international human rights treaties to enhance their image in the eyes of the international community while continuing to violate international norms. Activists appeal to international law, and the gaps between a government's words and deeds, as a source of political leverage in their struggles against national governments. Following the logic of the sovereignty bargain described in chapter 3, they seek to raise the legitimacy costs to governments wishing to preserve autonomy in ways that go against international norms. Patrick Ball's "hypocrisy thesis" describes this practice, which he sees as effective in promoting human rights outcomes over the long term (2000). More recently, Tunisian human rights activist Massoud Romdhani pointed to how international meetings were important spaces for activists to challenge repressive governments:

> It is noticeable that our government is rather more concerned about its reputation abroad than at home. That is one reason why I am glad to have done three interviews with the media while I was [at the European Social Forum]. Most governments . . . try to establish a wall between themselves and the rest of the world so that they can maintain the fiction that everything in the garden is lovely. (Quoted in Bechler 2004)

As globalization facilitates the flows of information across international borders, and as activists organize themselves to make strategic use of this information, the politics of shaming, of boomerangs, and of exposing hypocrisy will become more important to helping strengthen multilateralism. They will do so by serving to *domesticate* international law, a term legal scholars use to refer to the modification of national and local laws and practices to make them consistent with international obligations.

I have selected the following cases to illustrate the important contributions of democratic globalizers to the construction and strengthening of international law and institutions. While it is important to note that groups worldwide are working to domesticate international law in many different national contexts, I have selected two cases where activists target the U.S. government. As the world's most powerful country as well as a country admired for its historic leadership on democracy and human rights, the United States is especially vulnerable to criticism for its hypocritical actions on the global stage (Sands 2005). Like standing up to the bully on the playground, forcing the United States to respect international human rights norms would go a long way toward generating new momentum for multilateralism worldwide. Thus, activists in many countries have a huge stake in what happens in Washington.

This story of how different groups, operating both within and outside the United States, have tried to hold the world's most powerful government accountable to international norms illustrates how the democratic globalization network reinforces multilateralism. It does so by laying claim to rights established through international conventions that states have not fully implemented. These efforts also strengthen international law by highlighting the indivisibility of rights, so that civil and political rights cannot be seen as independent of broader economic and environmental rights, as they were during the Cold War.[1] These types of campaigns thereby radicalize human rights claims, making clear the ways economic globalization threatens the widely shared values of democracy and human freedom. Both campaigns also illustrate how social movement groups working within a broader transnational network have helped expand participation by groups not previously integrated into the network.

The Poor People's Economic Human Rights Campaign

In November 2000, a few hundred activists gathered at Riverside Church in upper Manhattan for the Poor People's World Summit to End Poverty. The Kensington Welfare Rights Union (KWRU) led this initiative as part of its Poor People's Economic Human Rights Campaign (PPEHRC). Launched in 1997 in response to drastic cuts in U.S. welfare provisions, the PPEHRC works to both domesticate international human rights law and to internationalize the struggle of poor people in the United States. This summit in New York brought U.S. activists together with their counterparts from as many as thirty other countries. They shared experiences and worked to build an international movement for economic human rights drawing explicitly on international treaties. Cheri

Honkala, director of the KWRU, opened the poor people's summit by asking participants to join hands and affirm their commitment to work for human rights by declaring, "we will know and claim our human rights." During the three-day meeting, participants attended workshops and plenary sessions or joined "reality tours" organized by local activists to make visitors aware of the crushing poverty in New York City.[2] Speakers at this meeting emphasized words like *dignity* and *inclusion,* words more commonly used by poor activists within and outside the United States than by middle-class ones.[3] Participants in the Poor People's World Summit took pride in the fact that they proved their critics wrong by successfully convening this meeting, despite their lack of funds.

The PPEHRC was inspired by a fortuitous meeting of two tireless organizers, Cheri Honkala of the KWRU[4] and Shulamith Koenig, the founder and director of People's Decade on Human Rights Education. Koenig had long been active in promoting human rights education and encouraging popular organizing around international human rights conventions. And Honkala was seeking a new approach to challenging the drastic U.S. welfare reforms of the mid-1990s, which antipoverty activists saw as part of a new and widening war against the poor in the United States (Ford Foundation 2004: 50). The PPEHRC was launched with KWRU's second annual March for Our Lives in June and July 1997, in which activists marched 125 miles from the Liberty Bell in Philadelphia to the doors of the UN. In 1998, the campaign launched a New Freedom Bus Tour, which, like the earlier civil rights movement's Poor People's Campaign, crossed the country to raise awareness of and to mobilize people around calls for economic human rights in the United States.[5] Along the way, activists collected documentation about economic human rights violations for use in the cases they planned to file with international human rights agencies.

The 1998 PPEHRC march became more explicitly international in focus. The March for the Americas took activists from around North and South America on a month-long march from Washington, D.C., to the UN headquarters in New York. The march's mobile Internet training unit helped cultivate skills in electronic communication among the participants, and daily Internet journals and photo albums helped spread activists' stories to observers in more than eighty countries.

Later in 1999, PPEHRC organizers brought the story of their Freedom Tour to a major international gathering of civil society groups working for peace and human rights, the Hague Appeal for Peace Conference, which marked the 150th anniversary of the intergovernmental Hague Peace Conference. Nearly ten thousand people from more than a hundred countries came together at the conference to claim that "peace is a human right," and KWRU used the opportunity to hold a formal screening of their documentary film on the Freedom Tour, *Outriders*. KWRU's links to international human rights organizations drew them to this conference, where many groups made explicit the links between poverty, globalization, and war. Activists discussed how to better integrate their efforts to prevent war while promoting economic justice. In a workshop entitled "Root Causes of War/Culture of Peace: Creating a New Vision for the 21st Century," Honkala argued: "We will no longer have the poor of one country fight the poor of another country in order to build the wealth for the richest 5% of the world." As one of the tiny number of poor people's organizations at a largely middle-class gathering of activists, PPEHRC organizers helped draw attention to the centrality of poverty to a host of other global problems while cultivating new alliances that would help globalize their struggle.[6]

The next stop in the campaign to globalize its efforts against poverty was Seattle in late November 1999, where Honkala and other PPEHRC activists participated in the preparations of the World Trade Organization (WTO) ministerial by providing testimony for the People's Tribunal on Corporate Crimes Against Humanity. They shared information about the impacts of corporate influence on the U.S. health care and pharmaceutical industries on poor people in the United States in general and in the Kensington neighborhood of Philadelphia in particular. They were joined by activists from the Philippines (speaking about sweatshop production tied to the Gap corporation), India (speaking about the impacts of U.S. agribusinesses on the economic devastation of small farmers), and Nigeria (testifying about the role of the Shell oil corporation in the repression of the indigenous Ogoni people). The organizers of the People's Tribunal explained the ways international war crimes laws can be applied to the activities of corporations, indicating that the Nuremburg principles allowed the legal extension of the concept of war crimes to include actions taken in peacetime and by actors other than governments and their armies.[7]

The KWRU and PPEHRC continued to build alliances with a wide range of groups within the United States as well as internationally as the global justice movement gained greater momentum in the aftermath of the Seattle WTO protests (Chabot 2005). For instance, Honkala was a key figure organizing in the 2000 Republican National Convention in Philadelphia, and she and other organizers for the PPEHRC have attended the World Social Forums (WSFs) since 2001.

In addition to strengthening its ties to other U.S. and international participants in the democratic globalization network, the PPEHRC has also worked to

generate sustained pressure on international human rights institutions such as
the UN Human Rights Commission and its regional counterpart in the Organization of American States (OAS). In late 1999, the campaign launched a petition
to the Inter-American Human Rights Commission[8] asking the organization to
rule that U.S. welfare reforms violated OAS human rights standards. The OAS
petition argues the U.S. Personal Responsibility and Work Opportunity Reconciliation Act of 1996 violates the American Declaration on the Rights and Duties
of Man (which defines the OAS human rights framework).[9] In particular the petition cites the requirement that

> 1) "the Member States agree that equality of opportunity, the elimination of extreme
> poverty, equitable distribution of wealth and income and the full participation of
> their peoples in decisions relating to their own development are . . . basic objectives
> of integral development," and that 2) every person has the right to the "preserva-
> tion of his (sic.) health through sanitary and social measures relating to food, cloth-
> ing, housing and medical care, to the extent permitted by public and community
> resources"; and 3) that every person "has the right to an education that will prepare
> him to attain a decent life, to raise his standard of living and to be a useful member
> of society."[10]

Not surprisingly, the petition has moved slowly through the OAS process, and
the PPEHRC has worked to maintain pressure on delegates to keep it active. In
January 2005, on the occasion of Dr. Martin Luther King Jr. Day in the United
States, the PPEHRC requested a general hearing in the OAS Inter-American
Human Rights Commission on the status of the right to adequate housing to
investigate housing rights violations in various OAS countries, including the
United States, Canada, and Brazil. Their request was granted, and members
of the coalition presented testimony to the commission in early March 2005.[11]
While the U.S. government will likely ignore the case in the short term, the
fact that human rights campaigns like this one are looking to international institutions to raise their concerns does generate new challenges to U.S. political
leadership. Such challenges to the legitimacy of U.S. policies come at a time
when U.S. influence in the region is being challenged by the rise of popular
leftist governments in several Latin American countries and by widespread con-
demnation of its military occupation of Iraq and treatment of prisoners. This
U.S. vulnerability increases the potential impact of this case.

In addition to work within the OAS, the campaign has brought the voices of
poor people to the UN. In April 2000, members of KWRU attended the 56th
Session of the UN Human Rights Commission in Geneva, where they deliv-

ered a statement to government delegates on behalf of the PPEHRC and their host organization, the International Peace Bureau. The statement highlighted the widespread poverty in one of the world's richest countries, identifying the welfare reforms of the 1990s as a cause of even greater misery. It emphasized the international ramifications of U.S. welfare policy and urged officials to back the PPEHRC petition in the OAS as well as to press the U.S. government to join international economic human rights conventions:

> To complement the existing debate around poverty and economic human rights which has focused mainly on important "developing" world issues like foreign debt, structural adjustment and lack of development, I would like to bring to your attention the extreme poverty that persists in the most "developed" countries. The reality of poor people in the United States, one of the richest countries in the world, is quite different from the image portrayed by both the US government and mainstream media. Downsizing, unemployment and poverty wage jobs exist in the shadows of the reported "US economic boom" . . . The social welfare reform bill passed by President Clinton in 1996 has effectively . . . limit[ed] economic human rights. Moreover, the American-style social reform is modeled and replicated throughout the developed world, therefore globally dismantling states' responsibility to provide for the basic needs of poor people. This is the American contribution to the global race to the bottom . . . Like the *desaparecidos* of Latin America, the poor of all colors in the United States are disappearing from the welfare rolls and unemployment statistics. As the criminalization of poverty and of poor people increases, prisons fill with the disappeared.[12]

With this statement, the campaign helped identify tensions between governments' commitments to protect human rights and policies that advance economic globalization. This point is further emphasized by the statement's reference to poor people in the United States as "disappeared." This phrase alludes to heinous examples of "disappearances" by Latin American dictatorships that were roundly denounced by the UN Human Rights Commission in the 1980s, implying parallels between economic and other rights abuses. The fact that the speaker represented a campaign led by poor people in the United States also helped undermine illusions that the kind of economic and welfare policies favored by the U.S. government were attractive models for poor countries.

International ties are important for a number of reasons. Not only do they provide necessary allies who can help bring the skills, resources, and people that help strengthen the campaign, but they also give U.S. antipoverty activists a perspective on the conditions for poor people elsewhere that they otherwise would not hear. These can be empowering relationships, in part because they can offer new insights into how poor people have organized to change their conditions. Many in the United States are surprised to find that conditions elsewhere are not as bleak, or at least the conditions of poverty are mitigated by stronger social organizations among the non-U.S. poor:

> While on a bus caravan in El Salvador, a Kensington resident's testimonial to her beleaguered situation startled their Southern sisters. "One woman began to cry," remembers Honkala. "Not only because she couldn't believe that poverty existed in the U.S, but, in contrast to her El Salvadorian community, "because of how little organization exists among the poor of the U.S." (Haddon 2000)

Transnational ties can also generate new ideas and strategies for U.S. antipoverty activism. For instance, learning about how poor people are organized elsewhere can inspire new initiatives as well as hope in communities in the United States. For European and other activists in the global North, evidence such as that presented by the PPEHRC demonstrates the failures of the more extreme neoliberal economic policies that the United States has pressed their governments to adopt. In short, the testimony of PPEHRC activists helps discredit claims made by critics that resistance to neoliberal globalization grows from misinformed, altruistic concerns raised by middle-class activists on behalf of the poor. It also helps make the case that poverty is endemic to the neoliberal economic order (for it is present in even the world's wealthiest and most pro-neoliberal country) and therefore is a threat to people in all parts of the world.

A key aim of the PPEHRC is to use the organizing frame of global human rights principles to help bring together many diverse struggles and to bring new leverage to efforts to eliminate poverty and the anti-poor policies in the United States and around the world. It remains, however, primarily a U.S.-based campaign with an expanding range of ties to a broad and diverse international network.[13] Because the corporate actors they found themselves confronting in their Philadelphia-based labor and health care struggles were transnational, KWRU organizers quickly learned that they needed to build their own global network. This theme permeates their discussions of economic human rights. For instance, their announcement for the 2004 March for Our Lives at the UN headquarters in New York proclaimed that the "poor of the United States call on the international community for help," and the campaign's participation in the 2005 WSF was framed as helping convey the "need for international support of resistance happening within the United States."[14] Another important consequence of the international human rights frame is that it enables a wide array of alliances with activist groups and professionals in the United States and elsewhere that would not be possible without a broadly inclusive framework based on notions of a common human identity.

A focus on international law not only helps nurture transnational alliances, but it also provides important substantive leverage for local activism. Activists in the PPEHRC work to help people "know and claim their rights" by devoting much of their attention to work that enhances popular awareness of the Universal Declaration of Human Rights, and in particular three of its key articles: Article 23—the right to work for just pay and the right to organize; Article 25—the right to health, housing, and security; and Article 26—the right to education. Activists attending PPEHRC events such as the 2000 Poor People's Summit in New York wore T-shirts displaying these articles. At its events and on its Web site, the campaign distributes resource packets and summaries of the Universal Declaration of Human Rights and other international human rights treaties. To help people claim these rights, the PPEHRC borrows strategies from other international human rights organizations, collecting individual reports on specific violations of international laws through both its Web site and its "tours." It aggregates these claims and presents them in various symbolic and strategic ways to international human rights bodies.[15]

The PPEHRC has attracted a wide array of antipoverty groups as well as students, social workers, and lawyers who brought new skills and approaches to the campaign to incorporate international human rights law into local, state, and national policies.[16] Within the United States, it is seeking a "second bill of rights" that reflects international norms and guarantees Americans' rights to food, education, health, housing, and the ability to make a living. At the same time, international partnerships bring comparative perspectives and lessons to the struggle, provide moral support and legitimacy, and expand international attention to the realities of poor people in the United States and elsewhere. The presence of poor activists in this international movement helps shatter popular American myths about the global superiority of the U.S. model of democracy and economic development (Josephson and Zoelle 2005), and it contributes to the global effort to strengthen all governments' commitments to both economic and political human rights.

U.S. civil rights activists sought to use a similar strategy when the Universal Declaration of Human Rights was in its infancy, but congressional officials repelled these efforts, equating them with the subversion of national law, communism, and even treason (Anderson 2003).[17] A recent Ford Foundation report on human rights activism in the United States notes that this history has long hindered human rights work in that country by excluding economic and social rights from citizens' notions of basic human rights:

> This brand of cold war politics sought not only to discourage U.S. activists from invoking human rights in their domestic work, but also to distort the very meaning of human rights for Americans by eliminating its economic and social dimensions . . . The development of a U.S. human rights movement is driven in part by the desire to reclaim the full legacy and meaning of international human rights. (Ford Foundation 2004: 7–8)

No government likes to have its dirty laundry aired in public. The power of shaming is the only mechanism we have for enforcing most international laws. For many activists appealing to international laws, the international arena is their only court of appeals and an important source of hope for changing the policies of their national governments. By bringing attention to the discrepancies between a government's practices and international standards, activists not only can help change the practices of their governments, but they also generate more of the needed scrutiny on the correspondence (or lack thereof) between local-level practices and global norms. This double-boomerang contributes to a stronger and more cohesive multilateral order.

Indigenous Peoples' Challenge to U.S. Climate Policy

The effects of climate change are becoming increasingly apparent, and the people most affected are those whose cultures have evolved in Arctic regions. Some of the most dramatic climate changes have occurred in the Arctic, where seasons are changing, permafrost is beginning to melt, and once stable ice shelves are breaking up. These changes signal important disruptions in ecosystems that depend upon long and cold winters to sustain human and wildlife inhabitants. Melting ice has limited the abilities of polar bears to hunt for food, threatening their very survival. And indigenous peoples living in these areas are finding that traditions they have followed for countless generations are endangered by changing weather patterns. Their ability to hunt for traditional food is constrained by thawing ice and by food sources that are facing extinction. Warmer temperatures are preventing them from building the traditional ice structures that keep them warm during extended hunts. Melting permafrost is destroying homes, roads, and other structures that support communities in this region.

Such realities were not often the subject of international human rights discourse, which has tended to focus on political and civil rights or at least to emphasize instances where perpetrators and victims were more clearly defined. But clearly the sorts of environmental changes happening in the Arctic have enormous implications for human rights. At least that is the claim being made by the Inuit Circumpolar Conference (ICC), in cooperation with environmental organizations. *This* ICC is a federation of Native nations representing about 150,000 people in Canada, Greenland, Russia, and the United States. It first proposed the idea of challenging climate change on human rights grounds at the 2003 Conference of the Parties to the Convention on Climate Change (COP) in Milan. At the time, official negotiations were being stymied by U.S. and Russian refusal to sign the Kyoto Protocol, and much of the discussion in both governmental and nongovernmental organization (NGO) circles focused on rather mundane or technical issues relating to science and policy. The ICC proposal generated renewed excitement and optimism (Gertz 2005).

The ICC consulted with environmental lawyers Martin Wagner of a U.S.-based environmental law group called Earthjustice and Don Goldberg of the U.S.-based Center for International Environmental Law, who were already working together to link climate change to human rights (Gertz 2005). Wagner and Goldberg helped the ICC draft a formal petition that could be filed with the Inter-American Commission on Human Rights, the most appropriate legal venue for the claims. By the time of the 2004 meeting of the COP, the ICC reported in sessions to other NGOs working on climate issues as well as in their meetings with national and international officials that, through existing decisions, the Inter-American Commission on Human Rights "has recognized indigenous peoples' right to a healthy and safe environment as integral to their right to life." It indicated that the Inuit would petition the commission concerning the impacts of climate change.[18]

As they worked to build the case for their petition, the ICC chair Sheila Watt-Cloutier also sought to bring U.S. government attention to the claims by meeting with officials at the U.S. Consulate General in Quebec City and testifying at a U.S. Senate hearing on climate change policy in the fall of 2004 (Gertz 2005). She also used the meetings of civil society groups during the COPs to build international awareness of their campaign and to cultivate allies. By the 2005 COP in Montreal, the ICC was prepared to formally file its petition with the OAS, and the announcement was met with great enthusiasm by activists long frustrated by U.S. intransigence in climate change negotiations. Some new approach was needed if there was to be any hope of real progress on international efforts to reduce greenhouse gas emissions.

The 163-page ICC petition draws upon the traditional knowledge of hunters and elders and peer-reviewed science, including the Arctic Climate Impact Assessment, a scientific study prepared by an intergovernmental panel and an NGO specializing in efforts to synthesize scientific knowledge of the effects of climate change on the Arctic.[19] Documenting the established links between climate change, emissions of greenhouse gases, and changes in the Arctic environment that threaten Inuit culture and livelihoods, the petition asks the commission to hold hearings to investigate the harm caused to Inuit by global warming and to declare the United States in violation of rights established in the 1948 American Declaration of the Rights and Duties of Man and other instruments of international law.[20] It seeks a commission recommendation to the United States that it adopt mandatory limits to its greenhouse gas emissions and that it cooperate with international efforts to prevent global warming. Finally, it requests that the commission declare that the United States has an obligation both to take into account the impact of its emissions on the Arctic and the Inuit before approving future major government actions and to work with the Inuit to develop a plan to help them adapt to the unavoidable impacts of climate change (Inuit Circumpolar Conference–Canada 2005).[21]

Like the climate activists seen in the previous chapter, the ICC and its allies are working to increase pressure on the United States to cooperate with international efforts to curb global warming. But rather than building pressure solely from the ground up, as Kyoto Now! groups were doing, this campaign works to bring pressure from the top down, by creating boomerangs through international legal institutions. Like the PPEHRC, this initiative seeks to help victims of abuses "know and claim their human rights," even as it seeks to expand popular awareness of how human rights law applies. As Sheila Watt-Cloutier observed, "I think this is really going to help to change the debate from technology to people . . . This petition is about opening this issue of climate change to humanity and human rights" (George 2005).

The ICC case certainly increased public attention to the OAS legal mechanisms. For instance, a Google search of the case in the weeks after its first announcement yielded nearly seven hundred hits, a majority of which were noncommercial news sites and Web sites of various environmental and human rights activist groups or indigenous communities.[22] These efforts depend to a large extent on work to expand public awareness of international human rights issues and of the positions of governments in international agreements. And each campaign thereby serves to alter the stakes for the United States in terms of its legitimacy vis-à-vis states and civil society for its continued refusal to cede some policy autonomy in global climate agreements.

What are the likely long-term consequences of this legal initiative? Groups behind the ICC petition acknowledge that a favorable OAS decision itself would have little direct bearing on U.S. policy, but they are pursuing the case because it would help advance international law by establishing a stronger legal foundation for connecting environmental policies and human rights. By bringing a rights-based approach to climate change discussion, it would set a legal precedent that advocates for environmental rights could use to shape decisions in other human rights bodies as well as in national courts. As Donald Goldberg, senior attorney with the Center for International Environmental Law, argued: "If the Commission finds the U.S. has violated human rights, it's a serious matter . . . States don't like to be classified as violators of human rights; and in any case, there is a domestic legal mechanism called the Alien Torts Claims Act which might allow us to use a Commission judgment in national litigation" (quoted in Black 2005). Also, examining the impact of OAS human rights decisions on human rights practices, Mendez and Mariezcurrena concluded that "pioneering decisions by Inter-American bodies have also inspired and given a solid legal footing to some of those [national human rights] enterprises" (1999: 85). If the case meets with some success, it may encourage Tuvalu to refile a similar claim against the United States in the International Court of Justice. Perhaps more important, however, by placing the enormous costs to human culture and livelihood at the forefront of the climate debate, this rights-based approach might give advocates of democratic globalization greater leverage against those who resist the Kyoto Protocol on the grounds that it would cost too much to implement.

Another interesting legal ramification from a favorable decision in the Inter-American Commission would be the notion that international institutions can make legal arguments regarding the decisions of governments to join specific treaty regimes. Given the human rights obligations to which the United States is committed by treaty and by customary law, the commission may find that the country is not legally free *not* to join the Kyoto Protocol. Here we see another double-boomerang, showing some of the many complex webs that make up international law, and revealing how advocacy groups are involved in helping construct these webs at the same time as they work to strengthen their impacts on government behavior.

In sum, the efforts of the PPEHRC and the ICC reveal several key ways that transnational networks of activists help to promote multilateralism. By bringing international legal claims into their struggles for social justice in particular settings, such campaigns amplify pressures on governments to conform to international standards. The campaigns also help extend and build the democratic globalization network by cultivating new constituencies for multilateral cooperation. In these cases, they have done so by politicizing claims to basic economic rights and by legitimating the claims of poor people and indigenous groups by linking them to widely recognized international norms. The PPEHRC in particular helps bring information about international law and human rights to people who are perhaps the least likely to be exposed to these ideas, namely the poor and other socially marginalized groups. Through their Web site, their Freedom Tours and marches, and other public educational events, the PPEHRC helps spread awareness of human rights and of the international institutions that are charged with promoting these rights. Their active national and international networking efforts are important for building and broadening popular support for multilateralism in the face of either indifference or hostility from local and national officials. The Inuit campaign is also important for strengthening ties of solidarity and trust between indigenous groups and other segments of the democratic globalization network, particularly environmentalists.

Finally, these campaigns help promote multilateralism by innovating new strategies for utilizing international legal mechanisms. While PPEHRC and ICC efforts to formally challenge the world's most powerful government in the OAS might seem quixotic and ultimately futile in legal terms, these efforts nevertheless help stimulate activists' "political imagination,"[23] nurturing understandings of the potential of international law and generating new ideas for campaigns that promote multilateral responses to the crisis of persistent poverty. In short, the actual legal outcome of the formal grievances the group files with international institutions matters less than its effect on the activists involved, for whom the processes of international law are made more transparent and accessible. Whether governments are listening or not, people touched by these campaigns are learning new ways to claim their internationally recognized rights and are gaining confidence as active global citizens. The cases chip away at the legitimacy of the predominant, state-centric order, providing glimmers of hope that—despite what appear to be overwhelming odds—eventually the balance of network power may tilt in favor of global human rights and democracy.

Connections between National and Global Political Arenas

While I have focused largely on the international dimensions of these two campaigns, it is worth commenting more specifically on the national and local roots of the PPEHRC in particular. This campaign is largely a network of local and national groups based in the United States, although as we have seen it maintains regular and important connections to other activist groups as well as to international officials. Moreover, the symbolism and language in much of the campaign's work is firmly grounded in American cultural traditions. For instance, the first PPEHRC March for Our Lives to the UN started from the Liberty Bell in Philadelphia. Organizers refer repeatedly in their speeches, newsletters, and other communications to traditional American ideals as a common reference point and legitimate aspiration for all poor people. Just as civil rights leaders appealed to the U.S. Constitution, so too do activists in the PPEHRC:

> Despite decades of neoliberal propaganda to the contrary, the founding documents of our nation still do not say that the purpose of government is to ensure the profits of large corporations. In fact, they don't even mention corporations . . . America was founded on a vision of human rights. That's what made what happened in 1776 not just the War for Independence, but the American Revolution. American history is the story of struggles to make that vision real. From the American Revolution to the abolitionist movement, from the fight for women's suffrage to the civil rights movement, all of these struggles mobilized massive numbers of people in the name of rights. In our call for economic human rights, the Kensington Welfare Rights Union is doing nothing more than what other Americans have done throughout history to succeed—rallying the American people to uplift the human condition, conditions that go well beyond those of Kensington. (Kensington Welfare Rights Union Education Committee 2002)

This illustrates the complex and multiple identities that transnational activism promotes (e.g., della Porta 2005). A focus on international political arenas and norms does not necessarily compete with a group's ability to relate to local and national contexts. So again I want to remind readers to beware of arguments that frame national and international politics in dualistic terms (see, e.g., Halperin and Laxer 2003: 16). The problem with these analyses is that they treat transnational and local-/national-level action as mutually exclusive instead of as nested arenas of action, as I have portrayed them in chapter 3.[24] They also overstate the extent to which the legal boundaries between local, national, and global are recognized and respected by activists who are concerned with addressing a problem rather than with following accepted lines of authority. In practice, fields of political action are fluid and interdependent, and people's actions do not always conform to the formal political and legal boundaries that many assume. The uses of boomerangs and double-boomerangs might involve action in international courts or national ones, sometimes simultaneously (Jacobson and Ruffer 2003).

My research, as well as that of many others, suggests that activists are very aware of the ways global processes define local possibilities for action, and they are constantly engaging in multiple levels of action with little concern for where boundaries lie (see, e.g., Stewart 2004). But the extent to which their struggles will bring them into international venues varies according to the availability of more localized legal venues (Jacobson and Ruffer 2003: 86). The following quote from a campaign to "Reclaim the United Nations" (see chapter 9) demonstrates this:

> This strategy of mobilisation should be developed at a variety of levels. There is no opposition between actions at the local level, national struggles for policy change and initiatives on international institutions. All civil society work at local, national or regional level needs a change in the international system of governance. A more democratic functioning of international institutions would open up spaces for change at the national and local level. Implementing the principle of subsidiarity would restore decision making power for national and local democratic processes. Building new solidarities would strengthen the search for alternatives in countries of the South. (Tavola Della Pace 2005b)

It is clear from looking at campaigns like the PPEHRC that activists can and do mobilize pressure on local and national authorities while they also cultivate intensive transnational alliances and networks. And the ICC case demonstrates that attempts to engage legal openings in international institutions also require efforts to mobilize international public awareness and pressure if they are to have real impact on government practice. Efforts in national and transnational arenas are thus complementary, providing activists with comparative analyses, mutual support and solidarity, and insights into the systemic causes of their grievances. To see them as either/or propositions both misrepresents the nature of these campaigns and obscures the strategic linkages between global processes and local political action. While they both demand time and resources from activists with little of either, there is no necessary competition between local and transnational struggles. Indeed, transnational campaigns can enhance local struggles in important ways (Stark et al. 2005). Moreover, local struggles that fail to account for global-level processes can be irrelevant or even counterproductive to local empowerment and democracy.

Conclusion

The cases I have examined here showed how activists challenge the neoliberal network by strengthening the salience of international human rights arguments, by demonstrating the indivisibility of rights and their relationship to economic practices, and by expanding and strengthening ties within the democratic globalization network.

By knowing and claiming their rights, activists broaden the appeal of human rights discourse, and they encourage its application across diverse policy areas. Thus the PPEHRC linked economic rights with human rights, while the ICC demonstrated the environmental dimensions of human rights. By doing so, these campaigns are seeking to do what Polanyi (1944) called "re-embedding" the economy in society. In other words, they are reminding people to question the fundamental purpose and priorities of social institutions. Are social institutions primarily designed to serve the economy, or are they—as democratic globalizers argue—designed to advance the human condition? Such questions often get lost in the everyday discourses and routines promoted by the neoliberal network, but democratic globalizers have sought to bring people back into political debates by engaging human rights discourse. By mobilizing in international arenas, activists working at local and national levels can bring respectability and urgency to their claims, altering the distribution of moral resources in the conflict. Mobilizing international legal arguments and institutions therefore helps alter the balance of power between the neoliberal and democratic globalization networks.

It is particularly significant that these campaigns target the U.S. government—which casts itself as a model of human rights promotion at the same time as it operates as a major proponent of neoliberal globalization. The PPEHRC and the ICC challenge the moral claims of neoliberal network advocates while giving voice to the needs and experiences of poor and indigenous people. Both campaigns highlight crucial failures of the neoliberal economic model in terms of its inclusivity, its sustainability, its effectiveness at reducing poverty, and its compatibility with other social values such as human rights. U.S. claims to human rights leadership depend upon a narrow definition of human rights that excludes substantial and widely accepted elements of international human rights law. Pointing to the hypocrisy of U.S. policy, PPEHRC and ICC activists challenge the human rights credentials of a government that takes pride in its human rights leadership and yet is content with a narrow conception of rights where everyone has the right to vote but not the right to eat, to drink safe water, or to have decent work that pays a living wage. They thus aim to diminish the "fund of moral re-sources" (Edwards and McCarthy 2004) of the neoliberal network.

The PPEHRC and the ICC petition also illustrate how effective campaigns can contribute to strengthening the democratic globalization network. In addition to helping extend and radicalize international human rights frames, the campaigns help draw new groups of people into the democratic globalization network, exposing them both to ideas about international law and to people from different cultures. The PPEHRC campaign serves as a broker between what are often locally oriented poor people's organizations and the broader transnational network for democratic globalization. It has helped train activists to help them participate effectively in global forums, and it has nurtured enduring ties among poor and middle-class activists. In this way it bridges an important social divide, strengthening and deepening the democratic globalization network. Through its sustained efforts to participate in the activities of the broader movement (such as the WSF) the PPEHRC helps provide poor and disabled activists with access to these forums that they otherwise would not have. The ICC campaign builds upon transnational ties between indigenous, environmental, and other global justice groups to both expand environmentalists' attention to the human rights aspects of their work while offering opportunities to build solidarity and trust across these diverse groups.

We also saw in these cases further examples of how social change networks use multifaceted strategies to shape the variety of agendas discussed in the previous chapter. Much of the PPEHRC campaign's energy seems to go to shaping public agendas, as illustrated by its participation in civil society meetings and actions such as the People's Tribunal in Seattle and in workshops at international civil society meetings such as the WSF. But the campaign targets other agendas as well. For instance, the Freedom Bus Tour sought to make national (and international) poverty a subject for local news coverage by staging media events in the cities where the tour stopped. While local media are likely to vary in how well they cover the international angle of a story, the fact that the bus tour ended at the UN most certainly helped link the local visit to the broader campaign themes. The PPEHRC was active at the Republican and Democratic National Conventions in 2000, building alliances with other national groups while hoping to shape the electoral and eventually governmental agendas. And its activities at the OAS and at the UN are aimed ultimately at shaping governmental agendas in the United States and worldwide.

The ICC campaign has thus far been mobilized primarily in international legal arenas, although in the process it has served to bring together the heretofore distinct international processes of international human rights and global climate treaty negotiations. Ultimately, the success of the effort will depend upon the ability of organizers to mobilize within U.S. media and public arenas to generate greater citizen awareness of the connections between fossil fuel consumption and the human rights of the Inuit people that can in turn bring political pressure on national officials in the United States.

These two efforts to apply human rights claims to economic and environmental policies illustrates an institutional dynamic explored further in the following chapter. Specifically, we find that many international organizations are organized around contradictory aims. The democratic globalization network has helped identify and rectify contradictions between institutions governing economic policy and those addressing broader social concerns.

Confronting Contradictions between Multilateral Economic Institutions and the UN System

> Despite what is written down in treaties and conventions and the laws of individual countries, even when they are generally upheld, rights are never absolute even in the most democratic societies . . . Capitalist globalization encourages states to reduce their duties and responsibilities to their citizens and to restrict them to the protection of those rights compatible with or not hostile to the interests of big business.
>
> —*(Sklair 2002: 312)*

The world's governments spend countless hours and resources to negotiate high-minded treaties that many have little intention of following. In fact, one might argue that much of the energy at international negotiating conferences is spent to ensure that international agreements cannot be adequately monitored or enforced. One frustrated official at the UN Commission on Human Rights proclaimed that institution, designed to monitor and implement international human rights agreements, "the most elaborate waste paper basket ever invented."[1] As Sklair observes, many international agreements allow national governments to suspend human rights protections when they determine this is necessary to protect national security interests. But all citizens are not equal when it comes to participating in decisions about what the "national interests" are, and the substantial influence of the transnational neoliberal network in many national political arenas ensures that the voices of business will dominate (e.g., Domhoff 1998).

Throughout history, an important objective of transnational citizen activists has been to give voice to visions of the national (and global) interest that differ from those advocated by the world's economic and military elite. As they opposed slavery, war, militarism, and myriad other injustices, citizen activists have proffered a vision of citizen-state relations that privileges human rights over military domination and economic exploitation (Boulding 1990; Chatfield 1997; DeBenedetti 1980). Observers of citizen activism in a variety of global settings have shown that citizen activists have consistently worked to expand government attention to the social issues that extend beyond questions about how many missiles to build (or not to build) or how much trade to allow (or not) across their borders (Smith et al. 1997; O'Brien et al. 2000). By 2001, these diverse efforts contributed to the emergence of the World Social Forum (WSF), which makes this objective more explicit and comprehensive. Within the democratic globalization network, we find many examples of efforts by ordinary citizens to challenge the hypocrisy of states and to demand that the human rights of all people be accorded greater weight than those of corporations.

Thus far we have considered how transnational activists have shaped global agendas and supported the development and strengthening of multilateral institutions and law. This chapter examines how transnational networks of activists have worked to point out the incompatibilities between the international economic agreements and practices of states and their social and ecological commitments. In pointing to the contradictions between the policies of the multilateral economic institutions and the peace and social welfare aims of the more universal institutions like the UN, some elements of the democratic globalization network seek to remedy fundamental incompatibilities in the global institutional order. To the extent that they succeed, they are contributing to the creation of a more effective and coherent, as well as a more democratic, global polity.

Institutional Contradictions and Their Causes

Legal experts acknowledge that the UN Charter clearly places ultimate global authority in the hands of the UN General Assembly, and the global financial institutions are therefore legally subordinate to this body (Urquhart and Childers 1996). However, in practice, the multilateral economic organizations have achieved far stronger capabilities to implement their policies, leaving the relatively toothless and resource-deprived UN incapable of exerting its own legal authority. Furthermore, the insulation of the multilateral economic institutions from other international institutions prevents systematic efforts to ensure that their policies are consistent with other international laws and that any incompatibilities are quickly identified and addressed (Charnovitz 2002). Such discrepancies in the basic principles that orient different international institutions abound, and they produce what analysts have called "institutional contradictions" (Friedland and Alford 1991). Friedland and Alford observe that diverse social institutions such as markets, family, state, and religion offer multiple and often competing logics that might guide people's actions. It is the contradictions among these logics that provide the fuel for social change (1991: 232).

The international system is populated by organizations with widely varying objectives and capacities to carry these out. Most international organizations are designed to solve problems that cross national boundaries. They help governments develop joint standards or rules to coordinate policies and action, thereby contributing to a more predictable and cohesive international order. However, not all international organizations can make legally binding laws. Even fewer are charged with actually monitoring systematically governments' compliance with agreements. And hardly any have very strong mechanisms for punishing those who violate international rules.

As a result of this institutional configuration, most international organizations can be seen as elaborate devices for dispensing advice, which they seek to reinforce with various forms of normative pressure. This is particularly true of institutions primarily concerned with social policy (including the UN), which must rely on moral suasion and argument to urge members to carry out their mandates (Levy et al. 1993). In contrast, the multilateral economic institutions have "some of the strongest rule-creating and rule-supervisory" authority, which they use to promote economic liberalism "with little concern for social policy" (O'Brien 2002: 144). In practice, this has meant that, for instance, countries borrowing money from the World Bank or the International Monetary Fund (IMF) must—if they want to receive loans and favorable credit ratings from these institutions[2]—enact particular economic policies, even if these policies undermine policies of democratically elected governments.[3] Debtor countries are especially vulnerable to international trade pressures, so adherence to World Trade Organization (WTO) rules is far more important for them than it is for countries with less trade dependence and/ or with a very diverse set of exports.[4] Thus, we find a significant power discrepancy between international organizations charged with addressing concerns of broad social significance and those defining the rules of the global economy. This discrepancy not only promotes the interests of profit making and international trade ahead of other social values such as equality or human and environmental health, but it also works to the advantage of the neoliberal globalization network.

The enforcement capabilities of different international institutions and the competing principles at work in different sectors create institutional tensions between markets and political negotiations as key determinants of policy. Moreover, the functionally defined organizational boundaries that structure international organizations hinder efforts to integrate these principles into a coherent whole. Table 9.1 summarizes some of the main contrasts among key elements of international trade, human rights, and environmental agreements. Not only do we see fundamental incompatibilities among these three areas, but also we find few arrangements to allow states or other members of the international community to come together to decide how to reconcile contradictions between competing international organizations and treaty systems.

Table 9.1 highlights some important challenges for those seeking a global order that is based upon a coherent set of broadly defined and inclusive principles that can provide a foundation for sustainable, humane, and peaceful coexistence. International trade agreements focus specifically and solely on matters of international trade, and organizations working in this area have no mandate to consider issues outside of this area. In fact, their mandates prevent them from addressing environmental or human rights concerns, since these are considered potentially illegal barriers to trade. The basic guiding principle of the trade bodies is to limit the role of government and to make public policy as least trade-restrictive as possible. Anything that may be seen as discriminating among trading partners is to be avoided, since it can trigger costly legal disputes in the WTO framework.

These antidiscrimination principles find strong defenders among both the corporate advocates of neoliberalism as well as among governments and even civil society groups in Southern states. The latter two groups tend to resist threats to national sovereignty from international institutions. To many in the global South, the global institutional order reproduces patterns of colonial domination, and thus multilateral cooperation is seen as a threat to the independence and self-determination of those in formerly colonized areas. Thus, these actors—who at times may align themselves with the broader interests of the democratic globalization network—oppose proposals such as that of introducing labor and environmental standards into the WTO legal framework (Khor 2000). They argue against expanding the range of issues over which this powerful institution—which they see as largely controlled by rich country governments of the global North—rules.

In contrast to the WTO principle that defines what governments *cannot* do, human rights and environmental organizations and treaties define guidelines

TABLE 9.1
Comparing International Legal Systems

	Trade	Human Rights	Environment
Main Goals(s)	Expanding international trade	Promoting respect for universal human rights (as a requirement for peace)	Developing common understanding of environmental effects of human activities and harmonizing national policies for environmental protection
Principal Target	States	States and individuals	States, individuals, and communities
Key Policy Guidelines	Least trade-restrictive	Primacy of human rights as source of peace, development	Precautionary principle
Other	Most favored nation (non-discrimination between trading nations)		Common but differentiated responsibilities
Guiding Principles	Non-discrimination between "like products" on the basis of process or production methods Emphasis on protection of individual property rights Subordination of local laws to global trade principles Special and differential treatment	Indivisibility of political rights form social, cultural, and economic rights Right to an effective remedy in an appropriate forum Right of participation of affected individuals and groups Positive discrimination/affirmative action	Polluter-pays principle Responsibility to future generations
Enforcement/ Monitoring Bodies	Legally binding, with trade sanctions and monetary fines (compensation) as potential penalties	Non-binding but universal (Universal Declaration of Human Rights) Other human rights conventions are legally binding where adopted under national laws or, in the case of the European Union, regional laws Monitoring mechanisms for the UN Charter (Human Rights Commission) and treaty-based agreements	Mix of legally binding (Kyoto and Montreal Protocols) and non-binding (Agenda 21) Enforcement mechanisms weak or nonexistent at international level Trade bans on such products as hazardous chemicals and endangered species permitted under some treaties Treaty secretariats act as ad hoc monitoring bodies but with no clear mandate
Conflict Resolution	Dispute settlement mechanism for WTO Independent (private) arbitration for bilateral investment treaties	None	None

SOURCE: Adapted from UNDP (2000: 87).

that *authorize* governments to act on behalf of widely shared goals such as environmental protection and respect for human rights. So, for instance, the human rights arena emphasizes respect for basic human rights as an overarching principle that helps advance other goals, such as the avoidance of armed conflict and other forms of international tension. In the environmental area, the precautionary principle calls on governments to take measures to prevent environmental damage even in cases where scientific evidence may be disputed. The principle grows out of the recognition that ecological damage often takes many years to become apparent, so that by the time we have clear evidence of a problem and its causes, it may be too late to rectify the damage. Thus, most people accept the idea that—given the importance of a healthy environment to human survival—governments should take action to prevent potential environmental problems even in the absence of indisputable evidence.

Another important principle that is at least nominally part of all of these three areas of international agreements is that of equity. Most international institutions provide some mechanism to ensure that there is fair representation from different parts of the world. Measures such as reserving specified numbers of positions for delegates from each geographic region, scaling financial obligations according to countries' ability to pay, and rotating leadership positions on committees and other bodies to maximize fairness in the representation of different interests are standard features of most multilateral institutions. In the environmental arena as well as in trade, we find the principles of "common but differentiated responsibilities" and "special and differentiated treatment," respectively. In the environmental area, the principle of common but differentiated responsibilities recognizes that the global South does not have the same financial and technical ability as the global North to address ecological problems, and these different capacities must be accounted for when defining treaty obligations. Moreover, the principle encourages the transfer of knowledge and resources from North to South as part of the shared effort to preserve the global environment. Behind this differentiation between North and South is an often tacit recognition that the early industrializing countries of the global North contributed far more than Southern countries to the world's environmental problems, even though the effects of ecological damage are broadly shared.[5]

The principle of special and differential treatment in the global trade area also acknowledges that the colonial history of many countries of the global South created long-term disadvantages for these countries with regard to their position in the international economy. Thus, this principle acknowledges that there should be room for governments to enact trade policies that help remedy historical injustices by providing special advantages to Southern countries. In practice, however, the special and differential treatment clause in the WTO agreement has not proved effective at overriding competing principles such as least trade-restrictive measures. For instance, as noted earlier, the United States successfully challenged the European Union (EU) practice of giving preferential access to its markets for small-scale banana producers in countries that were former European colonies. And efforts to allow poor countries to have access to patented medications that could help them manage major public health crises (such as HIV/AIDS) have been slow and unpromising (Wise and Gallagher 2006). In their analysis of the WTO's first decade of operation, Lori Wallach and Patrick Woodall conclude that the ability of poor country governments to claim their rights to special and differential treatment ultimately "comes down to issues of power" (2004: 95). By definition, then, this means that poor country governments (and especially the very poorest ones) must continue to struggle against long-term and systemic disadvantages in global trade as inequalities of global wealth and power increase.

How do such discrepancies come about? Don't diplomats carefully work through every word in the international treaties they negotiate? If so, how could they create such a contradictory mess of international laws? Much of the explanation for this lies in the fact that most international organizations were created to address a very specific function or task in global affairs. It is far easier to reach agreements on very narrowly defined and often technically oriented decisions, and governments tend to be reluctant to give up much of their control over national politics, particularly in areas of sharp disagreements. This piecemeal strategy, it was thought, would gradually foster trust and demonstrate for parties how international cooperation could advance their interests. This would eventually generate "transnational loyalties that would help integrate the system as people increasingly identified with international organizations and the services they provided" (O'Brien 2002: 146). While we might find some indications that transnational loyalties are indeed emerging, there certainly is not much evidence to suggest that this will automatically produce a more coherent global order. Beyond its failures to focus parties on the construction of a more comprehensive system for managing transnational problems, the piecemeal strategy has fostered a technocratic approach to global problem solving, which has served to exclude non-experts from important policy processes and has often generated "poor, even pathological policy outcomes" (O'Brien 2002: 147; see also Barnett and Finnemore 1999; Goldman 2005).

The ad hoc system of global institutional development the world has followed thus far has generated parallel systems of multilateral governance that do not speak to one another and that do not provide mechanisms for resolving conflicts between different principles, issue areas, and institutions. Thus, we find a long series of international environmental treaties establishing and reinforcing commitment to the precautionary principle. But this principle—achieved through many years of painstaking international negotiation and consensus-building—is undermined by a basic assertion in international trade agreements that WTO members cannot discriminate between similar goods based upon environmental or any other concerns. Because of this trade rule, the United States was barred from banning the importation of tuna caught with nets that also kill dolphins, an endangered species protected under the national Endangered Species Act. In another case, local governments have been penalized for refusing to allow international companies to invest in environmentally risky industries within their jurisdictions (Johnston and Laxer 2003; Wallach and Woodall 2004). And because the trade regime is the only one with substantial enforcement capacity, international trade law is allowed to take precedence over other international laws.[6] Yet another absurdity is found in the fact that, as the world's governments squabble over the commitments they will make to reduce their emissions of greenhouse gases under the Kyoto Protocol, the World Bank continues to lend money for projects that will more than cancel out any positive effect of the Kyoto agreement on limiting climate change.[7]

In the area of human rights, international treaties and the Universal Declaration of Human Rights have established a primacy of human rights in international law, while trade agreements give priority to property rights. Moreover, the enforcement mechanisms in the WTO require plaintiffs and defendants to retain expensive legal and professional counsel if they are to use these to their advantage. This arrangement privileges corporations and rich states while discouraging poor states and environmental or human rights advocates, who typically lack the resources or personal financial interests to challenge international trade laws on their own terms (Ostry 2007). Thus, companies can sue governments (either directly, as in the North American Free Trade Agreement's [NAFTA] Chapter 11 provision, or indirectly, as in the WTO) that obstruct their legal claims to property and related profits, but victims of human rights abuses are far more limited in their ability to use the international legal system to make claims regarding their basic rights to life, public safety, and freedom from abuses of various kinds.

In the early to mid-1990s, there was some hope that countries might overcome the compartmentalization of global politics to create mechanisms for addressing the relationships between issues such as environmental protection, economic development, and human rights. The UN launched a series of global conferences aimed at addressing global problems. The rapid succession of these meetings, coupled with the extensive preparatory meetings and background papers that were part of the conference process, helped focus governments' and civil society's attention on the intricacies of global interdependence. The conferences sought to generate programs of action that would guide national policies in complementary and forward-looking directions. They also aimed to provide a setting where countries could evaluate and agree upon the nature of scientific evidence about global problems and their solutions. And in the early years, the conferences appeared successful. However, by the time of the five-year review conferences scheduled to monitor governments' progress in achieving the goals of each major conference, many civil society groups were referring to these meetings as "Rio [or Copenhagen or Beijing] minus 5" rather than "+5." Governments simply were not keeping their word. Moreover, the conference process itself has been sidelined. As Meyerson observed:

> At an exciting time when science may be on the verge of merging diverse disciplines and data-sets towards an understanding of the complex interactions among population, development, and the environment, we appear to be moving backwards in terms of integrated international conferences that lead to action on these issues. (Meyerson 2002: 1)

In national settings, governments create coherence between different policy or issue arenas by fostering interagency dialogue and coordination through the executive branch of government, often at the cabinet level. This helps ensure that, on the whole, government agencies pursue common rather than competing agendas and that they complement rather than contradict or replicate one another. In the international system, we see no effective mechanisms for the coordination of different policy areas (O'Brien 2002: 150). Moreover, the power discrepancies between economic and other multilateral institutions have given the former few incentives to work cooperatively with other agencies. Not surprisingly, these organizations have demonstrated little capacity for responding to criticisms or for incorporating information from other international bodies (Broad 2006; Goldman 2005; O'Brien 2002; Stiglitz 2003).

Many of the pathologies of international organizations can be directly attributed to the insulation of international bureaucrats and decision makers and their lack of accountability to a wider public. A culture of exclusion tends to emerge in these settings due to the fact that bureaucracies favor technical expertise, while those lacking the recognized credentials are seen not only as ineligible for expressing a voice in the process but also as inferior (Markoff and Montecinos 1993). This kind of closure is anti-democratic in that it denies those who are affected by a given policy a voice in how that policy is defined and implemented. It also closes off possible feedback loops, inhibiting the system's ability to adapt policies to fit local needs. Moreover, by creating a closed system for the definition of relevant information, these arrangements prevent international officials from incorporating information that does not fit pre-conceived notions. This can obstruct the ability of the international community to respond to new or emerging threats that are inconsistent with the prevailing views of inside (powerful) "experts" (Barnett and Finnemore 1999; O'Brien 2002; Babb 2003). Significant failures of World Bank and IMF policies and their tragic consequences for people and ecosystems have been documented by both internal and external analyses, illustrating these organizational pathologies (Broad 2006; Goldman 2005; Rich 1994; Stiglitz 2003).

How can such a system be improved? Without denying that expertise is essential to many aspects of contemporary governance, it is important to emphasize that democratic governance requires the involvement of citizens as well as experts in the policy process. The policies of modern states and global institutions must account not only for new scientific information, but also for the competing interests of diverse stakeholders. Institutions that insulate officials from public scrutiny and that prevent public input into decisions that are political—relating to the distribution of costs, benefits, and risks—rather than purely technical, are undemocratic. An obvious way to address this democratic deficit is to expand participation in global policy making to include a wider range of stakeholders. While such an arrangement might seem less efficient, more cumbersome, and more costly, overall it is likely to generate policy that is both more responsive and appropriate to the complex situations it addresses as well as more coherent, effective, and legitimate.

Any effort to improve the ability of the multilateral system to effectively address a broader range of social problems ranging from unemployment to poverty to violent conflict must also confront the fact that we have created an unbalanced and contradictory system of international institutions that inhibit the development of a coherent and comprehensive global system, much less a democratic one. Moreover, the current arrangement privileges the interests of global capitalism over other social goods, and we are finding that these goals are increasingly in direct and dangerous competition. Without addressing this institutional flaw, those promoting alternatives to neoliberalism will have little long-term impact.

Sovereignty Bargains and Shifting Bases of Authority

Since states must operate on a single planet whose ecosystem and economic and social interactions transcend political boundaries, state autonomy must be exchanged for the resources and legitimacy needed to manage "problems without passports." This trade-off was described earlier as the sovereignty bargain. If a state cannot perform its key functions, it loses its sole purpose for existing, and therefore efforts to retain autonomy at the expense of legitimacy and capacity is often not a viable option, even for the most powerful states. For instance, no national government can manage climate change on its own, for even if it unilaterally reduced its own levels of greenhouse gas emissions, the emissions of every other state would continue contributing to global warming. But participating in international agreements to reduce the emissions of most, if not all, states is far more likely to allow them to control this environmental problem than unilateral action. Thus, the state must sacrifice some autonomy in exchange for control. With regard to national security, a state's ability to secure its borders from attack is impossible without cooperation with at least some other states. But to ensure that it has allies if it should come under attack, every government must work to win acceptance (legitimacy) from other states. This often means it must join agreements that help address other states' interests and otherwise contribute to a widespread sense of security. As civil society actors become more central to global negotiations and to the monitoring of international agreements, states must also take into account their standing among non-state actors if they wish to be seen as legitimate by other governments and their constituents.

Friedman and her colleagues analyzed the arguments raised by national governments and civil society activists during the major UN conferences of the 1990s, noting that the expanding participation of civil society actors in these conferences generated new emphases on the legitimacy component of the sovereignty bargain. It was easier for states to guard their autonomy and to control information about state capacity before many civil society actors were there to challenge them. As citizens' groups became more active during the 1990s, they helped shift the terms in which states defined each other's legitimacy. These changes helped produce a broader transformation of the terms around which states justified and defended their positions, from an emphasis on military security or economic issues to an increasing concern for social and cultural practices (Friedman et al. 2005). This should enhance the possibilities for civil society groups—which are poor in terms of coercive and economic power but richer in social and cultural terms—to influence global negotiations.

However, these scholars rightly note that economic and military power can more readily be substituted for legitimacy. Both can be used to shape ideology and sway the loyalties (through persuasion or manipulation, bribes, or coercion) of domestic populations and states away from the legitimating principles of democracy—participation, equity, and fairness. Through activities such as war, nationalism, co-optation, and what activists call "greenwashing" (making false claims about the social/ecological impacts of corporate activities), governments and corporations can seek to win the acceptance of civil society and/or of other states in the face of challenges from those promoting democratic visions of globalization (see chapter 4). The task of the democratic globalization network, then, must be to insist that government policies are consistent with fundamental democratic values that are defined in global rather than national terms. Below I illustrate how participants in the democratic globalization network have sought to do just this.

Defending UN Primacy in the Global Polity

As they participated in UN conferences and sought to influence international agreements, activists became aware of the institutional tensions that permeate the global political system. By the mid-1990s, there was an emerging discussion among civil society groups about the tensions between the UN Charter and the economic globalization model being advanced by the multilateral economic institutions. For instance, activists at the 1993 UN Conference on Human Rights and the 1995 World Summit for Social Development specified how the global financial institutions were undermining progress on human rights and development commitments that governments made in the UN (Friedman et al. 2005). And a 1995 survey of groups that were active in global conferences of the early to mid-1990s also showed fairly widespread concern among activists about the incompatibilities between the UN treaty system and the global financial institutions (Krut 1997).

In chapter 5, we saw that many activists have become disillusioned with the UN, as they have come to see it as simply reflecting the interests of the world's richest and most powerful countries. But while some have grown ambivalent about the UN and have channeled their energies in new directions, many groups remain committed to making the UN more consistent with the ideals of its Charter.[8] They do it out of a sincere belief in the organization's promise, or out of a sense that there is no alternative to some kind of UN organization. Their work is an important part of the struggle to change the world.

Here we examine just a few examples of how civil society has sought to keep governments from creating global institutions that privilege military security issues and markets over other social goals. Many observers have shown that civil society groups have tended to press for more broadly defined and socially grounded agendas than the more technical and limited ones preferred by negotiators focused on arms control, trade, or environmental agreements (Brysk 2000; O'Brien et al. 2000). So, for instance, activists at UN conferences on disarmament emphasized the long-term social costs of military expenditures, reflected in reduced welfare and education budgets (Atwood 1997). And groups targeting the World Bank focused on the deforestation and dislocation of communities caused by the projects it funded (Fox and Brown 1998; Structural Adjustment Participatory Review International Network 2002). As Porter observed in his analysis of civil society participation in global financial negotiations: "Where global civil society has been most successful at the global level it has combined highly detailed analysis of feasible policy options with insistent highlighting of the big-picture questions that official and other prevailing perspectives neglect" (Porter 2005: 151). Diplomats and their technically minded assistants who control the process of drafting and negotiating international agreements often have little expertise to address the more complex, systemic issues that activists raise. Moreover, the technocratic mindset that is encouraged in bureaucracies leads many in official positions to dismiss activists as unqualified and uninformed, and their claims as irrelevant and/or unrepresentative of the general public interest (Markoff and Montecinos 1993; O'Brien 2002). Recall that in bureaucracies, technical expertise replaces legitimacy as the main source of authority, leading many of those working in these settings to care little for what any member of the public might think of a given policy position.

Examining global financial institutions, Porter found that civil society groups had relatively less success in these arenas, largely due to the nebulous and technical nature of global financial governance as well as the strength of business organizations' influence in this sector (Porter 2005). This might help explain why we see the relatively more dramatic contradictions between the policy outcomes of the economic versus other multilateral institutions. It also suggests that our focus in this book on the relative strength of the neoliberal and democratic globalization networks can help us better understand how different institutions evolve over time. It may be that the influence of the neoliberal network over national governments, particularly in terms of the definition of economic models, has yet to be effectively challenged. It should not surprise us that global-izing politicians aligned with the neoliberal network are more prevalent in the multilateral economic institutions than they are in UN agencies focused on so-cial and environmental goals (Robinson 2004).

The reconciliation of incompatibilities between economic and other global in-stitutions depends upon a fundamental restructuring of power both among dif-ferent global institutions and between the democratic and neoliberal globaliza-tion networks. Where the neoliberal network is weakest is in the inconsistencies between the practices it advocates and the established values and principles of the broader society (e.g., human rights, democracy, and sustainability). By point-ing out these inconsistencies and by demanding public accountability of those in power, social change advocates can chip away at the ideological foundations of neoliberal power.

"Reclaiming" the UN

On 28 January 2005, several hundred activists gathered at the World Social Forum (WSF) under a banner reading: "Reclaim the United Nations." They heard analyses from campaign organizers and some of the principal groups involved in the effort, as well as from a representative of the Brazilian government, who conveyed support for the campaign from Brazil's president, Ignacio Lula de la Silva. At the time, over 140 organizations formally signed onto the campaign, which called for focused pressure on governments to end war, poverty, and uni-lateralism through greater support for the UN. A position paper listing the broad objectives of the campaign was distributed in Porto Alegre and debated by par-ticipants. The campaign was launched by an Italian peace organization called the Tavola della Pace (Peace Roundtable), which convened several meetings of hundreds of leading civil society organizers in the months prior to the WSF.[9] They sought to include a diverse range of organizations, from the Socialist Inter-national to the World Federalist Movement to the Landless Workers Movement in Brazil. They also worked closely with representatives on the WSF's Interna-tional Council to seek broader support for the campaign by WSF participants.

This meeting stood out as one of very few (and the only one with such broad representation from diverse civil society groups) campaigns to focus some of the energy of activists working within the WSF and the broader global justice movement on efforts to transform the UN.[10] The sentiments expressed in the discussion document prepared for the "Reclaim the United Nations" session in Porto Alegre were widely supported among those attending the meeting, and they reflect deep concern about the eclipsing of the UN by the global economic institutions:

> Strong unilateralism and uncontrolled neo-liberal globalisation are sidelining the only "common house" of humanity. The macro-economic functions of the UN have been taken away by the Bretton Woods institutions. A radical change of the IMF, World Bank, WTO and associated institutions, and their incorporation in the UN system is imperative . . . Only a comprehensive, radical and transparent reform of the UN will enable this system to fulfill its historical role for peace, development and international democratization . . . In an increasingly interdependent world we cannot expect to find solutions for our problems that are not global solutions. There are no human rights without international institutions able to enforce them. (Tavola Della Pace 2005a)

The primary emphasis of the Porto Alegre discussion was to urge groups to organize actions in their home countries to promote greater awareness of the UN and the ways it has been undermined by the World Bank, the IMF, and the WTO. The group called for a "global day of mobilization" on the eve of the meeting of heads of state at the UN's New York headquarters in September 2005. The actions aimed to press governments to do better at forging multilateral solutions to global problems such as war and poverty. They also sought a democratization of the world body to include not just national governments, but parliamentarians, local authorities, and other sub-national elected officials as well. And of course, the campaign also aimed for more systematic attempts to bring civil society's voices into UN processes.

The "Reclaim the United Nations" campaign specifies a concrete program of reforms to improve the UN. In doing so, it echoes key themes and reform proposals that have emerged from civil society groups' discussions of UN reform over many years.[11] First, it calls for the democratization of the organization through the placement of the General Assembly at the center of UN decision making, the empowerment of local authorities and parliamentarians to play a role in UN deliberations and policy, and the strengthening of relationships between the UN and civil society groups. It also calls for the elimination of the veto of the permanent members of the Security Council and a restructuring of the organization's financial arrangements to eliminate possibilities for powerful states to manipulate the UN by withholding dues payments. Second, it calls for efforts to "make human security the core mission of the UN system." It proposes the creation of a Human Security and Development Council that would be charged with overseeing the operations of the multilateral economic institutions and transnational corporations. And it calls for the strengthening of international mechanisms for upholding international law and protecting human rights, such as the International Criminal Court (Tavola Della Pace 2005b). The proposal is not for a strong, centralized world government, but rather for a democratically controlled global authority that can serve as a counterweight to transnational corporate power and to military threats from non-state actors and from unilateralist states.

In the context of Porto Alegre, the calls for "reclaiming the United Nations" had to compete with a long list of other calls to action. But the initiative gained an impressive amount of attention from a diverse array of participants in the forum, and the sentiments expressed in the working documents seemed to have wide resonance among activists attending the meeting and others with whom I spoke. Moreover, the campaign complemented another even more inclusive effort led by a very large, loose international alliance of hundreds of groups that launched a Global Campaign Against Poverty (GCAP).[12] GCAP links the calls for ending third world debt, transforming international trade relations, and improving progress toward achieving the Millennium Development Goals.[13] Participants in the campaign wore white arm- or wrist-bands during the 2005 WSF to show their intention during the coming year to put pressure on their own governments to carry out commitments on the UN's Millennium Development Goals. The campaign was linked to a series of concerts (dubbed "Live 8") designed to bring public pressure on Western governments to press them to follow through on the Millennium Development Goals at the G8 summit in July 2005.[14] GCAP also called on participants to wear their white bands and to contact relevant authorities during meetings of the G8 (July), the UN (September), and the WTO (December).[15] Its efforts earned the campaign the Inter Press Service news agency's 2005 International Achievement Award, which was presented at the UN (Schreinemacher 2005). An article in *The Guardian* highlighted the importance of the campaign:

> For all its shortcomings, the coming-of-age of the politics of global inequality is being driven by an important issue that will ensure it stays on the international agenda: at its heart is a question of legitimacy. The west's global dominance is being challenged as unjust—whether that is by the World Trade Organisation's new bloc of leading developing countries or even by the fanatical violence of the Islamist extremists. The huge wealth generated by globalisation, with its equally huge ecological footprint, cannot largely be for the benefit of a tiny proportion of the world's population. (Bunting 2006)

In short, by forcing questions of inequality to the forefront of political debates, and by highlighting the gaps between governments' words and actions in multilateral settings, the efforts of democratic globalizers press governments to respond constructively to the lack of legitimacy in global institutions. By highlighting the antipoverty commitments governments have made in various international forums, they help enhance the coherence of global institutions and their policies.

The claims of both the "Reclaim the United Nations" effort and GCAP are clearly consistent with the ideas and values expressed by many groups participating in the democratic globalization network. But what is different here is an attempt to turn movement demands into concrete proposals for institutional change. While many democratic globalizers remain understandably skeptical of institutional reform, many others see this as the only path to peaceful and democratic social change. As the Peace Roundtable working document states: "The UN remains the highest form of multilateralism available today. It is full of limitations, has been hijacked by powerful governments, but it is the only one we have" (Tavola della Pace 2005a). Efforts to democratize it and reclaim it for "We the Peoples of the United Nations" are therefore worthwhile.

Prioritizing Human Rights

Another important contribution of some groups that help make up the democratic globalization network is to maintain pressure on governments to prioritize human rights and human security in international policy. By human security, I refer to the basic physical needs people have for survival, including a healthy environment. Many have argued that the emphasis of neoliberal development economists and policy makers on promoting economic growth has compromised the quality of life for many people around the world. In 1990, the UN Development Programme launched its *Human Development Report*, offering a new index for measuring governments' progress on development by taking into account indicators other than growth. The human development index included measures of life expectancy, infant mortality, and literacy along with the more traditional economic measures, and it directly questions the assumed link between economic growth and human betterment.

Those seeking to amplify UN attention to human security impacted global negotiations at the World Conference on Human Rights in Vienna by demanding recognition for the "right to development" (Hamm 2001; Sengupta 2000; Skogly 1993). Activists at this meeting pressed governments to investigate apparent inconsistencies between the effects of World Bank and IMF structural adjustment programs and human rights commitments. The wording was ultimately rejected by governments and excluded from the final conference document, but those groups that were organizing around the Vienna meeting continued to focus on this tension between the UN's human rights machinery and the multilateral economic institutions (Friedman et al. 2005: 62). Since many of these groups were already active in the Human Rights Commission of the UN, this was a logical arena for pressing their case.

The first fruits of the labors of human rights advocates came in September 1998 with a resolution of the UN Commission on Human Rights, Sub-Commission on the Prevention of Discrimination and Protection of Minorities,[16] on "The Realization of Economic, Social and Cultural Rights; The International Economic Order and the Promotion of Human Rights."[17] The resolution makes reference to the massive popular mobilizations against an initiative of the Organization for Economic Cooperation and Development for a Multilateral Agreement on Investment (MAI), a treaty that would limit the abilities of local governments to regulate foreign investors and, activists claimed, adversely affect human rights and the environment (Barlow and Clarke 1998; Johnston and Laxer 2003; Sklair 2002: 287–290). It expresses concern that agreements like the MAI and other international trade policies might prevent governments from carrying out their human rights commitments and otherwise compromise the enjoyment of human rights by "creating benefits for a small privileged minority at the expense of an increasingly disenfranchised majority." The resolution stressed the "centrality and primacy of human rights obligations." In doing so it referenced a measure passed by the Committee of Economic, Social and Cultural Rights that noted that "the realms of trade, finance and investment are in no way exempt from human rights obligations and principles," and it called for relevant international organizations to "play a positive and constructive role in relation to human rights." In particular, the resolution called for a careful study of the potential impact of the draft MAI upon the enjoyment of economic, social, and cultural rights.

The resolution, in short, called upon governments and international bodies, including UN agencies, the World Bank, and the IMF, to take steps to ensure that their practices do not hinder governments' fulfillment of their human rights obligations. Also, demonstrating the important role civil society groups play in promoting international human rights, it

> encourages international, national and local human rights NGOs [nongovernmental organizations] to develop awareness of international trade, investment and fi-

nancial policies, agreements and practices, and capacity to effectively analyze and monitor the human rights impacts of such policies, agreements and practices. (UN Sub-Commission on the Prevention of Discrimination and Protection of Minorities, Resolution of 4 September 1998)[18]

While the sub-commission on its own has little power to act on its resolutions, it does carry moral weight, and also helps keep issues on the international agenda. This resolution contributed to activists' efforts to defeat the MAI and very likely heightened scrutiny over other international economic practices that might be deemed harmful to human rights.

In 1999 the Sub-Commission for the Promotion and Protection of Human Rights passed another resolution on the relationships between human rights and economic globalization, and this document was notably stronger than that of the previous year. Governments were called upon to consider the human rights implications of all their international economic policies (not just the MAI). It also called on the UN High Commissioner for Human Rights to intensify dialogue with the WTO (which was not mentioned in the previous year's resolution) and urge it to incorporate human rights in future negotiations. Again, the sub-commission

encourages the concerned civil society organizations to promote with their respective Governments the need for economic policy processes to fully incorporate and respect existing human rights obligations, and to continue to monitor and publicize the effects of economic policy that fail to take such obligations into account. (Resolution 1999/30)

These resolutions help recognize the legitimacy of activities of civil society groups, bringing them added leverage against governments, corporations, and international organizations that violate human rights. They also show the extent to which the UN relies upon allies in civil society to help carry out its work.

At its meeting in the late summer of 2000, the sub-commission heard the results of a detailed study of the impacts of neoliberal economic policies on human rights practices that was compiled by two expert jurists, J. Oloka-Onyango of Uganda and Deepika Udagama of Sri Lanka (E/CN.4/Sub.2/2000/13). The study concluded that the WTO "reflect[s] an agenda that serves only to promote dominant corporatist interests that already monopolize the area of international trade." It noted a neglect of human rights in the WTO charter and in its operations, calling the organization "a veritable nightmare" for many of the world's poor (Evans 2000). At that session, the sub-commission unanimously adopted

Resolution 2000/7, which warned of "apparent conflicts" between the agreement on trade-related intellectual property rights (TRIPS) of the WTO and international human rights laws such as the right of everyone to enjoy the benefits of scientific progress and its applications, the right to health, the right to food, and the right to self-determination.[19]

The discussions of the effects of the policies of multilateral economic institutions on international human rights practices have continued within the sub-commission and other human rights bodies within the UN, and by 2002 the discussion centered around questions of whether the economic institutions are even bound by international human rights laws, given that these are not explicit parts of their organizational charters. Many legal experts argue that human rights laws have priority over other international legal commitments.[20] This debate raises issues that are fundamental to the struggles between the neoliberal and democratic globalization networks. Ultimately, the main question is whether or not the institutions that have been created to help manage global affairs are indeed responsible for helping ensure that their policies contribute to—or at least do not obstruct—the ability of people to live with peace, health, and dignity. Individuals that are part of the democratic globalization network—whether they work in civil society groups, as individual activists, or as parts of government or international agencies (including the UN Human Rights Commission and its subsidiary bodies)—have been central to bringing these questions to the agendas of major international organizations. In doing so, they put neoliberal globalizers on the defensive, forcing them to offer legitimating rationale for policies that have been shown to undermine broad social goals. While these apparently small and symbolic victories might seem minor, if these are seen as part of the larger Lilliputian strategy of the democratic globalization network, they bring added reinforcement to the threads reining in the neoliberal Gulliver.

Conclusion

Global institutions are rife with internal inconsistencies. In part these reflect the difficulties of forging broad international agreements to manage complex problems. Sklair (2002) attributes this to fundamental incompatibilities between human rights and the interests of global capitalists, who enjoy much stronger support from national governments. Efforts of the democratic globalization network to alter this imbalance of protections have included campaigns that highlight the hypocrisies of states and that seek to make international practices more consistent with democratic principles and broader human rights norms. In fact,

Clark argues that the work of Amnesty International and other civil society actors has made it more difficult for states to ignore international criticisms of their human rights records (A. Clark 2003). By pressing states to address fundamental conflicts between different institutions, democratic globalization proponents help strengthen the correspondence between norms and practices, contributing to the construction of a more coherent, and ultimately stronger, multilateral system:

> The contrast between states' verbal support for norms and actual state behavior is sometimes a source of cynicism about whether legal norms have real meaning in the international system. Yet, if one recognizes that norms emerge in cyclical phases characterized by differing forms of activity, interaction, and communicative claims, one can see how state violations of principles can, and often do, become focal points for the articulation of changes in behavioral standards. (2003: 136)

In other words, as they highlight incompatibilities between the global economy and other aspects of global governance, participants in the democratic globalization network (either consciously or not) help reinforce the principle that the practices of the multilateral economic institutions should remain subject to the UN Charter. Democratic globalization proponents are participating in an ongoing struggle to define the norms of global society even as they help define and strengthen the institutions that defend these norms. As we have seen in the few examples listed above and in previous chapters, activists have used a variety of strategies to highlight the hypocrisies of governments and to insist that governments earn their legitimacy (vis-à-vis civil society and other states) by upholding broadly recognized principles. In doing so, they engage a transnational Lilliputian strategy that challenges neoliberal and governmental dominance of the international policy agenda while helping to strengthen multilateral institutions. This strategy may also be seen as a parallel to Polanyi's "double movement," which generated transformations in state practices to rein in the more destructive aspects of early industrial capitalism (e.g., Chase-Dunn 2002; Munck 2002).

A more subtle issue, though, is the privileging within the UN Charter of states' sovereign rights to determine their national interests and to act in defense of those interests. The groups working to "reclaim the United Nations" or to call for greater accountability of the multilateral economic institutions to international human rights law have not explicitly addressed how the legal notion of sovereignty in the UN Charter affects the prospects for realizing human rights. One possible response to this problem is to build upon the multifaceted conceptualization of sovereignty offered by Friedman et al. to emphasize legitimacy as a foundation for state sovereignty. Legitimate states are those recognized by others in the relevant community as conforming to accepted norms and standards. To the extent that democratic globalization proponents consistently reinforce and defend the norms and values of a human rights culture, they align definitions of statehood (and of national interests) with broad human rights principles. This reduces the possibility that states can ignore international criticisms with impunity. Moreover, as they educate mass publics about international human rights norms (and government violations thereof), they increase the likelihood that national officials will define national interests in terms that are consistent with these global norms.

The previous three chapters have focused on the ways transnational networks of organizations and activists have engaged in formal (i.e., intergovernmental) global institutional processes to promote the changes they seek. But increasing numbers of activists have been working outside global institutions to promote complementary aims. In the following chapter, I examine the work of activists to engage in bottom-up strategies for expanding the free spaces available for people to be active in global politics outside intergovernmental arenas.

CHAPTER TEN

Alternative Political Spaces

The World Social Forum Process and
"Globalization from Below"

Our global revolution requires no tumbrils, no guillotines, no un-
marked graves; no revanchist running dogs need be put against the
wall. We have within our hands already the means to a peaceful,
democratic transformation.

—(*Monbiot 2003: 67*)

Activist groups do not merely appeal to governments to solve their problems.
They have a long tradition of acting outside formal, governmental contexts to
plan and create their own visions of how to address problems. In this chapter,
I examine the World Social Forum (WSF) process as an example of how social
movements and their allies work to generate alternatives to government-led initiatives for world order.

The WSF process does a number of things that are relevant to nurturing an alternative to neoliberal globalization. First, it serves as a laboratory for experimentation with different forms of participation and representation in a large and diverse
global system. This experimentation builds upon lessons of past transnational
mobilization, and it contributes to the development and further testing of models for participatory and democratic global governance. Second, it creates opportunities for people to learn skills, share analyses and ideas, and cultivate transnational identities that are all central to the formation of a global political order.
Third, the WSF process creates spaces and focal points where diverse movements can come together to organize and expand their own initiatives to democratize the global economy and to hold transnational corporations accountable to
broader social norms. Analysts refer to these types of activities as "prefigurative

politics," since activists are enacting the lifestyles, values, and models of social organization that they hope to promote on a wider scale (see, e.g. Epstein 1991; Polletta 2002).

Before we examine in detail the WSF process, I discuss some of the difficulties the democratic globalization network faces in its efforts to empower people to be active and engaged *global* citizens. A key challenge for movement actors is to cultivate connections between local and global. They need to overcome the physical and cognitive distances between local and global spaces of action as well as the related, widespread lack of economic democracy in today's globalized economy.

The global political arena is far removed from the experiences of most of the world's people, and the challenge for those seeking to advance a global vision to rival the neoliberal network's is to connect their vision to people's everyday practices. While the various actors loosely contained within the neoliberal globalization network reinforce their global vision (consciously or not) through their daily efforts to make a living, those seeking a different kind of globalization must be more deliberate in their efforts to create new structures that help connect people's daily practices with their vision of a world governed by people rather than markets. Commenting on the ways activists make use of the Internet, Escobar emphasized this point:

> There is thus a cultural politics of cyberspace that resists, transforms, and presents alternatives to the dominant real and virtual worlds. Consequently, this cybercultural politics can be most effective if it fulfils two conditions: awareness of the dominant worlds that are being created by the same technologies on which the progressive networks rely; and an ongoing tacking back and forth between cyberpolitics and place-based politics, or political activism in the physical locations where networkers or netweavers sit and live. (Escobar 2003: 356)

Similarly, Richard Flacks pointed to this same problem as he analyzed the challenges faced by those who seek to confront the "power elite":

> Not only are "we" situated far from the centers of historical power, but efforts we may want to make to intervene in the historical process require a break with our own daily routines. Thus even if we were assured that our interventions could have effect (and of course we are never so assured), our effort to intervene entails the costs of interrupting the activities we normally pursue as role requirements. The "power elite" is in the unique position of being able to influence history while simultaneously maintaining and enhancing their own personal lives. For the rest of

us, historical intervention is experienced as entailing some degree of self-sacrifice and risk. (Flacks 1988: 6)

In Flack's analysis we see that the very power of the neoliberal, market-driven model of global order lies in the fact that so many of the world's people must spend so many of their waking hours working to reproduce that particular order. By following daily routines of going to work, supporting families, and consuming the goods produced through capitalist modes of production, even those who are critical of the power elite help sustain the flow of profits to corporate owners and shareholders. This allows neoliberal proponents to spend enormous amounts of money on marketing and lobbying to influence what and how people consume. It provides the surplus profits the power elite needs to spread its ideology and to cultivate networks of neoliberal sympathizers with connections to political, technical, and cultural institutions of society.

Given this analysis, any attempt to fundamentally challenge the neoliberal global vision must create different possibilities for people to make a living while supporting a different worldview. Drawing from Zapatista imagery, many speak of building new worlds within this one (Khasnabish 2005). Neoliberal advocates seek to organize the world around economic competition, and most people everywhere find few alternatives to engaging somehow in this competition. But those challenging neoliberalism are asking whether efforts to promote global economic competition are ultimately self-defeating, since many of the problems the world faces require cooperation and compromise. Many activists within the democratic globalization network have been engaged in a project to create autonomous spaces where people can enact this cooperative vision of the world through their daily routines. Without these kinds of efforts, attempts to promote a different kind of global system must rely upon the work of part-time activists who are extremely vulnerable to pressures from their employers and others in the neoliberal globalization network.

Few people—even those with very strong global civic-mindedness and economic autonomy—can devote all of their energies to trying to transform global institutions. This kind of work can be frustrating, it involves long-distance communication and cooperation, and it may frequently seem futile. Even minor shifts in the global policy arena can take years or even decades to realize, if they are realized at all. And often they involve so much compromise or so little in the way of enforceable policy that advocates of the changes question whether it is worth the effort. Perhaps most challenging is the fact that transnational cooperation lacks the frequency and intimacy of work with people who live in one's own neighborhood or region (email notwithstanding). Our social nature demands that we cultivate close ties to people around us, and much research on social movements shows the importance of close personal connections to movements' survival and effectiveness. Everyone must live somewhere, and it is often in localized settings that the results of activism can be most readily realized. While it is important that advocates for democratic globalization actively contest the neoliberal network in global political arenas, equally important are the substantial and growing efforts of activists around the world to create alternative ways for people to engage in political and economic life in their local settings.

Political and economic elites prefer to maintain the existing organizational and institutional arrangements that have served their interests well. They see no need, for instance, to seek major changes in the operation of political parties, campaign finance laws, or the regulation of the mass media. In fact, they actively resist attempts by challengers to modify these arrangements even slightly, although at times they find that they need to yield some ground in order to preserve the system. But although social movements have had some success in defending democratic rights and advancing democratic reforms within existing national and international institutions, it is clear that these efforts alone will not bring much progress in realizing the broader aim of a democratic world order. In addition to promoting institutional reforms, social movements are working outside existing institutional structures to develop alternatives to mainstream politics and economics. Enacting new repertoires of political *and economic* action, activists exercise what I discussed earlier as "political imagination" (Khasnabish 2004), giving people the alternative of choosing *not* to help reproduce a system that does not suit their needs. They are taking the first steps toward making these alternatives possible.

Such alternative political activities are important in two major ways. First, they help socialize large numbers of people by creating accessible, fun, and personally rewarding ways for them to be politically active. When people attend protest events of all kinds, they not only express political ideas, but they also learn about them at the same time as they cultivate networks of friends and other personal connections that can support their ongoing political engagement. By bringing politics to the spaces of people's everyday lives, activists help bridge the gaps between global institutional arenas and the locally lived experiences of individual citizens. In the words of C. Wright Mills, they help connect personal biographies with history (Mills 1956). Second, by experimenting with different kinds of political activities, activists help generate new ideas and programs for addressing global policy dilemmas. These activities have cognitive, social, and instrumental implications that help expand not just popular pressure for change but also introduce innovative ideas and practical proposals that can help overcome political inertia (Khasnabish 2004). They model and enact a different vision of how the world might be organized, thereby inspiring hope that another world is possible.

Throughout history, movements have engaged in efforts to create alternative social arrangements in which people might live out different social norms and values or directly challenge the dominant order. For instance, some religious groups deliberately live separately from mainstream society so that they can adopt lifestyles consistent with their values. But the democratic globalization network we are examining here has argued that its rival neoliberal network threatens this ability of people to either envision or choose alternatives, and that attempts to withdraw from the system without confronting it will ultimately fail. Neoliberalism itself must be challenged if any democratic alternative is to survive. Moreover, people do not need to fully isolate themselves from the neoliberal system in order to generate alternative ways of being. Some groups seek to build within the existing order new, autonomous spaces where people can make conscious choices about their daily lives—what they eat, how they consume, how they work, and even how they engage in political life. In fact, social movements themselves constitute such spaces for people to engage in political action that is not wholly defined by society's dominant institutions and discourses.

One of the claims made by those advocating a neoliberal model for global economic governance is that, if progress and development are to be achieved, *there is no alternative* to the global expansion of capitalism. Margaret Thatcher made this famous "TINA" claim very explicitly in her efforts to silence critics of neoliberalism. The fact that so many workers were either dependent upon corporations for their jobs and economic well-being or were exposed to mass media and widespread corporate advertising limited public debate about claims that markets were the logical and only efficient means of organizing economic life.

In many ways, the term *economic totalitarianism* applies to the neoliberal model of economic and political organization, since its expansionist imperatives lead it to displace all other modes of economic organization (e.g., Wolf 1982). Witness the attempts by indigenous peoples around the world to defend what remains of their cultures and ways of life in the face of coercive attempts by states and corporations to control the land, forests, and minerals of the territories on which these people have lived for countless generations. The Zapatista indigenous rebellion in Mexico—mobilized around the slogan of "one world with room for many worlds"—is just one very visible example of this conflict between different models for organizing economic and community life.

It is no coincidence that indigenous communities have played an important role both in inspiring leadership in the democratic globalization network and in helping guide the search for alternatives (Starr 2000). As communities that tend to live in greater harmony with the natural environment, they value diversity as a basic survival mechanism. Just as in the natural world we have found that biological diversity allows species to adapt to changing environments so that they can survive, more observers are recognizing that cultures work in similar ways (Diamond 2005). What many of those protesting against the predominant form of economic globalization are seeking is the space to develop and advance the diverse, "many worlds" they envision. These efforts, moreover, can be seen as social parallels to the biological processes found in natural selection and adaptation for survival. Freedom from the homogenizing forces of the global market economy is essential if these initiatives are to succeed.

An intellectual leader in the democratic globalization network, Walden Bello, has proposed the notion of "deglobalization" as a strategy for effectively advancing an alternative form of globalization to that offered by neoliberals. Bello developed his deglobalization concept through many years of research and dialogue among scholars, activists, and politicians. Deglobalization captures much of the various strands of thinking among different actors in the democratic globalization network even as it helps focus the ongoing debates and activities of activists. It is not anti-global in any sense, and its vision of world order corresponds with what I have labeled *democratic globalization*. Deglobalization celebrates global ties while seeking to expand the freedom and choice local communities have about how they will live. It encourages global solidarity and pluralism while relegating global economic relations to a subordinate role in society. But Bello argues that such a reorientation cannot happen within the current system of economic totalitarianism, which promotes a single global economy that denies alternative economic models the resources and protection they need to survive. Thus, deglobalization involves simultaneous efforts to *deconstruct* the existing institutions that support neoliberal globalization in order to create spaces for the *construction* of new ways of organizing economic life around the principles of tolerance of diversity (2003). The discussion of the WSF below will explore how activists in the democratic globalization network are engaging in both political and economic projects for deglobalization.

In Bello's vision, the struggle for deglobalization must take place both within and outside of institutions. As we saw in the previous chapter, if a global economy is to be embedded within a global society, then institutions that reinforce more comprehensive governance (i.e., the UN system) must be empowered over the more narrowly defined economic institutions. Such an institutional reconfiguration would create more spaces for human creativity, participation, and innovation. The neoliberal global economy is a force that centralizes and homogenizes. But it must constantly expand in order to survive, and thus it is vulnerable. Deconstructing this system will obviously be an immense struggle, but it is possible with greater global coordination by the democratic globalization network. Bello argues that by continuing to disrupt meetings of the global financial institutions and by increasing direct action that obstructs the operations of major corporations and governments supporting the corporate globalization agenda, social movements can help roll back the global capitalist order and open up spaces for advancing their preferred vision of global integration. Specifically, deglobalization involves:

- Reducing dependence on foreign investment and foreign financial markets by increasing reliance on locally available resources wherever possible
- Redistributing income and land to create the financial resources for investment
- De-emphasizing growth and maximizing equity in economic policy
- Abandoning market governance in favor of more democratic forms of economic decision making
- Subjecting the private sector and the state to constant monitoring by civil society
- Reorienting production to favor a diverse mix of local and national producers over remote ones
- Encouraging subsidiarity in our economies so that the production of goods takes place at the community and national level wherever possible (Bello 2003: 113–114)

Key elements of deglobalization are local empowerment, self-reliance or popular sovereignty, and participation. Their realization, however, requires institutions that reinforce values and practices that enable these things. Thus, activists must think about institutional arrangements and their impacts on practices while they help empower the individuals and groups in civil society to be active and engaged participants in a globalized society. As a diverse and broadly defined space for political action and active questioning, the WSF creates opportunities for activists to come together outside the contexts of state- and corporate-dominated institutions in what Mertes calls "the global university at Porto Alegre" (Mertes 2004). Their main purpose here is to cultivate globalized notions of citizenship as they share analyses about the effects of neoliberal globalization and develop strategies and capacities for globally relevant action.

Creating Spaces for Global Democracy: The World Social Forum Process

Just as was true with the emergence of democratic national states, a more democratic global political order requires that citizens have spaces where they can freely interact with other citizens, debate and discuss public questions, and cultivate alliances. If democracy is a political system that treats all members equally, all groups must have the ability to articulate their interests and concerns and be heard by others in society. No political order whose legitimacy is based on democratic premises can survive for long without conscious attempts to cultivate spaces where open, mutually respectful, and equitable discourse can happen. But the global economic system described above is notoriously lacking in this regard. Global policy arenas are, as we have seen, dominated by government and corporate actors, and there are no formal structures to enable democratic input and accountability. Without attempts to democratize this illegitimate system of global governance, it will become more subject to violent resistance and dependent upon coercion to maintain itself.

The WSF might be seen as a model for expanded citizen participation in the global polity. If political leaders respond to it in ways that encourage more interaction with the UN and other global institutions while supporting its autonomous and popular character, they might find a solution to the crisis of institutional legitimacy. The WSF is a self-consciously global project, attempting to bring people from diverse countries and cultural traditions together to consider alternative visions of how the world might be organized and to take action to realize these visions. It is essentially a global public meeting, which serves three crucial functions to help construct a foundation for a more democratic global order. Specifically, it contributes to the development of global identities, the cultivation of shared understandings of the world's problems and their appropriate solutions, and the building of capacities for citizens' groups to challenge existing global power relations.

The WSF first met in Porto Alegre, Brazil, in 2001, with considerable support from Brazil's Worker's Party. A team of French and Brazilian activists tied to various national groups in Brazil and France, as well as the international group ATTAC (the Association pour la Taxe Tobin pour l'Aide aux Citoyens) launched the idea for the WSF (Schonleitner 2003). Glasius and Timms describe the WSF as "an idea waiting to happen" (Glasius and Timms 2006: 191). Indeed, the initiative emerged at a crucial time when activists were debating the limitations of the strategy of "summit hopping," that is, moving from city to city to confront policy makers at the sites of their international meetings. The ease with which a small number of militants or agents-provocateurs could turn peaceful protests into scenes of vandalism and violence led many activists to seek other means of resisting neoliberal globalization. Given the nature of mainstream media in most countries, even very large and peaceful demonstrations were having limited effects on broader debates. Also, many—particularly those from the global South—found it difficult to maintain a consistently large presence at official meetings while also seeking to build local and national organizations to address both the causes and the effects of global neoliberal policies. And their sustained attention to global economic issues motivated them to develop more comprehensive thinking about how to struggle against the effects of neoliberalism.

When the invitation to participate in the WSF came, it was a welcome opportunity to shift the network's energies in new directions. The fact that the event was scheduled at the same time as, but across the world from, the annual World Economic Forum meeting in Davos, Switzerland, dramatized this strategic break. The symbolic link to the World Economic Forum highlighted the claims of the democratic globalization network that the global economy must be embedded within and governed by a broader system of norms and social relations.[1] The geographic location of the WSF in the global South also made an important statement about its intention to challenge the global organization of power.

The first WSF was an overwhelming success: organizers initially expected a few thousand participants, but more than 15,000 people attended. The second meeting in 2002 attracted more than 60,000, and the following year (also in Porto Alegre) drew at least 100,000. The WSF tested its wings in 2004 by moving the site to Mumbai, India, where a more economically and ethnically diverse collection of more than 100,000 people gathered. It returned to the incubator of Porto Alegre again for its 2005 meeting, drawing more than 155,000 registered participants from 135 countries to participate in more than 2,500 different sessions. The 2006 forum was a "polycentric" forum, which met sequentially in Africa, Latin America, and Asia (more on this below). And in 2007 organizers succeeded in bringing the global gathering to Africa (Nairobi). The 2008 global meeting was suspended to allow participants to organize local and regional forums.

The extraordinary success of the WSF lies in the fact that it emerged from an extensive history of transnational activism that had built a foundation of network ties capable of spreading the word about the initiative and of providing resources and motivation for participants. Now the forum contributes to this organizing base by providing "a venue in which churches and anarchists, punks and farmers, trade-unionists and greens can explore issues of common concern, without having to create a new web" (Mertes 2004: 244).

Youth have been an important element of the WSF from the beginning, even though they had to struggle to gain greater access to the WSF process. At the first WSF the youth camp was located far from the main forum site, while by 2005, the camp, which housed an estimated 35,000 participants, was the focal point of the "WSF Territory" in Porto Alegre's riverfront area. Youth initiatives have influenced the WSF process significantly, and the persistence of youth activists has been a key factor in holding the International Council accountable to the values of participatory democracy and an explicit rejection of hierarchy. For instance, a youth-led direct action to protest the presence of a VIP lounge at the first WSF led organizers to abandon the practice of establishing exclusive spaces for politicians and other luminaries. And youth have been most vocal in demanding that the WSF process generate more in the way of actions. Indeed, a central part of the youth programs at social forums has included "action laboratories" where activists enact direct action tactics during the forum itself and reflect on the limits and possibilities of particular actions (Juris 2008).[2]

The WSF was somewhat novel in that it constituted an autonomous gathering of civil society actors rather than one specifically targeting a particular intergovernmental forum. However, it was by no means the first such autonomous gathering, and indeed it built upon preexisting models to become what we might call a modular form of collective action (e.g., Tarrow 1995). This helps explain why it generated such immediate and widespread support. For instance, the basic format of the forum itself resembles in many ways the civil society conferences that paralleled UN global conferences of the 1990s. It also mirrors a model forged by feminist activists in Latin America, who gathered in what they called *encuentros*. These meetings familiarized activists with a common model for dialogue and exchange (Sternbach et al. 1992).[3]

> Encuentros are critical spaces where Latin American feminist activists exchange ideas, discuss strategies, and imagine utopias among themselves, along with "other" feminists who—although belonging to different countries, social classes, ethnic and racial groups, age groups, sexual preference, etc., with the most diverse personal-political trajectories and involved in the broadest array of political practices—share visions of the world and declare their political commitments to a wide gamut of feminist and social justice struggles. (Alvarez et al. 2003:200)

The *encuentro* as a form of action gained wider international attention when the Zapatistas called the First International *Encuentro* for Humanity and Against

Neoliberalism in 1996 as part of their efforts to expand their own struggle against the global sources of their grievances (Alvarez et al. 2003; Chesters 2004).

While the *encuentro* and the civil society conferences that paralleled the UN global conferences provided familiar templates for action, the scheduling of the WSF alongside a global meeting like the World Economic Forum meant that it occurred at a time when activists would be habitually seeking to act together. These overlapping understandings and expectations, which result from the history of social movement activism in general and transnational activism in particular, facilitated the rapid spread of attention to the WSF process as well as local attempts to replicate the process. In particular, one could also say that the successful diffusion of the WSF process is related to the more general "transnational resonance" of Zapatismo (Khasnabish 2005). The WSF links itself to the Zapatista struggle in both its organizing methods as well as by adopting as its own Zapatista slogans such as "another world is possible" and "against neoliberalism and for humanity."

Although the size of the WSF prevents much of the intimate exchange and consensus building that *encuentro* implies, it strives to remain an open space for activists to gather in large and small groups to exchange experiences, support each other's struggles, build transnational alliances, and coordinate strategies and actions. It explicitly rejects a representative role, and it makes no recommendations or formal statements on behalf of participants. It does require that participants adopt a general opposition to neoliberal globalization and a commitment to nonviolent struggle. These basic principles have allowed it to include many voices while minimizing major divisions and hierarchies.[4]

The substance of the WSF workshops and plenaries is understandably diverse. The WSF Charter of Principles specifies the broad definition of the aims of the WSF and principles for inclusion. Of course, the central elements of the Charter have generated debate, but there is broad acceptance of the notion that the forum is a space for those working to oppose neoliberalism in its various forms and that it seeks only to promote those forms of actions that do not intentionally harm people.[5] The first WSF was largely an "anti-Davos" people's assembly. The second WSF encouraged more explicit searches for alternatives to neoliberal globalization, and subsequent meetings have sought to articulate concrete steps toward achieving these alternatives. More recent forums have devoted extensive energy to questions about the connections between neoliberalism and U.S. militant and unilateralist foreign policy, while also broaching questions about what sorts of political institutions might help transform global relations (Adamovsky 2005). This latter, institutional question seems to have captured more focused attention in the WSF meetings of 2004 and 2005, although it is probably the least developed. Encompassed within this question are issues such as how the intergovernmental system might be democratized and made more effective, as well as how the WSF itself can be made more inclusive and responsive.

Struggles for Internal Democracy in the WSF

The leadership of the WSF consists of its International Council, which invites diverse groups to its membership in an attempt to bring representative leadership to the WSF while ensuring its continuity and basic principles. The International Council is plagued by the constant tensions between the demands of organizing annual meetings for more than a hundred thousand people while maintaining self-consciously inclusive and decentralized decision-making structures. It includes a wide range of organizations, and organizers explicitly seek to avoid exclusionary tendencies and to maximize space for expressions of diversity. However, the absence of a formal process designed to promote inclusive and nonhierarchical relations has generated the familiar "tyranny of structurelessness" (Freeman 1972).[6]

There will always be room for improvement with regard to representativeness and inclusion in the WSF, as is true with all representative structures. These two goals are in necessary tension, but WSF leaders may need to create a more explicit and formalized process for making collective decisions and statements in order to avoid exacerbating internal struggle while also creating de facto, unauthorized leaders. As the size of the WSF expands, many are calling for new approaches to facilitating global dialogue on a more manageable scale. There is also much discussion about how the location of this global meeting privileges some voices over others. Tensions remain over whether Porto Alegre should hold a special status as the WSF's birthplace, and how much to risk the continuity of the forum by moving it to locations that lack the physical and social infrastructures to support this immense gathering.

Another important challenge is the exclusion of activists who do not explicitly reject neoliberalism or the use of violence as a political tactic. Such exclusion is in tension with the broader democratic ideology of the movement as well as some activists' strategic thinking. While an expressed opposition to neoliberalism might be important for resisting attempts by the rival network to co-opt segments of the democratic globalization network, many activists wanting to attend the WSF may not have all the information they need to decide their position regarding global capitalism. Shouldn't the forum be a space where people can learn diverse views before they come to such a position? Similarly, with regard to the use of violence, some groups challenge the idea that dialogue with groups that use violence should be banned by WSF rules. In particular, as divisions between Arab and Palestinian peoples and the West become more strained, some argue that nonviolent activists must engage in efforts at dialogue with groups linked to violent struggles, even as they reject their tactics.[7]

The lack of a representative function of the WSF and the attempt by leaders to avoid making it a body that can speak on behalf of a global movement eliminates the possibility that the WSF could be used more effectively to mobilize activists around a shared global agenda. Moreover, there are tremendous pressures on activists to generate common statements, fueled in part by the mass media, which have complained about the failure of WSF organizers to provide a format that allows effective media coverage of the event. The mass media seeks spokespersons or leaders who can reflect the many common sentiments of the thousands of activists attending the forums, and many participants also want this process to be used to more effectively demonstrate their worthiness, unity, numbers, and commitment. Clearly a WSF that could speak for its participants and mobilize around key concerns of the various movements represented there would benefit the struggle to make "another world" possible.

Localizing the WSF Process

While the debate about how to routinize the WSF and to ensure that it attempts to be inclusive and open in its operations occupies considerable attention among some activists, there is little disagreement over the need to decentralize the efforts of the forum and to maximize connections to local organizers. And many of the networks involved in the WSF process have simply made the practical decision to devote their energies to addressing this problem directly. People cannot be represented if they are not involved in the WSF process, and many have yet to learn of the WSF process. So activists at local, national, and regional levels have organized social forums in these more localized settings, and these efforts have helped to decentralize the WSF process overall. Similarly, the WSF's notion that "another world is possible," and that this movement is about creating that world, has come to permeate the discourse and focus the creative attention of activists around the world. Thus, the slogan for the first U.S. Social Forum was "Another world is possible, another United States is necessary."

The 2005 WSF meeting was notable in that it reflected some decisive moves toward greater decentralization. Clearly there were always conscious efforts to prevent centralization among the leading players in the WSF process, and the ideology of openness and inclusion helped reinforce the legitimacy of those demanding more space for participation. But two important features of the 2005 WSF meeting helped create more structured possibilities for an even more open and participatory process.

First, the 2005 meeting helped strengthen efforts to mobilize social forums at regional and local levels by deciding to replace the global gathering in 2006 with a "polycentric" WSF of interlinked regional social forums in Caracas (Venezuela), Karachi (Pakistan), and Bamako (Mali). The decision to suspend the global meeting in 2008 further emphasizes organizers' interest in strengthening local and regional networks. The International Council called explicitly on WSF participants to organize local, regional, and national forums during the time when the global meeting would normally be held. These moves were largely in response to the difficulties of managing such a large global meeting as well as a flowering of more localized attempts to mobilize people around the ideals of the World Social Forum. Between 2001 and 2004 Glasius and Timms identified a minimum of 166 local social forums (not counting at least 183 in Italy and a similarly large number in Greece), 58 national social forums, and 35 regional and thematic social forums all explicitly linked to the WSF process (2006: 198). Clearly the WSF process has captured the "political imaginations" of activists. By encouraging activists to organize regional social forums, the International Council of the WSF hopes to reinforce the global process while also strengthening local organizing efforts.[8]

Second, in 2004 the International Council reorganized its methodology for soliciting participation in the global WSF, eliminating centrally organized panels and facilitating the use of its Web site by groups working to develop integrated proposals for panels before the forum and to disseminate proposals in its aftermath. While the process was far from perfect, and remains somewhat confusing,[9] by all accounts it was successful in fostering transnational dialogue and in making the forum more open and accessible (Albert 2003). Moreover, the process included efforts to generate from the huge variety of forum events some movement toward common positions. Daily assemblies were scheduled in each of the eleven thematic spaces to allow participants to highlight common themes and programs for action. This helped to focus different groups on the task of developing joint programs even in the planning stages of the forum. These experiences at transnational collaboration will have long-term effects on the capacities of the democratic globalization network, as subsequent forums have adopted and improved on them. They will certainly inform subsequent campaigns, reinforce trust between diverse groups, and encourage activists to develop important skills in transnational organizing.

While the WSF marks an important milestone in the development of the struggle for alternatives to neoliberal globalization, it builds upon a much longer tradition of activism within a global context. And as this discussion shows, it has been propelled by both global and local leadership, and the debates and tensions between these have contributed much to the WSF's evolution. Over recent years, civil society meetings with a global perspective are becoming larger (55 percent had more than ten thousand participants), are more coordinated across the globe, and are taking up a more diverse political agenda (Pianta and Silva 2003). The organizational data I reported in chapter 6, as well as the work of Pianta and Silva, show that more people are making conscious connections between economic issues and other demands such as democracy and peace. Pianta and Silva also report, based on their longitudinal survey of international groups attending different global civil society forums, that activist groups are becoming more outward-looking and they maintain a strong commitment to developing stronger and more diverse networks among global civil society organizations. The WSF process both reflects and contributes to this diversification and strengthening of global civil society networks.

The proliferation of local social forums demonstrates the power of the political imagination encouraged by the democratic globalization network as well as the capacities of the WSF process to integrate diverse groups. While many of these gatherings resemble those taking place long before the WSF was established, the WSF process allows people to imagine these kinds of events as part of a much bigger struggle. It encourages them to consider the linkages among diverse issues and campaigns and to feel themselves part of a much larger global effort. More important, the WSF process provides some of the few places where individuals can engage in global political deliberation and action, since global institutions lack formal mechanisms for promoting public engagement and participation.

Experiments in Global Democracy

Despite limitations to the WSF's representativeness and its failure to fully incorporate many of those most disadvantaged by neoliberal globalization, it remains without a doubt the most open and diverse space where global policy issues are considered. Even without formal designation as such, the WSF is a mechanism for helping people articulate and aggregate their demands for policy, and where activists can learn about each other's concerns while finding ways to improve communications. Thus, many observers have called it an "incubator" or a "laboratory" for global democracy. What is clear is that participants in the WSF process are helping articulate models of global participatory democracy that might contribute to a collective search for ideas about how to structure a more democratic global order (Juris 2008). As activists reflect on the process itself and seek to enhance its inclusiveness and representativeness, they are engaging in the essential steps of experimenting, refining, and elaborating plans for a more formal system for global democracy. More serious attention to how the WSF might relate to the broader multilateral system, however, might produce some important gains for global democracy.

Since the very origins of the UN, activists agitated for a "People's Assembly" or a "Global Parliament" to enhance the representativeness of the UN. These types of bodies would provide at least some formal mechanisms to link individuals and groups at local levels with global-level political debates, strengthening the connective tissues between local and global politics. A key challenge, however, has been in determining how to create a globally representative body that is also manageable and politically relevant. Some have suggested that a global parliament select its members from elected national legislatures. Another is to model the European Parliament, where representatives are elected directly by voters. But clearly the major impediment to efforts to expand representation in global bodies is government opposition.

Governments prefer to maintain maximum control over decisions in international political arenas, and thus they have long resisted attempts to democratize these spaces. By giving the multilateral economic organizations the capacities to enforce their decisions while denying such capacities to the UN General Assembly and other more inclusive and democratic bodies, they have supported a global order based on coercion over one based on consent (Monbiot 2003). But as I have argued earlier, such an effort is inherently unstable, as it violates a fundamental premise of modern political institutions that states derive their authority from the consent of the governed. In the face of this contradiction, activists themselves are creating structures to enable popular participation even over government opposition. Many believe that by continuing to foster public debates and proposals for global policy, social movements will eventually force governments to formally accept some form of participation by globalized civil society (Falk and Strauss 2001; Monbiot 2003). Indeed, a recent report by the UN Secretariat recommends some concrete steps for enhancing civil society's role in the organization, and democratic globalizers might unite behind efforts to actualize some of the report's recommendations (UN 2004).

In short, the WSF process reflects the efforts of the democratic globalization network to create autonomous spaces in which people can be active politically. But as much of this book has emphasized, the forum and other activities of the democratic globalization network go beyond purely political debates to promote efforts to better integrate the economy within society, challenging the (dys)functional boundaries between the UN and multilateral economic organizations (e.g., O'Brien 2002). Many commentators in the mainstream media and political circles have asked what critics of neoliberalism propose as alternatives to the current economic practices. The WSF promotes the notion that "another world is possible" by creating places for people to discuss what such a vision might look like as well as to encourage and support the concrete steps needed to realize an alternative to a neoliberal world.

Cultivating Global Collective Identities

By creating opportunities for activists to come together with counterparts from diverse sectors and parts of the world, the WSF process not only contributes to the elaboration of new modes of democratic global governance, but it also helps develop the networks and the sense of global community needed for the practice of global democracy. A Zapatista slogan used frequently by those in the democratic globalization network says that this effort is "against neoliberalism and for humanity." This phrase conveys the idea that this movement encourages people to think of themselves not just as citizens of a single country but as members of a global human community with many common values and concerns. Again borrowing from Zapatista writings that encourage values of equality and empathy, many WSF participants proclaim variations on the statement "we are all Zapatistas; we are all Subcomandante Marcos."[10] Every democracy requires that all of its members identify as part of a single community, and that every member recognizes and respects the rights of all other community members. Thus, a more democratic global polity requires that people think of themselves as part of a broader, human community. All movements engage in efforts to promote new collective identities, and these identities are negotiated and renegotiated by activists themselves, as group members work in an ongoing way to define a collective "we" and its relation to opponents (Gamson 1991: 40–41; McAdam and Paulsen 1993). In short, the WSF process creates a space that helps people overcome the geographic boundaries, limited shared experiences, cultural diversity, and high transaction costs that make it difficult to develop collective identities on a global scale.

Within the WSF, activists from more privileged backgrounds will frequently find themselves in dialogue (both face-to-face and indirect) with their organizational and activist counterparts from poor countries. They are also consistently challenged to consider how the WSF process and their own organizations might be excluding the voices of less privileged groups. This culture of inclusion and tolerance is widespread among WSF activists, and it is linked to their shared aim of promoting participatory democracy, which encourages practices of mutual respect, openness, and commitment to inclusive decision-making processes (della Porta et al. 2006; Polletta and Jasper 2001).

Amory Starr emphasizes the different roles of identity in contemporary struggles against neoliberalism and those of earlier identity movements, arguing that "the international invitation to be a Zapatista . . . is a moral solidarity around a political economic critique, not any kind of claim about interiority or essence" (Starr 2000: 167). Indeed, observers of the WSF process have noted the presence of multiple or ambiguous identities among activists who cross geographic and ideological boundaries on a regular basis in spaces such as these. Della Porta, for instance, found that activists in various social forums adopted "flexible identities and multiple belongings" that enabled them to make sense of the complex issues and political processes in which they were engaged (della Porta et al. 2006). Juris found a tendency for activists to use different identities in strategic ways within the various spheres of activism in which they operated. Activists who are particularly skillful in this regard frequently serve as "network bridgers," or brokers, who are essential to building diverse coalitions among activists from such a wide variety of backgrounds (Juris 2008; see also contributions in Bandy and Smith 2005; Tarrow 2005). Thus, we see contemporary activists responding to the need for more expansive and inclusive identities as they seek to mobilize in a global context.

Although many activists will never have the chance to attend a global WSF meeting, the WSF process encourages local groups to identify with a global movement and connect to transnational networks. Regional and local social forums serve as focal points that help dramatize and clarify the connections among diverse local and global struggles, helping to cultivate an "imagined global community" with its own agenda and culture. For instance, U.S. activists targeting the nominating convention of the Democratic Party organized the Boston Social Forum in 2004 to create space for U.S. activists to discuss their varied concerns and policy interests while encouraging and enabling them to understand connections between their own local struggles and those of other activists from around the world. New York activists have staged their own citywide social forums, one of which coincided with the 2002 meeting of the World Economic Forum in New York. This created new opportunities for groups working on global issues to connect with more locally oriented ones while encouraging local activists to see their problems and their struggles in global terms. These kinds of global identities and the related social forum culture are not likely to emerge from intergovernmental processes that are controlled by geographically defined states. Nor are they likely to disappear quickly, even if activists do not have regular opportunities to gather with their international counterparts. Together with the communication possibilities generated through the Internet, local social forums contribute to the breadth, depth, and intensity of global activist networks by helping activists see their work in global terms.

Developing Shared Analyses

WSF events focus on particular, issue-specific campaigns around which activists hope to build broad transnational coalitions; they seek to explore the connections between different problems such as environmental degradation, poverty, and neoliberal globalization policies; and they focus on practical questions about how to build a global movement to advance the various needs and objectives expressed in the forum. Many sessions devote substantial amounts of time to the sharing of experiences and analyses. Here, activists learn about how neoliberal policies impact people in different countries, as well as how activists from diverse regions define what policy changes are needed. Such exchanges sensitize activists to the complexities of global interdependence, and they help them develop joint strategies that address the concerns of activists in the global North as well as the South. For instance, while many Northern groups initially sought to integrate labor and environmental agreements into global trade negotiations, conversations with Southern activists convinced many of the dangers of such policies, which would further weaken the political voice of Southern countries while strengthening international financial institutions (see, e.g., Khor 2000; Waterman 2005). Also, much of the activity around the creation of local and solidarity economies (more on this below) is informed by the analyses of global capitalism derived from dialogues among activists in different parts of the world economy.

The WSF process has also created an important transnational place for activists to explore the potentially contentious theme of the connections between neoliberal globalization and the systematic use of violence by governments.[11] While peace movements have long had transnational components, the history of peace activism has shown that national boundaries and ideologies can impede transnational solidarity, particularly in wartime (Chatfield 1992; Cortright and Pagnucco 1997; Wittner 1997). Attention to the connections between militarism and neoliberalism is not something that began after the attacks on the United States in 2001 and the subsequent U.S. invasions of Afghanistan and Iraq. Even before the WSF process began, these connections were part of activist discourse in places like the May 1999 Hague Appeal for Peace Conference, where thousands of activists gathered months before the Seattle WTO protests to discuss, among other topics related to the theme of "peace is a human right," the connections between economic globalization and war. A significant number of sessions and organizational displays at the very first WSF focused on the connections between militarism and neoliberalism, and at that time particular attention was directed at the U.S. counter-narcotics operation called Plan Colombia. Such connections are particularly obvious for Latin American activists, even if many Northern activists have differentiated these issues in their analyses and organizing strategies.

The WSF process helped generate a General Assembly of the Global Antiwar Movement, which began in regional forums and convened at the 2004 WSF in Mumbai (Reitan 2007). The assembly provided spaces for antiwar activists around the world to exchange notes on their organizing experiences and to strategize for the future. Antiwar activists in the WSF helped launch the world's biggest demonstration against war on 15 February 2003, to protest the imminent U.S. invasion of Iraq. The WSF setting allows activists to develop shared understanding and mutual respect in a situation where the absence of direct communication could lead to suspicion and hostility. Activists from outside the United States have little opportunity to meet Americans who oppose official U.S. policy, but at the WSF they meet in a context where they can develop trust and mutual support. For instance, a Costa Rican delegate at the 2004 WSF meeting argued, "We must coordinate with American [antiwar] movements, not let ourselves be seen as anti-American, and not be seen as violent." And in another panel, Achin Vanaik, a prominent Indian nuclear weapons expert and founder of the Coalition for Nuclear Disarmament and Peace, called for international solidarity in the antiwar movement:

> To beat U.S. imperialism we must help struggles and resistances develop within each country. And we must recognise and explain to the people that there is a direct connection between U.S. empire-building, war and globalisation. We are trying to change the relationships between the forces against the United States [policy] and thus strengthen and unite the move[ment].[12]

As a space where people come together around their identities as activists rather than as nationals of particular countries, the WSF helps activists generate new understandings of the structures against and within which they struggle. It also helps them identify the commonalities in their struggles while they work to understand the causes of the problems they face. In the process, it helps nurture bonds of mutual trust and solidarity as activists learn to appreciate the experiences, knowledge, and determination of their counterparts in different parts of the world.

Socialization for Struggle

A huge amount of energy at the WSFs is devoted to enhancing the capacities of groups to both oppose neoliberal globalization and promote alternative visions. Thus, organizations use the WSF as a setting for their own organizational or campaign meetings, piggy-backing their efforts as they also did (and still do) during the UN conferences. By holding organizational meetings at the WSF, groups both conserve resources while improving their capacity to expand representation of their own members, since often they can obtain funding to bring members to a WSF meeting but cannot raise funds for internal organization building. More important, though, meeting at the WSF allows groups to envision their work in a broader context, and to familiarize themselves with the work and discourses of other activists. This can promote the building of coalitions among groups working on similar themes while preventing redundancy and enhancing complementarities in transnational organizing work. This is essential network-building work.

In addition to helping organizations envision themselves as part of a broader political process, the WSF creates opportunities for individual activists to expand their awareness of the various struggles and analyses of different people around the world and to cultivate skills in the various tasks surrounding transnational social change work. In 2005, for instance, women's groups organized special orientation sessions to help acquaint activists with the WSF process and to guide them in making effective use of their time at the forum. Groups leading particular campaigns also use the WSF process to help build broader awareness of and commitment to their programs. For instance, Amnesty International and collaborating organizations ran programs at both the European Social Forum and the WSF on their initiative to promote norms for businesses within the UN, explaining the UN processes in which they were working and identifying particular ways that other groups could help support the initiative by, for instance, pressing their own governments at the times of key votes or by referring to the draft norms in their own legal or activist work.

Generating Alternatives to Corporate-Led Globalization

The WSF process also generates new movement initiatives and campaigns. Even though it has not yet adopted a formal process through which it can take up joint campaigns, it has created spaces where groups can develop joint actions and further global campaigns. By creating a focal point for transnational activism, and by encouraging shared analyses and joint strategizing around global themes, the WSF supports new transnational relationships that in the past were fueled more by formal transnational organizations and by UN conference processes. Thus, we might expect in the future to see less energy devoted to the creation and maintenance of formal transnational organizations and more focused on cultivating more expansive and densely linked networks of activists pursuing common agendas. We are also likely to see more global leadership coming from groups acting outside formal governmental arenas.

Building Economic Democracy

Many critics of global capitalism point to the fact that it prevents citizens from participating in the most crucial decisions that affect their daily lives. Under neoliberalism, decisions about what kinds of jobs people have, where they can live, how much free time they have, what public services and spaces are available to them, and many other crucial quality-of-life issues are made far away from the people affected by these decisions. Many activists are working for a more democratic economy, and some claim that without such an economy, we cannot have a truly democratic political order. To democratize the economy means giving local communities real power to determine how they will organize their economic life. There is certainly a long history and abundant examples of these sorts of initiatives, many of which build upon the traditional forms of social and economic organization that were displaced with global capitalism (see, e.g., Mander and Goldsmith 1996; Schroyer 1997; Starr 2000). The WSF process has created spaces that allow more serious consideration of and experimentation with these models by a transnational collection of activists. This helps enable more cooperation among those working on such initiatives, thereby strengthening them as tools in the multifaceted struggle against global neoliberalism.

Democratic globalization advocates argue that global markets systematically exclude most of the world's poor simply because they lack the incomes to be consumers in these markets. Moreover, as governments cut back their spending on social services and turn these over to private, market-driven forces, these people's livelihoods are even more at risk. While markets might work for some things, critics argue, they alone cannot be allowed to regulate all decisions about how resources are used. Instead of allowing global markets and actors to determine what kinds of economic development will take place in a region or locale, citizens within this network have been combining their efforts to define their own local economies, which give preference to local over global market forces.[13]

The WSF process contributes directly to economic democracy by supporting local economic initiatives through its own operations. For instance, the bags distributed to participants at the WSF meetings are produced by local cooperatives, and preference is given to local producers in the allotment of displays and in the construction of temporary meeting spaces for the meetings. This has not only an immediate, pragmatic effect on the workers and cooperatives involved, but it also has long-term capacity-building and educational effects. By demonstrating the feasibility of organizing economic relationships in more equitable and environmentally sustainable ways, this practice encourages WSF participants to consider how they might better integrate their own political aims and values with their daily economic practices.

Activists attending the WSF thus become more sensitive to the possibilities for cooperative economies and learn about local economic initiatives. This contributes to efforts to build economic democracy by promoting and improving on models for local organizing. Examples include, for instance, local cooperatives and worker-ownership initiatives, community-supported agriculture, and local currency movements.[14] Other initiatives aimed at reorienting people's thinking about economic life are those that resist the culture of consumerism that is essential to global capitalism, including the voluntary simplicity movements, culture-jamming groups that critique the commodification of culture and of social life, and initiatives like "take back your time day" that seek to sensitize people to the trade-offs they make to be part of a globalized economy.[15] But despite the proliferation of initiatives for economic democracy, Jackson observes that few look at them in a comprehensive way, "usually focusing on one issue or another rather than promoting the green economy as a diverse and interconnected set of movements" (2005).

Reining in Transnational Corporations

Another way movements operating within the WSF process shape the prospects for economic democracy is by working to bring greater scrutiny to transnational corporations that have become less and less subject to regulation by democratic (or any) governments. The neoliberal globalization network has, according to numerous analysts, been very successful in recruiting political leaders willing to advance corporate interests by adopting policies that limit the role of government, privatize public assets, and maximize the role of global market forces in national policies. The network has successfully rolled back the capacities of national governments while strengthening those of global capital.

If democracy is to endure, however, the rising power of global capital must be met by a corresponding expansion in government capacities to ensure that all social actors—including corporations—adhere to global norms and principles of the global human community. Environmental and human rights agreements, for instance, have little relevance if transnational corporate behavior remains unchecked. But weakened states—particularly those in the global South—are now less able to regulate transnational corporations than they were in the past. Thus, leadership from outside governments is required to challenge corporate power and to reclaim the state as a defender of social aims. Ironically, social movements must become proponents of stronger national and local governments, even as they work to subject those governments to greater democratic oversight.

An important example of activism taking place within the WSF in this regard is the global anti-sweatshop campaign. While this campaign emerged long before the WSF process and helped shape the broader democratic globalization network, many groups promoting better and more consistent application of labor protections have been a key part of the WSF process. Among the groups helping focus attention on this particular campaign are global labor unions, whose transnational structures have helped sensitize them to the consequences of neoliberalism in local settings (Munck 2002; Waterman 2005; Waterman and Timms 2004).

At a time when governments are scaling back their regulatory policies to encourage international investment and trade, activists in the democratic globalization network are working directly to call on corporations to abandon the antisocial behaviors that unregulated markets encourage. Recognizing the vulnerability of local communities caused by the globalization of production, activists have used new information technologies and access to information to direct the public spotlight on companies whose production practices violate public sensibilities regarding child labor, worker safety, fair wages, and environmental protection (Greenberg and Knight 2004). They are helping to define the criteria and mechanisms for corporate governance at a time when governments have adopted—voluntarily or not—a hands-off approach. Despite the David-versus-Goliath nature of these sorts of campaigns and the enormous amounts of media and legal resources corporations can level against anti-sweatshop challengers, there is some evidence that they have generated some significant responses from corporations (Frith 2005).[16] While the monitoring and reporting efforts of activists alone will not have much impact on industry practices overall, these campaigns can help alter the balance of power among corporations, governments, and civil society groups. Also, as we saw with other examples above, this campaign is a necessary, if limited, part of the deglobalization strategy.

The anti-sweatshop campaign's work within the WSF context also demonstrates how activists have worked around a particular social problem to generate solutions that are suitable to the needs of diverse groups in different parts of the world. Earlier anti-sweatshop efforts focused on economic boycotts against offending companies, encouraging companies to abandon operations in areas targeted by activists rather than to improve the conditions of workers there. Following such experiences, and efforts of activists to prevent their campaigns from having harmful consequences on those they were seeking to help, new anti-sweatshop strategies emerged (Brooks 2005; Frith 2005). Instead of boycotting companies, activists began to build more diverse coalitions between labor and other movement groups that could bring pressure on companies to engage in efforts to improve labor conditions in the factories where their products were being produced.

But these sorts of agreements are limited in their abilities to improve actual conditions of workers in poor countries. To address the systemic problems of neoliberalism's intensified exploitation of the world's workers, we need systematic pressure on governments to be more proactive in defending social goods while providing models for better governance of global capital. Anti-corporate activists therefore need to envision their struggles within a broader context of global governance, and work to systematically transform power relations in ways that strengthen states and international institutions relative to corporations. An important example of one effort to do this is the work to establish a set of binding "UN Norms for Business." The initiative is being advanced by a coalition of groups including Rights and Accountability in Development, Amnesty International, and the Economic Social and Cultural Rights Action Network, together with other corporate accountability groups and coalitions (Amnesty International 2004; International Network for Economic Social and Cultural Rights 2005). This coalition has used the WSF and regional forums to promote information about these campaigns and to encourage groups to help make these norms legally binding by making reference to the draft norms in their own legal proceedings.

Conclusion

This chapter explored how the democratic globalization network works outside of formal governmental arenas to generate new possibilities for political activism at the global level. The WSF is an important example of how activists have come together to articulate and advance their visions of a democratic world. By gathering in spaces that are largely autonomous from governments and the UN, activists have helped foster experimentation in new forms of global democracy, encouraging the development of skills, analyses, and identities that are essential to a democratic global polity. At the same time, they have generated autonomous initiatives to corporate-led globalization. These activities prefigure, or model, a vision of the world that many activists in the democratic globalization network hope to bring about.

While independent from formal international institutions, the WSF process complements the work of international organizations like the UN in important ways. As a space that is autonomous from intergovernmental agendas, the WSF creates possibilities for more bottom-up, inclusive, and participatory analyses and initiatives around global problem solving to develop. It might be seen as an incubator for global change initiatives, providing a fertile setting for the exploration of new ideas and for the cultivation of networks of citizens who can help realize the proposals for change emerging from the WSF process. Some of these proposals will speak directly to existing multilateral institutions. Others provide alternative avenues for addressing the world's problems, and others challenge corporate power. We need pressure on all fronts to build more effective and responsive global institutions and to deny governments a monopoly over global institutional leadership.

Aside from the various campaigns and change initiatives that it encourages, the WSF process serves as an important educational space. Here people learn about global politics and develop the global awareness and identities as well as the knowledge and skills needed to be active and engaged global citizens. They are challenged to consider how their local concerns relate to struggles in other parts of the world as they imagine themselves as part of a larger political community. In the various world, regional, and local social forums, people can cultivate resources and networks for acting in a global polity. Polletta refers to this as the "developmental benefits of participatory democracy" (2002: 9). These contributions make the WSF process an important part of any effort to build a more democratic global order.

In short, while we might not yet have a truly global political system, the WSF process is an initiative of the democratic globalization network that clearly advances the globalization of politics. It does so by enabling people to imagine themselves as part of a global human community, even when the contexts within which people live reinforce local and national identities. It fosters global identities and values while serving as an incubator for new ideas about how to address the world's problems. Moreover, its self-consciously polycentric nature and its ideological aversion to hierarchy and exclusion reproduce a culture of networked politics that Escobar (2003) associates with "distributed intelligence." This kind of network structure, many argue, allows for more adaptation and innovation in response to an uncertain social and natural environment.

The effectiveness of the WSF may be limited if participants fail to find ways to resolve the tension between the need to be inclusive and representative of more of the world's people—especially those least able to participate in this sort of event. More deliberate efforts to relate the WSF process to the UN system, while avoiding the inevitable efforts of officials and corporate actors to try to co-opt it, can help the forum resolve the crisis of representation while also democratizing the global polity.

Conclusion

Network Politics and Global Democracy

Contemporary debates about how the world should be organized have centered around two competing visions. One view favors a global marketplace, where laws of supply and demand, structured within capitalist notions of private property, govern decisions about how the world's resources are distributed. Another view is more complex and less clearly defined, but it holds that the world should be organized around more human-centered institutions that enable people to participate in ongoing deliberations about policy. This view holds that markets should be subordinated to other social values and norms (see, e.g., Khagram 2004).

To the extent that these two visions fail to win broad popular support, anti-globalist visions—including militant fundamentalism, separatist movements, and imperialist/regressive tendencies—become more attractive (Glasius and Kaldor 2002). The interdependence of humanity that grows from our shared reliance on a single planet makes the neoliberal as well as imperialist and militant fundamentalist visions both dangerous and unsustainable. Thus, we need to find ways to advance an alternative, globalist view that is seen as legitimate by more people around the world.

The democratic globalization network—a very loose and mostly unselfconscious collection of actors seeking more participatory and responsive forms of global policy—is beginning to articulate such a vision. But the network lacks cohesion and has failed to clearly articulate a vision of globalization that can compete with that of its rival, neoliberal network. In this book, I have sought to highlight the work of some groups that are part of the democratic globalization network, illustrating how their campaigns have helped articulate and reinforce a more democratic world order. By supporting multilateral cooperation around shared social values rather than simply around market logics, social movements can help socialize global markets, embedding them in a global society governed by democratic processes. More serious thinking and strategizing along these lines are needed for such a project to succeed. The lessons of this book fall into two general categories. One relates to how democratic globalizers can better engage international and national institutions in their efforts to promote a more democratic world order. The other speaks to how they might enhance their own organizational strength. We might think of this as an effort to forge a "democratic globalization project" that can counter the neoliberal "globalization project" described by McMichael (2003) and advanced by the neoliberal globalization network.

Social Movements and Global Institutions

Many analysts have argued that a contemporary crisis of democratic institutions is reflected in declining rates of participation in traditional political organizations and low voter turnout (Norris 2002; Putnam 1995). Norris argues that this conclusion fails to capture important new developments. Changing forms of communication and association, she argues, have led to important shifts in how people engage in democratic action. While old forms of participation are in decline in some places, new forms have emerged, as citizens increasingly join new types of organizations, adopt new repertoires of political action, and expand the range of political targets. In the more established Western democracies, membership and participation in political parties have indeed declined. But at the same time, participation in new types of political organizations—specifically issue-oriented political organizations and increasingly transnational political organizations—is on the rise. And while fewer people may be voting, more people are involved in both protest politics and in "everyday" political behaviors such as recycling.

The social movement activism explored in this book reflects this shifting character of democratic participation. But while we might celebrate innovations in the forms of democratic participation, it is worth asking how and to what extent these have been able to enhance the representativeness and responsiveness of political institutions. *Do these new forms help reduce inequalities of access and influence, or do they signal a growing marginalization of citizens from national political processes that are increasingly enmeshed within a fundamentally undemocratic international political system?* Celebrating these "new" forms of politics without recognizing their origins in a system that increases political and social exclusion will undermine the potential for democratic change. It draws attention away from the problem of the failed representative institutions that pose serious long-term threats to democracy.

The key point of this book is that those hoping to bring about a more just, peaceful, and equitable world must work at many levels, not the least of which is within existing *global* institutions. This does not mean that advocates for global justice must moderate their aims, but rather that they must find ways to engage formal political institutions in ways that will prevent the further erosion of democracy around the world. By "reclaiming the United Nations" and bringing the power of massive popular mobilizations behind efforts to seriously transform this institution in democratic ways, transnational social movement networks can help expand possibilities for changing the world. Most important, popular movements must work more consciously to make the UN Charter and international legal instruments such as the Universal Declaration of Human Rights the key principles around which our world is organized. The world's financial institutions—especially the World Trade Organization (WTO), the World Bank, and the International Monetary Fund (IMF)—have been allowed to displace these more universal principles for governing society with principles that prioritize the maximization of wealth and profit. They have disembedded the global economy from a global society. They have done so with tragic and unsustainable consequences for people and ecosystems around the world.

To re-embed the global economy within a global society, social movements must focus attention on strengthening the institutions that can support a global *human rights culture*. We saw in chapter 4 how the neoliberal network worked to strengthen financial institutions as a means of advancing their vision of a global neoliberal economy, and it is clear that steps must be taken to roll back these neoliberal institutional advantages. Enhancing the UN as a principal center for making decisions about how the world should be governed can neutralize the neoliberal advantages in the financial institutions by prioritizing human rights and sustainability over financial aims. By advancing and supporting a global human rights culture, a stronger and more democratic UN would provide essential institutional support for a global society that can effectively manage a (more limited) global economy. Social movements must approach political institutions as potential allies in their struggle, while maintaining vigilance against possible co-optation by rivals using similar strategies.

This means that self-defeating internal debates about whether or not engaging existing institutions constitutes a moderation of tactics or even selling out should be abandoned. Because they represent society's weakest and poorest members, social movements have a strong interest in promoting institutions that can secure a rule of law that delegitimizes violence and other forms of coercion, protecting the weak from the strong. This is why most social movements—regardless of the specific issues they seek to influence—end up becoming advocates for democratization of some form or another. Thus, a stronger and more democratic and legitimate UN should be seen as an important element of any strategy to aid disadvantaged groups. Supporting multilateralism that prioritizes human rights and sustainability *is radical*. Moreover, given the hugely disproportionate distribution of financial and military power, it is the only feasible approach to advancing the vision of global order articulated by most global activists.

The history of transnational activism holds many lessons for how to advance this radical, pro-multilateral agenda, and many contemporary activists have built upon these lessons, as this study has shown. Much more can be done, however, to advance the project of building global institutions for human rights. Activists must come to see their efforts in broader, institutional terms. For instance, cases in this book demonstrate how movements have advanced global democracy by shaping global agendas, mobilizing constituencies for multilateralism, domesticating international norms, and promoting institutional initiatives that advance multilateral cooperation and prioritize human rights.

Democracy is a delivery system for human rights, and indeed without human rights, we do not have democracy. Thus, a more democratic world order is one that is organized to ensure the highest level of protection for human rights. Governments have shown that, left on their own, they are unlikely to make much progress in this regard. But there is growing evidence that the international system is at a point where it can no longer survive without addressing some of the fundamental inconsistencies in its structure. Specifically, the democratic deficits in global institutions are reaching a critical breaking point, and serious efforts must be made to address these deficits if we are to avoid some combination of anarchy and totalitarianism. The campaigns and organizations examined in this book illustrate how social movement actors can help bring about a more democratic form of global multilateralism.

In chapter 1, I identified five criteria for helping determine whether a particular campaign, actor, or event contributes to greater democracy in global settings. These include:

- Fostering participation and deliberation (strengthening the public sphere)
- Developing and publicizing alternative proposals
- Promoting access/voice to excluded groups
- Enhancing transparency/accountability
- Diminishing power inequities among states

Each example of transnational activism we examined in this book engaged in one or more of these activities, even if they did not consciously see themselves as working to democratize the global system. Greater awareness of how social movement efforts to advance particular goals contribute to the democratization of global institutions can help activists find more points of connection among their varied campaigns. Moreover, such thinking can generate more unified efforts to bring about the kinds of broad, systemic changes that are needed to achieve greater equality in the global system.

For instance, as the campaign against the Multilateral Agreement on Investment (MAI) showed, by simply expanding public discourse and spaces for debate about global issues, social movements diminish the ability of neoliberal globalizers to carry out the programs that lack broad popular appeal. By amplifying and promoting social change agendas such as the Kyoto Now! campaign has done, they create possibilities for progress on multilateralism where governments are stymied. By bringing excluded groups into the global policy process, they help make institutions more responsive to the needs of marginalized groups, such as the poor people and indigenous groups we saw in chapter 8. By increasing transparency and accountability in the global system, through initiatives such as the Indymedia Centers (IMCs) and through the kinds of public education efforts that were integral parts of most of the campaigns explored in the book, social movements help to hold public officials accountable in global settings.

Finally, activist campaigns can be crucial in helping diminish power inequities among states, thereby preventing the most powerful states from taking advantage of the weak. The Poor People's Economic Human Rights (PPEHR) and the Inuit campaigns to target the U.S. help make it easier for weaker governments to criticize U.S. failures to uphold international law. And the campaign to "reclaim the United Nations" seeks to formally restructure the UN to make it less possible for the United States or any other state to dominate others and to violate international laws with impunity.

Efforts to enhance democracy among governments, then, must be a key part of any broader strategy of strengthening civil society's role in global affairs. This lesson is particularly clear in recent attempts to constrain U.S. militarism. U.S. peace activists have found they have very little sway over U.S. foreign policy, even when they can mobilize enormous numbers of protesters and even when they have world opinion firmly on their side. A better strategy would be to help make the UN a more effective counterweight to U.S. power. Reforms to the Security Council and other organs of the UN would enhance democracy among the member states, making it harder for the U.S. or any other government to long defy international laws. John Clark, who has worked in civil society organizations as well as within the World Bank and UN, argues that U.S. activists in particular must focus more on helping Americans understand how U.S. foreign policy affects people around the world:

> Increasing resentment about US selfishness and double standards is fueling anti-Americanism around the world. US civil society has a pivotal role to play in ensuring that this mood translates to positive change rather than deepening anger. US [civil society organizations] have a duty to make sure Southern citizens' concerns are heard . . . They can use their very considerable access to media and politicians, their communications skills, and their vast resources to promote global responsibility, not unilateralism. (J. Clark 2003: 196)

Ironically, it is only by joining global campaigns to reform global institutions that U.S. activists can then exercise greater democratic control of their own government. By making it harder for the United States to act in unilateral ways, activists help ensure that their elected officials follow the laws embedded in international treaties that their elected officials have ratified. Similarly, activists in countries that have less influence in global affairs have much to gain from greater interstate democracy in the UN and other global institutions. Often, however, activists are stuck within a nationally oriented political framework that prevents them from seeing the ways global institutional dynamics either constrain or open up new possibilities for them to advance their goals.

The Role of the State

Another important lesson that emerges from the study here and from other analyses of transnational campaigns is that social change advocates must look more to the state as a solution to the problems they address. Many activists resist engaging the state or traditional political parties because they view them as hopelessly corrupt or fundamentally incapable of advancing progressive social reforms. But we saw in our analysis of the neoliberal globalization network how proponents of neoliberalism worked to transform the state for their purposes, systematically shifting public resources away from social welfare and into the control of corporate elites. Moreover, the neoliberal network cultivated alliances of states that could help it construct a transnational state, comprised of multilateral institutions and governments sympathetic with neoliberal objectives.

But in limiting the welfare-providing role of the state, the neoliberal ideology threatens the ability of any society to enjoy basic rights. States are the key arbiters of social conflicts and guarantors of rights for workers, minorities, and other marginalized groups. They help protect the poor and weak from abuses by the strong. Without strong and democratic states, we cannot have human rights (Guidry 2000; Seidman 2004; Tilly 1995; Wainwright 2003). Thus, the democratic globalization network must consider ways to generate institutional support for a transnational human rights state. Certainly key elements are there, but what is missing is consistent and widespread pressure on governments to ensure the primacy of human rights in global policy. This requires pressure to cultivate human rights norms both within multiple states as well as internationally. Thus, efforts to domesticate international human rights laws such as those seen in chapter 8 must be complemented by efforts to reconcile incompatibilities between human rights and other international institutions. And a strong global human rights culture supported by a densely connected and active civil society, such as that supported by the World Social Forum (WSF) process and related initiatives, provides an important source of motivation and innovation as well as a check against abuses of power.

Thus, just as efforts must be made to reclaim the UN, contemporary democrats must *(re)claim the state from neoliberalism*. Redefining the role of governments is crucial, and much of this effort must be waged on the ideological or cultural levels, just as the neoliberals waged their war against the state on cultural as well as political-institutional terrain. As Johnston and Laxer observe based on their analysis of the Multilateral Agreement on Investment (MAI) and Zapatista struggles, "while transnational activism is often romanticized as a goal of bottom-up globalization, our observations suggest that the gritty reality of the state as a legislative structure, an arbiter of violent conflict, and a potential redistributive agency remains critical" (Johnston and Laxer 2003: 71). Indeed, Luders's (2003) analysis of political violence against U.S. civil rights activists shows that such violence was more a product of the inaction of states than of proactive state policies. Some politicians found it expedient to allow white supremacists to serve as de facto "third-party 'administrators' of state policies" (2003: 44), advancing their aim of repressing the civil rights movement with minimal political costs. While the neoliberal network's "soft repression" strategies to neutralize its pro-democracy rivals involve less direct brutality than in the case Luders examines, there are important similarities here in regard to the enabling role the state plays in the nonviolent suppression of conflict. Reclaiming the state as an institution for the promotion and protection of human rights—rather than as an instrument for advancing economic growth—is essential to any strategy for resisting global neoliberalism.

The notion of internationalism introduced earlier in the book accounts for the reality that democracy is only possible where people are able to participate directly in deliberations about policy options. This is only feasible in relatively limited settings. Thus, a democratic global order is likely to be a federated system of democracies organized at regional, national, and sub-national levels. Thus, global activists might find that they must work to strengthen and support states rather than oppose them. This may seem odd, and it may be hard to motivate some activists on behalf of a campaign to "strengthen the state," but cast as a struggle to reclaim and strengthen democratic institutions for the cause of global democracy, there might be possibilities to organize pressures toward this aim. Korzeniewicz and Smith (2000) use the concept of "polycentric development coalitions" to refer to the alliances between civil society groups, government officials, and international agencies that seek to pursue development policies oriented toward greater equity rather than neoliberal objectives. The strategy of cultivating networks between activists and governmental and intergovernmental officials mirrors the strategy neoliberals used to advance their own global agenda. Thus, to reclaim the state and global institutions for the purpose of advancing human rights and equality, democratic globalizers must mobilize similar kinds of networks to transform—or democratize—national welfare states. This includes working to support stronger regional forms of multilateral cooperation, particularly ones that can counter-balance U.S. and neoliberal dominance in global affairs.

Strengthening the Democratic Globalization Network

In addition to sensitizing us to the ways social movements engage other actors in the broader society, the rival networks concept draws attention to relations among the wide variety of groups actively or potentially involved in social change efforts. The efforts to transform government policies and to otherwise democratize political institutions require conscious attempts to build democratic networks from the ground up. In other words, we might think of an essential part of all social movements as the construction and strengthening of strong "alliance systems" (Kriesi 1996). Diverse and cohesive transnational networks have proved important to achieving major policy shifts in the past, and contemporary activists can learn from these earlier campaigns (Khagram 2004). Considering links between contemporary thinking about global pro-democracy networks and Gramsci's prescription for countering the cultural hegemony of capitalism, Katz and Anheier observe:

Obviously, Gramsci didn't advocate network density, if only because the concept wasn't in existence in his time. However, Gramsci advocated the development of *a counter-hegemonic historic bloc which, he argued, to be of value should include all of the subaltern groups and interests, including workers and other groups.* When read with a network mindset, this translates into a dense network in the sense that *many of the ties that can possibly exist between those subaltern groups are actually in existence.* (2006: 247, emphasis added)

If past work to build transnational alliances and organizations has indeed generated the breadth of new network ties that these authors claim, then there is a firm base upon which to expand the democratic globalization network. More conscious efforts to both strengthen these ties and to mobilize them in a more self-conscious program for global democratic change is a key part of the work ahead.

Drawing upon the rival networks concept and the case study analyses in this book, I explore three key areas where participants in the democratic globalization network and their allies might focus their attention as they seek to counter anti-globalist movements while advancing the struggle against neoliberal globalization. First, I ask how the resources available to this network might be expanded. Second, I consider how the political opportunities for and constraints on more democratic forms of global mobilization might be altered to favor democracy over neoliberalism. Third, I ask what the preceding cases suggest about how the internal network dynamics among pro-democracy globalizers can be improved. I consider here not just the ways movement actors themselves might affect these factors, but also how governments and even the people who make up the neoliberal globalization network might find it in their interest to work more actively to alter the balance of power in favor of democratic globalization over its alternatives.

Resources and Political Opportunities

Democracy demands resources. Governing society through the involvement of citizens in major decisions about how the societies' resources will be used and how the risks and costs of policies will be distributed involve immense investments of money, time, and energy. Certainly more centralized and less participatory forms of governance are more "efficient," in economic terms, but we have a long history attesting to the major drawbacks and ultimate inefficiencies of this model. Thus, an abandonment of economistic notions of efficiency is imperative if we are to create a cultural foundation to support democracy. People and their elected officials must accept that investments in efforts to inform and educate citizens and to provide citizens with adequate time and space in their lives for democratic participation are valid and worthwhile if not essential to the common good. I have argued earlier in the book how neoliberalism threatens all of these by reducing state budgets for public services like education and health care, by limiting space for noncommercial media, and by reducing the economic security and leisure time available to workers. Democratic globalizers must confront these challenges on cultural as well as institutional and material levels.

The notion of a human rights culture can help us in this regard. Specifically, if advocates of global democracy can promote the notion that the ultimate purpose of government is to improve the human condition—rather than to secure the intermediary objective of promoting economic growth as a presumed means to human betterment—they can strengthen their challenges to global neoliberalism and help reorient the flow of society's resources toward the promotion of human rights rather than toward the enrichment of corporations and expansion of markets. This would make more resources available for the education of children and adults, enabling more people to be informed and engaged citizens. It would also legitimize the expenditures of public monies and individuals' time and energy in the everyday practice of politics. In other words, we need a culture that accepts the costs of democratic governance. This would complicate systematic efforts to disenfranchise citizens by, for instance, scheduling elections on work days, establishing prohibitive voter registration requirements, limiting public access to information, and other anti-democratic measures that are common in contemporary democracies. Such a culture would also quickly generate new pressures for institutional changes to democratize global-level politics, since it is increasingly apparent that no democratic state can exist within a fundamentally undemocratic interstate system.

To enhance the resources available for a global democracy project, democratic globalizers might think more systematically about what they can do to more effectively structure and expand "activist labor markets" (Minkoff and McCarthy 2005). How might resources be made available to allow citizens to be involved in politics on a more regular basis? How might citizens be better trained in the skills necessary to be active, critical citizens? And how might more career opportunities be made available for those wishing to devote their lives to efforts to expand and enhance democracy? Neoliberal globalizers have asked these questions and have devoted resources to creating opportunities for their routine participation and intervention in national and global politics. To what extent are democratic globalizers committing resources to ensure that people who share their vision can devote time to working toward it? How much energy does the network devote to training and socializing people into the ideas, values, and history of global pro-democracy work? Certainly there are many examples of such efforts—such as student internships and training fellowships, grants for paid organizing work, and programs such as the AFL-CIO's "union summer" project to help invite young people to be more actively engaged in the work of the network. But we can certainly ask whether even more could be done to help train and create real opportunities for the next generations of activists—in all parts of the world—to enable them to work effectively for a more democratic world.

Recognizing the centrality of democratic participation to the realization of a more equal and just world, democratic globalization network participants might also devote more of the resources at their own disposal toward enhancing more participatory forms of democracy in all parts of the world. The investment of movement resources toward fostering pro-democracy and pro–human rights work in local settings around the world is not a diversion from the broader project of promoting global justice—it is part and parcel of it. While local efforts at nurturing human rights and democracy are crucial, this does not mean that they alone are sufficient. The two-pronged deglobalization strategy offered by Bello must be borne in mind. Global democratizers must also work to shape broader institutional contexts that allow and enable the kinds of practices they seek, and as we have seen in this book, national and global institutions must be radically transformed to support a democratic version of globalization. Policies such as the structural adjustment conditionalities of the global financial institutions must be abandoned, and bilateral and multilateral lending practices must be made more transparent and accountable to democratic procedures. Democratic states must be nested within a democratic system of states, or they will cease to be democratic.

There are important political opportunities for proponents of global democracy to win new allies and supporters. The response of the neoliberal network and its governmental allies has been to repress all opponents of neoliberalism—both democratic and anti-democratic. The problem with such a policy is that, as neoliberalism continues to exclude greater and greater numbers from enjoying access to clean water, basic health care, and some minimum form of social security, the system will become ever more unstable and violent. It will cost both more money and legitimacy to sustain this system. Governments and neoliberals concerned with stability and security have an interest in changing their approach to open more spaces for democratic globalizers. Thus, democratic globalizers must seek to mobilize around those interests to promote institutional changes that will effectively create a more democratic world.

What kinds of institutional changes might the network seek? I think a primary one should be those changes that open new spaces for routine public involvement in global policy processes. For instance, in chapter 4 we saw how global institutions have responded to popular mobilization by limiting popular access to these institutions. And neoliberals have sought to challenge democratic globalizers by questioning their representativeness. A concerted demand for more formal systems of accountability and representation in global institutions can help undermine both of these threats to the democratic globalization effort. This means that we may be ready to think seriously about a global parliament and other mechanisms to ensure participation and accountability in global institutions. Although many will dismiss such an idea as inviting global chaos and inefficiency, it is the only tested means of enhancing the legitimacy of global institutions. Governments know that their authority depends upon the popular perception that they have been chosen in free and fair elections and that they are responsive to popular input. Campaigns that seek to broaden popular scrutiny of the global democratic deficit can quickly generate the political will to institutionalize global democracy. And democratic globalizers will find important allies among the officials of international institutions as well as in some national and local governments. In fact, democratic globalizers can appeal to some of the recommendations made by the recent UN Panel of Eminent Persons regarding UN–Civil Society Relations. Among those recommendations was a call for greater involvement of national elected officials in deliberation about global policies. This and other proposals would likely draw in new allies and would fundamentally transform global political processes (see UN 2004). And a global parliament might build upon existing proposals such as those by Monbiot (2003) and Falk and Strauss (2001). Any global legislative body, however, should be seen as a complement to—not a replacement of—the WSF, as the latter should remain an open space for the people and ideas that do not fit neatly within established institutional frameworks.

In addition to efforts to create spaces for democratic participation in global policy processes, democratic globalizers also must work to nurture and develop ongoing alliances within national, regional, and international political arenas. A clearer focus on the aim of constructing multilateral rules that emphasize social norms and fairness over market principles can help win over allies. And efforts to domesticate international norms such as those promoting social equity and human rights or environmental sustainability require concerted work within governments (e.g., Vasi Forthcoming). In short, efforts to build institutions at local, national, regional, and international levels must be seen as part of a project to enact a radical world vision that displaces the global market logic with that of a global society grounded in human rights.

Positive Network Dynamics

Enhancing the effectiveness of the democratic globalization network requires a more conscious effort to cultivate positive network dynamics. And essential to this is deliberate work at effective communication across the many different groups in the network. Peter Waterman argues that we should think in terms of a "new kind of internationalism" that emphasizes participatory democracy and dialogue (Waterman 1998, 2001). He sees dialogue as necessary because of: (1) the failures of top-down, centralized organizing models of past socialist movements; (2) the absence of a clearly defined, unambiguous working-class identity or other means of securing commitment and loyalty on the basis of one's economic position; (3) the increasing complexity of globalized capitalism; and (4) the interdependence between political reform and transformation (2001: xx–xxi). Thus, advocates for democracy must create spaces that allow for effective dialogue among people with varying amounts of power. This means that those with power must "provide space and allow voice to those on the margins of such" (2001: xxi).

Herein lies a crucial challenge. The kinds of changes that are required for a more democratic world require major shifts in the consumption patterns and assumptions of those in relatively privileged positions, especially in the North but also in the global South. Inequities that result from the long history of colonialism and neocolonialism, of urban-rural divisions, of racism, and of the Western development model's assaults on indigenous cultures shape contemporary social relations. Cultivating sensitivities to the histories of power and its multifaceted effects is a first step toward generating more positive network relations among democratic globalizers. Again Waterman's language is helpful, as he argues for "a complex solidarity for a complex globality," where solidarity is seen as

1) informed by and positively articulated with equality, liberty, peace, tolerance, and more recent emancipatory/life-protective ideals;

2) primarily a relationship between people and peoples, even where mediated by state, market and bureaucratic/hierarchical organizations;

3) an active process of negotiating differences, or creating identity (as distinguished from traditional notions of "solidarity as community" which may *assume* [a shared] identity). (2001: 235, emphasis original)

Waterman's notion of complex solidarity accounts for the many challenges that transnational organizing poses for those who would build alliances of mutual respect and trust. It learns from past mistakes by remaining sensitive to power dynamics, avoiding binary oppositions, and emphasizing mutual respect and tolerance as much as a shared commitment. It encompasses the notion that groups are committed to mutually respectful dialogue that aims at negotiating across differences to generate a shared foundation for collective action. Finally, and perhaps most important, this concept emphasizes the need for groups to pay attention to processes, remaining sensitive to the need to consciously create space for dialogue about differences and for building trust and a sense of collective identity within the group (Waterman 2001, 2005).

In short, the groups that I have labeled the democratic globalization network should work to see themselves as a part of a very broad network with a shared vision for a global society based on a human rights culture. Such a vision can help orient the diverse elements of the global justice movement in a common direction, and it can help participants see through the various strategic and tactical differences that have generated conflicts in the past. The case studies here and in other research on transnational organizing hold important lessons for how to build more effective and durable transnational coalitions that are capable of negotiating and sustaining cooperation despite their many differences (see, e.g., Bandy and Smith 2005; Jordan and van Tuijl 2000). These studies point to the central importance of efforts to understand how power operates and it is reproduced in broad social relations in cultivating respectful and enduring transnational coalitions.

Another important lesson is that attempts to expand democratic globalization networks must extend their appeal to those not completely convinced by critiques of global capitalism. And here is where a pro-democracy approach can be helpful in reaching out to new groups and creating opportunities for them to join in a broader struggle, even if they are not (yet) willing to embrace an anti-neoliberal stance. Seeking common ground in the desire for greater public participation and accountability in global institutions, democratic globalizers expand the possibilities for strengthening the network. Moreover, by fostering a democratic, human rights culture within the broad network, activists encourage more deliberate efforts to nurture constructive and respectful dialogue about the strengths and weaknesses of a variety of political and economic models, something that neoliberals have actively sought to avoid.

Finally, positive network dynamics will require that democratic globalizers avoid the trap of engaging in endless debates about the role of formal organizations in the movement. The WSF process has brought to the fore some key questions about the roles of political parties and governments in relation to this network, and many seek to create a firm boundary between all forms of institutionalized politics and the WSF process. Often this tension is framed as a struggle between the "horizontals" and the "verticals" (Glasius and Timms 2006), or between the proponents of "sovereign" state-oriented approaches and the "multitudes" seeking "non-sovereign" alternatives (Hardt 2004). Certainly there is a need for global civil society to manifest itself in spaces that are not defined by dominant institutions of society. Without this, there would be few possibilities for challenging power relations and for even imagining, much less realizing, alternatives to existing reality. However, activists must find ways to connect the politics of the WSF with the routines of people's everyday political lives, and this is likely to require explicit organizing work with parties, unions, governments, and other traditional organizational forms.

While formal organizations might tend to reproduce inequalities rather than challenge them, they also help remedy power imbalances within groups by creating formal mechanisms for accountability and ensuring equitable participation. Organization by and on behalf of "the multitude" can help overcome the enormous challenges posed by the neoliberal order within which democratic globalizers must organize. As Mertes notes in response to Hardt:

> The debate over the WSF needs to remember, too, the exhausting logistical problems that global organizing presents to the dispossessed. Time, money and a daunting sense of distance present real obstacles to students, activists, trade unionists and rural and urban poor—in stark contrast to the well-funded global infrastructures of the ruling class. For all his reservations about the Brazilian PT [Workers' Party], Hardt must acknowledge that, without its municipal government in Porto Alegre, the WSF would never have taken place. (2004: 246–247)

Important lessons one can take from observations of these sorts of movement debates is that activists should take advantage of the diversity within the democratic globalization network and appreciate the important division of labor therein. Often, more formalized and/or centralized groups can reach audiences and perform tasks that less formal and/or decentralized groups cannot. Conversely, less formalized and/or decentralized groups can appeal to different groups of people and engage in activities that centralized or formal groups cannot. They also can help nurture network identities and monitor boundaries, warning of risks of co-optation by adversaries. Acknowledging the strengths and weaknesses of different organizational structures can help organizers develop better strategies for mobilizing new groups and for targeting energies in efficient ways. For instance, strategic coordination can help make use of a "radical flank effect" wherein more militant activities of some groups force authorities to yield concessions to groups perceived as comparatively more moderate (Haines 1988).

There could be more systematic attention to the articulation and dissemination of a global human rights culture that encourages widespread awareness of global human rights instruments and nurtures appreciation of core democratic values. We saw in chapter 4 that an important part of the neoliberal network's strategy is the promotion of its own culture of consumerism. Moreover, important organizational entities that control substantial resources—the cultural fraction of the neoliberal network—are constantly engaged in the work of promoting this consumerist culture. What does the cultural fraction of the democratic globalization network look like? How could it be expanded? Can it co-opt resources now controlled by neoliberal globalizers? And how might a global human rights culture be better communicated? These are important questions to ask and address, and doing so may amplify significantly existing pro-democracy work.

In sum, the network imagery helps us envision the multifaceted and linked activities of activists in many different parts of the world to resist global neoliberalism and to promote democracy. One might summarize the lessons of this investigation as follows: First, seek friends among enemies. Challengers must seek political leverage in a number of places, and by rejecting involvement with the state or with political parties, they cede important ground to their opponents. The state is an important site of political contestation, and as we saw here it is necessary for the democratizing project envisioned by many contemporary activists. Moreover, complex multilateralism creates multiple venues and new possibilities for alliances with powerful actors, providing important political leverage for those challenging neoliberalism. Second, seek more friends among bystanders. Democratic globalizers can work harder to earn the sympathies of bystanders who are now uncommitted or more closely aligned with neoliberalism. By challenging the legitimacy of neoliberalism as an ideology and in its institutional manifestations, and by expanding the options people have for securing their physical livelihood, democratic globalizers can chip away at the network of support for neoliberalism, expanding their own network. Third, do not alienate your friends. Work harder to integrate actors in the democratic globalization network and develop organizational practices and routines to ensure that you avoid this. The network's strength is its diversity, and finding ways to cultivate unity while celebrating diversity is key to advancing the struggle. Fourth, think and act strategically and systematically about global institutions and democracy. More conscious work to build institutions that support a vision of globalization consistent with democratic values of equality, inclusion, tolerance, and nonviolence is key to the struggle to change the world. Finally, more focused cultural work to enhance understandings of and sensitivities to democratic and human rights principles will help advance democratic globalization and secure it from future anti-democratic threats.

A major study by Verba and his colleagues of why certain people do not participate in the U.S. political system provides important insights into how to enhance democracy everywhere (1995). They conclude that people do not participate in politics because they lack the time and resources, they lack the relevant knowledge or interest, and/or they were never taught or asked to participate. Global inequality contributes to all of these deprivations, producing a systematic bias in favor of conservative, pro-market policies and a systematic exclusion of disadvantaged groups. Conscious efforts by democratic globalizers to remedy inequalities in the resources, knowledge, and opportunities for political participation can dramatically enhance both national and global democracy. The activist initiatives explored in this book have laid the groundwork for a more expansive democratic globalization project. They have contributed new lessons and expanded the openings for people to engage in global-level politics. They have done so by promoting the public's access to skills and other resources for global political participation, by generating interest and knowledge of global issues, and by structuring invitations to participate through global campaigns and events such as the World (and local) Social Forums. More conscious dedication to the democratic globalization project—which involves more focused efforts to make global institutions more inclusive, responsive, transparent, and consistent with human rights values—will advance the vision of a more democratic world.

One • Contested Globalizations

1. Neoliberalism limits government roles in providing social welfare and regulating economic activities within and between nations, maximizing the role of market forces over political negotiations in shaping economic policies.

2. For instance, indigenous peoples have long resisted capitalist globalization, and major world religions have inspired resistance through their critiques of capitalism's materialism.

3. Many, however, are losing confidence in democracy as a political form. In Latin America and Eastern Europe, for instance, many link the transitions from more authoritarian forms of government to the introduction of neoliberal economic policies, and polls show a preference for economic well-being over democracy (see, e.g., Hoge 2004).

4. A few points of entry into this debate include Markoff's summary in the *Encyclopedia of Social Theory* (2004a); Linz and Stepan (1996); and on the role of social movements in the democratization process, see Tilly (2004) and Markoff (1996).

5. See, for instance, Glasius (2002), Nanz and Steffek (2004), and Coleman and Porter (2000).

Two • Rival Transnational Networks

1. Khagram (2004) demonstrates how transnational networking among elites helps advance particular agendas and visions of development. He traces how an "international big dam regime" (p. 6) formed to promote international financing of large and highly destructive dam projects around the world.

2. The transnational capitalist class consists of actors supporting the global spread of capitalism. Many local and national capitalists do not share the interest in promoting *globalized* capitalism, and thus some capitalists may favor national protection over global neoliberalism. Some capitalists may see their interests as complemented by those of democratic globalizers, whose ideology is not opposed to locally based and democratically accountable forms of capitalism.

3. I use the term *democratic globalization* to describe opponents of neoliberal globalization because—although their specific goals vary—most groups call for greater national and/or global democratization, often as a means of achieving some more specific policy objective.

4. NGOs refer to nongovernmental organizations of all kinds, including groups organized to promote social change (social movement organizations, or SMOs) in addition to recreational, professional, and business lobby groups. Thus, NGOs will appear in both rival networks.

5. Local politicians have organized to defend their authority to define local economic policy, such as regulations on foreign investment. They worked with others in the democratic globalization network to resist agreements like the Multilateral Agreement on Investment (MAI), establishing in some cases local "MAI-free zones" (Barlow and Clarke 1998; J. Smith 2002).

6. Compensation for NGO staff can differ greatly between the global North and South, and for some Southern activists, work in this sector is quite lucrative, in contrast to the North.

7. This makes the democratic globalization network more vulnerable to attempts at co-optation by rivals through, for instance, corporate grants and corporate sponsorship of activities.

8. Attempts to question the commitment of activists were also made in the 1960s, when media messages suggested that vast numbers of student activists ultimately joined the professional middle class. McAdam (1988) discredits such claims, showing that many civil rights activists remained active in movements throughout their adult lives.

9. Because corporate and government funding tends to moderate the activities of social movements (Brulle and Jenkins 2005), many groups limit or refuse such funding sources.

10. See, e.g., debate between Mertes (2004) and Hardt (2004).

11. This was despite the requirement in U.S. law that all relevant stakeholders be represented. One seat is formally allotted to an environmental representative, and this seat was left unfilled.

12. This has been a topic of widespread discussion in policy, academic, and activist circles. See, e.g., Herman (1995); Couch (2004); http://world-information.org/wio/info structure/; and www.fair.org, to name a few sources.

13. For instance, Adbusters was denied the right to purchase advertising space on all major U.S. broadcasting networks because its ad for "buy nothing day" contradicted the fundamental missions of the stations (Niman 2001).

14. Describing the "netwars" launched by contemporary groups such as the Zapatista rebels in southern Mexico, a Rand Corporation study refers to this as "the war of the swarm" (Arquilla and Ronfeldt 2001).

Three • Politics in a Global System

1. Following O'Brien et al. (2000), I use the term *multilateralism* to refer to the institutionalized settings containing both horizontal relationships (such as those among mul-

tiple states) as well as vertical ones (such as those between various combinations of states, non-state actors, and intergovernmental officials).

2. A particularly dramatic illustration of this occurred just after a 1990 Security Council vote on whether to authorize military action against Iraq's invasion of Kuwait. The U.S. envoy told the Yemeni ambassador that his vote would be "the most expensive 'no' vote you would ever cast," and the United States promptly cut its entire $70 million aid budget to Yemen (Deen 2002).

3. Of course, not all social movements promote progressive or redistributive political aims. Some—such as anti-immigrant or militant fundamentalism—promote *exclusive*, particularized, and often identity-based interests, and they may take on violent forms.

4. This figure hugely understates the numbers of groups relating their work to UN processes, including many local and national organizations that refer to UN conference declarations in their efforts to hold governments accountable to international commitments (e.g., Friedman et al. 2005; Riles 2001; Subramaniam et al. 2003).

5. However, a 2004 report on UN–civil society relations makes some concrete proposals in this regard, seeking to streamline but not limit civil society participation and to enhance access by allowing consultative relations with the General Assembly (UN 2004).

6. www.jwa.org/exhibits/wov/abzug/global.html, accessed 29 December 2005.

7. For a more detailed summary of the global financial institutions, see, e.g., Porter (2005); Dawkins (2003); Wallach and Woodall (2004); and Peet (2003).

8. The United States has as many staff members working *only* on WTO matters as more than a dozen of the world's poorest countries have to represent their interests in *all* of the more than twenty Geneva-based international organizations (Jawara and Kwa 2003).

9. In practice, nongovernmental organizations of private-sector business interests predominate in both formal and informal relations with these institutions. At the WTO meeting in Seattle, for instance, virtually all accredited "civil society actors" were industry lobbies or business-sponsored groups.

10. TOES was "a forum for the presentation, discussion, and advocacy of the economic ideas and practices upon which a more just and sustainable society can be built—'an economics as if people mattered.'" Language used here mirrors that of contemporary global justice activists. At http://www.cipa-apex.org/categories/toes/.

11. One can find this logic throughout contemporary U.S. conservative discourse. A recent example is found in Barr (2002). For a detailed analysis of U.S. conservatives' opposition to multilateralism, see Buss and Herman (2003).

Four • *Globalizing Capitalism*

1. This is not to say that the members of the TCC all share the same interpretation of the political and social environment. Many capitalists prefer nationally based to globalized markets, and different national cultures have generated distinct sensibilities about the appropriate rights and responsibilities of corporations (Ahmadjian and Robbins 2005; Hutton 2003). As the social and ecological costs of capitalist expansion become more apparent, we see more conflict within the neoliberal network about whether and how extensively to pursue the neoliberal agenda.

2. Figures compiled from various news accounts assembled through Lexis/Nexis search.

3. Southern governments were always far more repressive, and pro-democracy protesters there have faced far more arrests, brutality, and death at the hands of police (Podobnik 2005; Walton and Seddon 1994).

4. This has become even more evident as counterterrorist measures in the United States and elsewhere infringe on basic privacy rights of peaceful protesters and other citizens.

5. This strategy was not explicitly planned by participants in the neoliberal network. Nevertheless, uncoordinated efforts by different parts of the network constituted a multipronged effort to advance neoliberalism and stifle its critics.

6. Sklair (1997) uses this term to describe these very same organizations.

7. This compares with over $450 billion in military expenditures that year.

8. Some of these initiatives, such as a proposed UNICEF-McDonald's partnership and a UNDP plan to bring "two billion to market" (2B2M), were criticized and later abandoned. The larger failure to scrutinize UN relationships with business remains (Martens 2003).

9. See www.globalcompact.org.

10. Neoliberal advocates argue nevertheless that the Global Compact allows NGOs to police corporations (Rabkin 2003).

11. "Policy laundering" describes international counterterrorist activities of local and national security officials that aim to circumvent national laws protecting individuals' rights to privacy and association. The metaphor can be generalized to any attempt to cross national borders in order to bypass democratic procedures. See www.policylaundering.org/.

12. For instance, Wal-Mart established a "war room" from which it conducted strategic public relations campaigns to counter its critics. The company spent $1.4 billion on advertising in 2005 ($3.8 million per day), compared with the $1.8 million cost of the critical documentary, *Wal-Mart: The High Cost of Low Price* (Barbaro 2005).

13. Ironically, NGOs are the very sorts of organizations that many neoliberal proponents put forth as the solution to big government.

14. At www.aei.org/events/eventID.329,filter./event_detail.asp#, accessed 31 July 2005.

15. The papers are available on the American Enterprise Institute Web site: www.aei.org/events/eventID.329,filter./event_detail.asp#.

16. In my fieldwork I witnessed many lengthy discussions in large group meetings about how to improve accountability and representativeness within the movement. During the 1990s NGOs collaboratively generated some general guidelines for an "NGO Code of Conduct," which many groups have subsequently adopted (see www.gdrc.org/ngo/codesofconduct/infohabitat.html).

17. This is another example of isomorphism across these competing networks.

Five • *Promoting Multilateralism*

1. I focus here on organizations and treaties that are universal in membership, mainly the UN system. However, many multilateral arrangements base their membership on geography (e.g., the European Union), history (e.g., the Commonwealth), or interests (e.g., the G8).

2. This typology of relationships between movements and multilateral institutions draws from work I did with Charles Chatfield and Ron Pagnucco (1997).

3. This is not a comprehensive list, but it shows the most influential streams of transnational activism.

4. For examples of movements of this era, see, e.g., Keck and Sikkink (1998); Finnemore (1996); Boswell and Chase-Dunn (2000); Wittner (1997); Rupp (1997); and Chatfield (2007).

5. These accounts are from a survey of NGOs active at the UN conducted by the UN Panel of Eminent Persons on Civil Society. James Paul (1999) also reports on the rising hostility between governments and NGOs at the UN, and Meyerson (2002) reports on the disengagement of civil society groups from the UN in the early to mid-2000s.

6. Survey results based on five hundred responses, 54 percent of which were from organizations in the global South.

7. They do so, according to the criteria summarized in chapter 1, by raising public awareness, increasing the openness and representativeness as well as transparency in the global system, and improving both the fairness and effectiveness of the system.

8. For more detailed analyses of these various campaigns, see, e.g., Foster and Anand (1999); Mayo (2005); Mertes (2004); O'Brien et al. (2000); Reitan (2006); and Starr (2000).

Six • *Mobilizing a Transnational Network for Democratic Globalization*

1. This assumption of an adversarial relationship to states is also problematic at the national level (e.g., McCarthy and Wolfson 1992; Macdonald 1997)

2. Practitioners often use NGO to refer specifically to those formal organizations that maintain routine connections to official agencies and other elites (such as foundations), contrasting these with less formal (and often by implication less hierarchical) grassroots groups. This distinction is often problematic, however, as many grassroots groups can be quite undemocratic, while many groups with professional staff can be very informal and participatory in structure.

3. Khasnabish (2005) explains how ideas articulated by the Zapatistas help unify many diverse struggles around a common set of values, symbols, and slogans.

4. Jordan and van Tuijl (2000) conclude that effective coalitions are characterized by "political responsibility": that is, high-quality and regular flows of information, formalization of arrangements for resource allocation, explicit efforts to remedy inequities, and acknowledgment of the diversity of skills and resources in the network.

5. This characterization certainly applies to many NGOs, but it is often used to dismiss many groups that do not conform to this image.

6. The *Yearbook of International Organizations* is a census of all international organizations involving different national governments and/or citizens from at least three countries. *Yearbook* editors make extensive efforts to identify new and disbanded groups, and it details organizations' aims, membership, and ties to other groups. It is not a perfect census of all transnational organizations, and it is likely to exclude less formal as well as violent groups, but it remains the best record we have over a long period of time of transnational organizational activity.

7. This is consistent with other accounts (Krut 1997; Riles 2001). The leveling of growth in the numbers of ties between 1993 and 2003 may be due to the large number of new organizations, to a real decline in the formation of new inter-organizational ties, or both.

8. Bennett's discussion mirrors Lichterman's findings (1996) on U.S. environmental activism. Such lifestyle engagement, moreover, is tied to broader changes in work and family patterns: "busy people (and working women are the busiest of people) can better adapt personal schedules to volunteer activities than to the more arbitrary rhythms of organized groups" (1996: 9).

Seven • *Agenda Setting in a Global Polity*

1. Civil society mobilization alongside global trade negotiations parallels that in the UN, and IMC activists have reported on UN conferences since the group's founding in 1999. The format of the IMC might even be seen as replicating advocacy groups' practice of producing daily civil society newspapers.

2. www.imc.org.

3. Australia is the other Western state that has not ratified the Kyoto Protocol.

4. I am grateful to Bogdan Vasi for providing me with details about these cases.

5. www.rso.cornell.edu/kyotonow/index.html. The Kyoto Now! coalition built upon the organizing template established by another student environmental network, the Student Environmental Action Coalition's Youth Power Shift Campaign: "The Youth Power Shift Campaign aims to engage our schools, governments, and other institutions in a campaign to dramatically reduce their negative impact on the global climate, affected communities, and the environment as a whole" (www.seac.org/index.shtml). Kyoto Now! reports links to Greenpeace International as well as to the Climate Crisis Coalition, which promotes public education and advances a "people's ratification" of the Kyoto Protocol (www.climatecrisiscoalition.org).

6. The ICLEI's Local Governments for Sustainability issued a declaration at the 2005 Conference of the Parties to the Climate Change Convention agreeing to cut greenhouse gas emissions by 30 percent below 1990 levels by 2020 and 80 percent by 2050. Their declaration referenced the International Youth Declaration in setting those targets. As one observer noted: "Because of the steps that U.S. mayors are taking, the United States cannot solely be viewed as a stubborn obstructionist on climate change—the role that the Bush Administration would otherwise have America play. They are carving out a different role for the U.S. in the world" (S. Paul 2005).

7. A study of major U.S. newspapers showed that more than half (52.7 percent) of all stories gave equal attention to both the IPCC and industry-skeptical views, and just 35

percent emphasized the IPCC position while giving some mention to industry views. An additional 6.2 percent presented industry views only, with no mention of the scientific consensus (Mooney 2004).

8. Numerous Web sites track media ownership, including mediachannel.org, www.democraticmedia.org/, www.fair.org, and the Columbia Journalism Review (www.cjr.org).

9. The study was carried out by the Lear Centre Local News Archive at the University of Southern California (USC) Annenberg School for Communication and included 4,333 broadcasts. The study pointed out that the lack of attention to electoral campaigns by the news media forced candidates to rely more heavily on paid advertising to communicate their messages.

10. Iyengar's innovative study involved experiments that systematically compared how people interpreted and responded to information presented through televised news programs designed to emphasize either episodic or thematic coverage of different issues.

11. The World Trade Organization's General Agreement on Trade in Services (GATS) seeks to expand this kind of "trade." Countries of the global South have resisted the implementation of GATS, although elements of this have been brought into bilateral and regional trade agreements such as the Free Trade Area of the Americas (FTAA).

12. This calculation draws from Sklair's (2002: fig. 3.1) figure ranking the world's largest economic entities by revenues. Of these top 50, just 15 were governments, and fossil-fuel related industries were the largest single industry group represented in this ranking. Of the remaining 35, 7 were in financial/insurance industries, 6 were electronics, 4 retail, and 3 communications companies.

13. More details and youth reports from this meeting are available at www.itsgetting-hotinhere.org. Other youth-related activities reported there were podcasts of interviews by youth with conference delegates and a video entitled *Save Hockey: Fight Climate Change.*

Eight • *Domesticating International Human Rights Norms*

1. The Soviet Union emphasized economic, social, and cultural rights, while the United States and its allies emphasized civil and political rights.

2. "Reality tours" "thoroughly submerge visitors into an environment of decay, and [show] how globalization and national neo-liberal policies tie into it." As Honkala stated, "when the visitors from Sweden cried during these tours, it is not just for these dark scenes, but for the shock of how bad things have gotten in the U.S." (NYC Indymedia 2000).

3. I noted a number of other differences between this meeting and others I had attended, reflecting differences in organizing styles and life experiences from which these activists come. For instance, more effort was made by organizers to help participants with childcare and basic logistical matters. People spoke openly of the sacrifices they and their families and local communities made so that they could be at the meeting.

4. The Kensington Welfare Rights Union (KWRU) was formed in 1991 by a group of poor women who came together to oppose welfare cuts. Information on KWRU and the PPEHRC history comes from the KWRU Web site, www.kwru.org, author fieldnotes, and informal interviews with participants.

5. The bus tour makes an explicit link to the civil rights movement and its failed attempt to frame its struggle in terms of human rights rather than civil rights.

6. The discourse at this meeting showed that activists were clearly making connections between militarism, poverty, and economic globalization.

7. The use of international tribunals dates to the Vietnam War era, and they seek not to uncover answers about the legality of particular actions but rather emerge "from a conviction that the institutions of the state, including the UN, have failed to act to protect a vulnerable people" (Falk 2005). Popular tribunals focusing on corporate actors extend back at least to the 1993 meeting of the G7 (Asia Pacific Resource Center 1994).

8. The OAS, rather than the UN, is targeted because the United States is not party to relevant UN treaties and also because the principle of subsidiarity requires that cases be filed in the most local jurisdiction possible, which in this case is the regional body.

9. The U.S. government has signed very few international human rights treaties, including the international Convention on Social, Economic and Cultural Rights. Thus, U.S. citizens cannot use reporting mechanisms within those treaty bodies to draw international scrutiny to U.S. policies.

10. "Economic Human Rights Petition Filed before the Inter-American Commission on Human Rights against the United States Government for Violations against the Poor" (2000) at www.kwru.org/ehrc/ehrc.html.

11. www.economichumanrights.org/updates/oashearing.htm, accessed 31 March 2005.

12. At www.kwru.org/updates/geneva.html, accessed 19 December 2006.

13. In this sense it reflects what I described in chapter 6 as a trend toward more decentralized and network-like structures that connect local- and global-level organizing efforts. While KWRU remains deeply rooted in its local action to help respond to housing and other poverty-related emergencies of its membership, its leadership has been able to maintain a consistent effort to build and sustain international ties. So while the PPEHRC focuses much of its attention on getting the United States (and other OAS countries) to adhere to international human rights commitments, it also is working through the World Social Forum process to cultivate alliances with other U.S. and international antipoverty groups and to help build a global movement on the "right to health."

14. At www.kwru.org/internat/, accessed 31 March 2005.

15. The claim form that activists can obtain from the PPEHRC Web site is based on the templates developed by human rights groups to help them bring claims to international legal bodies.

16. For instance, assisting the campaign on its international legal work are students from various New York City law schools, the National Employment Law Service, the Urban Justice Center, and the Center for Constitutional Rights.

17. Kolb argues that human rights language had some traction in the executive branch, but not in Congress, where Southern members rejected international law outright (Kolb 2007).

18. At www.iisd.ca/climate/cop10/enbots/15dec.html, accessed 4 January 2006.

19. www.acia.uaf.edu.

20. The specific rights in the OAS Declaration that are cited by the ICC petition include: the right to life (art. I); the right to residence and movement (art. VII); the right to

inviolability of the home (art. IX); the right to the preservation of health and to well-being (art. XI); the right to the benefits of culture (art. XIII); the right to work and to fair remuneration (art. XIV); and the right to property (art. XXIII).

21. In December 2006, the OAS turned away the Inuit petition, arguing that there was "insufficient evidence of harm." But it changed its position just a few months later, and a hearing was held on the petition in early March 2007 (Sieg 2007).

22. The search was conducted in Google on 14 January 2007 on the terms "Inuit OAS petition."

23. Political imagination is "impetus and processes involved in envisioning and articulating political projects" to promote social change (Khasnabish 2005).

24. In describing legal arenas, Jacobson and Ruffer (2003) use the same concept of nested institutions to describe relationships between courts operating at local, national, regional, and global levels. They see a thickening of the "legal webbing" over time that has generated a stronger and more unifying human rights emphasis throughout the system.

Nine • *Confronting Contradictions between Multilateral Economic Institutions and the UN System*

1. The quote is from John Humphrey, an early director of the UN's Division on Human Rights and one of the key architects of the Universal Declaration of Human Rights (quoted in Alston 1992: 141).

2. The World Bank and IMF determine the credit-worthiness of a particular government, affecting that state's ability to attract private loans and investment. They thus have far more influence on these countries than the amounts of their loan packages would suggest.

3. Elected legislative officials in borrowing countries typically do not have access to the text of loan agreements until they are binding on their countries.

4. Many poor countries rely on a small number of exports, whereas richer countries tend to have a more diversified range of exports. Moreover, regardless of domestic needs, borrowing countries *must* produce goods for export in order to earn foreign exchange to pay back international loans.

5. The global South is doubly victimized by the fact that many ecological problems—such as deforestation, climate change, and desertification—have far more devastating consequences for people in the global South.

6. But Sands (2005) sees some hope that appeals processes may remedy this.

7. See Friends of the Earth International (2004).

8. In fact, Hill (2004) argues that the newest, "third" generation of transnational activism is best characterized not as outside the UN (as is true in Bennett's characterization of it [2005]) but as participating in "partnerships" between the UN, national governments, and private-sector actors. However, many civil society groups are reluctant to join such partnerships out of concern that these are not designed to ensure equal accountability and transparency. And some groups that entered into partnerships have become disillusioned and withdrawn from these arrangements. I suspect that far more groups have adopted what we might call a "loyal opposition" stand that is critical of UN relationships

to corporate actors while committed to helping the institution better fulfill the aims of its Charter.

9. A meeting in November 2004, for instance, drew over six hundred organizers from more than two dozen countries (Tavola Della Pace 2005b).

10. I have reviewed World Social Forum programs and attended two forums, finding very little focused attention to work within the UN. Of the more than 2,500 sessions that made up the 2005 WSF, just a handful addressed proposals for targeting the UN.

11. See, for instance, Foster and Anand (1999) and the Non-government Liaison Service *Go-Between* and *NGLS Roundup* (at www.un-ngls.org/). Also, extensive discussion of human rights and economic globalization appear on the Web site of the People's Movement for Human Rights Learning (www.pdhre.org).

12. See www.whiteband.org.

13. The Millennium Development Goals (MDGs) are eight specific antipoverty targets governments accepted in the 2000 Millennium Summit at the UN. They include: (1) eradicate extreme poverty and hunger; (2) achieve universal primary education; (3) promote gender equality; (4) reduce child mortality; (5) improve maternal health; (6) combat HIV/AIDS, malaria, and other major diseases; (7) ensure environmental sustainability; and (8) create a global partnership for development.

14. As is often true of these sorts of movement-sponsored concerts, activists find that their ability to influence the discussion of issues is eclipsed by musicians, who can often claim the media spotlight despite their limited knowledge of the issues. Activists have complained that G8 leaders took credit for making new promises to address poverty, but that they have not followed through on these, now that celebrities' and public attention has subsided (Schlosberg 2006).

15. One of the GCAP white band days corresponded with that of the "Reclaim the UN" effort's international day of action to mark the opening of the 2005 UN General Assembly, which opened with a review of progress on achieving the Millennium Development Goals. The third white band day during the 2005 WTO meeting generated more than a quarter-million email petitions to authorities emphasizing MDG commitments.

16. This sub-commission is the main subsidiary body of the UN Commission on Human Rights. It is composed of twenty-six independent human rights experts, acting in their personal capacity, elected by the commission with due regard to equitable geographical distribution. It was renamed in 1999 the Sub-Commission for the Promotion and Protection of Human Rights.

17. Resolution dated 4 September 1998, available at www.pdhre.org/involved/uncommission.html.

18. The full text of the resolution can be found at www.globalpolicy.org/socecon/un/uncohr.htm.

19. Reported in *NGLS Roundup*, no. 61, September 2000, Human Rights Sub-Commission Holds 2000 Annual Session. At www.unsystem.org/ngls/documents/text/roundup/, accessed 21 July 2005.

20. Roundup 90—May 2002: Human Rights Approaches to Sustainable Development, at www.un-ngls.org/documents/pdf/roundup/ru90hrsd.pdf.

Ten • *Alternative Political Spaces*

1. For more detailed analyses of the WSF process, see, e.g., Fisher and Ponniah (2003); Reitan (2006); Sen et al. (2003); Teivainen (2002); and Smith et al. (2008).

2. The direct action laboratories have also generated strong criticism even from youth activists themselves, since these sessions tend to draw those more concerned with doing civil disobedience than with serious reflection on the choice of tactics.

3. On the explicit connections between the *encuentro* form and the World Social Forums, see, e.g., Escobar (2003); Chesters (2004); and Fisher and Ponniah (2003).

4. Disagreements remain among WSF participants over basic questions such as whether or not the forum should make common statements and whether and how to involve governments, political parties, and private entities such as foundations and corporations. But these conflicts have not prevented the forum from convening and providing space for participants to act on shared goals (see Smith et al. 2008).

5. For a discussion of the debates surrounding these principles, see Sen (2003); Patomäki and Teivainen (2004); and Smith et al. (2008).

6. Activists actively discuss this dilemma, and more than once I have heard people reference Freeman's article.

7. Walden Bello made this argument in a speech at the European Social Forum in London in 2004. Of course, such a position is problematic on many levels, not the least of which is that critics of the movement will use such contacts to discredit the entire movement. And in the context of the "global war on terror," such contacts are likely to bring repressive responses from nominally democratic governments.

8. Discussions at the WSF and at the European Social Forum revealed strains over the difficulties activists found in hosting very large meetings while also working to build local activism. However, many participants in these discussions did not want to abandon regular meetings at the broader regional or global levels, for fear of losing the global orientation of the forum process. The decisions of the International Council to host a polycentric forum in 2006 and then to suspend the world meeting in 2008 in order to encourage local and regional organizing reflect its effort to respond to these tensions.

9. I participated in the 2005 World Social Forum in Porto Alegre as a coordinator for a delegation from the international group Sociologists Without Borders. In this capacity, I coordinated and registered our delegation through the WSF Web site, and consulted with other registered groups to develop a joint program for the actual WSF meeting. I learned to appreciate the difficulties involved in attempts to organize transnationally within the WSF process, as well as the possibilities.

10. During the first WSF in Porto Alegre, French farmer-activist José Bové was arrested for "decontaminating" a genetically modified crop test plot. As the news of his arrest and imminent deportation was announced, organizers passed around stickers with the Zapatista-inspired phrase, "Somos todos José Bové" (We are all José Bové).

11. This includes not only international war making but also internal repression and the expansion of what activists call the "prison industrial complex" of modern, neoliberal states.

12. Antiwar speakers quoted in Hayden (2004).

13. Because the existing legal context often prevents action to restrict international investments or trade that might undermine local economies or damage the environment, these actions must be supplemented with attempts to roll back neoliberal policies at the global level, as seen in the deglobalization strategy discussed earlier.

14. Global Exchange, a U.S.-based group with extensive transnational ties that has also been a key node of the global democratic network in the United States, has devoted considerable effort to these sorts of economic democracy programs in the years since the Seattle protest (Jackson 2005).

15. For just two examples of these cultural initiatives, see www.simpleliving.net/time day/; www.adbusters.org/home/.

16. Frith (2005) reports, for instance, "The Gap cancelled contracts with 136 factories after the report disclosed details of child labor, the virtual slavery of workers and working weeks in excess of 80 hours. Levi Strauss, the jeans company, is now being praised by anti-sweatshop campaigners for working with unions and activists to improve conditions in its factories."

Adamovsky, Ezequiel. 2005. "Beyond the World Social Forum: The Need for New Institutions." In Opendemocracy.net, vol. 2005.

Ahmadjian, Christina L., and Gregory E. Robbins. 2005. "A Clash of Capitalisms: Foreign Shareholders and Corporate Restructuring in 1990s Japan." *American Sociological Review* 70:451–472.

Albert, Michael. 2003. "The WSF: Where to Now?" Pp. 323–328 in *Challenging Empires: The World Social Forum*, edited by J. Sen, A. Anand, A. Escobar, and P. Waterman. At www.choike.org/nuevo_eng/informes/1557.html.

Alger, Chadwick F. 1963. "United Nations Participation as a Learning Experience." *Public Opinion Quarterly* 27:411–426.

Alston, Philip. 1992. "The Commission on Human Rights." Pp. 126–210 in *The United Nations and Human Rights: A Critical Appraisal*, edited by P. Alston. New York: Oxford University Press.

Alvarez, Sonia, Nalu Faria, and Miriam Nobre. 2003. "Another (also Feminist) World is Possible: Constructing Transnational Spaces and Global Alternatives from the Movements." Pp. 199–206 in *Challenging Empires: The World Social Forum*, edited by J. Sen, A. Anand, A. Escobar, and P. Waterman. At www.choike.org/nuevo_eng/informes/1557.html.

Amnesty International. 2004. "The UN Human Rights Norms For Business: Towards Legal Accountability." Amnesty International, London. At http://web.amnesty.org/library/pdf/IOR420022004ENGLISH/$File/IOR4200204.

Anand, Anita. 1999. "Global Meeting Place: United Nations' World Conferences and Civil Society." Pp. 65–108 in *Whose World Is It Anyway? Civil Society, the United Nations and the Multilateral Future*, edited by J. W. Foster and A. Anand. Ottawa: United Nations Association in Canada.

Anderson, Carol. 2003. *Eyes off the Prize: African-Americans and the Struggle for Human Rights, 1948–1954.* New York: Cambridge University Press.

Anheier, Helmut, and Hagai Katz. 2005. "Network Approaches to Global Civil Society." Pp. 206–221 in *Global Civil Society 2004/5*, edited by H. Anheier, M. Glasius, and M. Kaldor. London: Sage.

Arquilla, John, and David Ronfeldt, eds. 2001. *Networks and Netwars: The Future of Terror, Crime, and Militancy.* Santa Monica, CA: Rand Corporation.

Arrighi, Giovanni. 1999. "Globalization and Historical Macrosociology." Pp. 117–133 in *Sociology for the Twenty-First Century,* edited by J. L. Abu-Lughod. Chicago: University of Chicago Press.

Asia Pacific Resource Center. 1994. *The People vs. Global Capital: The G-7, TNCs, SAPs, and Human Rights—Report of the International People's Tribunal to Judge the G-7.* Tokyo: Asia Pacific Resource Center.

Atwood, David. 1997. "Mobilizing Around the United Nations Special Session on Disarmament." Pp. 141–158 in *Transnational Social Movements and Global Politics: Solidarity Beyond the State,* edited by J. Smith, C. Chatfield, and R. Pagnucco. Syracuse: Syracuse University Press.

Ayres, Jeffrey M. 1998. *Defying Conventional Wisdom: Political Movements and Popular Contention Against North American Free Trade.* Toronto: University of Toronto Press.

———. 2004. "Framing Collective Action Against Neoliberalism: The Case of the 'Anti-Globalization' Movement." *Journal of World Systems Research* 10:11–34.

Babb, Sarah. 2003. "The IMF in Sociological Perspective: A Tale of Organizational Slippage." *Studies in Comparative International Development* 38:3–27.

Babones, Salvatore J., and Jonathan H. Turner. 2003. "Global Inequality." Pp. 101–121 in *Handbook of Social Problems,* edited by G. Ritzer. Malden, MA: Blackwell.

Baiocchi, Gianpaolo. 2003. "Emergent Public Spheres: Talking Politics in Participatory Governance in Porto Alegre, Brazil." *American Sociological Review* 68:52–74.

———. 2004. "The Party and the Multitudes: Brazil's Worker's Party (PT) and the Challenges of Building a Just Social Order in the Globalizing Context." *Journal of World Systems Research* 10:199–215.

Ball, Patrick. 2000. "State Terror, Constitutional Traditions, and National Human Rights Movements: A Cross-National Quantitative Comparison." Pp. 54–75 in *Globalizations and Social Movements: Culture, Power, and the Transnational Public Sphere,* edited by J. A. Guidry, M. D. Kennedy, and M. N. Zald. Ann Arbor: University of Michigan Press.

Bandy, Joe, and Jackie Smith. 2005. *Coalitions Across Borders: Transnational Protest and the Neoliberal Order.* Lanham, MD: Rowman & Littlefield.

Barbaro, Michael. 2005. "A New Weapon for Wal-Mart: A War Room." *New York Times,* 1 November. At www.wakeupwalmart.com/news/20051101-nyt.html.

Barber, Benjamin. 1995. *Jihad vs. McWorld.* New York: Random House.

Barlow, Maude, and Tony Clarke. 1998. *MAI: The Multilateral Agreement on Investment and the Threat to American Freedom.* New York: Stoddart.

Barnett, Antony. 2005. "The Man Who Fought for the Forgotten: Peter Benenson, 1921–2005, Founder of Amnesty International." In *Observer/UK.* London. 27 February. At observer.guardian.co.uk/uk_news/story/0,6903,14266,00.html.

Barnett, Michael, and Martha Finnemore. 1999. "The Politics, Power, and Pathologies of International Organizations." *International Organization* 53:699–732.

Barr, Bob. 2002. "Protecting National Sovereignty in an Era of National Meddling." *Harvard Journal on Legislation* 39(2):299–324.

Bechler, Rosemary. 2004. "Islam and Politics Don't Mix: Massoud Romdhani Interviewed." In *Open Democracy*, vol. 2004.

Bello, Walden. 1999. *Dark Victory: The United States and Global Poverty.* London: Pluto.

———. 2000. "UNCTAD: Time to Lead, Time to Challenge the WTO." Pp. 163–174 in *Globalize This! The Battle Against the World Trade Organization and Corporate Rule,* edited by K. Danaher and R. Burbach. Monroe, ME: Common Courage.

———. 2003. *Deglobalization: New Ideas for Running the World Economy.* London: Zed.

Benchmark Environmental Consulting. 1996. "Democratic Global Civil Governance Report of the 1995 Benchmark Survey of NGOs." Royal Ministry of Foreign Affairs, Oslo.

Bendell, Jem. 2004. "Flags of Inconvenience? The Global Compact and the Future of the United Nations." Nottingham University Business School, Nottingham, UK. At www.globalpolicy.org/reform/business/2004/flags.pdf.

Bennett, W. Lance. 2003. "Communicating Global Activism: Some Strengths and Vulnerabilities of Networked Politics." In *Cyberprotest: New Media, Citizens and Social Movements,* edited by W. van de Donk, B. D. Loader, P. G. Nixon, and D. Rucht. London: Routledge.

———. 2004. "Branded Political Communication: Lifestyle Politics, Logo Campaigns, and the Rise of Global Citizenship." In *The Politics Behind Products: Using the Market as a Site for Ethics and Action,* edited by M. Micheletti, A. Follesdal, and D. Stolle. New Brunswick, NJ: Transaction.

———. 2005. "Social Movements Beyond Borders: Understanding Two Eras of Transnational Activism." Pp. 203–226 in *Transnational Protest and Global Activism,* edited by D. della Porta and S. Tarrow. Lanham, MD: Rowman & Littlefield.

Bennis, Phyllis. 1997. *Calling the Shots: How Washington Dominates Today's UN.* New York: Olive Branch.

———. 2006. *Challenging Empire: How People, Governments, and the UN Defy US Power.* Northampton, MA: Olive Branch.

Black, Richard. 2005. "Inuit Sue US over Climate Policy." *BBC News,* 8 December. At news.bbc.co.uk/2/hi/science/nature/4511556.stm.

Bob, Clifford. 2004. "Contesting Transnationalism: Anti-NGO Mobilization and World Politics." Presented at the American Political Science Association Annual Meeting.

Boli, John. 1999. "Conclusion: World Authority Structures and Legitimation." Pp. 267–302 in *Constructing World Culture: International Nongovernmental Organizations Since 1875,* edited by J. Boli and G. M. Thomas. Stanford: Stanford University Press.

Boli, John, and George M. Thomas. 1999. *Constructing World Culture: International Nongovernmental Organizations Since 1875.* Stanford: Stanford University Press.

Bonacich, Edna, and Richard Applebaum. 2000. *Behind the Label: Inequality in the Los Angeles Apparel Industry.* Berkeley: University of California Press.

Boswell, Terry, and Christopher Chase-Dunn. 2000. *The Spiral of Capitalism and Socialism.* Boulder, CO: Lynne Rienner.

Boulding, Elise. 1990. *Building a Global Civic Culture.* Syracuse: Syracuse University Press.

Brecher, Jeremy, Tim Costello, and Brendan Smith. 2000. *Globalization from Below: The Power of Solidarity.* Cambridge, MA: South End.

Broad, Robin. 2006. "Research, Knowledge, & the Art of 'Paradigm Maintenance': The

World Bank's Development Economics Vice-Presidency (DEC)." *Review of International Political Economy* 13:387–419.

Brooks, Ethel. 2005. "Transnational Campaigns Against Child Labor: The Garment Industry in Bangladesh." Pp. 121–140 in *Coalitions Across Borders: Transnational Protest and the Neoliberal Order*, edited by J. Bandy and J. Smith. Lanham, MD: Rowman & Littlefield.

Brulle, Robert J., and J. Craig Jenkins. 2005. "Foundations and the Environmental Movement: Priorities, Strategies, and Impact." In *Foundations for Social Change: Critical Perspectives on Philanthropy and Popular Movements*, edited by D. Faber and D. McCarthy. Lanham, MD: Rowman & Littlefield.

Bruno, Kenny, and Joshua Karliner. 2002. *Earthsummit.biz: The Corporate Takeover of Sustainable Development*. Oakland: Food First.

Brysk, Allison. 2000. *From Tribal Village to Global Village: Indigenous Peoples' Struggles in Latin America*. Stanford: Stanford University Press.

Bunting, Madeleine. 2006. "Last Year, the Politics of Global Inequality Finally Came of Age." In *Guardian/UK*. At *www.guardian.co.uk/comment/story/0,,1676369,00.html*.

Burawoy, Michael. 2004. "The World Needs Public Sociology." *Sosiologisk tidsskrift* (Journal of Sociology, Norway). At *http://sociology.berkeley.edu/faculty/burawoy/burawoypdf* PS.Norway.pdf.

Buss, Doris, and Didi Herman. 2003. *Globalizing Family Values: The Christian Right in International Politics*. Minneapolis: University of Minnesota Press.

Byerly, Carolyn M. 2006. "Those Missing Media Voices." In TomPaine.com At www .tompaine.com/articles/2006/11/20/those_missing_media_voices.php.

Campbell, John L. 2004. *Institutional Change and Globalization*. Princeton: Princeton University Press.

Castells, Manuel. 1996. *The Rise of the Network Society*. Cambridge: Blackwell.

Cavanagh, John, and Jerry Mander. 2004. *Alternatives to Economic Globalization: A Better World Is Possible*. 2nd ed. San Francisco: Berrett-Koehler.

Chabot, Sean. 2005. "Activism across Borders, Dialogue across Differences: A Freirean Reinvention of Scale Shift and Transnational Contention." Manuscript.

Charnovitz, Steve. 1997. "Two Centuries of Participation: NGOs and International Governance." *Michigan Journal of International Law* 18:183–286.

———. 2002. "Triangulating the World Trade Organization." *American Journal of International Law* 96:28–55.

Chase-Dunn, Christopher. 1998. *Global Formation, Updated Edition*. Boulder, CO: Rowman & Littlefield.

———. 2002. "Globalization from Below: Toward a Collectively Rational and Democratic Global Commonwealth." *The Annals of the American Academy of Political and Social Science* 581:48–61.

Chatfield, Charles. 1992. *The American Peace Movement: Ideals and Activism*. New York: Twayne.

———. 1997. "Intergovernmental and Nongovernmental Associations to 1945." Pp. 19–41 in *Transnational Social Movements and World Politics: Solidarity Beyond the State*, edited by J. Smith, C. Chatfield, and R. Pagnucco. Syracuse: Syracuse University Press.

———. 2007. "National Insecurity: From Dissent to Protest Against U.S. Foreign Policy."

Pp. 456–516 in *The Long War: A New History of U.S. National Security Policy since World War II,* edited by A. J. Bacevich. New York: Columbia University Press.

Chesters, Graeme. 2004. "Global Complexity and Global Civil Society." *Voluntas: International Journal of Voluntary and Non-Profit Organizations* 15:323–342.

Chicago Council on Foreign Relations and Program on International Policy Attitudes. 2004. "The Hall of Mirrors: Perceptions and Misperceptions in the Congressional Foreign Policy Process." University of Maryland, College Park, MD.

Chua, Amy. 2003. *World on Fire: How Exporting Free Market Democracy Breeds Ethnic Hatred and Global Instability.* New York: Anchor.

Clark, Ann Marie. 2003. *Diplomacy of Conscience: Amnesty International and Changing Human Rights Norms.* Princeton: Princeton University Press.

Clark, John D. 2003. *Worlds Apart: Civil Society and the Battle for Ethical Globalization.* Bloomfield, CT: Kumarian.

Clayman, Stephen E., and Ann Reisner. 1998. "Editorial Conferences and Assessments of Newsworthiness." *American Sociological Review* 63:178–199.

Cobb, Roger, Jennie-Kieth Ross, and Marc Howard Ross. 1976. "Agenda Building as a Comparative Political Process." *American Political Science Review* 70:126–138.

Coleman, William D., and Tony Porter. 2000. "International Institutions, Globalization and Democracy: Assessing the Challenges." *Global Society* 14:377–398.

Coleman, William D., and Sarah Wayland. 2004. "Global Civil Society and Non-Territorial Governance: Some Empirical Reflections." *Global Governance* 12(4):523–526.

Cortright, David. 1993. *Peace Works.* Boulder, CO: Westview.

Cortright, David, and Ron Pagnucco. 1997. "Limits to Transnationalism: The 1980s Freeze Campaign." Pp. 159–173 in *Solidarity Beyond the State: The Dynamics of Transnational Social Movements,* edited by J. Smith, C. Chatfield, and R. Pagnucco. Syracuse: Syracuse University Press.

Couch, Colin. 2004. *Post-Democracies.* Cambridge: Polity.

Cullen, Pauline. 2005. "Obstacles to Transnational Cooperation in the European Social Policy Platform." Pp. 71–94 in *Coalitions Across Borders: Transnational Protest and the Neoliberal Order,* edited by J. Bandy and J. Smith. Lanham, MD: Rowman & Littlefield.

Daly, Herman E. 1996. *Beyond Growth: The Economics of Sustainable Development.* Boston: Beacon.

———. 2002. "Globalization versus Internationalization, and Four Economic Arguments for Why Internationalization is a Better Model for World Community." At www.bsos. umd.edu/socy/conference/newpapers/daly.rtf.

Davenport, Christian, Hank Johnston, and Carol Mueller. 2005. *Repression and Mobilization.* Minneapolis: University of Minnesota Press.

Davis, Gerald, Doug McAdam, W. Richard Scott, and Mayer Zald. 2005. *Social Movements and Organizational Theory.* New York: Cambridge University Press.

Dawkins, Kristin. 2003. *Global Governance.* Toronto: Seven Stories.

DeBenedetti, Charles. 1980. *Peace Reform in American History.* Bloomington: Indiana University Press.

Deen, Thalif. 2002. "US Dollars Yielded Unanimous UN Vote Against Iraq." *Inter Press Service,* 11 November. At *www.globalpolicy.org/security/issues/iraq/attack/2002/1111dollars.htm.*

della Porta, Donatella. 2005. "Multiple Belongings, Tolerant Identities, and the Construction of 'Another Politics': Between the European Social Forum and the Local Social Flora." Pp. 175–202 in *Transnational Protest and Global Activism*, edited by D. della Porta and S. Tarrow. Lanham, MD: Rowman & Littlefield.

della Porta, Donatella, Massimiliano Andretta, Lorenzo Mosca, and Herbert Reiter. 2006. *Globalization from Below: Transnational Activists and Protest Networks*. Minneapolis: University of Minnesota Press.

della Porta, Donatella, and Herbert Reiter. Forthcoming. "The Policing of Transnational Protest: A Conclusion." In *Policing Transnational Protest in the Aftermath of the "Battle of Seattle,"* edited by D. Della Porta, A. Peterson, and H. Reiter. Lanham, MD: Rowman & Littlefield.

della Porta, Donatella, and Dieter Rucht. 1995. "Left-Libertarian Movements in Context: A Comparison of Italy and West Germany, 1965–1990." Pp. 229–272 in *The Politics of Social Protest: Comparative Perspectives on States and Social Movements*, edited by B. Klandermans and C. Jenkins. Minneapolis: University of Minnesota Press.

Diamond, Jared. 2005. *Collapse: How Civilizations Choose to Fail or Succeed*. New York: Penguin.

Diani, Mario. 2003. "Introduction: Social Movements, Contentious Actions, and Social Networks: 'From Metaphor to Substance?'" Pp. 1–19 in *Social Movements and Networks*, edited by M. Diani and D. McAdam. Oxford: Oxford University Press.

Diani, Mario, and Ivano Bison. 2004. "Organizations, Coalitions and Movements." *Theory and Society* 33:281–309.

DiMaggio, Paul J., and Walter W. Powell. 1991. "The Iron Cage Revisited: Institutional Isomorphism and Collective Rationality in Organization Fields." Pp. 63–82 in *The New Institutionalism in Organizational Analysis*, edited by W. W. Powell and P. J. DiMaggio. Chicago: University of Chicago Press.

Doherty, Brian, and Timothy Doyle. 2006. "Friends of the Earth International: Negotiating a Transnational Identity." *Environmental Politics* 15:860–880.

Domhoff, G. William. 1998. *Who Rules America: Power and Politics in the Year 2000*. Mountain View, CA: Mayfield.

Economist, The. 2000. "A Survey of the New Economy." *The Economist* (23 September):11–19.

Economy, Elizabeth C. 2004. *The River Runs Black: The Environmental Challenge to China's Future*. Ithaca: Cornell University Press.

Edwards, Bob, and Michael Foley. 1997. "Social Capital and the Political Economy of Our Dissent." *American Behavioral Scientist* 40:668–677.

Edwards, Bob, Michael Foley, and Mario Diani, eds. 2001. *Beyond Tocqueville: Social Capital in Comparative Perspective*. Lebanon, NH: University Press of New England.

Edwards, Bob, and John D. McCarthy. 2004. "Resources and Social Movement Mobilization." Pp. 116–151 in *Blackwell Companion to Social Movements*, edited by D. A. Snow, S. A. Soule, and H. Kriesi. New York: Blackwell.

Ellison, Katherine. 2002. "Kyoto, U.S.A.: Tackling Climate Change at the Local Level." *Grist Magazine: Environmental News and Analysis*, 31 July.

Epstein, Barbara. 1991. *Political Protest and Cultural Revolution: Nonviolent Direct Action in the 1970s and 1980s*. Berkeley: University of California Press.

Ericson, Richard, and Aaron Doyle. 1999. "Globalization and the Policing of Protest: The Case of APEC 1997." *British Journal of Sociology* 50:589–608.

Escobar, Arturo. 2003. "Other Worlds Are (Already) Possible: Self-Organisation, Complexity, and Post-Capitalist Cultures." Pp. 349–358 in *Challenging Empires: The World Social Forum,* edited by J. Sen, A. Anand, A. Escobar, and P. Waterman. At www.choike.org/nuevo_eng/informes/1557.html.

Escobar, Arturo, and Sonia E. Alvarez. 1992. *The Making of Social Movements in Latin America: Identity, Strategy, and Democracy.* Boulder, CO: Westview.

Evans, Peter B. 1997. "The Eclipse of the State? Reflections on Stateness in an Era of Globalization." *World Politics* 50:62–87.

Evans, Robert. 2000. "UN: Report Calls WTO 'Nightmare.'" *Reuters,* 11 August. At http://corpwatch.org/article.php?id=659.

Evans, Susan M., and Harry C. Boyt. 1986. *Free Spaces: The Sources of Democratic Change in America.* New York: Harper & Row.

Faber, Daniel. 2005. "Building a Transnational Environmental Justice Movement: Obstacles and Opportunities in the Age of Globalization." Pp. 43–68 in *Coalitions Across Borders: Transnational Protest and the Neoliberal Order,* edited by J. Bandy and J. Smith. Lanham, MD: Rowman & Littlefield.

Falk, Richard 2005. "The World Speaks on Iraq." *The Nation,* 1 August. At www.thenation.com/doc/20050801/falk.

Falk, Richard, and Andrew Strauss. 2001. "Toward Global Parliament." *Foreign Affairs* 80(1):212–220.

Farrell, Mary, Bjorn Hettne, and Luk Langenhove. 2005. *Global Politics and Regionalism.* London: Pluto.

Ferree, Myra Marx. 2005. "Soft Repression: Ridicule, Stigma, and Silencing in Gender-Based Movements." Pp. 138–158 in *Mobilization and Repression,* edited by C. Davenport, H. Johnston, and C. Mueller. Minneapolis: University of Minnesota Press.

Ferree, Myra Marx, William A. Gamson, Jurgen Gerhards, and Dieter Rucht. 2002. *Shaping Abortion Discourse: Democracy and the Public Sphere in Germany and the United States.* New York: Cambridge University Press.

Ferree, Myra Marx, and Beth B. Hess. 1985. *Controversy and Coalition: The New Feminist Movement.* Boston: Twayne.

Ferree, Myra Marx, and Carol Mueller. 2004. "Feminism and the Women's Movement: A Global Perspective." Pp. 576–607 in *The Blackwell Companion to Social Movements,* edited by D. A. Snow, S. A. Soule, and H. Kriesi. New York: Blackwell.

Fetner, Tina. 2001. "Working Anita Bryant: The Impact of Christian Antigay Activism on Lesbian and Gay Movement Claims." *Social Problems* 48:411–428.

———. Forthcoming. *Fighting the Right: How the Religious Right Changed Lesbian and Gay Activism.* Minneapolis: University of Minnesota Press.

Finnemore, Martha. 1996. *National Interests in International Society.* Ithaca: Cornell University Press.

Finnemore, Martha, and Kathryn Sikkink. 1998. "International Norm Dynamics and Political Change." *International Organization* 52:887–917.

Fisher, Dana R., Kevin Stanley, David Berman, and Gina Neff. 2005. "How Do Organizations Matter? Mobilization and Support for Participants at Five Globalization Protests." *Social Problems* 52:102–121.

Fisher, William, and Thomas Ponniah, eds. 2003. *Another World Is Possible: Popular Alternatives to Globalization at the World Social Forum.* New York: Zed.

Flacks, Richard. 1988. *Making History: The American Left and the American Mind.* New York: Columbia University Press.

Florini, Ann. 2003. *The Coming Democracy: New Rules for Running a New World.* Washington, DC: Island.

Ford Foundation. 2004. "Close to Home: Case Studies of Human Rights Work in the United States."

Foster, John W. 1999. "Civil Society and Multilateral Theatres." Pp. 129–195 in *Whose World Is It Anyway? Civil Society, the United Nations, and the Multilateral Future,* edited by J. W. Foster and A. Anand. Ottawa: United Nations Association of Canada.

———. 2005. "The Trinational Alliance Against NAFTA: Sinews of Solidarity." Pp. 209–230 in *Coalitions Across Borders: Transnational Protest and the Neoliberal Order,* edited by J. Bandy and J. Smith. Lanham, MD: Rowman & Littlefield.

Foster, John W., and Anita Anand, eds. 1999. *Whose World Is It Anyway? Civil Society, the United Nations, and the Multilateral Future.* Ottawa: United Nations Association of Canada.

Fox, Jonathan. 2002. "Assessing Binational Civil Society Coalitions: Lessons from the Mexico-U.S. Experience." Pp. 341–417 in *Cross-Border Dialogues: U.S.-Mexico Social Movement Networking,* edited by D. Brooks and J. Fox. La Jolla, CA: Center for U.S.-Mexican Studies, University of California–San Diego.

Fox, Jonathan, and L. David Brown. 1998. *The Struggle for Accountability: The World Bank, NGOs, and Grassroots Movements.* Cambridge, MA: MIT Press.

Frank, Robert H. 2000. *Luxury Fever.* Princeton: Princeton University Press.

Freeman, Jo. 1972. "The Tyranny of Structurelessness." Pp. 285–299 in *Radical Feminism,* edited by A. Koedt, E. Levine, and A. Rapone. New York: Quadrangle.

Friedland, Roger, and Robert R. Alford. 1991. "Bringing Society Back In: Symbols, Practices, and Institutional Contradictions." Pp. 232–263 in *The New Institutionalism in Organizational Analysis,* edited by W. W. Powell and P. J. DiMaggio. Chicago: University of Chicago Press.

Friedman, Elisabeth Jay, Ann Marie Clark, and Kathryn Hochstetler. 2005. *Sovereignty, Democracy, and Global Civil Society: State-Society Relations at the UN World Conferences.* Albany: State University of New York Press.

Friends of the Earth International. 2004. "World Bank Spins Renewable Energy Conference." Press Release, 3 June . At www.foe.co.uk/resource/press_releases/world_bank _spins_renewable_03062004.html.

Frith, Maxine. 2005. "The Ethical Revolution Sweeping Through the World's Sweatshops." *Independent,* 16 April. At www.commondreams.org/headlines05/0416-01.htm.

Gaer, Felice D. 1996. "Reality Check: Human Rights NGOs Confront Governments at the UN." Pp. 51–66 in *NGOs, the UN, and Global Governance,* edited by T. G. Weiss and L. Gordenker. Boulder, CO: Lynne Rienner.

Gamson, William A. 1991. "Commitment and Agency in Social Movements." *Sociological Forum* 6:27–50.

————. 1992. *Talking Politics*. Cambridge: Cambridge University Press.

————. 2004. "Bystanders, Public Opinion, and the Media." Pp. 242–261 in *The Black-well Companion to Social Movements*, edited by D. A. Snow, S. A. Soule, and H. Kriesi. Oxford: Blackwell.

Gamson, William A., David Croteau, William Hoynes, and Theodore Sasson. 1992. "Media Images and the Social Construction of Reality." *Annual Review of Sociology* 18:373–393.

Gamson, William A., and David Meyer. 1996. "The Framing of Political Opportunity." Pp. 275–290 in *Political Opportunities, Mobilizing Structures and Framing: Social Movement Dynamics in Cross-National Perspective*, edited by D. McAdam, J. McCarthy, and M. Zald. New York: Cambridge University Press.

Gamson, William A., and Antonio Modigliani. 1989. "Media Discourse and Public Opinion on Nuclear Power." *American Journal of Sociology* 95:1–37.

George, Jane. 2005. "ICC seeks legal ruling against U.S. on climate change: ICC petition alleges violation of Inuit human rights." Nunatsiaq News, vol. 2006. At www.nunatsiaq.com/news/nunavut/51209_04.html.

Gerhards, Jurgen, and Dieter Rucht. 1992. "Mesomobilization Contexts: Organizing and Framing in Two Protest Campaigns in West Germany." *American Journal of Sociology* 98:555–596.

Gertz, Emily. 2005. "The Snow Must Go On: Inuit Fight Climate Change with Human-Rights Claim against U.S." *Grist Magazine: Environmental News and Commentary* (Online), 26 July. At www.grist.org/news/maindish/2005/07/26/gertz-inuit/index.html.

Giddens, Anthony. 1990. *The Consequences of Modernity*. Stanford: Stanford University Press.

Gillham, Patrick F. 2003. "Mobilizing for Global Justice: Social Movement Organization Involvement in Three Contentious Episodes, 1999–2001." Ph.D. Dissertation, University of Colorado, Boulder.

Glasius, Marlies. 2002. "Expertise in the Cause of Justice: Global Civil Society Influence on the Statute for an International Criminal Court." Pp. 137–169 in *Global Civil Society Yearbook, 2002*, edited by M. Glasius, M. Kaldor, and H. Anheier. Oxford: Oxford University Press.

Glasius, Marlies, and Mary Kaldor. 2002. "The State of Global Civil Society: Before and After September 11." Pp. 3–34 in *Global Civil Society Yearbook, 2002*, edited by M. Glasius, M. Kaldor, and H. Anheier. Oxford: Oxford University Press.

Glasius, Marlies, and Jill Timms. 2006. "The Role of Social Forums in Global Civil Society: Radical Beacon or Strategic Infrastructure." Pp. 190–239 in *Global Civil Society Yearbook 2005/6*, edited by M. Glasius, M. Kaldor, and H. Anheier. Thousand Oaks, CA: Sage.

Goldman, Michael. 2005. *Imperial Nature: The World Bank and Struggles for Social Justice in the Age of Globalization*. New Haven: Yale University Press.

Goldstone, Jack A., ed. 2003. *States, Parties and Social Movements*. New York: Cambridge University Press.

Gowan, Peter. 2004. "UN=U.S." In *Presentation at the European Social Forum*. London.

Greenberg, Josh, and Graham Knight. 2004. "Framing Sweatshops: Nike, Global Production, and the American News Media." *Communication and Critical/Cultural Studies* 1:151–175.

Greenberg, Michael R., David B. Sachsman, Peter M. Sandman, and Kandice L. Salomone. 1989. "Risk, Drama and Geography in Coverage of Environmental Risk by Network TV." *Journalism Quarterly* 66:267–276.

Guardian, The. 2005. "Editorial: Climate Change: US Grassroots Revolt," 17 May. At www. guardian.co.uk/climatechange/story/0,12374,1485651,00.html.

Guidry, John A. 2000. "The Useful State? Social Movements and the Citizenship of Children in Brazil." Pp. 147–180 in *Globalizations and Social Movements: Culture, Power, and the Transnational Public Sphere*, edited by J. A. Guidry, M. D. Kennedy, and M. N. Zald. Ann Arbor: University of Michigan Press.

Guidry, John A., Michael D. Kennedy, and Mayer N. Zald. 2000. "Globalizations and Social Movements: Introduction." Pp. 1–32 in *Globalizations and Social Movements: Culture, Power, and the Global Public Sphere*, edited by J. A. Guidry, M. D. Kennedy, and M. N. Zald. Ann Arbor: University of Michigan Press.

Haddon, Heather. 2000. "Poor People's Summit Grounds Global Community in NYC." Independent Media Center, New York, 20 November. At http://projects.is.asu.edu/ pipermail/hpn/2000-November/001995.html.

Haines, Herbert. 1988. *Black Radicals and the Civil Rights Mainstream, 1954–1970.* Knoxville: University of Tennessee Press.

Halperin, Sandra, and Gordon Laxer. 2003. "Effective Resistance to Corporate Globalization." Pp. 1–23 in *Global Civil Society and Its Limits*, edited by G. Laxer and S. Halperin. New York: Palgrave Macmillan.

Hamm, Brigitte I. 2001. "A Human Rights Approach to Development." *Human Rights Quarterly* 23:1005–1031.

Hanagan, Michael. 2002. "Irish Transnational Social Movements, Migrants, and the State System." Pp. 53–74 in *Globalization and Resistance: Transnational Dimensions of Social Movements*, edited by J. Smith and H. Johnston. Boulder, CO: Rowman & Littlefield.

Hannan, Michael T., and John Freeman. 1977. "The Population Ecology of Organizations." *American Journal of Sociology* 82:929–964.

Hardt, Michael. 2004. "Today's Bandung?" Pp. 230–236 in *A Movement of Movements: Is Another World Really Possible?* edited by T. Mertes. London: Verso.

Hayden, Tom. 2004. "Talking Back to the Global Establishment." *Alternet*, 18 January. At www.alternet.org/story/17593/.

Herman, Edward. 1995. *Triumph of the Market: Essays on Economics, Politics, and the Media.* Boston: South End.

Herman, Edward, and Noam Chomsky. 1988. *Manufacturing Consent.* New York: Pantheon.

Hertz, Noreena. 2001. *The Silent Takeover: Global Capitalism and the Death of Democracy.* New York: The Free Press.

Hill, Tony. 2004. "Three Generations of UN–Civil Society Relations: A Quick Sketch." *Civil Society Observer*, April.

Hippler, Jochen. 1995. *The Democratisation of Disempowerment: The Problem of Democracy in the Third World.* East Haven, CT: Pluto with Transnational Institute.

Hobbs, J., I. Khan, M. Posner, and K. Roth. 2003. "Letter to Louise Fréchette raising concerns on UN Global Compact," 7 April. At http://web.amnesty.org/pages/ec_briefings _global_7April03.

Hochschild, Adam. 1998. *King Leopold's Ghost.* New York: Houghton Mifflin.

Hoge, Warren. 2004. "Latin Americans Losing Hope in Democracy, Report Says." *New York Times*, 22 April, 3A.

Hutton, Will. 2003. *A Declaration of Interdependence: Why America Should Join the World.* New York: W. W. Norton.

Imig, Doug, and Sidney Tarrow. 2001. *Contentious Europeans: Protest and Politics in an Integrating Europe.* Lanham, MD: Rowman & Littlefield.

Indigenous Peoples' Caucus. 2000. "Indigenous Peoples' Seattle Declaration." Pp. 85–91 in *Globalize This! The Battle Against the World Trade Organization and Corporate Rule,* edited by K. Danaher and R. Burbach. Monroe, ME: Common Courage.

International Forum on Globalization. 2002. *Alternatives to Economic Globalization: A Better World Is Possible.* New York: Berrett-Kohler.

International Network for Economic Social and Cultural Rights. 2005. "History of UN Norms for Business Campaign." At www.escr-net.org/EngGeneral/unnorms1.asp.

Inuit Circumpolar Conference—Canada. 2005. "Inuit Petition Inter-American Commission on Human Rights to Oppose Climate Change Caused by the United States of America." Vol. 2005.

Iyengar, Shanto. 1991. *Is Anyone Responsible? How Television Frames Political Issues.* Chicago: University of Chicago Press.

Jackson, Hunter. 2005. "The Blossoming of the Green Economy." *Global Exchange Newsletter* 64(3):3.

Jacobson, David, and Galya Benarieh Ruffer. 2003. "Courts Across Borders: The Implications of Judicial Agency for Human Rights and Democracy." *Human Rights Quarterly* 25:74–92.

Jawara, Fatoumata, and Aileen Kwa. 2003. *Behind the Scenes at the WTO: The Real World of International Trade Negotiations.* New York: Zed and Focus on the Global South.

Jenkins, J. Craig, and Charles Perrow. 1977. "Insurgency of the Powerless: Farm Worker Movements." *American Sociological Review* 42:249–268.

Joachim, Jutta. 2003. "Framing Issues and Seizing Opportunities: The UN, NGOs and Women's Rights." *International Studies Quarterly* 47:247–274.

Johansen, Robert C. 2006. "The Impact of US Policy toward the International Criminal Court on the Prevention of Genocide, War Crimes, and Crimes Against Humanity." *Human Rights Quarterly* 28:301–331.

Johnston, Josee, and Gordon Laxer. 2003. "Solidarity in the Age of Globalization: Lessons from the Anti-MAI and Zapatista Struggles." *Theory and Society* 32:39–91.

Jordan, Lisa, and Peter van Tuijl. 2000. "Political Responsibility in Transnational NGO Advocacy." *World Development* 28:2051–2065.

Juris, Jeffrey Scott. 2004. "Digital Age Activism: Anti-Corporate Globalization and the Cultural Politics of Transnational Networking." Ph.D. Dissertation, University of California–Berkeley.

———. 2008. *Networking Futures: The Movements Against Corporate Globalization.* Durham, NC: Duke University Press.

Kaldor, Mary. 2003. *Global Civil Society: An Answer to War.* Cambridge: Polity.

Karliner, Joshua. 1997. *The Corporate Planet: Ecology and Politics in the Age of Globalization.* San Francisco: Sierra Club.

Katz, Hagai, and Helmut Anheier. 2006. "Global Connectedness: The Structure of Transnational NGO Networks." Pp. 240–265 in *Global Civil Society 2005/6,* edited by M. Glasius, M. Kaldor, and H. Anheier. London: Sage.

Keck, Margaret, and Kathryn Sikkink. 1998. *Activists Beyond Borders.* Ithaca: Cornell University Press.

Kelly, Dominic. 2001. " 'Markets for a Better World?' Implications of the Public-Private Partnership Between the International Chamber of Commerce and the United Nations." International Studies Association Annual Meeting, Chicago, 22–24 February.

Kensington Welfare Rights Union Education Committee. 2002. "Why We're Fighting for Economic Human Rights." Independent Media Center, Philadelphia (*www.phillyimc.org*), 10 April. At *www.nasw-pa.org/displaycommon.cfm?an=1&subsrticlenbr=62* (Archived).

Kent, Deirdre. 2005. *Healthy Money Healthy Planet: Developing Sustainability Through New Money Systems.* Nelson, New Zealand: Craig Potton.

Keraghel, Chloe, and Jai Sen. 2004. "Explorations in Open Space: The World Social Forum and Cultures of Politics." *International Social Science Journal* 182:483–494.

Khagram, Sanjeev. 2004. *Dams and Development: Transnational Struggles for Water and Power.* Ithaca: Cornell University Press.

Khasnabish, Alex. 2004. "Globalizing Hope: The Resonance of Zapatismo and the Political Imagination(s) of Transnational Activism." Working Paper, Institute on Globalization and the Human Condition, McMaster University, Hamilton, Ontario. At http:// globalization.mcmaster.ca/wps/Khasnabish.pdf.

———. 2005. " 'You Will No Longer Be You, Now You Are Us': Zapatismo, Transnational Activism, and the Political Imagination." Ph.D. Dissertation, McMaster University, Hamilton, Ontario.

Khor, Martin. 2000. "How the South is Getting a Raw Deal at the WTO." Pp. 7–53 in *Views from the South: The Effects of Globalization and the WTO on Third World Countries,* edited by S. Anderson. Chicago: Food First.

Kielbowicz, Richard B., and Clifford Scherer. 1986. "The Role of the Press in the Dynamics of Social Movements." Pp. 71–96 in *Research in Social Movements, Conflict and Change,* vol. 9, edited by L. Kriesberg. Greenwich, CT: JAI.

Kim, Sunhyuk, and Phillippe C. Schmitter. 2005. "The Experience of European Integration and Potential for Northeast Asian Integration." *Asian Perspective* 29:5–39.

Kingdon, John W. 1984. *Agendas, Alternatives and Public Policies.* Boston: Little, Brown.

Kingfisher, Catherine. 2003. *Western Welfare in Decline: Globalization and Women's Poverty.* Philadelphia: University of Pennsylvania Press.

Kitchelt, Herbert. 2003. "Landscapes of Political Interest Intermediation: Social Movements, Interest Groups, and Parties in the Early Twenty-First Century." Pp. 81–104 in *Social Movements and Democracy,* edited by P. Ibarra. New York: Palgrave Macmillan.

Klein, Naomi. 1999. *No Logo: Taking Aim at the Brand Name Bullies.* New York: Picador.

Kolb, Felix. 2005. "The Impact of Transnational Protest on Social Movement Organizations: Mass Media and the Making of ATTAC Germany." Pp. 95–119 in *Transnational*

Protest and Global Activism, edited by D. della Porta and S. Tarrow. Lanham, MD: Rowman & Littlefield.

———. 2007. *Protest, Opportunities, and Mechanisms: A Theory of Social Movements and Political Change.* New York: Campus Verlag.

Koopmans, Ruud. 2005. "Repression and the Public Sphere: Discursive Opportunities for Repression against the Extreme Right in Germany in the 1990s." Pp. 159–188 in *Mobilization and Repression,* edited by C. Davenport, H. Johnston, and C. Mueller. Minneapolis: University of Minnesota Press.

Korten, David. 1996. *When Corporations Rule the World.* West Hartford: Kumarian.

———. 1997. "Memo to United Nations General Assembly President, Mr. Razali Ismail." People Centered Development Forum. At *www.pcdf.org/1997/UNfacs.htm.*

Korzeniewicz, Roberto Patricio, and Timothy P. Moran. 1997. "World Economic Trends in the Distribution of Income, 1965–1992." *American Journal of Sociology* 102:1000–1039.

Korzeniewicz, Roberto Patricio, and William C. Smith. 2000. "Poverty, Inequality, and Growth in Latin America: Searching for the High Road to Globalization." *Latin American Research Review* 35(3):7–54.

———. 2001. "Protest and Collaboration: Transnational Civil Society Networks and the Politics of Summitry and Free Trade in the Americas." North-South Center, University of Miami, Miami.

Kriesberg, Louis. 1997. "Social Movements and Global Transformation." Pp. 3–18 in *Transnational Social Movements and World Politics: Solidarity Beyond the State,* edited by J. Smith, C. Chatfield, and R. Pagnucco. Syracuse: Syracuse University Press.

Kriesi, Hanspeter. 1996. "Organizational Development of New Social Movements in a Political Contexts." Pp. 152–184 in *Political Opportunities, Mobilizing Structures and Framing: Social Movement Dynamics in Cross-National Perspective,* edited by D. McAdam, J. McCarthy, and M. Zald. New York: Cambridge University Press.

———. 2004. "Political Context and Opportunity." Pp. 67–90 in *The Blackwell Companion to Social Movements,* edited by D. A. Snow, S. A. Soule, and H. Kriesi. Oxford: Blackwell.

Kriesi, Hanspeter, Ruud Koopmans, Jan Willem Duyvendak, and Marco Giugni. 1995. *New Social Movements in Western Europe: A Comparative Analysis.* Minneapolis: University of Minnesota Press.

Krut, Riva. 1997. "Globalization and Civil Society: NGO Influence on International Decision Making." UN Research Institute for Social Development, Geneva.

Kunstler, James Howard. 1996. "Home from Nowhere." *Atlantic Monthly* 278(3):43–66.

Langman, Lauren. 2005. "From Virtual Public Spheres to Global Justice: A Critical Theory of Internetworked Social Movements." *Sociological Theory* 23:42–74.

Laxer, Gordon, and Sandra Halperin. 2003. *Global Civil Society and Its Limits.* New York: Palgrave Macmillan.

Levy, Marc A., Robert O. Keohane, and Peter M. Haas. 1993. "Improving the Effectiveness of International Environmental Institutions." Pp. 397–426 in *Institutions for the Earth: Sources of Effective International Environmental Protection,* edited by P. Haas, R. Keohane, and M. Levy. Cambridge, MA: MIT Press.

Lichbach, Mark, and Paul Almeida. 2001. "Global Order and Local Resistance: The Neoliberal Institutional Trilemma and the Battle of Seattle." Manuscript, University of California, Riverside.

Lichterman, Paul. 1995. "Piecing Together Multicultural Community: Cultural Differences in Community Building Among Grass-Roots Environmentalists." *Social Problems* 42:513–534.

———. 1996. *The Search for Political Community: American Activists Reinventing Commitment.* New York: Cambridge University Press.

Linz, Juan J., and Alfred Stepan. 1996. *Problems of Democratic Transition and Consolidation: Southern Europe, South America, and Post-Communist Europe.* Baltimore: Johns Hopkins University Press.

Lipsky, Michael. 1968. "Protest as a Political Resource." *American Political Science Review* 62:1144–1158.

Livezey, Lowell W. 1989. "U.S. Religious Organizations and the International Human Rights Movement." *Human Rights Quarterly* 11:14–81.

Luders, Joseph. 2003. "Countermovements, the State, and the Intensity of Racial Contention in the American South." Pp. 27–44 in *States, Parties and Social Movements,* edited by J. A. Goldstone. New York: Cambridge University Press.

Macdonald, Laura. 1997. *Supporting Civil Society: The Political Role of Non-Governmental Organizations in Central America.* New York: St. Martin's.

———. 2005. "Gendering Transnational Social Movement Analysis: Women's Groups Contest Free Trade in the Americas." Pp. 21–42 in *Coalitions Across Borders: Transnational Protest and the Neoliberal Order,* edited by J. Bandy and J. Smith. Lanham, MD: Rowman & Littlefield.

Malamud, Andres. 2004. "Regional Integration in Latin America: Comparative Theories and Institutions." *Sociologia—Problemas e Practicas* 44:135–154.

Malhotra, Kamal, and others. 2003. *Making Global Trade Work for People.* London: Earthscan in cooperation with the United Nations Development Program, Heinrich Böll Foundation, The Rockefeller Foundation, and The Wallace Fund.

Mander, Jerry, and Edward Goldsmith. 1996. *The Case Against the Global Economy and for a Turn Towards the Local.* San Francisco: Sierra Club.

Maney, Gregory M. 2001. "Rival Transnational Networks and Indigenous Rights: The San Blas Kuna in Panama and the Yanomami in Brazil." *Research in Social Movements, Conflicts and Change* 23:103–144.

Markoff, John. 1996. *Waves of Democracy: Social Movements and Political Change.* Thousand Oaks, CA: Pine Forge.

———. 1999. "Globalization and the Future of Democracy." *Journal of World-Systems Research* 5:242–262.

———. 2001. "The Internet and Electronic Communications." Pp. 387–395 in *Encyclopedia of American Cultural and Intellectual History,* vol. 3, edited by M. K. Cayton and P. W. Williams. New York: Scribner's.

———. 2004a. "Democracy." In *Encyclopedia of Social Theory,* volume II, edited by G. Ritzer. Thousand Oaks, CA: Sage.

———. 2004b. "Who Will Construct the Global Order?" Pp. 19–36 in *Transnational Democracy,* edited by B. Williamson. London: Ashgate.

Markoff, John, and Veronica Montecinos. 1993. "The Ubiquitous Rise of Economists." *Journal of Public Policy* 13:37–68.

Marks, Gary, Liesbet Hooghe, and Kermit Blank. 1994. "European Integration and the State." American Political Science Association Meetings, New York, 1–3 September.

Martens, Jens. 2003. *Precarious "Partnerships": Six Problems of the Global Compact between Business and the UN.* New York: Global Policy Forum. At *www.globalpolicy.org/reform/business/2004/0623partnerships.htm.*

Marullo, Sam, Ron Pagnucco, and Jackie Smith. 1996. "Frame Changes and Social Movement Contraction: U.S. Peace Movement Framing After the Cold War." *Sociological Inquiry* 66:1–28.

Massamba, Guy, Samuel M. Kariuki, and Stephen N. Ndegwa. 2004. "Globalization and Africa's Regional and Local Responses." *Journal of Asian and African Studies* 39:29–45.

Mayo, Marjorie. 2005. *Global Citizens: Social Movements and the Challenge of Globalization.* New York: Zed and Canadian Scholars' Press.

McAdam, Doug. 1982. *Political Process and the Development of Black Insurgency.* Chicago: University of Chicago Press.

———. 1988. *Freedom Summer.* New York: Oxford University Press.

McAdam, Doug, John D. McCarthy, and Mayer Zald, eds. 1996. *Comparative Perspectives on Social Movements: Political Opportunities, Mobilizing Structures and Cultural Framings.* New York: Cambridge University Press.

McAdam, Doug, and Ronnelle Paulsen. 1993. "Specifying the Relationship between Social Ties and Activism." *American Journal of Sociology* 99:640–667.

McAdam, Doug, and Dieter Rucht. 1993. "The Cross-National Diffusion of Movement Ideas." *The Annals of the American Academy of Political and Social Science* 528:56–74.

McAdam, Doug, Sidney Tarrow, and Charles Tilly. 2001. *Dynamics of Contention.* New York: Cambridge University Press.

McCarthy, John D. 1987. "Pro-Life and Pro-Choice Mobilization: Infrastructure Deficits and New Technologies." Pp. 49–66 in *Social Movements in an Organizational Society,* edited by M. Zald and J. D. McCarthy. New Brunswick, NJ: Transaction.

———. 1994. "The Interaction of Grass-roots Activists and State Actors in the Production of an Anti-Drunk Driving Media Attention Cycle." Pp. 133–167 in *New Social Movements: From Ideology to Identity,* edited by E. Larana, H. Johnston, and J. Gusfield. Philadelphia: Temple University Press.

———. 1996. "Constraints and Opportunities in Adopting, Adapting and Inventing." Pp. 141–151 in *Comparative Perspectives on Social Movements: Political Opportunities, Mobilizing Structures and Cultural Framings,* edited by D. McAdam, J. McCarthy, and M. Zald. New York: Cambridge University Press.

McCarthy, John D., Clark McPhail, and Jackie Smith. 1996b. "Images of Protest: Selection Bias in Media Coverage of Washington, D.C. Demonstrations." *American Sociological Review* 61:478–499.

McCarthy, John D., Jackie Smith, and Mayer Zald. 1996a. "Accessing Media, Electoral and Government Agendas." Pp. 291–311 in *Comparative Perspectives on Social Movements: Political Opportunities, Mobilizing Structures and Cultural Framings,* edited by D. McAdam, J. McCarthy, and M. Zald. New York: Cambridge University Press.

McCarthy, John D., and Mark Wolfson. 1992. "Consensus Movements, Conflict Movements, and the Cooptation of Civic and State Infrastructures." Pp. 273–300 in *Frontiers in Social Movement Theory,* edited by A. Morris and C. M. Mueller. New Haven, CT: Yale University Press.

McChesney, Robert W. 1999. *Rich Media, Poor Democracy: Communication Politics in Dubious Times.* Champaign-Urbana: University of Illinois Press.

McCright, Aaron, and Riley Dunlap. 2003. "Defeating Kyoto: The Conservative Movement's Impact on U.S. Climate Change Policy." *Social Problems* 50:348–373.

McKenna, Brian. 2005. "Dow Chemical Buys Silence in Michigan." *Counterpunch,* 18 April 2005.

McMichael, Philip. 2003. *Development and Social Change: A Global Perspective.* 3rd ed. Thousand Oaks, CA: Pine Forge.

Meade, Geoff. 2005. "'McLibel' Campaigners Win Legal Aid Battle." *Independent.* UK. At http://news.independent.co.uk/europe/article11256.ece.

Mendez, Juan E., and Javier Mariezcurrena. 1999. "Accountability for Past Human Rights Violations: Contributions of the Inter-American Organs for Protection." *Social Justice* 26:84–107.

Mertes, Tom. 2004. *A Movement of Movements: Is Another World Really Possible?* London: Verso.

Meyer, David, and Suzanne Staggenborg. 1996. "Movements, Countermovements, and the Structure of Political Opportunity." *American Journal of Sociology* 101:1628–1660.

Meyer, John W., John Boli, George M. Thomas, and Francisco O. Ramirez. 1997. "World Society and the Nation-State." *American Journal of Sociology* 103:144–181.

Meyerson, Frederick A. B. 2002. "Burning the Bridge to the 21st Century: The End of the Era of Integrated Conferences?" *Population, Environmental Change and Security Newsletter (PECS):*1, 12.

Mills, C. Wright. 1956. *The Power Elite.* New York: Oxford University Press.

Minkoff, Debra C. 1995. *Organizing for Equality: The Evolution of Women's and Racial Ethnic Organizations in America, 1955–1985.* New Brunswick, NJ: Rutgers University Press.

Minkoff, Debra C., and John D. McCarthy. 2005. "Reinvigorating the Study of Organizational Processes in Social Movements." *Mobilization* 10:401–421.

Moghadam, Valentine. 2000. "Transnational Feminist Networks: Collective Action in an Era of Globalization." *International Sociology* 15:57–85.

———. 2005. *Globalizing Women: Transnational Feminist Networks.* Baltimore: Johns Hopkins University Press.

Monbiot, George. 2003. *The Age of Consent: A Manifesto for a New World Order.* London: Harper Perennial.

Moody, Kim. 1997. *Workers in a Lean World: Unions in the International Economy.* New York: Verso.

Mooney, Chris. 2004. "Blinded by Science." *Columbia Journalism Review.* Vol. 6. At www.cjr.org/issues/2004/6/mooney-science.asp.

Morris, Douglas. 2004. "Globalization and Media Democracy: The Case of Indymedia." In *Shaping the Network Society: The New Role of Civil Society in Cyberspace,* edited by D. Schuler and P. Day. Cambridge, MA: MIT Press.

Munck, Ronaldo. 2002. *Globalization and Labour: The New Great Transformation*. London: Zed.

Murphy, Gillian, and Margaret Levi. 2004. "Coalitions of Contention: The Case of the WTO Protests in Seattle." Seattle, WA.

Nanz, Patrizia, and Jens Steffek. 2004. "Global Governance, Participation and the Public Sphere." *Government and Opposition* 39:314–335.

Nelson, Paul. 1995. *The World Bank and Nongovernmental Organizations: The Limits of Apolitical Development*. New York: St. Martin's.

———. 2001. "Multilateral Development Banks, Transparency and Corporate Globalization." Presented at International Studies Association Annual Meeting, Chicago, 21–24 February.

Nepstad, Sharon Erickson. 2002. "Creating Transnational Solidarity: The Use of Narrative in the U.S.-Central America Peace Movement." Pp. 133–152 in *Globalization and Resistance: Transnational Dimensions of Social Movements*, edited by J. Smith and H. Johnston. Lanham, MD: Rowman & Littlefield.

Niman, Michael I. 2001. "Buy Nothing Day." Alternet, 12 November. At http://alternet.org/story/11901/.

Nimtz, August. 2002. "Marx and Engels: The Prototypical Transnational Actors." Pp. 245–268 in *Restructuring World Politics: The Power of Transnational Agency and Norms*, edited by S. Khagram, J. Riker, and K. Sikkink. Minneapolis: University of Minnesota Press.

Norris, Pippa. 2002. *Democratic Phoenix: Reinventing Political Activism*. New York: Cambridge University Press.

NYC Indymedia. 2000. "Report on New York City Poor People's Summit." November. New York Indymedia. At www.indymedia.nyc.org.

Nye, Joseph S., Jr. 2002. *The Paradox of American Power: Why the World's Only Superpower Can't Go It Alone*. New York: Oxford University Press.

Oberschall, Anthony. 1980. "Loosely Structured Collective Conflict: A Theory and an Application." *Research in Social Movements, Conflict and Change* 3:45–68.

O'Brien, Robert. 2002. "Organizational Politics, Multilateral Economic Organizations and Social Policy." *Global Social Policy* 2:141–161.

———. Forthcoming. *The Global Labour Movement*.

O'Brien, Robert, Anne Marie Goetz, Jan Aard Scholte, and Marc Williams. 2000. *Contesting Global Governance: Multilateral Economic Institutions and Global Social Movements*. New York: Cambridge University Press.

Oliver, Pamela E., and Hank Johnston. 2000. "What a Good Idea! Ideologies and Frames in Social Movement Research." *Mobilization: An International Journal* 5:37–54.

Olsen, Thomas. 2005. *International Zapatismo: The Construction of Solidarity in the Age of Globalization*. New York: Zed.

O'Neill, Kate. 2004. "Transnational Protest: States, Circuses, and Conflict at the Frontline of Global Politics." *International Studies Review* 6:233–251.

Ostry, Sylvia. 2007. "The World Trade Organization: System Under Stress." In *Globalisation and Autonomy*, edited by S. Bernstein. Vancouver: University of British Columbia Press.

Otto, Dianne. 1996. "Nongovernmental Organizations in the United Nations System: The Emerging Role of International Civil Society." *Human Rights Quarterly* 18:107–141.

Pagnucco, Ron, and Jackie Smith. 1993. "The Peace Movement and the Formulation of U.S. Foreign Policy." *Peace and Change* 18:157–181.

Paine, Ellen. 2000. "The Road to the Global Compact: Corporate Power and the Battle over Global Public Policy at The United Nations." Global Policy Forum. At www.globalpolicy.org/reform/papers/2000/road.htm.

Parsons, Craig. 2003. *A Certain Idea of Europe.* Ithaca: Cornell University Press.

Patomäki, Heikki, and Teivo Teivainen. 2004. "The World Social Forum: An Open Space or a Movement of Movements?" *Theory, Culture & Society* 21:145–154.

Paul, James. 1999. "NGO Access at the UN." Vol. 2005. New York: Global Policy Forum.

Paul, Scott. 2005. "Mayors Look to Youth and Forge Ahead." At www.itsgettinghotinhere.org/archives/106.

Pauly, Louis. 1997. *Who Elected the Bankers? Surveillance and Control in the World Economy.* Ithaca: Cornell University Press.

Peet, Richard. 2003. *Unholy Trinity: The IMF, World Bank and WTO.* New York: Zed.

Peoples' Global Action. 2000. "Worldwide Resistance Roundup: Newsletter 'Inspired by' Peoples' Global Action." London.

Peterson, Luke Eric. 2004. "Bilateral Investment Treaties and Development Policy-Making." International Institute for Sustainable Development and Swiss Agency for Development and Cooperation, Winnipeg. At www.iisd.org/publications/pub.aspx?id=658.

Pianta, Mario, and Federico Silva. 2003. "Parallel Summits of Global Civil Society: An Update." Pp. 387–394 in *Global Civil Society Yearbook, 2003,* edited by H. Anheier, M. Kaldor, and M. Glasius. London.

Podobnik, Bruce. 2005. "Resistance to Globalization: Cycles and Evolutions in the Globalization Protest Movement." Pp. 51–68 in *Transforming Globalization: Challenges and Opportunities in the Post 9/11 Era,* edited by B. Podobnik and T. Reifer. Boston: Brill.

Polanyi, Karl. 1944. *The Great Transformation.* Boston: Beacon.

Polletta, Francesca. 2002. *Freedom is an Endless Meeting.* Chicago: University of Chicago Press.

Polletta, Francesca, and James Jasper. 2001. "Collective Identity and Social Movements." *Annual Review of Sociology* 27:283–305.

Porter, Tony. 2005. *Globalization and Finance.* Malden, MA: Polity.

Powell, Walter W., and Paul J. DiMaggio. 1991. *The New Institutionalism in Organizational Analysis.* Chicago: University of Chicago Press.

Price, Richard. 1998. "Reversing the Gun Sights: Transnational Civil Society Targets Land Mines." *International Organization* 52:613–644.

Pring, George W., and Penelope Canan. 1996. *SLAPPs: Getting Sued for Speaking Out.* Philadelphia: Temple University Press.

Putnam, Robert D. 1992. *Making Democracy Work.* Cambridge: Cambridge University Press.

———. 1995. "Bowling Alone: America's Declining Social Capital." *Journal of Democracy* 6:65–78.

Rabkin, Jeremy. 2003. "Why The Left Dominates NGO Advocacy Networks." Presented at conference, "We're Not from the Government, but We're Here to Help You Nongovernmental Organizations: The Growing Power of an Unelected Few." Washington D.C.: American Enterprise Institute. At http://www.aei.org/events/eventID.329,filter./event_detail.asp#.

Radcliff, Benjamin, and Patricia Davis. 2000. "Labor Organization and Electoral Participation in Industrial Democracies." *American Journal of Political Science* 44:132–141.

Reimann, Kim D. 2002. "Building Networks from the Outside In: International Movements, Japanese NGOs, and the Kyoto Climate Change Conference." Pp. 173–189 in *Globalization and Resistance: Transnational Dimensions of Social Movements*, vol. 6, edited by J. Smith and H. Johnston. Lanham, MD: Rowman & Littlefield.

Reitan, Ruth. 2006. *Activism Goes Global: The Internationalization of Activism against Neoliberal Globalization and the Role of the World Social Forum in This Process*. London: Routledge.

———. 2007. "The Global Anti-War Network and the World Social Forum: A Study of Transnational Mobilization." Presented at the International Studies Association (ISA) Convention, Chicago, 28 February–3 March.

Renner, Michael. 2006. "Worldwide Mergers and Acquisitions 1980–1999." At www.globalpolicy.org/socecon/tncs/tables/mergdata.htm.

Revkin, Andrew C. 2005. "Youths Make Spirited Case at Climate Meeting." *New York Times*, 9 December. At www.nytimes.com/2005/12/09/international/americas/09climate.html?ex=1291784400&en=b68ab9c01737c0f8&ei=5089&partner=rssyahoo&emc=rss.

Rich, Bruce. 1994. *Mortgaging the Earth: The World Bank, Environmental Impoverishment and the Crisis of Development*. Boston: Beacon.

Riles, Annelise. 2001. *The Network Inside Out*. Ann Arbor: University of Michigan Press.

Risse, Thomas, Stephen C. Ropp, and Kathryn Sikkink. 1999. *The Power of Human Rights: International Norms and Domestic Change*. New York: Cambridge University Press.

Robinson, William. 1996. *Promoting Polyarchy: Globalization, U.S. Intervention and Hegemony*. Cambridge: Cambridge University Press.

———. 2004. *A Theory of Global Capitalism*. Baltimore: Johns Hopkins University Press.

Rochon, Thomas. 1998. *Culture Moves: Ideas, Activism, and Changing Values*. Princeton: Princeton University Press.

Rootes, Christopher. 2002. "Global Visions: Global Civil Society and the Lessons of European Environmentalism." *Voluntas: International Journal of Voluntary and Nonprofit Organizations* 20:411–429.

———. 2005. "A Limited Transnationalization? The British Environmental Movement." Pp. 21–43 in *Transnational Protest and Global Activism*, edited by D. della Porta and S. Tarrow. Lanham, MD: Rowman & Littlefield.

Rose, Fred. 2000. *Coalitions Across the Class Divide: Lessons from the Labor, Peace, and Environmental Movements*. Ithaca: Cornell University Press.

Rosenthal, Naomi, Meryl Fingrutd, Michele Ethier, Roberta Karant, and David McDonald. 1985. "Social Movements and Network Analysis: A Case Study of Nineteenth-Century Women's Reform in New York State." *American Journal of Sociology* 90:1022–1054.

Rothman, Franklin Daniel, and Pamela E. Oliver. 2002. "From Local to Global: The Anti-Dam Movement in Southern Brazil 1979–1992." Pp. 115–131 in *Globalization and Resistance: Transnational Dimensions of Social Movements*, edited by J. Smith and H. Johnston. Lanham, MD: Rowman & Littlefield.

Rucht, Dieter. 1996. "The Impact of National Contexts on Social Movement Structures: A Cross-Movement and Cross-National Comparison." Pp. 185–204 in *Political Opportunities, Mobilizing Structures and Framing: Social Movement Dynamics in Cross-National Perspective*, edited by D. McAdam, J. McCarthy, and M. Zald. New York: Cambridge University Press.

————. 2000. "Distant Issue Movements in Germany: Empirical Description and Theoretical Reflections." Pp. 76–107 in *Globalizations and Social Movements: Culture, Power, and the Transnational Public Sphere*, edited by J. A. Guidry, M. D. Kennedy, and M. N. Zald. Ann Arbor: University of Michigan Press.

————. 2003. "Social Movements Challenging Neo-liberal Globalization." Pp. 211–227 in *Social Movements and Democracy*, edited by P. Ibarra. New York: Palgrave Macmillan.

————. 2004. "Movements, Allies, Adversaries, and Third Parties." Pp. 197–216 in *The Blackwell Companion to Social Movements*, edited by D. A. Snow, S. A. Soule, and H. Kriesi. Oxford: Blackwell.

Rudra, Nita. 2002. "Globalization and the Decline of the Welfare State in Less-Developed Countries." *International Organization* 56:411–445.

Ruggie, John G. 2002. "The Theory and Practice of Learning Networks: Corporate Social Responsibility and the Global Compact." *Journal of Corporate Citizenship* (Spring): 27–36.

Rupert, Mark. 2000. *Ideologies of Globalization: Contending Visions of a New World Order.* New York: Routledge.

Rupp, Leila J. 1997. *Worlds of Women: The Making of an International Women's Movement.* Princeton: Princeton University Press.

Ryan, Charlotte. 1991. *Prime Time Activism.* Boston: South End.

Sands, Philippe. 2005. *Lawless World: America and the Making and Breaking of Global Rules—From FDR's Atlantic Charter to George W. Bush's Illegal War.* New York: Viking.

Sassen, Saskia. 1998. *Globalization and Its Discontents.* New York: The New Press.

Schell, Jonathan. 2005. "Faking Civil Society." *The Nation,* 25 April. At www.common dreams.org/views05/0407-21.htm.

Schlosberg, Justin. 2006. "The Day the Music Failed: A Reflection on 6 Months after the Live8 Concerts, the Broken Promises and Bob's Unusual Silence." CommonDreams .org. At www.commondreams.org/views06/0105-35.htm.

Schonleitner, Gunther. 2003. "World Social Forum: Making Another World Possible?" Pp. 127–149 in *Globalizing Civic Engagement: Civil Society and Transnational Action*, edited by J. Clark. London: Earthscan.

Schor, Juliet B. 1993. *The Overworked American: The Unexpected Decline of Leisure.* New York: Basic.

————. 2004. *Born to Buy: The Commercialized Child and the New Consumer Culture.* New York: Scribner.

Schreinemacher, Elisabeth. 2005. "IPS Honours Anti-Poverty Alliance." *Inter Press Service News,* 8 December. At www.ipsnews.net.

Schroyer, Trent. 1997. *A World that Works: Building Blocks for a Just and Sustainable Society.* New York: Bootstrap.

Schulz, Markus S. 1998. "Collective Action Across Borders: Opportunity Structures, Network Capacities, and Communicative Praxis in the Age of Advanced Globalization." *Sociological Perspectives* 41:587–617.

Seidman, Gay W. 2000. "Adjusting the Lens: What Do Globalizations, Transnationalism, and the Anti-apartheid Movement Mean for Social Movement Theory?" Pp. 339–358 in *Globalizations and Social Movements: Culture, Power, and the Transnational Public*

Sphere, edited by J. A. Guidry, M. D. Kennedy, and M. N. Zald. Ann Arbor: University of Michigan Press.

———. 2004. "Deflated Citizenship: Labor Rights in a Global Era." Pp. 109–129 in *People Out of Place: Globalization, Human Rights, and the Citizenship Gap,* edited by A. Brysk and G. Shafir. New York: Routledge.

Sell, Susan K. 2003. *Private Power, Public Law: The Globalization of Intellectual Property Rights.* Cambridge: Cambridge University Press.

Sen, Amartya. 1999. "Democracy as a Universal Value." *Journal of Democracy* 10:3–17.

Sen, Jai, Anita Anand, Arturo Escobar, and Peter Waterman. 2003. Challenging Empires: The World Social Forum. Third World Institute. At: www.choike.org.

Sengupta, Arjun. 2000. "Realizing the Right to Development." *Development and Change* 31:553–578.

Shiva, Vandana. 2000. "War Against Nature and the People of the South." Pp. 91–125 in *Views from the South: The Effects of Globalization and the WTO on Third World Countries,* edited by S. Anderson. Chicago: Food First.

———. 2005. *Earth Democracy: Justice, Sustainability, and Peace.* Boston: South End.

Sieg, Richard. 2007. "At International Commission, Inuit Want To See Change in U.S. Policy on Global Warming." *Vermont Journal of Environmental Law* 8. At www.vjel.org/news/NEWS100058.html.

Sikkink, Kathryn. 1986. "Codes of Conduct for Transnational Corporations: The Case of the WHO/UNICEF Code." *International Organization* 40:815–840.

Sklair, Leslie. 1997. "Social Movements for Global Capitalism: The Transnational Capitalist Class in Action." *Review of International Political Economy* 4:514–538.

———. 1999. "Competing Conceptions of Globalization." *Journal of World Systems Research* 5:143–162.

———. 2001. *The Transnational Capitalist Class.* Cambridge: Blackwell.

———. 2002. *Globalization and Its Alternatives.* New York: Oxford University Press.

Skogly, Sigrun. 1993. "Structural Adjustment and Development: Human Rights—An Agenda for Change?" *Human Rights Quarterly* 15:751.

Slaughter, Anne-Marie. 2004a. "Disaggregated Sovereignty: Towards the Public Accountability of Global Government Networks." *Government and Opposition* 39:159–190.

———. 2004b. *A New World Order.* Princeton: Princeton University Press.

Smith, Christian. 1996. *Resisting Reagan: The U.S. Central America Peace Movement.* Chicago: University of Chicago Press.

Smith, Jackie. 2000. "Framing the Nonproliferation Debate: Transnational Activism and International Nuclear Weapons Negotiations." Pp. 55–82 in *Research in Social Movements, Conflict and Change,* vol. 22, edited by P. Coy. Greenwood, CT: JAI.

———. 2002. "Globalizing Resistance: The Battle of Seattle and the Future of Social Movements." Pp. 183–199 in *Globalization and Resistance: Transnational Dimensions of Social Movements,* edited by J. Smith and H. Johnston. Lanham, MD: Rowman & Littlefield.

———. 2004. "Exploring Connections between Global Integration and Political Mobilization." *Journal of World Systems Research* 10:255–285.

———. 2005a. "Building Bridges or Building Walls? Explaining Regionalization among Transnational Social Movement Organizations." *Mobilization* 10:251–270.

———. 2005b. "Transnational Social Movement Organizations." Pp. 226–248 in *Social Movements and Organizational Theory*, edited by G. Davis, D. McAdam, W. R. Scott, and M. Zald. New York: Cambridge University Press.

Smith, Jackie, Charles Chatfield, and Ron Pagnucco, eds. 1997. *Transnational Social Movements and Global Politics: Solidarity Beyond the State.* Syracuse: Syracuse University Press.

Smith, Jackie, and Tina Fetner. 2007. "Structural Approaches in the Study of Social Movements." In *Handbook of Social Movements: Social Movements Across Disciplines*, edited by B. Klandermans and C. Roggeband. New York: Springer.

Smith, Jackie, Marina Karides, Marc Becker, Dorval Brunelle, Christopher Chase-Dunn, Dontatella della Porta, Rosalba Icaza, Jeffrey Juris, Lorenzo Mosca, Ellen Reese, Peter Jay Smith, and Rolando Vásquez. 2008. *Global Democracy and the World Social Forums.* Boulder, CO: Paradigm.

Smith, Jackie, John McCarthy, Clark McPhail, and Boguslaw Augustin. 2001. "From Protest to Agenda-Building: Description Bias in Media Coverage of Protest Events in Washington, D.C." *Social Forces* 79:1397–1423.

Smithson, Shelley 2002. "Big Plan on Campus: Universities Combat Climate Change." *Grist Magazine: Environmental News and Commentary*, 31 July.

Snow, David, E. B. Rochford, S. Warden, and Robert Benford. 1986. "Frame Alignment Processes, Micromobilization and Movement Participation." *American Sociological Review* 51:273–286.

Snow, David A., Louis A. Zurcher, and Sheldon Ekland-Olson. 1980. "Social Networks and Social Movements: A Microstructural Approach to Differential Recruitment." *American Sociological Review* 45:787–801.

Snyder, Anna. 2003. *Setting the Agenda for Global Peace: Conflict and Consensus Building.* Burlington, VT: Ashgate.

South Commission. 1989. *Redefining Wealth and Progress: The Caracas Report on Alternative Development Indicators.* New York: Bootstrap.

Starhawk. 2001. "Response to 'Manifest of Anti-capitalist Youth against the World Social Forum.'" Electronic Communication.

Stark, David, Balazs Vedres, and Laszlo Bruszt. 2005. "Rooted Transnational Publics: Integrating Foreign Ties and Civic Activism." *Theory and Society* 35:323–349.

Starr, Amory. 2000. *Naming the Enemy: Anti-Corporate Movements Confront Globalization.* New York: Zed.

Stearns, Linda Brewster, and Paul D. Almeida. 2004. "The Formation of State Actor–Social Movement Coalitions and Favorable Policy Outcomes." *Social Forces* 51:478–504.

Steinberg, Marc W. 1995. "The Roar of the Crowd: Repertoires of Discourse and Collective Action among the Spitalfields Silk Weavers in Nineteenth-Century London." Pp. 57–88 in *Repertoires and Cycles of Collective Action*, edited by M. Traugott. Durham: Duke University Press.

Sternbach, Nancy Saporta, Marysa Navarro-Aranguren, Patricia Chuchryk, and Sonia E. Alvarez. 1992. "Feminisms in Latin America: From Bogota to San Bernardo." Pp. 207–239 in *The Making of Social Movements in Latin America: Identity, Strategy, and Democracy*, edited by A. Escobar and S. E. Alvarez. Boulder, CO: Westview.

Stewart, Julie. 2004. "When Local Troubles Become Transnational: The Transformation of a Guatemalan Indigenous Rights Movement." *Mobilization* 9:259–278.

Stiglitz, Joseph. 2003. *Globalization and Its Discontents.* New York: W. W. Norton.

Structural Adjustment Participatory Review International Network (SAPRIN). 2002. "The Policy Roots of Economic Crisis and Poverty." Washington, DC: SAPRIN.

Subramaniam, Mangala, Manjusha Gupte, and Debarashmi Mitra. 2003. "Local to Global: Transnational Networks and Indian Women's Grassroots Organizing." *Mobilization* 8:335–352.

Swarts, Heidi J. 2003. "Setting the State's Agenda: Church-Based Community Organizations in American Urban Politics." Pp. 78–106 in *States, Parties and Social Movements,* edited by J. A. Goldstone. New York: Cambridge University Press.

Tarrow, Sidney. 1988. "National Politics and Collective Action." *Annual Review of Sociology* 14:421–440.

———. 1995. "Cycles of Collective Action: Between Moments of Madness and the Repertoire of Contention." Pp. 89–116 in *Repertoires and Cycles of Collective Action,* edited by M. Traugott. Durham: Duke University Press.

———. 2005. *The New Transnational Activism.* New York: Cambridge University Press.

Tavola Della Pace. 2005a. "Call for Global Day of Mobilisation against Poverty, War and Unilateralism." Call to mobilization on September 10, 2005, vol. 2005. At www.un-ngls .org/cso/cso6/appeal.htm.

———. 2005b. "Reclaim Our UN." Porto Alegre, Brazil. At www.un-ngls.org/UN -reform-Tavola%20della%20pace%20-%20WSF%202005.doc.

Teivainen, Teivo. 2002. "The World Social Forum and Global Democratisation: Learning from Porto Alegre." *Third World Quarterly* 23:621–632.

Tharoor, Shashi. 2001. "Are Human Rights Universal?" *New Internationalist,* March. At www.findarticles.com/p/articles/mi_moJQP/is_332/ai_30144069.

Tilly, Charles. 1978. *From Mobilization to Revolution.* Reading, MA: Addison Wesley.

———. 1984. "Social Movements and National Politics." Pp. 297–317 in *Statemaking and Social Movements: Essays in History and Theory,* edited by C. Bright and S. Harding. Ann Arbor: University of Michigan Press.

———. 1990. *Coercion, Capital and European States, AD 990–1990.* Cambridge: Blackwell.

———. 1995. "Globalization Threatens Labor Rights." *International Labor and Working Class History* 47:1–23.

———. 2004. *Social Movements, 1768–2004.* Boulder, CO: Paradigm.

ul Haq, Mahbub. 1989. "People in Development." Pp. 17–25 in *Redefining Wealth and Progress: The Caracas Report on Alternative Development Indicators,* edited by South Commission. New York: Bootstrap.

UN. 2004. "We the Peoples: Civil Society, the United Nations and Global Governance: Report of the Panel of Eminent Persons on United Nations–Civil Society Relations." UN Secretary General, New York.

UN Development Programme. 2000. *Human Development Report 2000: Overcoming Human Poverty.* New York: UNDP.

———. 2001. *Human Development Report 2001: Making New Technologies Work for Human Development.* New York: Oxford University Press.

———. 2002. *Human Development Report 2002: Deepening Democracy in a Fragmented World.* New York: Oxford University Press.

———. 2004. *Human Development Report 2004: Cultural Liberty in Today's Diverse World.* New York: Oxford University Press.

———. 2005. *Human Development Report 2005: International Cooperation at a Crossroads.* New York: Oxford University Press.

UN Food and Agriculture Organization. 2005. "State of Agricultural Commodity Markets." UN Food and Agriculture Organization, Rome.

Urquhart, Brian, and Erskine Childers. 1996. *A World in Need of Leadership: Tomorrow's United Nations.* Uppsala, Sweden: Dag Hammarskjold Foundation.

Vasi, Ion Bogdan. Forthcoming. "Thinking Globally, Planning Nationally, and Acting Locally: Institutional Spheres and the Diffusion of Environmental Practices."

Verba, Sidney, Kay Schlozman, and Henry Brady. 1995. *Voice and Equality: Civic Volunteerism in American Politics.* Cambridge, MA: Harvard University Press.

Wainwright, Hilary. 2003. *Reclaim the State: Adventures in Popular Democracy.* London: Verso, Transnational Institute.

Wallach, Lori, and Patrick Woodall. 2004. *Whose Trade Organization? A Comprehensive Guide to the WTO.* New York: The New Press.

Wallerstein, Immanuel. 1976. *The Modern World System.* New York: Academic.

Wallerstein, Immanuel, ed. 2004. *The Modern World-system In The Longue Duree.* Boulder, CO: Paradigm.

Walton, John, and David Seddon. 1994. *Free Markets and Food Riots: The Politics of Global Adjustment.* Cambridge: Blackwell.

Wapner, Paul. 2002. "Defending Accountability in NGOs." *Chicago Journal of International Law* 3:197–205.

Waterman, Peter. 1998. *Globalization, Social Movements, and the New Internationalisms.* Washington, DC: Mansell.

———. 2001. *Globalization, Social Movements and the New Internationalisms.* New York: Continuum.

———. 2005. "Talking across Difference in an Interconnected World of Labour." Pp. 141–162 in *Coalitions Across Borders: Transnational Protest and the Neoliberal Order,* edited by J. Bandy and J. Smith. Boulder, CO: Rowman & Littlefield.

Waterman, Peter, and Jill Timms. 2004. "Trade Union Internationalism and a Global Civil Society in the Making." Pp. 175–202 in *Global Civil Society 2004/5.* London: Sage.

Whitaker, Chico. 2005. "The World Social Forum: Towards a New Politics?" Presentation at World Social Forum panel, Porto Alegre, Brazil.

Wiest, Dawn, and Jackie Smith. 2007. "Explaining Participation in Regional Transnational Social Movement Organizations." *International Journal of Comparative Sociology* 48:137–166.

Willetts, Peter. 1989. "The Pattern of Conferences." Pp. 35–63 in *Global Issues in the United Nations Framework,* edited by P. Taylor and A. J. R. Groom. New York: St. Martin's.

———. 1996. "Consultative Status for NGOs at the United Nations." Pp. 31–62 in *The Conscience of the World: The Influence of NGOs in the United Nations System,* edited by P. Willetts. London: C. Hurst.

———. 2000. "From 'Consultative Arrangements' to 'Partnership': The Changing Status of NGOs in Diplomacy at the UN." *Global Governance* 6:191–213.

Wise, Timothy A., and Kevin P. Gallagher. 2006. "Doha Round and Developing Countries: Will the Doha Deal Do More Harm than Good?" Research and Information System for Developing Countries, New Delhi.

Wittner, Lawrence. 1997. *Resisting the Bomb: A History of the World Nuclear Disarmament Movement, 1954–1970*. Vol. 2. Stanford: Stanford University Press.

Wolf, Eric. 1982. *Europe and the People without History*. Berkeley: University of California Press.

Wolfson, Mark. 2001. *The Fight Against Big Tobacco: The Movement, the State, and the Public's Health*. Hawthorne, NY: Aldine de Gruyter.

Wood, Lesley Julia. 2004. "The Diffusion of Direct Action Tactics: From Seattle to Toronto and New York." Ph.D. Dissertation, Columbia University, New York.

———. 2005. "Bridging the Chasms: The Case of Peoples' Global Action." Pp. 95–119 in *Coalitions Across Borders: Transnational Protest and the Neoliberal Order*, edited by J. Bandy and J. Smith. Lanham, MD: Rowman & Littlefield.

World Commission on the Social Dimensions of Globalization. 2004. "A Fair Globalization: Creating Opportunities for All."

World Health Organization. 2000. "Tobacco Company Strategies to Undermine Tobacco Control Activities at the World Health Organisation." World Health Organization, Geneva. At www.who.int/genevahearings/inquiry.html.

Wuthnow, Robert. 1989. *Communities of Discourse: Ideology and Social Structure in the Reformation, the Enlightenment, and European Socialism*. Cambridge, MA: Harvard University Press.

———. 1998. *Loose Connections: Joining Together in America's Fragmented Communities*. Cambridge, MA: Harvard University Press.

Zald, Mayer, and John D. McCarthy. 1987. "Religious Groups as Crucibles of Social Movements." Pp. 67–95 in *Social Movements in an Organizational Society*, edited by M. Zald and J. D. McCarthy. New Brunswick, NJ: Transaction.

Zoelle, Diana, and, Jyl J. Josephson. 2005. "Making Democratic Space for Poor People: The Kensington Welfare Rights Union." Pp. 55–74 in *Beyond Global Arrogance: Transnational Democracy and Social Movements*, edited by J. Leatherman and J. Webber. New York: Palgrave Macmillan.

A Funeral
in Mantova

Books by David P. Wagner

The Rick Montoya Italian Mysteries
Cold Tuscan Stone
Death in the Dolomites
Murder Most Unfortunate
Return to Umbria
A Funeral in Mantova

A Funeral in Mantova

A Rick Montoya Italian Mystery

David P. Wagner

Poisoned Pen Press

First Edition 2018

10 9 8 7 6 5 4 3 2 1

Library of Congress Control Number: 2017946815

ISBN: 9781464209512   Trade Paperback
ISBN: 9781464209529   Ebook

Poisoned Pen Press
4014 N. Goldwater Blvd., #201
Scottsdale, AZ 85251
www.poisonedpenpress.com
info@poisonedpenpress.com

Printed in the United States of America

For Bill Oglesby, fellow writer, intrepid travel companion,
and *zuppa inglese* expert, with thanks for
all the help and encouragement,
right from the beginning.

The body rolled off the planks and slipped into the water with barely a splash. It sank a few inches, bobbed back to the surface, and was immediately embraced by the river's steady current. A man stood watching, his form casting barely a shadow in the weak light of the morning. He took in three short breaths, gaining his composure after the exertion of the struggle. The fishing pole lay where it had been placed, ready to be stowed in the boat that was tied a few feet away. He moved his eyes from the body, now almost invisible in the dark water, and surveyed the scene. Leave it as it is. He turned and walked away.

The small wooden dock jutted out at a point where the Mincio widened before turning into a virtual lake at Mantova. After passing the city it would squeeze back to normal size before emptying into the mighty Po for the final kilometers to the Adriatic Sea. Once the border between Venice and Milan, where the armies of those two powerful city states clashed in mortal combat, the river ran through land now known more for food than violent history. This was the eastern tip of the region of Lombardy, its point shaped like a local cheese knife.

On this morning, like so many mornings in the northern Italian winter, the water and the land were covered with dense Lombard fog. It made driving treacherous, sometimes nearly impossible, but the Mantovani accepted it as a fact of life. The locals also believed, with some justification, that the moist air contributed to the quality of what the land produced, and helped age the cheeses and cure the meats for which the area was famous. Stumbling through zero visibility in the winter was a small price to pay.

The body glided under the layer of fog as it moved into the center of the river. It was too early in the day for any boats, which was why the dead man had always found this hour, just before dawn, to be the perfect time for fishing the dark waters. Usually his first cast was at a small bend where trout often congregated. They were huddled there now, just above the mud, but on this morning there would be nothing to tempt them.

In the distance a string of lights outlined the Via dei Molini causeway which connected Mantova's medieval center with flat farmland to the east. The water of the Lago Superiore narrowed toward the single passage under the causeway, taking the body with it. The lifeless figure swept slowly over the small dam that ran under the roadway, twirled for a few moments in the eddy below, and continued toward the middle of the Lago di Mezzo. The next barrier was another causeway, the last obstacle of any length between the city and the Po. But the capricious currents in this part of the river would keep the body here, as if they had decided the man should not be allowed to stray far from his home, even in death. The dark figure floated toward the shore and came to rest against the rocks below the walking path along the river's edge.

The grim ramparts of Castello di San Giorgio looked down on the scene. Even in its modern role as a museum, the gray stone exuded cold malevolence. There was a time in Mantova's history when a body floating past its walls had been as normal as a farmer trudging to market—but this was not the fifteenth century.

The young jogger who found the body would have nightmares for weeks afterward.

Chapter One

Rick felt the faint vibration of his cell phone before hearing the ring. He pulled it from his pocket and saw that the number was from the States, though not an area code he recognized. Given the hour in Rome, the caller had to be an earlier riser—very early, if calling from the West Coast. He moved to the side of Piazza Navona and took a seat on one of its stone benches.

"Montoya."

"Mr. Montoya, my name is Alexis Coleman. I am in the employ of Angelo Rondini."

The voice was smooth and efficient. "In the employ" was an expression more appropriate for use in a nineteenth-century British novel than by a woman whose American accent Rick could not place. He prided himself on detecting accents, both American and Italian; it came with being a professional interpreter. But he couldn't decide what part of the country she was from. More intriguing was her tone. It implied that he would know who Angelo Rondini was.

"Good morning, Ms. Coleman. How can I help you?"

"Mr. Rondini would like to contract your services."

"I'm always glad to hear such words. How did he find out about my services? If I might ask."

"It is a perfectly reasonable question. The chief of the economics section in the embassy recommended you."

The economics counselor at the embassy in Rome was a good friend of Rick's father from an earlier assignment in their careers. It always helped to have friends in high places.

"Mr. Rondini spoke with Mr. Treacy?"

"Mr. Rondini spoke with the ambassador, who gave him Mr. Treacy's name. I called Mr. Treacy."

Aha. Not just anyone, Rick knew, could pick up the phone and talk to the American ambassador in Rome. Perhaps, like the ambassador, Mr. Rondini had been a major contributor to the president's election campaign. Whoever this Rondini guy was, he had clout. And he was above speaking to anyone lower than the ambassador in the embassy pecking order.

"What kind of interpreting would Mr. Rondini like me to perform for him?"

"Can you please hold for a moment, Mr. Montoya?"

Before he could answer she was replaced by classical music. Boccherini. Rick kept the phone to his ear and looked around the piazza. It was the usual mix of tourists and locals, most on their way to lunch, many stopping to watch the waters of the four rivers noisily recycle through Bernini's fountain. After a full three minutes, she returned.

"Sorry about that. Mr. Rondini is making a trip to Mantova, Italy, to attend a funeral and make contact with his family there. You will be his guide."

Not would, but will. He also noticed that she used the Italian "Mantova" instead of the anglicized "Mantua" that would be found on most maps in the States. The woman must have done her homework.

"It sounds interesting, Ms. Coleman, but I'm afraid that kind of thing is really not my usual—"

"I checked your website and saw your daily rate, Mr. Montoya. Mr. Rondini will double that. And cover your expenses, of course."

He looked at the phone and decided he'd heard right. "When will Mr. Rondini need me, and for how long?"

"The funeral is next Thursday, so he is planning on arriving that morning. He can't be away for more than a week. I will send you the logistical details by e-mail today. I trust that will work with your schedule?"

At that moment Rick was working on a series of academic translations. It was boring sitting over his keyboard with a dictionary trying to make sense of someone's turgid Italian and then transforming it into equally turgid English. He was anxious to have a live interpreting job, and this one sounded intriguing as well as lucrative.

"Certainly. I'll juggle my schedule, but it can work."

"Excellent. My e-mail will have contact information, but you can call me at this number if absolutely necessary. Good-bye, Mr. Montoya." She was gone before Rick could think of any other questions, let alone return her good-bye.

He looked up at the gray sheet of clouds that covered the city, perhaps portending another afternoon rain. The call had partially brightened his day, which needed some brightening. Not only was his work at the moment dull, his relationship with Betta Innocenti had been sliding into a predictable routine. Is this what happens when two people spend too much time together? A trip alone to Mantova might be just what he—and Betta—needed. She was immersed in a case of stolen paintings with the art police, so she might not even notice he was gone.

He kept the phone in his hand and scrolled through the numbers in his address book before hitting the one for the embassy. After talking to the switchboard operator and one secretary, he got through to the counselor for economic affairs.

"*Ciao*, Rick. I thought you might be calling."

"First, John, thanks for the recommendation. But tell me who this guy Rondini is. Besides being a friend of the ambassador."

Treacy laughed. "You found that out. They were both on the board of the U.S. Chamber of Commerce, but I don't think they're close friends. That Coleman woman's a piece of work, isn't she? Like talking to some kind of automaton."

"You think? I found her quite charming. Especially when she told me what Rondini was going to pay me. Listen, I'll look up Rondini on the Internet so as not to waste your time. You have better things to do. But thanks again for giving her my name. I'll let you know how it goes."

"Please do. And give my best to your mom and dad next time you Skype with them."

Rick promised he would. A few minutes later he was in his apartment, searching on his laptop for information about Angelo Rondini. He didn't have to go far, and began to scribble notes on a yellow legal pad as he read the screen.

Angelo Rondini, 78, born Voglia, Italy, widowed, one daughter, residences in Chicago and Marco Island, Florida, semi-retired from Rondini Enterprises (malls and shopping centers), serves on boards of directors at numerous corporations and national charities, art collector.

The photograph on the screen showed a man in a tuxedo with two other people who looked equally wealthy and of the same age, all holding champagne flutes. He had thinning but long white hair and wore glasses which were lightly tinted yellow. The event was a fund-raiser for the Chicago Symphony Orchestra, and these three looked like just the type of persons any community organization would kill for to have in attendance at their events. Nothing could be deduced from the expression on Rondini's face, not in this photo or any of the others that came up in the search. No kindly smile, but no stony expression either. Rick would have to wait until he actually met his temporary employer to make an assessment of the man. What was most intriguing was that Rondini had been born in Italy. There had to be a story in that.

Rick called his uncle. Commissario Piero Fontana was not at his desk at police headquarters, but the call was answered by his faithful secretary, Signora Rocca. It was a running joke in the building that she had started working in the *questura* when Rome became capital of Italy in the nineteenth century, using family connections to King Vittorio Emmanuele to get the job. She wasn't quite that old, but she did have connections, something Piero used sparingly and only when dealing with the most sensitive issues.

"Your uncle is out on a case, Riccardo. You can call him on his *telefonino*."

Not when he's working a case. "Thank you, Signora, please tell him that I'll be going to Mantova on Wednesday. He can call me when he's free and I'll explain."

"I'll tell him. And how is that lovely little friend of yours?"

It was another of Signora Rocca's traits, an interest in the personal life of everyone she met. Not that she was nosy; it was a benign interest, like that of a maiden aunt or a grandmother. Importantly, she didn't share what she knew with others, which meant that police in the building came to her with personal problems, knowing it would go no farther than her desk. Her advice was usually sound. The Ann Landers of police head-quarters. Today, Rick was not in the mood to share.

"Betta is fine. Working hard."

"You must bring her by some time so I can meet her."

After he hung up, Rick reluctantly returned to his transla-tion. An hour later he put his computer on sleep and pulled out his red guide book for Lombardia. As he expected, there was a long entry on Mantova.

Rick's overnight train from Rome arrived in Verona on time, saving him any worry about making his rendezvous with Rondini. The sleeping compartment gave him what he needed: a firm mattress, the regular clatter of the rails to put him to sleep, and a sink for him to wash up and shave when he awoke. The porter had tapped on his door at exactly the time he'd requested, holding a *caffè latte* and *cornetto* on a small tray. So much more civilized than flying. Poor Rondini would be a basket case after a flight from Chicago, with a plane change somewhere else in Europe before arriving in Verona, the nearest airport to Mantova.

Even without his morning run, Rick was in excellent spirits when he stepped off the car and started walking along the platform. Everyone else coming off the train seemed to be in more of a hurry. They rushed past him, suitcase wheels rumbling along the pavement, leading him down the steps, under the tracks and into the terminal. Like most Italian train stations, it was cavernous and bustling with people. The only ones not hurrying along had stopped to scan the massive schedule board or were talking on cell phones. He immediately spotted a strategically placed man in a blue suit holding a hand-lettered sign: MONTOIA. Close enough.

"I'm Riccardo Montoya." Rick extended his hand.

The handshake was firm, the smile genuine. "*Piacere*, Signor Montoya. Marco Bertani."

The driver was older than Rick by at least a decade. Gray streaks had begun to work themselves in among the long, dark hair, and there was the hint of a stomach. He was clean-shaven, and his shoes were shined to perfection. He wanted to make a good first impression on Rondini.

"You can be more formal with our employer, Marco, but please call me Riccardo."

"Riccardo it is." He gestured toward the door. "I'm parked just outside. Do you need help with the bag?"

"I'll get it, thanks. Are you from here, Marco? I'm always trying to identify local accents."

"In fact I was born in the Verona suburbs south of the city, but I've lived here in Verona most of my life. So I suppose my accent is more Vernonese city than of the countryside around it, not that there's much difference."

A large modern square greeted them when they emerged into the open. The day was cloudy with patches of sky, and the temperature noticeably colder than what it had been when Rick had left Rome. That would be expected this far north of the Apennines and in the shadow of the Alps, especially in late autumn. He tightened the wool coat that he wore over his blazer. They reached the parking lot and Bertani led Rick to a shiny black Mercedes S-class sedan parked away from the other vehicles. The car was a few years old, but had been so well kept up that looked like it had just rolled off the line at Stuttgart. Bertani popped the ample trunk and stowed Rick's bag. He went to the rear passenger door to open it but Rick waved him off, opened the front door, and climbed in. The driver brought the diesel engine to life and they eased into the street.

"You are making me look like a country bumpkin, Marco," Rick said. *Burino* was not a word he used often in his interpreting work, and he was pleased to have remembered it.

The driver glanced from the road to Rick. "I hadn't noticed anything but your cowboy boots. Are you from Texas? I've always wanted to visit there."

"I lived close to Texas. I went to university in New Mexico, the next state west of Texas."

"I had clients once from Santa Fe. That's in New Mexico, isn't it?"

"*Bravo.* The state capital. You have a lot of clients from America?"

"Yes. I suspect Mr. Rondini found out about my company from one of them. The word gets around."

"So your English must be fluent."

"Not totally fluent as is your Italian, Riccardo, but I am able to defend myself."

Less work for me, Rick thought. The car began to weave its way through the city as only a local driver could do, sometimes on major streets, other times getting off them to avoid traffic. They crossed the river, passed railroad yards, and moved into the suburbs which, as in most of Italy, were more drab than the upscale historic center. This may have been where Marco had grown up, but Rick didn't ask. They drove parallel to the *autostrada* and went underneath it as airport signs, with the international airplane symbol, began to appear.

"I was told you would have the flight information, Marco."

The driver grunted an assent as he wheeled off the street toward the terminal. His Mercedes passed the terminal entrance and the parking lot, coming up to a gate manned by a uniformed guard. He rolled down his window but the guard merely greeted him with a "*Ciao*, Marco," and waved the car past. Rick was impressed, but noticed they were parking far from the terminal. Just ahead, the tarmac spread out in front of the windshield. A mid-sized Lufthansa plane had just pushed away from the terminal and was making its way out to the runways.

"We can wait here," said Marco. "I'll check on their arrival, but it should be in just a few minutes." He got out of the car, pulled a cell phone from his suit pocket, and walked a few steps before dialing.

Rick opened his door and stepped to the cement. He stretched and looked around, his nostrils taking in the coarse odor of burning airplane fuel that always hung over runways. After so many plane trips as the son of a diplomat, he knew it well. They were close to a door at one end of the terminal where, he assumed, they would go in to meet Rondini at the gate. Better than going through a crowded terminal. Marco clearly knew his way around; he must have done this count-less times when meeting other clients. Through a break in the clouds, Rick could see snow on the mountains, making him think of the upcoming ski season. Perhaps he could meet Flavio again for a ski vacation. The clouds closed in and his thoughts returned to the present. The Lufthansa plane was now at the end of the runway, gunning its engines, almost close enough to make Rick cover his ears. It lurched forward, picked up speed, and suddenly climbed sharply into the air. After it disappeared into the clouds, Rick heard the distant sound of another plane coming from the opposite direction. As he was turning to find it, the driver came back to the car.

"I have a friend who works in the control tower." Marco gestured toward the terminal. "The plane should be here at any moment."

"It's probably the one I just—" Rick's sentence was interrupted by the sound of the Lobo Fight Song coming from his pocket. He extracted his cell phone and flipped it open. "Commissario Fontana, it is an honor to speak with you." It was his standard response when receiving a call from his uncle.

"And how is my nephew?" said the voice at the other end of the line. "Have you been to the castle yet?"

"Still in Verona, Zio. At the airport. The man's plane should be here momentarily. Did you solve the case that has kept you so busy the last few days?"

"I'm afraid not, and we are running out of time." He paused. "Riccardo, did you speak with Betta before you left last night?"

Rick rubbed his eyes. It was the kind of question a mother would have asked, but perhaps Piero had begun thinking that he should be his sister's stand-in. Despite his affection for Piero, he was annoyed by this kind of meddling. Or was he annoyed because the relationship with Betta was going sour?

"I left her a message."

Even over the phone Piero could sense that his question was not appreciated. He let it drop. "Everything is on schedule up there in the north?"

"With typical northern efficiency, Zio." Rick turned away from the tarmac, hunched over, and raised his voice as the engines from the arriving plane got closer. "The driver is waving at me; it must be time to go into the terminal. Talk to you later. *Ciao.*"

Marco was gesturing for Rick to return to the car. When Rick got in, he put it in gear.

"Are we driving back to the terminal, Marco? I thought we'd be going in through that door."

"No terminal for us, Riccardo."

The Mercedes drove through an open gate onto the tarmac as the plane was directed to its parking place by an airport employee wielding two brightly colored paddles. Rick chuckled and shook his head as they parked off the left wing. He didn't know much about private jets, but he knew this was a Gulfstream, that it could easily fly direct from Chicago to Verona, and that if you had to ask what it cost, you couldn't afford one. The name RONDINI ENTERPRISES was centered under the seven oval windows, large enough to read but small enough to be tasteful. As they sat waiting for the plane engines to stop, a small Fiat Panda with a flashing light on its roof pulled up next to them and a man in a blue suit holding a briefcase got out.

"Passport and customs," said Marco without looking at Rick.

The two engines whined to a stop and the door of the plane opened. As soon as the stairs dropped to the ground, the official scurried up into the plane holding tightly to his briefcase. Rick and the driver got out of the car and leaned against its hood while they waited.

"Nice way to travel," Rick commented.

The formalities didn't take long. The man came down the steps, got back into his car, and drove off toward the terminal. As the car departed, a woman dressed in blue slacks and a white blouse looked out from the plane door. She gazed at the snow on the mountains to the north before noticing Rick and giving him a wave. He waved back. A few more minutes passed before Angelo Rondini himself appeared, shaking hands with the pilot and copilot. Rondini slapped one of them on the back and took in the mountain view before starting down the steps.

The society photo had not flattered or aged him. Except for a brown suit and tie rather than a tuxedo, it was the guy in the picture, down to the yellow-tinted glasses. He looked like he had recently lost some weight but hadn't bothered to get himself a suit that fit better. An Italian with that much money would have worn a perfectly tailored suit, but, apparently, appearance was not that important to Angelo Rondini. His eyes locked on the two men on the tarmac who now moved toward the plane, and Rick could feel himself being sized up.

"You must be Montoya," Rondini said as he shook Rick's hand. "There's a certain American aura about you. I haven't seen boots like that since I opened a shopping mall in San Antonio. The person wearing them almost cost me the deal. And this guy is our driver, I suppose?"

"Yes, sir."

He was about to make introductions, but Marco took the cue and stepped forward to offer his hand. "Marco Bertani, Mr. Rondini, at your services. It is my pleasure."

The English was accented but clear.

"Sounds to me like this guy speaks good English," Rondini said. "So tell me, Montoya, why did I hire you? I'll have to have a talk with Lexi. That's all right; I'll find something for you to do."

"Mr. Rondini, if you want to end my services now—"

The man clapped Rick on the shoulder just as he'd done with the pilot. "I always like to throw a curve ball when I first meet people. See how they react. It's never failed me in business, and as you can see, I've done all right." He didn't feel the need to gesture toward the plane to help make his point. "I think we'll get along just fine, Montoya. Despite the cowboy boots. Now if we can get Lexi off the plane, we can get the hell out of here."

"I didn't realize Ms. Coleman was coming along. She never mentioned that in her e-mails."

"Probably didn't think you needed to know. That's just like her. But I never go anywhere without Lexi, even to a funeral. Plus, she keeps contact with the office. Never know what trouble those assholes back there will get themselves into."

Rick looked up at the empty airplane doorway. Great. Not only do I have to deal with a millionaire with an ego, I have to put up with his supercilious special assistant. Perhaps I should have negotiated for three times my usual fee.

A male crew member came down the steps carrying bags and stowed them in the trunk of the car. He hustled back up the stairs and returned with another set. Angelo Rondini walked toward the tail of the plane to get a better look at the mountain. Rick pulled out his cell phone and checked the time.

Finally, Alexis Coleman appeared at the top of the steps, gripping a leather briefcase as if it held the nuclear codes. Jet-black hair in a natural cut framed an oval face, its smooth skin the color of a *caffè macchiatto*. The frames of her glasses subtly matched the burgundy hue of her lipstick, and if there was other makeup, it had been applied with perfection. He had been unable to estimate her age from the few words she'd spoken on the phone, but now Rick guessed mid-thirties, or perhaps younger, given the perfect complexion. He moved his eyes from the face to a slim figure which showed itself through the opening of a long wool coat.

Had it not been for her all-business manner, he might have looked forward to working with Alexis Coleman.

She extended her hand when she reached the bottom of the stairs.

"I assume you are Rick Montoya." It was a serious handshake, matching her expression.

"My pleasure, Alexis."

"Everyone calls me Lexi." It sounded more like an order than a clarification. "And this is our driver, Mr. Bertani?"

Marco mumbled a few words and shook her hand.

Rondini watched it all with a large smile on his face. "Can we get this show on the road, Lexi? The only funeral I want to be late for is my own."

Chapter Two

The drive from the airport to Mantova was short and mostly quiet. Rick was expecting Rondini to ask questions about the area of his birth, but instead he spent most of the half hour looking silently out the window at the flat countryside on either side of the *autostrada*—which made sense if he hadn't been back to Italy in a while. Or had he been back at all? Rick had a few questions of his own for Rondini, many about the reasons that his family left Italy for America. Italian emigration was something that had always fascinated Rick, the personal histories of desperation and hope. He would wait for the right time to ask.

While Rondini, deep in thought, watched the farms zipping by, Lexi tapped away at her tablet, sending and receiving e-mails that had stacked up during the flight. A question sneaked into Rick's head, but it was one he would never ask: how much of the operation did she run? Rondini had complete trust in the woman, that was clear, but what was the extent of her real power? Rick recalled something his father had told him about working in the bureaucracy of the State Department: the trick was knowing when to make a decision yourself and when to consult your boss. Lexi, it appeared, knew the trick. The personality of the boss was the key, and while Rondini did not strike Rick as a micro-manager, he was definitely in charge. So how much leeway did Ms. Coleman have? It would be fascinating to watch the two interact.

Marco eased the car off at the Mantova exchange, paid the toll, and headed west into town. As they neared their destination, the number of buildings increased—low boxy structures that included factories and gas stations along with residences. Beyond clumps of trees and bushes on both sides of the road, the lake suddenly appeared, stretching in both directions and dotted with floating patches of morning fog. They drove onto a long, two-lane causeway that separated the Lago di Mezzo on the right from the Lago Inferiore on the left. In the distance the skyline of Mantova began to appear through the morning mist, the round dome of Sant'Andrea and a medieval tower its first identifiable shapes. Halfway across the water the squared-off lines of the Gonzaga castle took form, and eventually overpowered the view. The Mercedes turned left when the causeway ended, drove between the fortifications and the lake, then eased into Mantova itself. Once inside the historic center, it passed over a narrow canal and started down a long, straight street before pulling to a stop in front of the hotel.

Rick estimated the buildings on the street dated from the nineteenth century. All were two to three stories with plain stucco fronts, neat and well maintained. As they entered he found that the interior of the hotel was very much of the present century, starting with the reception area. White walls contrasted with a décor of glass, shiny metal, and dark wood, the result of a restoration that was so spotless it could have been finished the previous day. Rick was certain that the efficient Ms. Coleman was not one to dip under five stars when choosing accommodations for her boss, so this place had to be the best in Mantova. The reception staff was young, spoke passable English, and fully checked them in while Rondini was still standing out on the street talking with the driver. When he got inside, Lexi handed him his key card.

"You are in the suite on the third floor, Mr. Rondini, and I'll be a few doors down. Rick is one floor below. Our bags are being taken to the rooms. The funeral is set for eleven, an hour and a half from now. I assume it will start on time?" She looked at Rick.

"The ones I've been to always have," Rick answered.

Rondini did not appear to have heard what was being said. His eyes were on a framed abstract print on the wall. "I was just chatting with our driver and he seems to know his Mantova art. Comes from taking tourists around the town over the years. That will come in handy." He turned to Lexi and Rick. "I'm going to rest for a bit and change into a dark suit. I'll see you down here at quarter to eleven. Knock on my door if I'm late." He turned and walked to the elevator.

"Mr. Rondini is very interested in art," Lexi said to Rick. "It is another reason he wanted to make the trip, besides attending the funeral of his cousin, of course."

"Lexi, that's the first I've heard whose funeral we're attending. Why don't we have a cup of coffee and you can tell me about what's going to happen during the next few days?"

She looked at her watch and then studied Rick's expression. "I suppose you're right. You don't really know much about all this. I have to make some calls so let's do it quickly."

They walked into the breakfast area where a couple was finishing their coffee and rolls. A girl appeared and Rick ordered a *caffè latte* for him, a *cappuccino* for Lexi.

"Do you want something to eat?" Rick asked as they sat at one of the tables. The buffet was so well stocked it looked as if it had just opened.

"No, I was well fed on the plane. But you go ahead."

He did, taking a yogurt and sweet roll from the groaning board. It had been a while since the train and he wasn't sure when he'd see food again. He walked back to the table and saw that Lexi was stealing a look at her cell phone. She glanced up at him and slipped it into an outside compartment of her briefcase.

"The funeral is for Mr. Rondini's cousin, Roberto Rondini," she began, as if making a presentation to a board. "Obviously, their fathers were brothers."

"Were the cousins very close?"

"On the contrary, they'd never met. Mr. Rondini came to the U.S. as an infant and has never felt very close ties with Italy. His parents thought it important that he embrace his new nationality, and they made a point of speaking English in front of him when he was growing up. Not that he feels any ill will toward his native country, but the whole Italian-American thing was never his style."

"So he doesn't wear a baseball cap that says 'Kiss Me, I'm Italian.'"

She looked hard at Rick, then shook her head. "No."

The coffees arrived and Rick stirred sugar from a small bowl on the table into his. She sipped hers without adding anything.

"Roberto Rondini's daughter, whose name is Livia Guarino, called the morning he died and I spoke to her. Her English is halting. She wanted Mr. Rondini to come to his cousin's funeral. She was very compelling and I put her through to him."

Rick swallowed a bite of the sweet roll. "So he was convinced."

"Yes. He didn't tell me what she said and I didn't ask. He just told me to make the arrangements."

"You said something about his interest in art."

"Yes." She took another sip of her coffee. "Mr. Rondini is an art collector, and lately his interests have shifted from modern to more classical genres. Not that he can afford to purchase any Botticellis or Raphaels, but he wants to see some of the great Italian painters other than those in museums in the States. So he sees this trip as a way to do that. Naturally, we won't say that to the family."

"But he must have some interest in his roots."

She gave him a faint shrug. "I know him as well as anyone outside his family, but I'm not sure."

"Perhaps the art thing is just an excuse to find out about his family, rather than the other way around."

Lexi brushed back her hair and he caught sight of one of her earrings, gold with a pearl pendant. "I never thought of that." She drained her cup and got to her feet. "I really have to make those calls. I'll see you in the lobby in about an hour."

Rick watched her walk away, still clutching her briefcase. Her coat had been sent up to her room with the luggage, so he could get a full view of her slender figure. The elegant pants suit fit perfectly, but Alexis Coleman would have looked good wearing a sweat suit three sizes too large. If only her temperament was as attractive as her looks.

On the way to the church, the driver gave his passengers background on what they were going to see, but since it was just a few blocks away, Marco wasn't able to say very much.

"Even though the Duomo is the city's cathedral, Sant'Andrea is the more famous because it was designed by one of the greatest architects of the fifteenth century, Leon Battista Alberti. In fact, it was the last work designed by Alberti. Construction on it started in 1472, the year he died. You will see immediately how Alberti used classical elements, beginning with the Roman arch. The facade of Sant'Andrea is filled with them."

"Is there any art of importance inside, Marco?" Rondini asked. "I couldn't care less about architecture."

"The tomb of Andrea Mantegna is decorated by his *aiuti*—what is it in English, Riccardo?"

"His assistants," Rick said from the front seat.

"You finally earned your pay, Montoya," said Rondini. "I should let you take the rest of the day off, but I may need you at the funeral, and it looks like we've arrived."

The car parked across the piazza from the church where people dressed in dark clothing were beginning to climb the steps.

"You want to come in, Marco?"

"I should remain with the car, Signor Rondini. And the funeral would be a painful memory of one I attended recently."

The three of them got out and walked across the pavement. Rondini was dressed in a black suit with a gray tie over a white shirt. Lexi had changed into a blue print dress, covered by the same long, wool coat, but for the first time since getting off the plane she was without her briefcase. Rick wore his only suit, with a suitably somber tie, and his dress cowboy boots.

He looked at the facade and understood what Marco had meant about the architect's use of classical design—the arches and columns could have been taken from a building in imperial Rome. Because of the buildings which hemmed in the basilica, he was unprepared for its cavernous interior. A barrel vault ceiling covered with deep, square coffers seemed miles above their heads, and tall chapels running along the sides under their own vaults added to the vast sense of space. It was also empty, or at least most of it. The single-wide nave was bare of seating until directly in front of the main altar where rows of chairs had been set up. Rick, Rondini, and Lexi walked slowly toward the chairs that were starting to fill with silent mourners. Unlike the others who kept their eyes on the ground, the three could not help but take in their surroundings as they walked. When they were close to the chairs, Rondini spoke into Rick's ear.

"How am I going to find Roberto's daughter?"

Not many strangers would show up at her father's funeral with a black woman and a guy wearing cowboy boots, Rick thought. But he said: "I'm sure she'll find you."

At that moment they saw a woman quietly greeting people at the end of the aisle that ran between the rows of chairs. She wore a black dress and her head was covered with a veil of the same color. She smiled weakly at each of the people, who in turn embraced her and murmured into her ear. When it was Rondini's turn, he stepped forward, unsure what to say.

"My dear Uncle Angelo, I thank you for coming." She wrapped her arms around him and kissed him on both cheeks.

"You recognized me."

"How could I not? The resemblance with my father is…"

She searched for a word and found it. "Striking." She looked at Rick and Lexi.

"This is my assistant, Alexis Coleman," Rondini said, "and my interpreter for the visit, Mr. Montoya."

"My condolences," said Lexi as she took Livia Guarino's hand.

Rick was next, and offered his condolences in Italian.

She shook his hand and stayed in the same language. "I'm glad you're here. My English is abominable and it is nonexistent among my family." She said something about seeing them after the service and turned to the group forming behind them.

The three took seats in the fourth row from the front just as a voice began to sing in Latin from somewhere out of sight. The mournful words echoed off the walls and faded into the dome high above them. Ahead, between the rows of chairs and the altar, sat the dark casket, its top covered with a tight blanket of white carnations. Rick listened to the music and let his eyes move around the space. He remembered the few funerals he'd been to in Italy, starting with two for his Italian grandparents, who had died within months of each other in Rome. It had been a difficult year for his mother and uncle, and, by extension, for all the Montoya family. Those masses had been celebrated in the same parish church where he, his mother, and his sister had been baptized, and where his parents had exchanged vows. It could have fit in one corner of Sant'Andrea.

The priest and two altar boys appeared, and the mass began. The eulogy was full of vague descriptions of the dead man, and many allusions to the afterlife. In case Angelo might want to know what was said, Rick tried to remember them since taking notes would have been inappropriate. At the end everyone rose and the casket was rolled between the chairs toward the door, accompanied by six men and followed by Livia Guarino and several others. As they passed up the aisle, those watching began to applaud.

"What the hell is this?" Rondini whispered to Rick.

"Sign of respect. Italians often do it at funerals."

Rondini nodded and began to clap. "I like it."

As the casket took its slow journey toward the large doors of the church, the people emptied the rows and followed behind them, talking softly to one another. Rondini walked to one side and stopped to look into one of the chapels, Lexi at his side. Rick watched, remembering what Lexi had said about Rondini's interest in art. The man was starting already.

"Signor Montoya?"

The person who spoke must have been sitting behind them, since Rick had studied the profiles of everyone in the rows ahead while listening to the priest. The man's fatigued eyes were even with Rick's, putting him over six feet, and his plain, dark suit was well filled out. Too well filled out. *Could it be that this guy…?*

"I am Inspector Giulio Crispi."

He is. A cop.

"Your uncle and I worked together a few years ago, and I was speaking to him this morning. He mentioned that his nephew was in our city."

"That's right. I'm working as an interpreter for the American cousin of Roberto Rondini. He flew in this morning. Did you know the deceased well, Inspector?"

"Never met him."

No doubt the *questura* sent an official representative to the funerals of prominent locals, and Inspector Crispi had drawn the short straw. Rick was about to ask if that were the case, when he saw that Rondini was looking around for him.

"Inspector, it was a pleasure to meet you, but I must be on my way."

"Signor Montoya, we suspect that Roberto Rondini was murdered."

Crispi was a man of few words, but they got Rick's attention. "I…I had no idea."

"There is no reason you would. Since you will be spending some time with the family of Signor Rondini, I would be most grateful if you could be observant, now that you know of our suspicions." He handed Rick a card. "I can be reached at any hour at this number. The address of the *questura* is also there. Good day, Signor Montoya."

When the Mercedes fell in line behind the hearse, clouds were beginning to move in from the west. They were the vanguard of a cold front that had originated south of Geneva, descended to Turin, and now widened as it moved through the Po River Valley toward the Adriatic. The weather system could eventually bring rain or snow, but, for the moment, served to remind the Mantovani that winter was on its way. The fields on either side of the road had given up their crops weeks earlier; for them a white winter blanket would be welcome. For the townspeople, not as much.

"Who were you talking to in there, Language Man?"

They were the first words Rondini had spoken since the car had driven across the lake. Rick had been fingering Inspector Crispi's card in his overcoat pocket while deciding how to handle the policeman's request. The inspector suspected foul play. What better way to gather information about the dead man and his family than from Riccardo Montoya, who was working for a member of the family? Crispi also must have known, from talking to Piero, that Rick had assisted the police in the past. The problem for Rick was his present employer. Working on the side with the police wasn't something he could keep from Rondini; that would be unethical, not to mention impossible. Now was not the time to explain, and there hadn't been time in the church to get any details of the case out of Crispi. Rick could meet the policeman later, when he had a break from his translation duties. Before that, he'd talk to Rondini.

"His name's Crispi, a work colleague of my uncle. He found out I was here and stopped me to say hello."

Marco kept his eyes on the road, and Rick wondered how much of the conversation he was getting, since Angelo had a fast, choppy way of talking. It was a speech pattern that many foreigners would have trouble following. That was likely what Roberto Rondini's daughter meant when she said how pleased she was to have Rick's assistance.

"You have a big family, Montoya?"

An interesting question from someone who'd never bothered to meet his own cousin. Was the funeral bringing out some feelings of guilt in Rondini? Well, that was fine; it wasn't too late for him to get to know what was left of his family. Rick turned in his seat to answer.

"The cliché would be that my Italian side, my mother's family, would be much more numerous than those on my father's American side. But in fact it's just the opposite. I have an Italian aunt and uncle, and one cousin, that's all. Back in New Mexico, there are Montoyas everywhere."

Rondini listened and nodded before returning his eyes to the countryside passing the window. As if mesmerized by the monotony of the terrain, he was still staring out when he spoke again.

"I suppose being an only child had its advantages, like getting all the attention from my parents. All my friends in the neighborhood had big families, so there was no lack of kids to play with or fight with. They even had grandparents, which I didn't, but the old folks didn't speak much English and I didn't speak any Italian, so I stuck with my own generation. When I went off to college, the size of your family was never something anybody talked about. Still isn't."

The Mercedes slowed, pulled over, and stopped, keeping its place in the line of cars which were now emptying of their passengers. The casket was removed from the hearse by eight of the men; there would be no wheeled cart as in the church. They carried it carefully through the iron gate of a tall, stone wall, followed by mourners who kept their eyes to the ground as they walked. Once inside, Rick saw that the wall was made up of horizontal tombs, like catacombs, most of them sealed by stone squares etched with names and dates. Beside the gravel path next to the wall, the ground held traditional graves marked by gravestones, many with small black-and-white photographs of the deceased. Wilting flowers drooped from metal vases attached to the grave markers on the ground and the wall. The only sound was the crunch of shoes on the gravel path as the procession walked to a far corner where the freshly dug grave awaited. Rick noticed that three graves in the same row had the names Rondini etched on their surfaces. From the dates below the names, he concluded they were the dead man's parents and wife. He whispered in Rondini's ear while he inclined his head toward the grave markers. Angelo looked at the names of his aunt and uncle and nodded. The priest began to speak.

Perhaps because of the ominous clouds, the ceremony was brief. The thick walls, filled with stacked tombs, protected the circle of mourners from a wind that stirred the air, bringing with it the scent of wet leaves. When the ceremony ended, everyone gathered around Roberto Rondini's daughter and exchanged more embraces. Rick and Lexi hung back while Angelo joined in offering his condolences. They watched Livia Guarino speak into Angelo's ear, after which he nodded and gave her another hug. Then he shook hands with the man whom Rick assumed was Livia's husband. The man's awkward demeanor indicated to Rick that he didn't speak much or any English, but he did pass something to Angelo, earning a nod.

"We're invited back to their farm," said Rondini when he got back to Rick and Lexi. He held up the card. "This is the name of the place. Our driver should know how to get there. It will be family and close friends, so Lexi, you can go back to the hotel and get some work done." He looked at Rick. "But not you, Language Man. Time for you to go to work."

Rick remembered Inspector Crispi.

In more ways than one.

Chapter Three

The driver knew exactly where the Rondini dairy farm was located. In an area of Lombardy where numerous cheese producers thrived, Rondini's was known by everyone as one of the largest and most successful. Much of its production came from its own cows, but it also bought milk from other farmers in the area. Rondini cheese could be purchased throughout Italy and was exported to other countries in the European Union, and while the farm's lead product was Parmigiano-Reggiano, it made other cheeses that were less regulated and less expensive. All this required acreage and equipment, and Latteria Rondini had more than enough of both. The farm's clean, white buildings lined one side of a large parking lot where trucks and tractors were neatly parked. Behind them, level fields dotted with cows stretched for kilometers. Marco drove past the farm entrance to a modern house separated from the business operation by a row of thick trees. Cars from the funeral were already parked in front and people were walking up to the house. The Mercedes slowed and entered a long, circular driveway, coming to a stop at the walkway that led to the door.

The driver got out and opened the door for Rondini, who disengaged himself from the seat with some effort. Rick stood and looked around him, taking in a rural smell that mixed the strong odor of hay with the fragrance of the few flowers that still bloomed along the driveway. The sky continued to threaten, but it was impossible to know if anything would come of it. Those who'd spent all their lives in the Po Valley might know, but he didn't.

Rondini leaned down and spoke through the open driver window. "Lexi, call me if there's any movement with the guy in Memphis, but I have the feeling it's not going to happen. If you talk to him, tell him we need the decision by yesterday." He stood up and looked toward the house. "Marco, you should have time to get something to eat before you come back. This may take a while."

Marco got back in the car and drove toward the road with Lexi in the back seat.

"Mr. Rondini, before we go in, I need to talk to you about something."

Angelo, who had been straightening his tie, stopped and eyed Rick. "You can't ask for a raise, you haven't done anything yet."

"No, sir. It's something else. The man I was talking to in the church? He's a policeman."

"He's not a friend of your uncle, like you said?"

"I said he's a colleague of my uncle, and my uncle is with the police in Rome."

"That could come in handy if I get into trouble on this trip." He chuckled while watching the Mercedes pull out onto the road. "So what's the big deal?"

Rick took a breath before answering. "Inspector Crispi thinks there is a chance your cousin was murdered."

"Whoa." He scanned the house, where the door was open and visitors were entering. "Does Livia know that?"

"He didn't give me any details, since there wasn't time to talk."

"Why would he tell you this?"

"I've worked with the police in the past. He knew that."

The man's face showed that what had been confusing was starting to make sense. "And he wants you to work with them again. He knows you'll be around people who were close to Roberto but might not be forthcoming with him."

"That's correct. But my contract is with you. If you don't want me to help him, I won't. Just say the word."

Rondini rubbed a hand over his chin and squinted his eyes in thought. "He really thinks Roberto was murdered?"

"That's what he said."

"Are they going to pay you?"

It was a logical question from a businessman, but something that never entered Rick's mind. He shook his head. "They haven't before."

Rondini had run out of questions. Rick guessed that this was not an issue he usually faced in his business dealings, most of which dealt with the bottom line. Complicating it was the new family connection, a foreign culture, and a little jet lag. But the man had not become successful by avoiding decisions.

"Yes, do it. He was my cousin, after all, the least I can do is not stand in the way of an investigation if he was murdered. But here are the conditions. It can't interfere with what you are doing for me. When I need you to interpret for me, you have to be there."

"Of course."

"And you will keep me in the loop with anything you find out from these people."

Rick agreed, but interpreted "these people" as the family and friends of Roberto Rondini, not the police. He didn't want to share what Inspector Crispi might know, unless forced to.

"And finally, Roberto's daughter must not know what you are up to. This is just between you, me, and the cops."

"Understood." Rick stretched his arm toward the walkway up to the front door. "Shall we go in?"

A man wearing an ill-fitting suit took their coats inside the door. Rick guessed he was someone who worked elsewhere on the farm and had been pressed into service for the event. They walked into an ample rectangular living room, beyond which he could see a dining room, its round table set with trays of food. The dining room chairs had been pushed to one side, under windows that looked out on the grass lawn and fields beyond. About two dozen people mingled between the two rooms, most with glasses in their hands, a few with small plates of food. The voice level was higher than it had been in the church, but still muted. Some looked up when Rick and Angelo approached, one being Livia Guarino, who had been talking with her husband and a man with the ruddy complexion of someone who worked in the open air. She walked over to them and took Angelo's hand in both hers.

"So good to see you, Uncle. May I call you that? It was kind of you to come all the way from America. I know you must be a busy man."

"I wish we had met under other circumstances, Livia. As I wish I had met your father."

Rick decided he wasn't needed and didn't want to listen in on their private conversation. He excused himself, encouraged by Livia to partake of the food and drink. After lifting a glass off a passing tray, he surveyed the group like an embassy officer at a diplomatic reception. Why not start with Livia's husband and the man with the tan? He was curious about both. He took an initial taste of his wine, a dry, dark red, and walked to them.

"You must be Livia's husband." Rick shook the younger man's hand.

"That's correct; Francesco Guarino," he answered, before turning to the man next to him. "Carlo, this is Riccardo Montoya, Angelo Rondini's interpreter. Riccardo, Carlo Zucari is the manager of the dairy farm." His eyes darted toward the door where an elderly man was making his way in from the hallway. "Can you excuse me a moment? Livia is busy and I should greet the new arrivals."

He hurried off, leaving Rick to wonder if the man was just shy and nervous, or thought he should greet an important visitor rather than mix with the hired help.

"This is quite an operation," Rick said as he shook Zucari's hand.

"It is the largest family-owned dairy in the area. With a few exceptions, all the others are cooperatives. We keep busy."

"Now the ownership passes to his daughter, I suppose?"

"You suppose correctly. Livia and her husband. I doubt if things will change much for the workers. Signor Rondini had not been very involved for years. He left it up to me to run the place. He only became involved if there was a long-range decision about the direction of the operation."

Rick looked around the room. "But he was here."

Zucari frowned in non-comprehension, then smiled. "Ah. You mean he lived here. Yes and no. One wing of this house is his, but he also had an apartment in Mantova. The last several years, since his wife passed away, he was spending more and more time in town. He would sometimes drop in to see me in the morning after fishing, but he didn't get involved in the day-to-day operation of the farm and the cheese-making."

"His death was sudden?"

"A fishing accident? I would say so."

"I don't know anything about the circumstances of his death. We only arrived here this morning."

"Of course, you wouldn't." He took a sip from his wine-glass. "He slipped on the dock and fell into the river. His body washed up near the castle in town."

"He always fished in the same place?"

Zucari's look made Rick wonder if he was probing too much.

"He tied up his boat at a dock at the edge of the property. I don't know where on the river he fished since I'm not a fisherman. Never had the time or the inclination. Running a place like this keeps me busy."

It was the second time the man had noted that he was busy, contrasting with the deceased owner, who apparently spent his time fishing or in Mantova. Rick had been keeping an eye on

Angelo, who now waved him over. He was standing next to Francesco Guarino.

"My *capo* is calling, Signor Zucari, and needs his interpreter. It was nice to meet you."

"Come back, if you have time, and I'll show you around the farm."

"I'd enjoy that, thank you."

As he walked to his boss, Rick thought about the times he'd visited relatives in the States when he was young. Being introduced to cousins and other relatives for the first time was always the same; they weren't quite sure what to think of him. Most had never met anyone who lived outside New Mexico, never mind another country, making him very exotic. Angelo wasn't getting any of that, these northern Italians were very much used to foreigners in their midst.

Rick noticed the relief on the faces of both his boss and Livia's husband when he reached them.

"I was asking Francesco here about what he does for a living, but I'm not sure he understood the question. I think he said something about cheese, so he must be part of the dairy."

"Signor Rondini was inquiring about your work," Rick said in Italian to Guarino.

"I think I understood that, but I could not explain well. I am an inspector for the Parmigiano-Reggiano Consortium. My territory is this part of Lombardy. But of course someone else inspects the cheese of Latteria Rondini."

Rick interpreted, and with him in the middle, a conversation began between the two men.

"The quality control is pretty tight for the cheese?"

"We have a most rigorous process to assure that the Parmigiano-Reggiano meets the highest of standards before it can display the stamp of the *Consorzio*. You can be assured that any cheese with the stamp burned into its rind has passed those tests." He pointed at a wooden board holding a large slice of the cheese. Protruding from it was the distinctive teardrop-shaped knife not used with any other kind of cheese. "You must try some. This is a *stravecchio* made here."

"Are you sure it's okay, even though you didn't inspect it?"

Even after Rick's translation, Guarino wasn't sure if Angelo had been joking or not. He wedged out two chunks and passed them to Angelo and Rick. He then got one for himself and popped it into his mouth. "It is one of the few foods we eat with our fingers."

"This is good cheese," said Angelo after eating his bite. "Now that your father-in-law is gone, Francesco, will you be leaving your inspector job and taking over the cheese-making here?"

The question took Guarino by surprise, and the nervousness he had shown to Rick earlier returned.

"I—I haven't thought about that. Livia is the owner now, so it will be up to her on how to proceed. With everything going on, we haven't discussed it." His eyes darted around the room, as if he were searching for an escape route. Rick provided it.

"I think Signor Rondini might want to taste some of the other cheeses."

"Yes, yes, of course. There are many good things to eat, please do."

Rick and Rondini stood by the table and surveyed the spread, which included small sandwiches, various kinds of salami and other cold cuts, and a variety of cheeses. Everything was local.

"Kind of a strange duck, that one." Rondini picked up a small plate and began to fill it. "Livia seems like a very intelligent young woman, but he doesn't seem like her type. Who were you talking to?"

"Carlo Zucari. He's the manager of the farm. He told me that your cousin had pretty much turned the operation over to him to run a while back. He'd show up occasionally but was hands-off on a day-to-day basis. He invited us to tour the place, by the way."

Rondini nibbled a miniature *panino*. "Livia did as well,

and we'll have to do that. These sandwiches are good. If I eat enough of them I won't need dinner."

Rick took another chunk of Parmigiano-Reggiano, noting its perfect consistency—an advantage of getting it at the source. "He told me that your cousin was drowned after he slipped on the dock when he was going fishing."

"She said that, too, but didn't go into details." He rubbed his eyes. The time change was starting to catch up with him. "She also asked a favor of me, which I found somewhat curious." He looked around to be sure no one was listening, though it was unnecessary since they were conversing in English. "Apparently her father was considering selling a plot of land to a developer. She said the people she trusts have no expertise on such things, and those who do have it, would have a stake in the decision. The manager of the farm is dead set against it, thinks it should be used to expand production. She knows that development is my business and asked my advice. I'm a bit bothered by her request."

"Why is that?"

"Don't you see? I thought she asked me to come over for the funeral because I was family, but she may just have wanted to pick my brain."

"Maybe a bit of both, Mr. Rondini, don't you think?"

Angelo had been giving his wineglass a hard look. "Yeah, maybe you're right. Way in the back of my mind is that my parents never talked much about my father's side of the family. Don't get me wrong, they never said anything against those who'd stayed in Italy. But I never sensed a warmth, if you know what I mean. Sometimes I wonder what was behind that." He glanced over Rick's shoulder. "Who's this guy?"

A large man holding a glass of red wine was marching toward them. His eyes indicated that the glass had been filled a few times, and his tie was slightly askew, something rare among Italians. Like the farm manager, his face was tanned and well creased.

"You are Mr. Rondini?" he said to Angelo, like it was an accusation. The English was as rough as the man's complexion, so Rick intervened in Italian.

"This is Signor Angelo Rondini, the cousin of the deceased. I am his interpreter. And you are?"

The answer was in Italian. "I'd heard there was a rich relative from America. I am Emilio Fiore. I own the farm to the east." He jerked his free thumb eastward before turning to Angelo and bowing dramatically. "My deepest condolences, Signor Rondini, on the passing of your cousin."

Rick translated, including the part about the rich relative.

"This guy's a piece of work," said Angelo to Rick as he returned the bow. "But since he's been softened up by Livia's wine, he may be able to answer some questions."

Rick managed to contain a smile. His concern that his employer would be against involvement in the murder investigation had been unwarranted; the man was embracing it. He went into his interpreter's routine.

"You must have known the deceased well, being his neighbor."

Fiore drained his glass and looked around for a refill. Fortunately for him, the girl with the tray was in the vicinity, and she swapped his empty for a full one. "I knew him well enough, but it is no secret that we didn't get along. But I will not speak ill of the dead, especially here, today."

"It is perfectly natural for neighbors to have disagreements," said Angelo after hearing the translation. "What was the nature of yours?"

"That is not a secret either. It was over his parcel of land on the river, quite a large number of hectares. It's been fallow for years, the same number of years I've been trying to purchase it from him so I can expand my dairy farm. Right now it's wasted, but he didn't care. Then word got out a few weeks ago that he was going to sell it to developers to build a factory, or something worse. We don't need any more factories creeping onto agricultural land. Agriculture is the backbone of our community, always was and always will be."

"What will happen to the land now?" Rick wasn't sure if Fiore had heard the question; the man was staring out the window at the expanse of flat fields.

"Let's just say I hope Livia has more sense than her father." He took another gulp of the wine.

"When did you see Roberto Rondini last?"

"Haven't seen him in weeks, but he was spending most of his time in town." A malevolent grin split his face, accentuating the wrinkles. "Can't say I blame him."

Fiore excused himself, shook hands again, and moved on. Rondini sidled back to the table to put more food on his plate, with Rick at his side.

"Did you catch that comment?" Rondini asked.

Rick nodded. "I did. But did it get garbled in my translation for you?"

"I don't think so. My cousin was spending time in town with someone, and it wasn't his priest."

Thanks to the wine and the lapsed time since the burial, the sound level in the room had risen, and serious faces had been replaced with normal ones and even smiles. People came over and introduced themselves to Angelo, ostensibly to pass on their condolences, but also curious to meet the *Americano* and his exotically booted interpreter. Many told him of relatives in the States, most asked how long he was going to be in Italy, and all encouraged him to see the art and architecture for which Mantova was known. He assured them he would.

Rondini was showing fatigue from the trip, despite sleeping on a real bed in his jet. "How long do you think we should stay?" he asked Rick during a break in the action. "You know the local customs."

"People are starting to leave, and Livia knows you've been traveling all night, so I think you can head back whenever you want. You'll be seeing her again, of course?"

"She wanted to have lunch tomorrow at a restaurant near here. I agreed but said I was inviting them. You'll need to be there since her husband hardly speaks any English."

They said their good-byes. Outside, Marco was leaning against the car and scanning the low horizon. Clouds still covered the sky but in a less-menacing manner, and the wind had died down to a light but chilling breeze off the river. When he saw Rick and Rondini approaching, he bent down and opened the rear door for his employer.

"Back to the hotel, Mr. Rondini?"

"Yes, Marco, but we're going to make a stop on the way. I need to check out a piece of land that may be for sale."

Rick noticed the bewildered look on the driver's face, and could almost hear the gears working in the man's head. The rich American comes back to his birthplace for a funeral and finds a parcel of land for sale. What better way to return to one's roots than to buy land where they were once planted? It made sense to Rick, but it might be the farthest thing from Angelo's mind.

"Go out to the road and turn left, toward the river." Rondini got into the Mercedes, followed by Rick and the driver. The car drove slowly along the driveway and stopped momentarily before turning onto the road. Fences lined both sides of the pavement, those on the left marked periodically with the R of the Rondini property. Just as the water became visible, Rondini tapped Marco on the shoulder.

"Pull up at that gate and we'll get out. I always like to walk when I'm looking at a property."

The driver obliged, slowing to a stop. The metal gate was a narrow one, opening on a path rather than a road. Farm equipment would have to get into this field from another direction, though it appeared that this part of the farm had not seen a tractor, or any other machinery, in some time. The ground was covered with a green stubble that looked like it was attempting to grow back after its last cutting. Perpendicular to the path, dirt rows ran between the green in the direction of the river, their lines blocked here and there by scraggly brown weeds.

Rondini emerged from the back seat, adjusted his glasses, and looked in all directions. He pulled the belt of his overcoat around him after a cold gust tried to force it open.

"Not exactly like the wind off Lake Michigan, though it's trying." The gate was closed but not locked. Rondini pulled the latch and it swung open with a low creak. "Let's check it out, Montoya." The two men walked through the gate into the field while the driver leaned against his car and watched. His face showed concern, which Rick assumed was worry that mud might find its way to the floor of his immaculate Mercedes.

As Rondini's eyes moved, he spoke. "The main factor, Montoya, is location, depending on what kind of business they might put here. If it's a factory, there has to be easy access to the highway to get the product out, and that road where we're parked could be widened to accommodate the traffic. If they're selling, the public has to have a way to get in, so the same concerns. Depending on what you're selling, you have to be close to your market. Is this place near enough to Mantova to get people here if they put up some mega-store? I don't know. You'd need a marketing study of the demographic. Or is there enough of a rural population to support a business here? The idea that you build it and they will come is crap. You'd have to know what you can expect before anyone would sink a dime into construction."

Rondini was in his element, making Rick feel like a young resident following a veteran doctor on his hospital rounds. They turned to the right and walked down between rows of dormant plants toward the river. The sky had darkened to a color that signaled a change in weather, but Rondini was oblivious to the possibility of getting wet.

"Assuming electricity, sewerage, and water are not a problem, this could work. Its flatness makes it very easy to build on. But there are too many questions that I can't answer. Look how scenic the river is from here."

They had reached the end of the row and ascended a small hill. Through breaks in the trees they could see the waters of the Mincio, its width beginning to open as it flowed toward the city.

"I can see why my cousin liked to come here. I've never been into fishing, or for that matter any pastime other than golf, and I only play it for the business contacts. But somehow, looking at that water, I get it. Ironic, isn't it, that it's here that he met his end? Or perhaps poetic is the right word. Come on, let's get back. I've done what Livia asked, but if I were her, I'd keep it as farmland."

As they turned to retrace their steps, Rick noticed, through a break in the trees, a small dock jutting into the river. It was at the end of the road where the car was stopped. Rondini didn't spot it, and Rick said nothing. Nor did he mention a pickup truck that was idling at the far end of the field on the opposite side of the road. It was too far away for Rick to make out the face of the driver, and as he was trying to do just that, the person drove slowly through the field and out of view.

The return drive was mostly silent except for a few drops of rain that hit the roof of the car. Rondini went back to staring out the window at the passing scenery, deep in thought. Rick mused about what little he had garnered from talking to the people at Livia's place, and decided it didn't amount to much. Roberto Rondini had lost interest in running his *latteria*, and spent perhaps most of his time in town. Did the widower have someone on the side in Mantova? The most curious tidbit was the sale of the acreage they had just surveyed. Was there a connection between that sale—or non sale—and his demise? The dock he'd seen through the trees—could it be where the murder took place? If it was, it couldn't be any closer to the plot of land. It wasn't much, but it was all he had to go on. Perhaps some of it would click with Inspector Crispi.

It was midafternoon when they walked into the lobby of the hotel.

"I'm going to check in with Lexi to see what's going on in Chicago, then get some quick shut-eye. I'll meet you down here in an hour. We're going to make a visit to the house of Mantegna."

"The painter."

"Good for you, Language Man. You don't just read dictionaries. I did some research on him and thought it would be fun to see where he lived before we see his masterpiece tomorrow. I should say Lexi did the research and I read it. The house is now a museum. You've got something to do until then?

"I'll go talk to the inspector."

"Of course. You have things to tell him."

The woman at the front desk armed him with a map marked with a yellow highlighter to show him the route, insisting it would take no more than ten minutes. He was ready for a walk; it would give him a chance to get the feel of the town that peering from car windows couldn't provide. He could also try to plot a route for his morning run. He walked briskly, breathing in the heavy humidity in the air and enjoying the moisture on his skin. Fall was the best time of year in all the places he'd lived on both sides of the Atlantic. In New Mexico it meant aspens turning yellow on the mountains, and in Italy it marked the end of the harvest and meals with mushrooms and truffles. The street crossed the canal that had once been a defensive barrier, a piece of Venice dropped into a corner of Lombardy. He was now in the oldest section of Mantova, and the street narrowed accordingly before bursting into the open space of the Piazza delle Erbe that ran along the side of San'tAndrea, where they'd been for the funeral. The daily market held in the square had folded up and moved on hours earlier. Now its only inhabitants were two women pushing baby carriages.

Passing under an arch between buildings, Rick looked up to see a small door surrounded by a metal cage clinging high up on the side of an ancient tower. He'd seen them in other cities, a place of cruel punishment for criminals or enemies of those in power. It crossed his mind to ask Inspector Crispi if the police were still putting it to use, but the man had seemed humorless when he stopped Rick in the church. Probably not a good idea.

He turned the corner and found himself at one end of the magnificent Piazza Sordello. The city had banned vehicles from its cobblestones, keeping the long square—at least visually—in the golden age of the Gonzaga dynasty. The Palazzo Ducale, home of the dukes, ran along most of one side. Across from it was the cathedral which looked drab compared to Sant'Andrea—Marco the driver had been correct about it playing second fiddle to the more famous church. Immediately on Rick's right, at the corner, was the police station. It was simple to spot the *questura* in any city, since armed police were always stationed in front, and Mantova was no exception. He walked to the entrance and pushed through the doors.

Rick was expected. A uniformed corporal glanced at his identification and immediately took him up a set of steps to the second floor. Halfway down a drab corridor he tapped on a partially open door and looked in.

"*Ispettore? E' arrivato Signor Montoya.*"

The inspector ignored the policeman, but came around his desk and shook Rick's hand.

"Thank you for coming in, Signor Montoya. Please sit down."

Rick had not had much time in the dark church to size up the inspector, but he could see now that the man was, in his appearance, the complete opposite of his Uncle Piero. Crispi's unshaven face was not an attempt to be fashionable, but simply the result of not seeing a razor for too long. His suit looked to be a size large, but he was on his way to filling it. The hair needed cutting and combing, falling down on both sides of his forehead. At least his shoes were shined. Rick wondered how well Piero knew the guy.

"I hope I can be of help, Inspector."

"So do I," answered Crispi as they both sat.

"Perhaps you could begin by telling me what you know about Roberto Rondini's death. At the gathering I just came from, all I found out was that he drowned. No one said anything about foul play."

"I wouldn't expect his daughter to say something. I told her we were investigating, but she got it in her head that because of the nature of the death, such an investigation is a required formality. She dismissed any possibility other than a tragic accident." He paused. "The autopsy showed that Signor Rondini had a blow to the head, but that his death was by drowning. The medical examiner surmised that the head trauma caused him to lose consciousness, at which time he fell into the river and subsequently drowned. He frequently went fishing early in the morning, and kept a boat tied up at the river at one corner of his farm. We went to the dock and found blood stains on the wood. Given the fact that the dock was slippery from the morning mist, it is possible that he did indeed slip, lose his balance, hit his head, and fall into the water. He was in good physical health, but he was in his late sixties, so it could have happened that way."

"But you're not so sure."

"The wound analysis was inconclusive, the result of spending too much time in the water. The medical examiner could not say for sure if it was made only by impact on the dock, or if he was struck with something and then the head hit the wood, leaving the traces of blood. Or the head could have been purposely pressed to the dock to make it look like he slipped, after which he was pushed, unconscious, into the water to drown."

To Rick it seemed like thin gruel to justify the launch of an investigation, and he said so.

Crispi did not appear to be annoyed by his visitor's frankness. Nor was he pleased. The man was so lacking in emotion that he almost seemed to be on tranquilizers. His neutral expression never changed, including the eyes, which were locked on Rick's.

"Perhaps. But Signor Rondini was not universally loved. That fact was not featured at the funeral, as we both know, and I suspect it didn't come up in the events afterward. But he had that reputation." He waited for Rick to respond, and when he didn't, Crispi continued. "So far I have told you a great deal. Did you manage to glean anything from your contacts with the family that you would care to share?"

Rick couldn't decide if he liked Crispi or not. After this initial conversation the jury was still out, and it might stay out for a while.

"There was a neighbor, the man who owns the farm adjoining the Rondini property. Emilio Fiore, if I remember correctly. He freely admitted that he and the deceased did not always get along. He mentioned a plot of land that Rondini owned and was thinking of selling for development, a sale which he strongly opposed, partly because he wanted to buy it himself."

Crispi's eyebrows furrowed, not a radical change in his demeanor, but at least it was something. "I think I remember reading about it in the *Gazzetta*." His eyes strayed to the ceiling as he tried to recall. "A factory, was it? Or a furniture chain store? That kind of development happens frequently around here, and there are always those who oppose it. They want to keep the land pristine, either dotted with cattle or waving with corn."

"That would characterize this man Fiore."

The phone on the desk rang and Crispi leaned over to answer it. Rick gestured to ask if he should step out, but the inspector shook his head. While the policeman talked, Rick got to his feet and walked to the window. The office looked out over a rectangular courtyard that under previous owners may have been filled with grass and flowers, but now was paved and stuffed with police vehicles. The rest of the room was what Rick had seen before in the offices of other police stations, though more orderly than most. Crispi's desk was a model of neatness: a shelf behind it held books in a straight row, and a healthy potted plant was perfectly centered on the windowsill. Quite a contrast with the man's appearance. As Rick began studying the still-threatening sky, Crispi hung up the phone.

"Where were we? You were telling me about Rondini's neighbor?"

"Right," said Rick. "Fiore also mentioned that the deceased had been spending very little time on his dairy farm. Mostly he was here in town, where he had an apartment. The farm manager, Carlo Zucari, said the same thing."

"I spoke to Zucari."

"Fiore made an off-hand comment which I took to mean that Rondini had a lady friend of some sort here in town, which was why he was always here."

Inspector Crispi leaned forward and pulled a folder from the neat stack. "I know about her. Letizia Bentivoglio is her name. Younger than Rondini, as one might expect. I'm going to interview her this afternoon."

"So the word on her was already around."

"This is not Rome, Signor Montoya—there are few secrets here." He paused to let his bit of wisdom sink in. "What about the daughter, Signora Guarino?"

"I only exchanged pleasantries with her. But I spoke briefly with her husband."

"Yes, Francesco Guarino. I met him only in passing, but I got the sense that it is his wife who makes the decisions in that family. She will inherit the farm, of course."

"But Guarino could take over running it, I would assume. He's now a cheese inspector, so I would imagine he has the expertise."

Crispi declined to comment on Rick's assumption. "You said you met the manager. Any words of interest from him? He couldn't tell me much. It was he who took me to the dock where Rondini met his fate."

"If you've talked to all these people, Inspector, why have you asked me to help you?"

Crispi was unfazed. "A valid point. I thought your proximity to the family could yield some valuable information that they would be reluctant to pass to the authorities. They may let their guard down when around you and your employer. Already you have discovered the issue of the possible land sale. There may be nothing there, but it is worth exploring." He didn't try to hide a glance at his watch. "Signor Montoya, as I told you, I have made an appointment to interview Signora Bentivoglio. Thank you again for coming in." He rose and extended his hand. His face had not changed.

Later, as Rick walked back to the hotel, he tried to analyze his mixed feelings about the policeman. *Simpatico*, Crispi was not, but more importantly, did he know what he was doing? Did he even have enough evidence to warrant a police investigation? Maybe the guy just had a hunch, or someone had put a bug in his ear.

Rick had a little time before meeting Rondini, and when he got to the bridge over the canal he stopped to enjoy the view. Water ran happily under the bridge on its way to the lake, oblivious to the dark skies above, that could soon swell the flow into a torrent. All along it, the backs of stone houses were in a colorful competition for how many red and white geraniums could be packed into their window boxes. He pulled out his phone to take a picture, but decided against it. Instead, he hit some buttons and held it to his ear. It was answered after two rings.

"I thought you'd be calling," said Commissario Piero Fontana. "You have met Crispi?"

"Just got out of a meeting with him at the *questura*."

"And you are puzzled. That is the usual reaction people have when they first meet him. It was mine. But let me tell you a bit about the inspector."

"Please do, Zio." Rick leaned on the stone railing and spotted some tiny fish working against the current. "I have a few minutes before I must go back to work for my employer."

"Crispi doesn't look it at first, Riccardo, but he is one of the more brilliant police minds I have encountered. I was his supervisor when he was on a case here in Rome several years ago, and while it took me a good while to understand him, I came away impressed. I won't go into the particulars of the case now, I'll save that for some time when we dine together, but suffice to say it was a complicated one. He sorted out all the details and brought it to a successful conclusion."

"If he is so brilliant, Zio, how is it that he's only an inspector in Mantova?"

"It is always charming, dear nephew, when you drop the Italian subtlety and take on your American directness. But surely you have already discovered the answer to your question. It's very simple, really. Crispi does not interact well with his colleagues, and, something unusual in us Italians, he is not adept at office politics. In a word, he drives his co-workers and supervisors *pazzo*. And that is not the way to advance in any Italian bureaucracy, including the *Polizia dello Stato*."

Since Piero said he had supervised the inspector, Rick assumed that his uncle was one of those driven crazy. "But he's competent, Uncle?"

"More than competent."

"And honest."

"In my experience, yes."

"That's good enough for me. And I have an advantage over his fellow policemen: I don't have to work with him permanently."

"Indeed."

"Perhaps I can get him to smile."

"I wouldn't bet on it."

Chapter Four

Inspector Crispi paused on the street and looked up at the windows of the building. Letizia Bentivoglio lived in a walk-up apartment at the eastern edge of the city's ancient center. At one time it had been the residence of one well-to-do family, but today the building was divided into three rentals, hers being the one on the top floor. The advantage was that she had an unencumbered view of the lake from her back windows, since only a parking lot and some grass separated the building from the water. The disadvantage was the stair climb to reach it, but when her door opened, Crispi could see that this was not an issue for the woman, who looked to be the picture of health. She was about forty-five, her hair color appeared natural, and the figure under the jeans and sweater was slim. He assumed that the initial attraction to her for the deceased Roberto Rondini was the obvious one, but wondered if there might be something else. That could come out in the interview, but at the moment, Crispi's main interest was what happened in the period before the death.

"I'm glad you called on my day off. I wouldn't have wanted a policeman showing up at the office."

She led the way into the small living room and took a seat in one of its two chairs. An empty cup perched on the side table next to it, made him wonder if she would offer him something. He hoped not, since it would only waste time. He made a fast assessment of the surroundings to confirm what he already assumed. The wear on the furniture and the type of decorations in the room indicated that she had been living alone for some time, perhaps her entire adult life. There were no masculine touches to be seen; everything had an aura of neatness and regularity. What would have caused a woman like this to take up with an older man? There could be a dozen reasons, but likely none had any bearing on the case. He had no cause to include her as a suspect, at least up to this point.

"Where do you work?" He knew the answer, and she knew he knew, but it was an easy way to begin the interview.

"The large farm equipment company just south of the city. That's how I met Roberto. He came in one day with his farm manager because they needed a new cattle truck and some other machinery. I do the paperwork for our sales. I'd expected that once he'd made the decision on what he wanted he'd send Carlo—that's his manager—to deal with the details, but instead he came back himself. We became friends. It turned out that he had an apartment in town very close to mine, so we used to have dinner a few times a week. Sometimes I'd make dinner here, but mostly he'd take me out. He liked to go to nice places."

It was more information than the question deserved. She was ready to talk, so he decided to let her do so.

"Tell me about Signor Rondini."

Her sigh was close to a shudder. "He was not what most people thought of him. Oh, I know you're wondering how I know what people thought of him, but it's because he told me. He laughed about it. But to me he was kind and generous, always. He was lonely after his wife died several years ago, and I could see it when I met him that day. I could sense it. He needed companionship, which is something he didn't get from his family, and he could talk to me."

"When did you see him last?"

She looked out the window at the darkening sky, thinking

about an answer, but he knew she had to have been ready for the question.

"The night before the…" Her lips trembled almost imperceptibly. "The night before, we had dinner here."

"Did he seem any different from your previous meetings?"

She looked at the cup next to her, and he thought she might get up to fill it. Instead she pondered the question while Crispi waited.

"Not different from how he'd been for the last few weeks. About a month ago, when he began considering the sale of some property, he was surprised to find that people were against it. Not just his manager, he'd expected that, but people he'd never met. He thought it was none of their business and brushed it off as nothing, but I could tell he was bothered by it. I was the only one who could see this side of him. To everyone else he was just someone who had money and wanted to make more of it. He wasn't like that, Inspector."

She got up, walked stiffly to the window, and stared out across the water. Her hands were clasped tightly and pressed against her chest.

"Also in the last few months," she continued, "he did a lot of thinking about his father."

"I don't understand."

She continued looking at the lake. Did she know that the body was discovered on the shore almost within view of her window?

"I suspect it had something to do with the anniversary of his father's death. Twenty years ago the man had died when he was the age Roberto was about to reach. I suppose it's natural to think about those things. He talked about what his father had done in his lifetime and compared it to his own accomplishments."

"Did he tell you what were his conclusions?"

She didn't answer immediately. "No. No, he didn't. Perhaps he didn't come to any. Contemplating one's mortality is never easy, I suppose. And just a few weeks before his own death, Roberto went to a funeral, which made him even more depressed. Apparently, the family either didn't know who Roberto was, or if they did, they didn't think he should have appeared at the funeral. It's difficult enough when friends your own age start dying...."

Crispi looked at his watch and decided it was time to wrap up the interview.

"Signora Bentivoglio, is there anything that would lead you to believe that his death was not an accident?"

She turned quickly. "It was not an accident, Inspector."

"You seem very sure."

"Roberto had been going fishing in the same place for years, even decades. As he often told me, he had his routine, it was a comfort to him. Always arriving at the same time, no matter the weather, always with the same fishing pole; he even fished in the same place along the river. Some spot only he knew, where he claimed the big fish hid. It was a joke with us. He said he couldn't tell me where it was, since I might sell the secret to someone." A smile appeared on her face for the first time, but it disappeared quickly. "No, Inspector, he didn't have an accident."

Crispi didn't point out that accidents could happen to anyone, especially at Rondini's age. He had seen this reaction before in people close to victims—denial that fate could have simply done its work.

"If it wasn't an accident, who could be responsible? Did he ever talk about enemies he had? Someone who could want him dead?"

She didn't try to hide her agitation. "As you already know, Inspector, he was not well liked. If such dislike could reach the point of murder, I have no way of knowing. I sensed that he and Carlo had reached an understanding. Neither liked the other, but Roberto trusted Carlo and let him run things. There was a neighbor he didn't get along with. I think the man wanted to buy that piece of land. The price might have been right, but Roberto had no intention of selling it to the man. As far as his daughter, I think their relationship was normal, but he said a few times how her husband was weak."

"Weak?"

"Well, you know, not a strong personality like Roberto. He looked down on people he thought had no backbone. How his son-in-law felt about him, I have no idea. I never met him. Nor his daughter, for that matter."

Crispi rubbed a hand across the stubble of his chin, trying to decide whether to ask Signora Bentivoglio an obvious question: Why had Rondini, a widower many years removed from the mourning period, not carried on openly with the woman? He needed female companionship and she was certainly respectable, so why treat her like a mistress? That was the way the family viewed her, it seemed, since she was not at any of the events connected with the funeral. No, better to get an answer from someone else; the question would be too painful for her right now. He could pose it to her later, if needed, but likely would not. It was simply not important to the investigation. He got to his feet.

"You are back at work tomorrow, Signora?"

"Yes." She turned from the window. "We open at seven, and often our clientele is outside waiting. Farmers keep early hours."

Just like fisherman, Crispi thought.

"There is some debate," said Marco, "as to whether Andrea Mantegna in fact designed his own palazzo, but regardless of who did, it remains a spectacular structure. The combination of the circle and the square, which you see so much in the positioning of figures in Renaissance painting, is utilized here in a simple but powerful way."

The driver, along with Rick, Rondini, and Lexi, stood on the damp stones of the Casa Mantegna's open courtyard looking upward. The four sides of the building's outer shell framed the circular opening to a clouded sky. From it, an almost invisible mist of rain fell on their faces. The walls surrounding the open space were an austere brick, broken by doors leading to the inner rooms. Everything about the building, from the drab outside to the floor plan, was rigidly geometric.

"Not exactly warm and inviting," said Rondini, "but it might be better on a sunny day. The circle in the square is intriguing, I have to admit."

Lexi pointed at the curved walls. "My image of Italian Renaissance architecture was always ornate marble and rounded columns, in the classical tradition. This is not like that at all. The four doors are framed classically, and the sun design on the stone floor adds something, but the rest is quite plain."

"Perhaps Mantegna himself was a rather plain guy," said Rick. He looked through one of the open doors into one of the rooms of the gallery. "The exhibit inside doesn't look very plain."

Swaths of bright color filled a large canvas on the wall opposite the door. Angelo scowled. "I can find better abstract works in Chicago; that's not what I came to Italy to see. Lexi, you and Marco go in and check it out. I need to talk to Language Man here."

Lexi and the driver exchanged looks and walked through the door.

"Tell me what happened with the cop," Angelo said, once the other two were inside. "He really thinks my cousin was murdered?"

"Yes, he does." Rick explained the head injury that preceded the drowning, and Crispi's suspicion that it was not caused by a fall.

"Who does he think could have done it?"

"I know you want me to be frank. Am I correct?"

"You better be."

"Well, Mr. Rondini, it appears that your cousin was not universally loved. Whether that was enough for someone to do him in remains to be seen, but there is no lack of people who could be considered suspects. It might be better to begin with who could have gained from not having your cousin around. And that starts, unfortunately, with his daughter and her husband. They inherit the farm."

Rondini's expression remained the same. "Makes sense. Go on."

"The manager of the farm, Zucari, could be out of a job if Livia's husband takes over running the operation and wants to be more hands-on than your cousin was. Zucari didn't agree with selling the plot, as Livia told you, but that doesn't appear to be a big deal. Then there is that neighbor, Emilio Fiore."

"The drunk."

"The one who had too much wine, yes. He even admitted to us that he didn't get along with Roberto Rondini, and was very much against him selling that property for development. In my mind, he's the strongest suspect."

"It all seems a touch weak to build a murder case, don't you think? But if he was killed, maybe Roberto was just mugged by someone who knew he went fishing every morning. It happens all the time in Chicago."

"The inspector didn't mention if his wallet was missing, and I think he would have."

Rondini squinted at Rick. "You think this guy knows what he's doing?"

"I would have had my doubts if I hadn't spoken to my uncle afterward. He told me Crispi is a first-class policeman, and I can assure you my uncle would have said so if it were the other way around."

They looked upward at the same time. The small drops were beginning to get bigger, but the rain felt good on their faces.

"Montoya, after hearing all this I feel like I don't know enough about my cousin and the rest of the family. We need to find out more, but the kind of questions I have now I wouldn't want to ask Livia. See what you can get from the cop. By the way, what about Roberto's friend in town? Did he mention her?"

"He was on his way to interview her."

The thought of his cousin's extra-curricular activities made Rondini smile. He looked over to see Lexi and the driver come back through the doorway into the courtyard.

"A local artist on her way up," she said, "or trying to. Nothing very original."

Rondini was not paying attention. "Marco, I need to find out more about my family. Is there some kind of genealogical society here that could help?"

The question startled the driver.

"I don't know about such societies, Mr. Rondini. If I were you, I would start at the *Gazzetta*. It is the oldest newspaper in Italy and I think they have…" He turned to Rick for help. "*Un archivio?*"

"Archives," Rick said.

"Yes, that's it. Perhaps you could go there, Mr. Rondini."

"You mean perhaps Language Man could go there." He looked up. "Is the car parked nearby? It's starting to rain harder."

"I found a place near the door. I'll get it unlocked so you don't get wet." Marco walked briskly toward the entrance.

"I'm surprised he didn't know about genealogy stuff," Rondini said as the driver disappeared out the door. "Don't a lot of Americans come here in search of their roots? I would think it would be something a guy who works with tourists would know. Am I right, Language Man?"

"Yes and no. The vast majority of Americans of Italian descent trace their roots to the south, people who left to escape poverty in what has always been the least developed area of Italy. During the time of the great migrations, at the end of the nineteenth and the beginning of the twentieth centuries, the boats left from Naples and Palermo. Here in the north it was relatively prosperous, certainly relative to the *mezzogiorno*, as they call the south. So there was less emigration from around the northeast. It's still one of the richest areas of Italy—actually of Europe."

"It makes me wonder why my parents left here. They never talked much about it, and by the time I was curious about it, they were gone and I couldn't ask them." He looked at Rick and then back at Lexi. "Today's advice to both of you from an old man: ask questions now, while you can."

Lexi's expression gave Rick the idea that Rondini was acting out of character.

"We will be sure to take that advice, Mr. Rondini. But perhaps Rick can find out something at this newspaper Marco mentioned. And if needed I can get on one of those ancestry websites and find out what I can there."

When they emerged onto the sidewalk the Mercedes was waiting, Marco holding open the rear passenger door for Rondini and Lexi. Rick put his hand on the handle of the front door and noticed a paper folded under the wiper in front of his seat. He reached over to take it out.

"Were you parked illegally, Marco?" he said. "You may have a ticket."

The driver's head jerked up to look at the signs along the sidewalk. "That's impossible."

As Angelo and Lexi got settled into the back seat Rick unfolded what was more of a card than a piece of paper. The message on it, written in a crude hand with red ink and slightly blurred from the rain, was brief and to the point. He passed it to Marco, who stiffened when he read it.

"What's it say?"

Rick turned to face the back seat. "Short and sweet, Mr. Rondini. The simple translation is 'Go back to America or face the consequences.' Someone is not happy with our presence in Mantova."

Marco stared at the paper, still gripped in his hand. "What shall we do, Mr. Rondini?"

"Drive back to the hotel, of course."

Five minutes later Marco had been dismissed and the three stood in the lobby of the hotel. No words had been exchanged on the way back from the museum, making Rick suspect that Rondini did not want to say anything in the presence of the driver. That was the case.

"Does this happen often, Language Man?"

"Threatening notes?"

"Yeah. 'Yankee go home,' that kind of thing? Is this a hotbed of Communism?"

Lexi stood silently next to her boss and waited for Rick's reply. She maintained her usual stone composure.

"I'd like to say it is, but it doesn't seem likely at all. The only reason I can think of is that someone saw you out in the field and put two and two together to think you wanted to buy it."

Had Lexi not been there, he would have brought up what Inspector Crispi had said about opposition to the sale. Rick had to assume that Rondini was keeping the police involvement between him and Rick. Her next words confirmed it.

"That's the piece of property Ms. Guarino asked you to look at?"

"Yeah. But who would have known that I was going out there to see it?"

"Her husband," said Rick. "The manager of the farm. Probably other people who were there. Someone may have overheard her asking you. I don't think she was trying to keep it a secret, do you?"

"I suppose not. This reminds me of the time outside St. Louis when that group protested one of our developments, and it got ugly. Some kind of bird migration issue."

"The police took care of that without much trouble," said Lexi. "Should the local police be notified now?"

Rondini held his room keycard between two fingers and snapped it with his thumb. "Some scribbled note? I don't think so. What about you, Language Man? You're our authority on local customs, including the police."

"If it happens again, perhaps. But I'd let it go for now."

"Okay, done. I am going to my room and stay there for the night. The spread at Livia's should hold me until breakfast, but if I get hungry I'll get room service. Language Man, I want you to take Lexi to a nice restaurant and get her to talk about something other than business, if that's possible." He laughed and shuffled toward the elevator.

Rick rubbed his eyes. *That will be about as easy as teaching her to speak Italian.*

• • ● ● •

"All right," Rick said, "let's have the truth. Who are you, and what have you done with Alexis Coleman?"

Lexi's giggle was not the first of the evening, though the first since the second bottle of wine had arrived at the table. The restaurant, in the heart of Mantova, was almost full. The clientele was local and affluent, which reflected the prosperity of this part of Italy. Tables in the middle of the large dining room were each discreetly lit by a single shaded fixture which hung from the ceiling. Thanks to the reservation called in by the hotel, Rick and Lexi were ensconced in a corner booth with a view of the other diners. The atmosphere was low-key and elegant, broken only by table conversation and a barely audible classical CD.

"I like to unwind when I get off work, Rick. Don't you? I love working for Angelo, but I have to clear my mind. You must have the same thing after spending hours doing a translation, or interpreting for someone. I can't even begin to imagine how exhausting that must be. Poor dear." She reached across the small table and patted his hand.

"A translator's lot is not an easy one." He furrowed and then raised his brow. "But every so often someone like you brings a few rays of sunshine into a life of drudgery."

This night's rays included a glimmering gold pendant just visible above the top button of a silk blouse which clung perfectly to Lexi's body. As she laughed, gold hoop earrings quivered as if trying to distract him. He was not distracted. At that moment the waiter cleared away the pasta dishes and carefully placed the menu in front of each of them. She thanked him while trying unsuccessfully to wipe the smile from her face.

"You mean we're going to eat more? I have to say that the idea of ravioli filled with pumpkin sounded very strange, but I'm sure glad you talked me into it. With the butter sauce and sage, that ravioli was amazing, but it was a meal in itself."

"*Those* ravioli, my dear. I believe we each got three. If you'd had only one it would be a *raviolo*."

"I love it when you talk in tongues, Rick. This wine is also amazing, by the way."

"All the better to loosen your tongue, Lexi. I'm waiting for you to tell me more about your boss."

She pulled a face. "Okay, but first, what will we have next to eat?"

The hotel concierge had told him that one of the restaurant's specialties was a warm capon salad. Lexi admitted she'd never eaten capon, and only recalled hearing about it in Shakespearean plays—which seemed a good enough reason to try it. The waiter left with the order and Rick filled her wineglass.

"You were about to tell me more about Angelo, which you seem to call him now, when he's out of earshot. But how did you come to be working for him?"

She sipped her wine and gazed at him over the rim of the glass before setting it back down.

"Angelo Rondini is a complicated man, but I will try to simplify. Only child in an immigrant family very much committed to the American dream. He grew up in the Bronx, went to Fordham on scholarship, started at a construction firm and slowly worked his way up until getting into an argument with his boss and starting his own business. He's been burned enough times in business deals that he's very wary of people's motives. Made his money by doing things his way and making his own decisions. And you can't argue with success."

Rick held up a hand. "You don't need to return to your daytime self, Lexi. You can do this without going all serious on me."

Another giggle. "Sorry." She took more than a small sip of wine. "Angelo is difficult to work for because he has trouble trusting his staff to do the right thing, the right thing being the way he would have wanted to do it. He doesn't micromanage, he second-guesses. It drives people nuts. Some quit every few months, a few are fired."

"He seems to trust you, Lexi. He told me when he got off the plane that he never goes anywhere without you."

The grin showed a perfect row of white teeth. "He said that? How sweet. Well, Rick, we have a special relationship, thanks to Nikki."

"Nikki?"

"Nikki Rondini, his daughter."

The second courses arrived and were placed carefully in front of them on bone white plates. The dishes were as simple as the plates: a few leaves of lettuce topped by white slices of capon breast and drizzled with a vinaigrette sauce that included red raisins. Before departing, the waiter filled their glasses.

"He hasn't asked me yet if everything is tasting all right," said Lexi as she gazed at the plate.

"They don't need to do that here in Italy." Rick waited for her to pick up her fork before taking his in hand.

"This looks fantastic, Rick. Remind me again what capon is. It looks like chicken."

"It is. So what about Rondini's daughter?"

She waited to finish her first bite. "Wow. That is something. Just the right light tang in the sauce, doesn't overpower the pure taste of the capon. And it goes perfectly with this white wine. What is it again?"

He pulled it out of the bucket and checked the label. "*Oltrepó Pavese pinot grigio*. It comes from west of here, near Pavia. *Oltrepó* means the other side of the River Po. So you know his daughter?"

"Rick, you keep plying me with exotic food and drink. How can you expect me to stay on topic?"

"No one has ever accused me of plying."

"Someone should have, you're very adept at it." She took another small bite of the capon and savored it before continuing. "All right, Nikki Rondini. We were roommates our first year at Northwestern and became best of friends. Still are. She took me home one weekend, since she lived right in Chicago, and I became almost a member of the family. The summer before my senior year Angelo took me on as an intern at Rondini Enterprises. That led to a job offer when I graduated, and I ended up as his special assistant. Now let me get back to this chicken."

"Capon. You were a business major?"

"No," she said through a mouthful. "Chemistry. But Angelo said I had a knack for business, whatever that means."

"Plus he trusts you, being a member of the family and all. And Mrs. Rondini?

"She died about five years ago. Wonderful woman of Irish ancestry, so she was able to give as well as she got from Angelo. It took him more than a year to get over her passing, if one ever truly gets over that kind of loss."

"Do you have much time for a personal life, what with having to jet around the country all the time?"

She tilted her head at Rick and smiled. "That sounds like a leading question, Mr. Montoya, and one I will decline to answer. It is also not one you will hear me asking you."

His mind churned in an unsuccessful attempt to interpret her comment; he'd had too much wine.

"Fair enough. And now, since you have almost finished your *secondo*, it is time to return to the business at hand, which is the possibility of ordering something else. I understand they make an excellent banana split here."

"Rick, that's not even funny. Pour us the rest of that bottle and let's take our leave."

A few minutes later Rick was helping her on with her coat inside the door of the restaurant. They agreed that after the warmth of the restaurant the chill night air would feel good on their faces, but they did not expect what they saw on stepping outside. While they had dined, a windless cold front had parked over the city, coating everything with a light layer of snow. The flakes were still coming down softly, glimmering as they caught the rays of the streetlights and dropping silently to the ground. The street, always quiet at this late hour, was made more silent by the insulating whiteness.

"I can call a taxi," Rick said.

"Absolutely not. Look how pristine the snow is. In Chicago it turns to dirty slush even before it reaches the ground. No, we walked here and we'll walk back." She looked down to check out their footwear. "We're both dressed for it."

She took his arm and they started down the street, their boots leaving the only marks in the snow until a single car slowly passed. After two corners they emerged onto the piazza where Rick had been earlier in the day. Two police cars sat empty in front of the *questura* and a young armed policeman stood next to the door trying his best not to look cold. Many public buildings in Italy had guards; would Lexi know that it was the police station? Rick opted not to point it out.

"Rick, do you think that note on the car is really nothing to worry about?"

Perhaps she did recognize the building.

"Like I said to Mr. Rondini, I suspect it was just some silly prank, perhaps tied to the possible land sale, perhaps totally unrelated. If it happens again we'll rethink it."

"How would they know about Angelo being a developer?"

"After that sparkling phone conversation I had with you, I got online and found out all sorts of things about your boss. Anyone who has even minimal English could have done the same."

"I suppose you're right. Angelo doesn't get upset about these things. I'm sure he's sleeping like a baby now."

"And you will too, Lexi."

They had left the piazza and reached a block of covered sidewalk, its shops shuttered and dark. At the end of the street Lexi clutched Rick's arm as they stepped back into the open, noticing that the flakes were now smaller and fewer. By the time they reached the hotel the snowfall had stopped. They stamped their feet on the mat outside and pushed through the doors.

"I am in the habit of taking a run every morning." Rick brushed the snow from his hair and coat while Lexi did the same. "But I don't think the streets will be cleared by tomorrow. I doubt if the city of Mantova has much snow-removal infrastructure."

Lexi brushed a final bit of snow from his shoulder. "Don't be a wuss, Rick. I run every day in Chicago, no matter what the weather."

A picture of Lexi Coleman in running tights formed in his head. "How about a nightcap in the bar to warm us after the long march across the Lombard tundra?"

"I'd love to, but I have to go up and check the messages that piled up while we were enjoying our capon. Oh, I remembered where I'd read about capon. Jaques' monologue in *As You Like It* about all the world being a stage. One of the ages of man is…" She closed her eyes tightly as she thought. "The justice, wasn't it? 'In fair round belly, with a good capon lined.' That's us tonight, even the round belly part."

"I'm impressed that a chemistry major would remember that."

"My minor was English Lit." She kissed two fingers and touched them to Rick's lips. "Thank you for a wonderful dinner, Rick." She walked to the elevator while he watched.

He hadn't thought about Betta the entire evening.

Chapter Five

Rick chose his steps with care, trying to avoid the few ice patches left on the sidewalk from the previous evening. He could see his breath, but in the last hour the temperature had climbed enough to begin to melt the snow. With no clouds, the sunshine would make quick work of it. It was turning into a pleasant morning, but he was annoyed nonetheless. If he'd not been on a job, he would have taken his morning run, snow and ice or not, but the risk of twisting an ankle or worse was not worth taking when he was on Rondini's payroll. He tried not to think what Lexi would say when she found out he'd skipped the run. At least the newspaper office was close to the hotel. Some of the sidewalks had been cleared and others were in the process. Either the Mantovani were fastidious about the walkways in front of their homes or there was a city ordinance that required them to be. He reached the corner, crossed a busy street at the light, and came to the entrance to *La Gazzetta di Mantova*.

The building was not what he expected—the oldest newspaper in Italy was housed in what had to be the city's most modern building. Steel, glass, and sharp edges caught the rays of the morning sun and bounced them off dripping tree branches and the cars driving by. The glass door of the main entrance was marked with the newspaper name. Underneath, in a smaller font, was a simple *Fondata nel 1664*. No big deal.

He pushed the door and entered an open space, its only furniture a tall dark desk behind which a woman sat on a stool. A telephone and laptop were lined up neatly in front of her on the wood surface. She looked up from her screen and smiled at Rick.

"*Desidera?*"

In this context the word meant, simply, "Can I help you?" But since it was a form of the verb "to desire," Rick always found it a wonderfully Italian way to say something so mundane.

"*Buon giorno.* I am doing some family genealogical research. Is it possible to have access to your archives?"

"Of course. Just sign in here." She turned a clipboard in his direction and slid it across. "And if you could give me your identification, please?" She pulled a badge from beneath the table and put it next to the clipboard as Rick wrote. He finished writing, passed his ID to her, and clipped the badge to his coat collar.

"Take the elevator to the basement and follow the signs. Dottor da Feltre will help you."

When he got to the basement, signs for the *archivio* took him down a long corridor to a set of glass doors. The ceiling was low, giving it the feeling of a crypt, which would be appropriate for a place where ancient texts were kept. The lighting was dim, in contrast with the brightness of the atrium just one story above. Rick pushed open the door and once again was surprised. He'd expected rows of shelves, extending deeply into the basement, on which editions of the *Gazzetta* would be bound and stacked, their browned pages reaching back centuries. Instead, two cubicles, each with a chair and computer, were positioned against one wall. Ahead, three imposing doors were marked with the warning: No admittance to unauthorized persons. Unlike the corridor, the room was bright with the light of fixtures set into the ceiling. On the side opposite the cubicles a man sat hunched over the morning's edition. The newspaper was the only item on his desk except for a nameplate, its letters carved from a wood block: VITTORINO DA FELTRE.

The man looked up from his paper when Rick pushed open the glass door. Only a green eyeshade was lacking to give him the central casting image of an archivist: thinning gray hair, thick glasses, and a wrinkled shirt and tie. Rick was disappointed to find that the fingers were not stained with newsprint.

"You lost?"

"Not if these are the archives," Rick answered.

The eyes widened, their outlines blurred through the glasses. "Really?" He closed the newspaper and pushed it to one side of the desk. "I haven't had anyone in here in a week. And he was looking for the boiler room. What are you searching for?" He took off his glasses, pulled a dirty handkerchief from a jacket pocket, and began to clean them while squinting at Rick.

"Background on the Rondini family."

The glasses were replaced. "The guy who just died." He tapped the newspaper in front of him. "I read the paper pretty closely every day. You a reporter? You don't look familiar. Not that the reporters come down here much. They do their research online." He raised his eyes and pointed to the upper floors.

"I'm not a reporter. Is everything you have online?"

"No, not everything, only back to 1875. The older stuff is in there." He pointed his chin toward the doors along the back wall. "You need anything before 1875?"

"I wouldn't think so," said Rick.

"If you do, let me know. Just turn on one of those computers and you're into our system. There's an instruction sheet in each cubicle on how to get in and do a search. By word, dates, whatever. It's pretty easy. There's a printer if you need to make copies, but if you do a lot of them, I'll need to charge you. There's paper if you want to make notes." It was an instructional speech recited by rote. When he finished, the man studied Rick for a few moments, decided that this visitor would not be a problem, and returned to his newspaper.

Rick followed the instructions and quickly found the obituary of Roberto Rondini. It had nothing unexpected, but he took notes on the basics anyway. Son of Enzo and Pina Rondini, long deceased, husband of Berta Rondini, who died four years earlier. Daughter Livia Rondini Guarino. A cousin, Angelo Rondini, lived in America. Owner of the Rondini dairy farm and cheese producer. Italian obituaries, he noted, were considerably shorter than the ones he remembered reading in the *Albuquerque Journal*. There was a photograph which showed more than a strong resemblance to Cousin Angelo. Further searches brought up passing mentions of Roberto Rondini buried inside news stories, mostly related to the dairy industry or the associations of cheese producers. Rick got the sense that his participation in such groups was minimal. Not so with the local fishing club, of which the deceased was active to the point of serving as an officer. The man knew his priorities. Fishing was apparently considered a sport by the newspaper, since a story about the fishing association election appeared in the back pages of the sports section, after all the soccer news. In the same election in which Rondini had been voted onto the board, the previous president resigned from it. Probably not much there, Rick concluded, but worth mentioning to Crispi. He copied down the name of the disgruntled fisherman: Sandro Bastoncini.

Next, he searched Livia and Francesco Guarino. Of Roberto's daughter there was almost no mention, other than her marriage to Francesco. For the husband, Rick found numerous articles in connection with the Parmigiano-Reggiano Consortium, mostly participation in industry meetings or boards involved with production standards. Francesco was a bureaucrat.

It was in a previous Rondini generation that things got interesting.

Enzo Rondini, the father of the deceased, had been a prominent politician in his day, but his prominence had been gained without the support of the *Gazzetta*. From the selection of stories and the tone of the reporting, it was clear that the newspaper had it in for the man. First mention was of Enzo as a student activist, in what the paper considered the wrong political party. His initial foray into politics was on the campaign of a city councilman, then as part of the man's staff when the election was successful. Enzo steadily moved up and eventually gained elective office himself. Rick scrolled quickly through the pages, finding one article after another which insinuated shady dealings, or out-and-out corruption. If the stories were to be believed, Enzo Rondini had used his political clout to go from being a small-time farmer to owning large tracts of land. One of the losers had been a farmer who'd fallen on bad times, been unable to pay his taxes, and had his land confiscated. When it was put up for sale, it was Rondini who managed to put in the winning bid, something the paper did not believe was by chance. On another occasion, posters of a political opponent had disappeared from the walls of the city, with suspicion placed on Rondini's campaign workers. No one was ever charged. The newspaper finally was successful in thwarting his political career when he lost an attempt to get into the national parliament. At that point Enzo Rondini retired from politics and concentrated his efforts on making money from cheese. The paper, still showing animosity, covered allegations that Rondini had bribed dairy inspectors, but Rick could find nothing to show he was ever charged.

Rick looked at the clock on the wall and pushed back his chair. One thing was sure, the *Gazzetta di Mantova* and Enzo Rondini did not get along. But was it something personal between an editor and Rondini? Or could it simply have been a tiny local skirmish in the national political war of that time between the Christian Democrats and the Communists? Hard to know. He reluctantly turned off the computer and got to his feet.

The archivist looked up from the sports pages. "Find what you needed?"

"I found quite a bit. But I'll have to come back."

"You don't need a reservation."

The horse showed impatience, its face lowered and the hoof of one muscular leg raised slightly from the ground. The groom had a hand on the saddle, his expression showing no concern as he chatted with a friend standing next to him. Two large dogs stood next to the horse, tense and ready to jump if the huge white animal next to them showed any more signs of aggression. The animals were more excited than their human masters; they knew they would soon be bounding over the flat fields of Lombardy, the wind in their faces and the smell of the countryside surging into their lungs. It was what they enjoyed most. It was the day of the hunt.

"Bottom line," Rick said, "if what I read is to be believed, your Uncle Enzo was no angel."

Angelo kept his eyes on Mantegna's hunting party for a few more seconds, then craned his neck to study the work on the ceiling. A peacock and several winged *putti*, framed by blue sky and clouds, looked down with curiosity at the group standing in the center of the square room. The uniformed museum guard stood to one side. He worked in the most famous collection of art in the city, but he kept his eyes on the visitors, not the walls.

"It sounds like he might have broken a few rules, Language Man. Sometimes you have to do that to make it in this world. I wonder if any of that was passed on to my cousin, either through the genes or in the upbringing. I've often thought about that with my parents. They were simple, hard-working people, your classic immigrants. I wouldn't call them overly ambitious; they just wanted the best for me. And look how I turned out. I couldn't have been more different."

"You turned out well, Mr. Rondini," said Lexi.

"I bent the rules a few times, Lexi, and as you well know, I've made a good number of enemies." Angelo was looking now at the court scene, the seated Ludovico Gonzaga surrounded by family and courtiers. A trusted aide was whispering something in the duke's ear. "Look at this guy. You don't think he stayed in power by following all the rules, do you? My Uncle Enzo was just following the local customs."

"We should be on our way if you want to go back to the hotel before meeting your niece for lunch, Mr. Rondini."

The Lexi of business hours had returned, without so much as an acknowledgment to Rick that she'd ever been away. On the way to the museum she had sat in the back seat and continued briefing her boss on issues from the home office in Chicago uncovered during the night. Rick wondered if she'd gotten any sleep, not that her appearance indicated it. Quite the contrary.

A few minutes later they had descended into the courtyard where Marco and the car were waiting.

"You enjoyed the castle, Signor Rondini?"

"Immensely, Marco, and they saved the best for last."

"I never tire of seeing those walls."

"I should have asked you to come in with us. Next time." He looked up at the castle stone. "I wonder if the Gonzagas felt cooped up in this place."

"Mr. Rondini, we really must—"

"I know, Lexi. We'll drop you at the hotel so you can get back to work. That's really why you're in such a hurry, isn't it? You can get to your computer and work while Language Man and I go off to have a leisurely lunch, Italian-style."

They all got into the car. Marco drove them back through the winding streets to the hotel where Rick jumped out and opened the back door for Lexi. She unfolded her long legs, stood at the curb, and bent down to look through the open door. As always, she was clutching her briefcase.

"Have a nice lunch, Mr. Rondini."

Her boss waved.

Rick said, "Lexi, don't work so hard that you forget to have something sent up to your room for lunch. You need your sustenance."

She frowned, saw that Rondini could not see her face, and gave him a wink before walking to the door of the hotel. Rick watched her go in and took her place in the back seat.

"I worry about that girl," said Rondini when the car turned onto the street that ran along the water. A few patches of snow clung to the grass where the trees provided shade, but most of it had long melted away, soaking into the ground or trickling down to the lake. "She's all business, which is one reason I have her as my assistant, but I wonder if she has any kind of social life. It's something she never talks to me about, not that it's any of my affair."

"Maybe she just wants to keep business and her private life separate."

"Could be. I've asked my daughter—they're good friends—and she tells me not to worry. Did you get bored to death having dinner with her last night?"

"Not at all. We had a nice conversation."

"Good. Perhaps there's hope for Lexi."

Angelo looked out the window as the car drove under the shadow of the castle and along the city wall before turning onto the causeway separating the Lago Superiore from the Lago di Mezzo. Once across the water, the view was of flat fields, their lines broken only by an occasional farm structure, all the way to the horizon. The restaurant was in Goito, about a dozen kilometers from Mantova. The town and the restaurant itself sat on the western side of the same river which downstream spread into the lake at Mantova. At this stretch it was less than a hundred feet wide and crossed by a two-lane bridge that gave the restaurant its name, Il Ponte. Marco dropped them at the door.

The main dining room was half full, mostly with men in casual but elegant clothing whom Rick took to be businessmen or owners of the farms and dairies in the area. The soil around Goito and Mantova was the most fertile in Italy, producing some of the finest crops in Europe and making the locals wealthy. From looking at the people sitting at the tables, and what they were dining on, one would think that Italy had no economic woes. But this was not representative of the country as a whole, not even close.

They spotted Livia Guarino at a table near the wide window that looked out over the river. Her face showed the same fatigue as the day before, as if she still had not been blessed with a good night's sleep. Her dress was dark and plain, not quite mourning attire, but close to it. She looked up and waved.

"I thought her husband was going to be here," muttered Anglo. "That's why I wanted you along to interpret."

They reached the table and Angelo, now well into the local routine, bent over to kiss his niece on both cheeks. Rick shook her hand and took the seat between them, with Angelo directly across from Livia. As soon as they were seated a waiter appeared and placed menus before them.

"I hope we aren't late, Livia," said Angelo.

"No, not at all. I just arrived."

Angelo opened the menu. "I was expecting to see Francesco."

Livia's smile tightened. "Something…*imprevisto*." She turned to Rick for help.

"Unforeseen."

"Yes, unforeseen. Thank you, Riccardo. An important meeting. When he dropped me here he asked me to send his regrets. And could you give me a ride home after lunch?"

"Of course, Livia. I'm sorry we won't see him."

She took a drink from her water glass. "He's been working too much these last few weeks. Late hours. I haven't seen enough of him." She seemed to be deciding whether to say more. Her eyes did not meet Angelo's, and now they moved to the window. "I hope you enjoy this restaurant. It was a favorite of my father. He loved the river, of course, and this being directly on it…"

And it was in its waters where he found his end, Rick thought. The Mincio would be a constant reminder to her of her father's death, but she was doing her best to associate the river with pleasant aspects of his life. Would she ever succeed?

"It is a beautiful setting, Livia," said Angelo, perhaps with the same thought in his mind. "And I'm sure the food will live up to the setting. You both will have to help me with the menu. What do you suggest, Livia?"

"It is cold outside, a good day for a risotto." She pointed to a line on Angelo's menu. "*Risotto mantecato alla salsiccia tipico goitese.* That's what I'd like. Riccardo, can you translate?"

"Risotto with the local sausage. *Mantecato*, I think, means that butter and cheese are added to make it creamy. I'll have it, too. Shall we make it three?"

Angelo agreed, and the waiter was pleased to take the order. A dry *Lambrusco Mantovano* to go with your risotto? The suggestion was accepted without hesitation.

"Uncle, I have to tell you that the police think my father was murdered." Rick and Angelo exchanged glances but said nothing. She continued, "At first I thought it was absurd. My father was not universally liked, but who would want him dead? But ever since I talked to the police it has been in my thoughts. It is not something I can talk to Francesco about, he would think I was *pazza*. I hope you don't mind that I tell you. I have nobody else I can trust."

"I'm glad you feel that way, Livia." Angelo reached across and squeezed his niece's hand. He glanced at Rick and then turned his attention back to her. "Why are you having second thoughts?"

"Just…the way he died. That he fell into the water at a place where he had been fishing for so many years. His physical condition was good for a man of his age. He would not have, uh, *scivolato*."

"Slipped," said Rick. "But do you suspect anyone?"

"I told the policeman that I could think of no one. I still can't. Unless—"

They were interrupted by the arrival of the wine. The waiter filled their glasses, set the bottle in an ice bucket on the table, and retired. After a toast, the three took sips, though Livia's was more of a gulp.

"Unless," she continued, "it had something to do with that terrible piece of land."

"The one you asked me to look at."

"Yes. What did you think, Uncle?"

Angelo took a deep breath before answering. "If it were located in America I would know exactly what to recommend, Livia, but it is more difficult here. If someone wanted to develop it they would need water, sewerage, electricity, paved roads—all those things. I don't know what the cost would be here, but I assume it could be done. If you really want to sell it, a good real estate agent…" He noticed the look on her face and let Rick translate the term. "A good real estate agent who deals in commercial properties would know if it is feasible and be able to put a market price on the land. Unless you're thinking of developing it yourself."

"I hadn't thought of that, Uncle. My inclination is to keep it and expand the farm." She took another drink of her wine. "Francesco thinks I should sell."

Rick noticed the use of "I" instead of "we." Was that significant? "Since your father died," he said, "has anyone talked to you about buying the land?"

"My husband takes care of the mail, and Francesco said that a letter came from someone who my father must have been dealing with on the possible sale of the land. I didn't read it, but Francesco said it was a note of condolences. Other people don't need to talk to me about it, I know their opinions already."

"Such as the manager?"

"Yes. Carlo thinks we could use it to expand our storage capacity, that it would pay for itself in a few years, but my father didn't want to take on the expense. My father worried that the prices of milk and cheese would drop and he would end up with a loss. That was the kind of thing they would argue about."

"It appears that my cousin was not a risk taker."

"Not just that. He didn't want to upset his routine. The dairy ran itself, under Carlo's management of course, and the money flowed in from the cheese, so why make any changes? Life was good enough for him, and of course he had his fishing. Perhaps he was right."

The risotto arrived, creamy yellow rice in low bowls, a small stack of sausage pieces in its center. A sprig of rosemary stuck out of the sausage like a feather. Strong, earthy aromas rose from each plate with tufts of steam. The waiter warned that the dishes were hot and sprinkled grated Parmigiano-Reggiano over each plate. After an exchange of the traditional *buon appetito*, they took up their forks and tasted.

"*Buon appetito* was one of the few Italian phrases my parents taught me," Angelo said. "By the time I was old enough to talk, they spoke enough English to insist it be the language of the house, though I heard them speaking Italian between themselves. Now I wish they had taught me Italian."

"It's not too late to learn, Uncle."

Angelo shook his head. "An old brain like mine? I don't think so."

Conversation paused while they ate their risotto.

The restaurant had filled, but the elegant surroundings put the diners on their best behavior and kept the noise level to a low murmur. A large truck carrying hay passed over the bridge, silently to them, thanks to the thick glass of the picture window. The color of the massive bales matched the mud that caked the wheels and mud flaps. Had it not been for the freshness of the food, the people eating their lunch might not have known they were in the heart of a gritty agricultural zone, with all the dirt and odors that go along with it.

Rick put down his fork on the now empty dish. "Is there anyone else you might suspect, assuming your father was murdered?"

"He and our neighbor—Emilio Fiore—argued frequently, but I always had the sense that it was normal since they were competitors to a certain extent. Each thought their cheese was better than the other's, kind of like two men who argued over soccer teams. And they both could be...*stizzosi?*"

Rick stepped in. "Cranky, irascible."

"I got that impression when we met him yesterday," said Angelo. "But I thought it was partly due to the wine."

"Emilio does enjoy his wine. But I can't imagine him and my father fighting. Arguing, yes, but not to the point of physically attacking each other."

As much as Rick wanted to run other suspects past her, such as her farm manager, or mention her father's lady friend, he knew he couldn't. And it was time to order a second course, since the *primi* had not been as filling as they feared, given the small portions. The waiter cleared the dishes and again set menus before them. Fortunately, the list was not long, so Rick was able to translate it quickly for Angelo, who settled on the perch with *polenta*. Livia ordered the *fiori di zucca ripieni di ricotta di bufala, menta e erba cipolina su passata di pomodoro e basilico*. Rick told Angelo that the name of the dish—zucchini flowers stuffed with ricotta, mint and spring onions over a tomato and basil puree—could prove more of a mouthful than the dish itself. Rick was last, requesting *carpaccio* with *grana padana*, and black truffles. The waiter checked the wine bottle, saw that it was still half full, and left. No hard sell.

"I don't know what to do about the land, Uncle. Francesco is anxious to sell it, but I'm not sure." Her eyes fixed on Angelo.

"There is no urgency, I assume? If I understand correctly it has stood idle for years, and could continue idle for a few years more. This is not a time, when you are grieving, to make a decision like this. Take your time."

"I'm so pleased you're saying that, it makes me feel much more tranquil. When I talk with you it's almost like talking to Babbo. That's what I called him." Again her eyes moved to the water flowing outside the window. "This would have been a good fishing day for him. He always told me that after a storm the fish were anxious to be caught."

"Did you ever go fishing with him?" Angelo asked.

She shook her head. "No, for him it was a solitary activity. He was a member of a fishing association, but when it came time to fish, he preferred to be alone. I asked him once, had I been a boy rather than a girl, if he would he have taken me out on the boat. He swore that he would have treated a son the same, but his answer was slow in coming."

"So you've never been to the dock?" After he said it, Rick worried that he'd made a mistake, but she was not bothered by the question.

"I know where it is, and I used to walk down there in the summer when I was a girl and dip my toes into the river. It is a beautiful spot. I understand why my father loved to go there."

"I'd like to see it," said Angelo.

"It's hard to find. If you continue past the lot you visited yesterday, look for a turn to the left to a narrow road. After a few bends it goes through some trees and comes out to the river."

"I'll do that before I leave." He pulled the bottle out of the ice bucket and, starting with Livia's, filled up the three glasses. Then he held up his. "We have not toasted your father, Livia. It seems a good place to do it, in one of his favorite restaurants, next to his beloved river."

Her eyes misted as she raised her glass. "To Babbo."

They tapped crystal and drank. When they had finished, the main courses arrived at the table.

Portions once again were small but elegantly presented. Livia's plate displayed three closed zucchini flowers that had been dipped in a light batter and quickly fried, giving parts of it a brown color to contrast with the yellow. A bit of the cheese filling oozed out of the green ends, flowing into the thin layer of tomato sauce under it. Angelo's perch filets had been steamed and placed on a layer of creamy, yellow *polenta* and topped with capers and herbs. The simplest of the three dishes was Rick's carpaccio, its paper-thin raw beef covering the plate. Equally thin slices of the hard cheese dotted the meat along with the occasional shred of dark truffle that gave off its distinctive aroma. Olive oil crisscrossed it all. After taking in the artistic qualities of their own plates, each of them studied the other two before silently picking up their forks. The first sound was the crunch of Livia's first zucchini flower.

"I can see why my cousin enjoyed coming here," said Angelo before taking a taste of perch. "And I can taste why."

"Babbo did love to eat, but never cooked himself. Fortunately, my mother was an excellent cook." She finished another bite of the zucchini flower. "She passed away several years ago, before I met Francesco. I thought for a long time that my father would never recover from her death, but eventually he did."

Rick expected something about her father's woman friend. She had to have known about Letizia Bentivoglio, but something kept her from saying anything to Angelo. Perhaps if Rick had not been present, Livia would have opened up more. Or Rick was an easy way to justify, in her own mind, avoiding any mention of the other woman. He turned his attention to the *carpaccio*, one of his favorite dishes, and wondered why the chef had decided to use *grana padana*, the cheaper and less-renowned cousin of Parmigiano-Reggiano. The difference of taste between the two cheeses was difficult to pinpoint. If anything, the *grana* was a touch sweeter, which might be a reason to combine it with the sharp flavor of the raw beef. Just as likely the reason was more mundane, such as that the chef had a friend who produced *grana padana*.

Angelo patted his lips with his napkin and looked down at his dish where only a few specks of yellow *polenta* remained. "Excellent fish, and it goes perfectly with the *polenta*. I will have to recommend it to the owner of my favorite Italian restaurant at home, but since it doesn't have some kind of red sauce, he won't want to put it on the menu." He gestured toward their plates, also empty. "Just this lunch alone has opened my eyes to what Italian food really is."

"There is still *dolce* or *frutta*, Uncle."

"That sounds like dessert. I will, if you will."

As the waiter cleared the dishes Livia asked if they had *frutti di bosco*. When he said they did, she got a nod from Rick and ordered three, con *zucchero e limone*. As the waiter exited, his place was taken at the table by a large man whom Rick recognized as Livia's neighbor. Emilio Fiore wore a corduroy jacket that barely covered his girth. Under it was a plaid shirt open at the collar, exposing the thin line of a gold chain. He looked down at the two men as if they had sneaked into his private club.

Rick and Angelo got to their feet as Fiore bent over, took Livia's hand in his, and extended further condolences. Then he shook hands with the two men.

"Mr. Rondini," said Rick, "you remember Signor Fiore?"

"I do—Livia's neighbor."

"I hope you are enjoying our region, Mr. Rondini." Fiore had decided to try out his English, perhaps because he hadn't had as much wine as the day before. It was passable but highly accented. "You have seen our, um, *bellezze?*"

"Sights, beautiful things," Rick interpreted. Remembering the truck in the distance during the previous day's visit to the empty plot, he wondered if Fiore meant the artwork or the land. Angelo understood it to be the former.

"We were at the castle this morning to see Mantegna's masterpiece, among other art."

"Yes, his *capolavoro*. We are proud to have it in our city. Will you be staying long in Italy?"

It would have been an innocent question, but his emphasis on the word "long" made it sound otherwise.

"Not nearly long enough, Mr. Fiore. I have to get back to my work."

"You construct things, I am told."

"That is one way to describe my work."

"Here we grow food. Some of the best in the world. Is that not so, Livia?"

"The very best, Emilio."

The man smiled and inclined his head toward the corner. "I must return to my guests. Germans. They love our Italian cheeses. Livia, I will be seeing you tomorrow evening. I look forward to it. Good day." He bowed slightly and walked away. Rick and Angelo sat back down.

"Thank goodness he mentioned tomorrow, with all that's going on, I'd forgotten to tell you. The local cheese consortium is holding an event at seven at the Palazzo Te, in honor of my father. Of course you are invited."

"It will be an honor to attend," answered Angelo. He looked back at Fiore who was at his table with the Germans. "I think I like him better when he's had more wine," he said, eliciting a laugh from his niece.

"Emilio is traditional in all ways. He sees the land as our…" She struggled to find the word and did without Rick's help. "Our heritage, as well as our future. And he is very good at what he does, which is produce Parmigiano-Reggiano cheese. That was the main part of the rivalry with my father, if that is the correct term for their relationship. But what I think annoyed Emilio more was that my father, in the years after my mother's death, didn't care about keeping up the rivalry. Our dairy made good cheese, and Babbo knew it was good, but he wasn't obsessive about it."

"Fiore is obsessive."

"Most definitely, Uncle. And he enjoys a good argument."

The waiter arrived and placed small glass bowls of berries before each of them. Tiny wild strawberries, blueberries, and raspberries were coated with lemon juice and sprinkled with sugar. A small cookie sat on the plate under each bowl.

"I can picture local children with baskets picking these a few hours ago in the forest," Angelo said after tasting his first spoonful. "The lemon and the sugar, I never would have thought of that. Wonderful."

"This is the only time of year you can get them," she said. "And with the snow last night, these may be the last."

"I will have to come back next year."

"I hope you'll come many times before then, Uncle."

Twenty minutes later, after they had accepted *espressos* and declined *grappas*, they walked to the parking lot where the driver was waiting. Marco looked puzzled when he saw Livia Guarino walking with them.

"We will be giving my niece a lift back to her home, Marco."

The driver nodded silently and went to the other side to open the door for her. When she and Rondini were seated in the rear, Rick took his place in the front passenger seat. The engine roared to life and the Mercedes pulled out of the lot into the road.

Chapter Six

"Thank you for the lunch, Uncle."

"You're welcome, Livia." His eyes moved out across the fields where a midafternoon breeze kicked up a brown cloud behind a small tractor making its way along a dirt road. "That guy, Fiore, is right, you do make some great food around here. And you really know how to cook it." He settled back into the seat, but continued enjoying the view. Trees and bushes intermittently blocked it, but when they cleared, more fertile land spread out on either side of the road. "What does that say, Language Man?"

Rick turned his head to see a hand-lettered cardboard sign. "*Vendita Miele.* Honey for sale. Do you want to stop?"

"No. I have to bring something back for my daughter, but a jar of honey wouldn't cut it. She'd prefer something made of leather or gold."

"You must tell me about your daughter, Uncle."

"Nikki is wonderful young woman, Livia, and you two would get along famously. She was raised well, thanks to her mother, since I didn't spend as much time on it as I should have. But I'm trying to make up for it now. You will have to come to America to meet her.

"Or she could come here."

Something caught Rondini's eye and he tapped the driver on the shoulder. "What's that, Marco? I didn't notice it on the way to lunch."

The car rose gently as it went over a bridge. Blue water flowed under it along a cement canal that reminded Rick of the storm channels in Albuquerque built for the monsoon rains.

"The river is diverted at several places, Mr. Rondini. The water is used on the crops."

Rondini was now noticing new vegetation on his side of the car, low plants with dark leaves hanging from wires strung above them. "Those are grapes, aren't they?"

"That's right, Uncle."

"Is there anything that doesn't grow here?"

The car slowed to make a turn at an intersection marked by two arrowed signs, both black and yellow, indicating an industry or other business. The top one read *Latteria Agricola Rondini*, and below it was *Latteria Agricola Mincio*, which Rick guessed to be the dairy farm across the road, owned by Emilio Fiore. The other two signs on the post were pointed ahead, one blue and white for Mantova, the other with the distinctive green, meaning that an *autostrada* entrance was to be found in that direction. Cows grazed on either side, unfazed by the passing car. It was dairy country.

Rick noticed that Marco had pushed lightly on the brake. He looked up to see a crowd of people milling around on the road ahead. Cars, and a few mopeds, were parked along the side. The Mercedes passed the entrance to Fiore's property and slowed more as the people got closer.

"*O Dio,*" said Livia. "They have returned."

Angelo leaned forward for a better view. "What's going on?"

"Several weeks ago, when the news got out that my father was going to sell out to a developer to build a shopping center, they appeared. Some kind of environmental group. They want to keep the land natural, but of course, only they can decide what is natural."

"What should I do, Signora?" Concern was evident in the driver's voice.

"Drive in, of course."

The reply earned her a smile from Rondini. "They won't dare touch your car, Marco. If they do, we'll call the police." He leaned back in the leather seat. "Try not to hit any of them."

The crowd had now noticed the car and all their faces were turned toward it. When Marco put on his turn signal, there was a visible change in the group dynamic, led by one man who pushed himself forward, brandishing his sign above his head. He wore his gray hair long, matching an unkempt beard. The group began to chant, but Rick had trouble making out the words. Something *si*, something *no*. They needed more practice in their chanting, and also weren't clear on what to do about a car turning onto the property. Everyone except the leader moved aside to allow the Mercedes to enter the open gate. He stood defiantly in front of the car's circular hood ornament as Marco crept forward, but finally moved to the passenger side. As the car slid past, the man stared at Rick with wild eyes, leaving the shouting to his colleagues. The car picked up speed and drove to the front of the house. Marco and Rick got out and opened the doors for the rear passengers.

"I'm sorry you had to witness that, Uncle."

"Not a problem, Livia. It made me feel at home."

"There is a path you can take through the fields that we use for trucks that will get you back to the road so you can avoid them."

Marco perked up with the comment, but was disappointed by his boss' reply.

"Not a chance. We don't want them to think we're taking them seriously."

"And you will come back tomorrow to visit the farm? I think you will find the cheese-making fascinating."

"I would like that very much," answered Rondini.

They said their good-byes and the men waited until Livia got to the door before getting back in the Mercedes. Rick sat in the rear with Rondini.

"Marco," said Rondini, "turn left when you get out to the

road, drive past the field we stopped at yesterday, I want to see the place where Roberto Rondini used to go fishing."

The driver looked in the mirror. "It may start raining, Mr. Rondini. Are you sure you'd like to go there?"

"I just told you, didn't I?"

"Yes, sir." He started the engine.

The crowd came to life again as the car approached the gate. Their leader may have given them a pep talk, since their chant—NATURE YES, CEMENT NO—was clear and loud. They were also more reluctant to give way to the car as it approached, but did move to the side after Marco tapped his horn twice and edged slowly ahead. Once again the bearded leader was in the forefront.

The car turned back onto the road that formed a straight line between the Rondini dairy and the property of Emilio Fiore. Cows on both sides faced toward the road, checking each other out between bites of browned vegetation.

"At least the assholes took a break for the funeral," Angelo said. "I hope Livia doesn't have to get caught up in that every time she goes out. But that's the way you have to deal with these people—ignore them and go about your business. That's what we did that time in St. Louis, which just pissed them off and they got violent, so we had an excuse to bring in the police. That group back there didn't look like they'd get violent, but that old guy better be careful he doesn't get run over." Rondini looked out at where they had walked the day before. "All because of that plot of land, which isn't even very large by American standards."

Rick leaned forward and looked as they passed the field. "It was interesting that she said her husband wanted to sell it. Do you think Francesco can talk her into it?"

"Livia has her head on straight, Rick. She will eventually make the right decision on that land. Whatever it might be."

The comment didn't require a reply. Rondini, as he had done most of the time spent in the car, settled into silent contemplation while staring out the window at the fields. Just before the road bent to the right to go parallel to the river, the car turned onto a narrow dirt path. It ran along a thick line of trees that bordered the river, then turned where there was a break between them. Branches brushed against the car as it made its way through the passage to the riverbank before stopping in a circular clearing. Between the parking area and the river spread open ground. It was carpeted with short grass and dropped gradually to the water, its descent broken only by a few small mounds and scruffy bushes on one side. The Mincio at this point had expanded beyond the width it had been held to at the restaurant, getting ready to spread into a lake on the east side of Mantova. The only sign of human activity on either bank was the dock at the end of a path running from the clearing to the water. Rick and Angelo got out and walked down the path while the driver leaned against the car, his eyes on the darkening sky. A cold gust of wind blew toward them from a black cloud that formed in the distance.

The dock was only a few meters longer than the boat floating next to it on the upstream side. Lines from both ends of it were tied to the dock posts, but the steady current of the river also kept it in place. Angelo walked ahead of Rick, stepping out onto the planks and surveying the scene. His coat flapped open in the wind and he buttoned it while looking out over the choppy water. Rick stood back on the path watching his boss. Rondini had become increasingly contemplative since arriving in Italy. It would make sense; returning to one's roots had to make a profound impression on even the most cynical of people, and Angelo, at least outwardly, played the part of the cynical businessman. This trip was giving Rondini a lot to contemplate, not only because it was Italy, but the Italy of his parents. The likely murder of his closest Italian relative had added another layer to the experience. He'd wanted to visit this site to see where his cousin had spent many happy hours, but also because it was the site of the murder. Rick could almost hear the man's mind processing it all.

"It's beautiful here. I can understand why my cousin loved coming to this spot. There's something to be said for getting close to nature." He walked back to the shore, bent down, and touched the surface of the water. Ripples ran around his fingers and continued downstream. He stood and stared across the river in silence before turning.

"What do you think, Montoya? Could it have happened like the cop said?"

Rick descended to the dock and squatted at the edge, rubbing his hand over the wood. "This surface doesn't seem that slippery now, but it could have been that day, enough to make him fall and hit his head. Either an accident or a homicide is plausible."

Angelo stared down at the eddies formed by the water passing around the dock supports. "Your uncle the cop, he ever talk to you about his cases?"

"Often."

"What would he think of this?"

"Hard to say. But I know he has confidence in the opinion of Inspector Crispi."

"It's time for you to see this Crispi again to find out what's going on."

"I was going to make another visit to the newspaper archive, but I'll call him when we get to the hotel."

"Do it."

Out on the water's surface a dark line pushed toward them, the front edge of a gust bringing not just a chill but rain. A few small drops began to fall, followed immediately by larger ones. Rick heard footsteps and turned to see Marco rushing down the path, holding an open umbrella. Angelo met him halfway and took it, gesturing for Rick to join him underneath while the driver ran ahead. By the time they got to the car and jumped inside it was a full-blown storm.

"You'd better get us onto the pavement quickly," shouted Angelo over the noise of the downpour on the metal roof.

Marco needed no urging. He started the engine, made a quick turn, and got back onto a road that was rapidly turning from dirt to mud. By the time they bumped onto the blacktop a few minutes later, the Mercedes had fishtailed twice on the slick surface. He drove slowly through the storm while his passengers sat silently. The only sound beside the rain itself was the whomp-whomp of the wipers trying to keep up with it. When they passed the gate to the Rondini dairy, there was no sign of the demonstrators. The storm had driven them away. Halfway back to the city, the clouds disappeared as quickly as they had formed, allowing rays of sunlight to play on the lake as they drove into Mantova.

●　●　●　●　●

The archive room had not changed since the morning, even down to the newspaper that da Feltre was reading, though it appeared he was on the final pages. Rick wondered if the man paced his reading to make it last the entire day, in conformity with Parkinson's Law. Did he ever leave? He scanned the desk for a telltale crumb indicating a bag lunch, and finding none decided that the man might in fact go somewhere else for his midday meal. There was no sign on the glass door giving hours, but perhaps da Feltre taped a "back in an hour" note when he took his lunch break. He squinted through the thick lenses and a trace of a grin appeared when he recognized Rick.

"My most loyal customer," he said.

"I just can't stay away," Rick answered, and gestured at the work station. "May I?"

"Be my guest." Rather than return to the newspaper, the man kept looking at his visitor.

"Is there something else, Signor da Feltre?"

The man rubbed his finger over his nose, slightly dislodging the glasses. "Yes. Yes, there was. After you left I recalled that someone was here about a month ago, also looking for information about the Rondini family. Strange, isn't it?" After the rhetorical question, his eyes dropped to the paper and Rick walked to his cubicle.

Strange, indeed. But of any significance? Rick tucked the information into the back of his mind and turned on the computer, thinking that he had not yet read the recent stories about the death of Roberto Rondini. Calculating when the murder must have taken place, he quickly found the edition which broke the story. It ran an interview with the jogger who had found the body, including a staged photograph of him pointing to the water's edge near the castle, grotesquely enjoying his fifteen minutes of fame. The next day's paper mentioned Inspector Crispi, who refused to be specific about the cause of death, though that did not stop the reporter from assuming it was a fishing accident since the victim was known to be active in a local sport fishing association. No mention was made by the policeman, nor the reporter, of the fishing dock. Both stories mentioned the Rondini dairy operation and that Livia Guarino was the next of kin to the deceased. Other than the formal death notice, which Rick had read that morning, those were the only stories he could find in the paper about Roberto Rondini's death. He scrolled back to check if he'd missed something in earlier editions about the man before the death, but the same stories caught his eye.

With one exception.

Ten days before the body was found, a report on the inside pages covered a water pollution protest staged in a park area beside the lake. A photo showed a small group of protesters holding signs and shouting for the camera. They were concerned, wrote the reporter, about any development which could dump bad things into the Mincio, and they wanted the government to prevent it. From its size and signs, the group could have been the same one that Marco's Mercedes had squeezed past in and out of the Rondini dairy. It also had the same leader, identified as Domenico Folengo, the man who had glared through the car windows as his compatriots yelled.

Rick took notes and set the search to a couple decades earlier. He wanted to get more information for his boss on the elder Rondini, the man who started the dairy operation that Roberto Rondini had inherited and would now pass to Livia Guarino.

The paper had no lack of stories about Enzo Rondini and again showed the paper's dislike for the man. Rick skimmed over those he'd read on his first visit but found enough new ones to occupy him. The one that jumped out immediately told of the family that had been displaced when Enzo had worked the deal to have their property taken over for lack of tax payments. The head of the family was forced to pack up his family and head north to Verona where a dreary factory job would be his only chance of employment. The paper described him and his bitter wife driving off in a battered car, children squeezed into the back seat with the family belongings. The account made Enzo Rondini into a modern Italian Simon Legree, but Rick assumed much of it to be journalistic license until he saw the photo of a child staring blankly from the rear window of a car.

He was searching for another Rondini story when he heard the muffled sound of the Lobo Fight Song coming from his coat pocket. He pulled out the cell phone and saw that it was an 0376 area code number for Mantova. Signor da Feltre didn't look up.

"Montoya."

"Montoya, this is Crispi."

"Yes, Inspector. I was just going to call about coming to see you again."

"I hope you have something to tell me."

Rick looked at the ancient archivist, who seemed oblivious to the conversation. "Probably nothing of any consequence, but a few details." In truth he had nothing but hunches and conjecture, but he didn't want to say that he'd promised Rondini to get anything new on the case from the policeman. "Shall I come to the *questura* now?"

"Where are you at the moment?"

"In the archives of the *Gazzetta*."

If Crispi was intrigued by Rick's location, it didn't show in his voice. "I am not at the *questura*. I will send a car for you. It will be there in five minutes." He hung up.

Inspector Crispi as his usual loquacious self.

The police car arrived four minutes later, just as Rick was coming through the glass doors of the building. He got in the front seat, and after a short exchange of greetings, the car made a sharp U turn and drove away from the center of the city. He considered asking the driver where they were going, but the policeman didn't appear to be the chatty type. What would be the reason to meet at someplace other than the police station? The car took them quickly to the edge of the city where even a decade or two earlier there would have been fields rather than structures. The houses they passed were cement boxes devoid of personality, despite attempts to add color and life through window boxes and shrubbery. They were almost into exclusively agricultural land when the car slowed down. Rick could see a police vehicle parked in front of a house that looked like it had originally been part of a farm rather than new construction. Age was difficult to judge in farmhouses, but this one looked to date from early in the twentieth century, or even the late nineteenth. In a few more years it would be surrounded by newer construction, even a housing development, as the city seeped outward. The house consisted of two stories, like a square two-layer wedding cake, with a balcony running around the entire second floor. Separate from the house sat a garage, which could have originally been a storage shed, and behind that, rose a tall metal windmill like the old ones Rick had seen in New Mexico. A quarter of its blades were missing, the vane was rusted, and it looked like it hadn't turned in years. Three people stood at the base of the windmill: a woman, a uniformed policeman, and Inspector Crispi. They were looking up at a man sitting on the small platform next to the blades, his legs dangling over the edge.

"What's going on?" Rick asked when he reached Crispi.

The inspector turned his attention from the man above to the new arrival. "Afternoon, Montoya. He won't come down."

The sitter stared back toward the city, oblivious to the group below. He was dressed in canvas work overalls, the knees wrapped with orange strips that caught the sun as the legs swung back and forth. Heavy boots, a dark blue sweat shirt, and a knit cap completed the outfit of a highway construction worker.

"Excuse me, Inspector," Rick said, "but what does this have to do with the murder of Roberto Rondini?"

In reply he got a puzzled look from Crispi. "Rondini? Nothing, of course. Do you think I have the luxury of dealing with only one case at a time? I needed to talk to you and this is where I happen to be at the moment." He jerked his thumb upward. "Here with Lando."

"Why is he up there?"

He glanced at the woman. "Let's go over to the house and I'll tell you." They had started to walk when Crispi stopped and turned back to the windmill. "You've made your point, Lando," he shouted up at the man who continued to stare at the horizon. When they were out of earshot of the group, Crispi stopped and took a deep breath which spoke more than words about the present situation.

"He came home early from work because of a water main break and found his wife with the neighbor."

Rick looked around, wondering in which of the few houses he saw the neighbor might have resided. "*In flagrante?*"

"They were having coffee in the kitchen. Both fully clothed."

"But Lando is the jealous type."

"It appears so."

Rick dug his hands into his coat pocket. The temperature was noticeably lower out in the country than in town. Perhaps the cold would get Lando off his perch. "Do you have some news on the Rondini investigation, Inspector?"

"We were contacted by your hotel about an hour ago. Someone called and left a threatening message for your *capo*. 'Tell the American that he should leave immediately or he will be in grave danger,' was what the desk clerk remembers. It was a man's voice. Of course the American could be you, but I doubt it. There are no other Americans registered in the hotel at the moment except you, Rondini, and his secretary. I wanted to talk to you before we speak with Mr. Rondini."

"There was a similar message yesterday, written on a note and left under the wiper of the car."

For an instant Crispi's normally bland expression changed almost imperceptibly to a frown. "And you didn't tell me?"

"It didn't appear serious enough to waste your time. It could have just been a prank."

"My time will now be wasted on it. Did you keep the note?"

"I think the driver threw it away."

Crispi nodded his head slowly. "And now the prankster has returned, likely annoyed that his first message wasn't taken seriously."

They were interrupted by the shrill voice of Lando's wife. Rick couldn't make out what she'd said, but from the tone and the way she was shaking her fist he concluded that her words did not convey much tenderness.

"So you will talk with Rondini?"

The reply was another nod. "With your help. My English is minimal. This threat is just another small detail added to an already murky case, making it messier but no more conclusive. I am not in the good graces of my superior for pursuing it, since he preferred Roberto Rondini dying in a tragic accident. I'm not sure how he will react to this development."

Rick recalled what his uncle had said about Inspector Crispi's relationships with the rest of the police force. It was impossible to read anything into the inspector's comment, to know if he was concerned about his boss, or with anything else. The words were said as if he was describing what he'd had for breakfast.

"What else have you found since we last spoke?"

Rick looked back at the windmill before answering. All the players were still in their places, looking up at Lando. "Rondini had lunch today with Livia Guarino, and I was present. She is coming around to the possibility that her father was murdered."

"Which would argue for taking her off the list of suspects. Go on."

"The lunch was mostly about family and how her father loved the river, but she did talk about that plot of land. She doesn't know what to do about it, and asked Rondini's advice. Their neighbor, Fiore, was against any kind of development, and the two men used to argue about it. By coincidence, Fiore was having lunch at the restaurant and came to our table."

"And?"

"The normal exchange of pleasantries, as you would expect. He asked Rondini if he'd seen the sights. He knows that Rondini is a developer, and I'm guessing he made a connection in his mind between Rondini's appearance and the possible sale of the land to build a shopping center or factory."

"Is there a connection?"

"Pure coincidence, as far as I can see, but I'm still not Italian enough to see plots behind everything."

"Just give yourself time, you'll come around to it. What else of interest?"

"After the lunch there was something. We gave Signora Guarino a ride home, since her husband didn't make it because of an appointment, and had dropped her at the restaurant. When we got to her farm there were demonstrators at the gate."

"I heard they were back. Any problems?"

"We got in without incident, dropped off the *signora*, and got out without a problem, though they squeezed in close to the car. By coincidence, when I was looking up Rondini family stories in the *Gazzetta* just now, I came across a photo of the man who appeared to be the leader of the demonstrators. The caption with the photo said his name is Domenico Folengo."

"Yes, Folengo. He is, as the saying goes, known to the police. We have never actually arrested him, but he has been detained temporarily for getting too boisterous in his demonstrations. The issue is always the same, what he sees as environmental destruction in any and all forms. We had a case of vandalism early this year, some construction equipment had tires slashed and windows broken, and we suspected it was Folengo's doing, but couldn't find evidence to justify bringing him in."

"What does he do when he's not demonstrating?"

"Not much. He lives off an inheritance from a wife who died a few years ago. He spends all his time saving the world. It would be nice to have family money, wouldn't it?"

Rick assumed that Crispi's question didn't require an answer. "Something else I found in the archives was interesting, regarding the fishing association that Roberto Rondini was active in."

"I knew that he was a fisherman, of course. What did you find?"

"When Rondini was elected to the board, the former president resigned. The man's name is Sandro Bastoncini." Rick passed him the piece of paper with the name. "I couldn't tell if it was in protest to Rondini's election, or something totally unrelated, but he might be someone you'd want to talk to. If nothing else, he can tell you about Rondini's activities in the fishing group."

Crispi studied the name and then slipped the paper into his pocket. "Another person who likely won't be of any help. But you are correct, it may at least give me some more insight into the fascinating private life of Roberto Rondini."

"In that regard, how did the interview with the woman go?"

"As expected. Add Letizia Bentivoglio to the list of those who think it couldn't be an accident. She said Rondini was getting moody in weeks before, set off, she thinks, by the anniversary of his own father's death. Concerned with his own mortality. Going to some funeral a few weeks before he died didn't help his mind-set. He was also bothered by the uproar when people found out he was thinking of selling that plot of land."

"The demonstrators? This guy, Folengo?"

"Must have been." Crispi looked over at the scene around the windmill. Nothing had changed. "I did a background check on Signora Bentivoglio and didn't find anything out of the ordinary. She's never done anything to bring her to the attention of the authorities. I also checked on Roberto Rondini's farm manager, Carlo Zucari, but that was different."

"How so?"

"About twenty years ago he was arrested for assault and did prison time after an argument in a bar that led to violence. He almost killed a man in a rage. He somehow got himself a job at the Rondini farm after he was released, and he worked his way up to the manager position. We don't often find instances of an ex-convict turning himself around, but that was the case with Zucari. I can't help but wonder if he really is a changed man, or if the violence was simmering below the surface."

"What would be his motive?"

Crispi looked at his watch and up at the man on the windmill. "That's what puzzles me. Rondini gave him a chance after prison, so why would he want to do in his benefactor? It also puzzles me why Rondini gave him the job in the first place, but we'll likely never know. Maybe he's ready to jump."

The last sentence was uttered after they heard some commotion coming from the windmill. Lando had taken his eyes from the horizon and was now engaged in an animated conversation with his wife. At one point he waved his arms wildly, almost losing his balance, and she screamed. Their voices lowered and the uniformed policeman, who had been joined by Rick's driver, edged away from the metal ladder that extended up to the platform, to give them privacy. Slowly, as Rick and Crispi watched, the man began climbing down the ladder. When his feet were about ten feet off the ground, the woman said something that Rick couldn't make out, and Lando's head jerked around, causing him to lose his balance and start to fall head-first toward the ground. His wife screamed again as the nearby policemen rushed toward the base of the windmill. Crispi stood and watched. It was Lando's turn to scream as his left ankle caught in a rung, keeping him from falling all the way to the ground but causing great pain. Grunting and struggling, the two policemen managed to extract the foot from the ladder and get him down without further complications. It was a toss-up as to which was now louder, Lando's groans or his wife's admonitions. Crispi walked to the small group, gave orders to the two policemen, and returned to Rick.

"They'll get him into one of our cars and take him to the hospital. They should examine his head as well as his ankle, when he gets there."

The two policemen got Lando to his feet, put his arms over their shoulders, and he hobbled on one foot between them toward one of the cars. The scene reminded Rick of an injured linebacker being taken off the gridiron with a torn ACL, his wife following behind in the part of the team doctor. After Lando was squeezed into the back seat of one of the police cars, his wife got in the front and they were driven off toward the city.

"I'm not sure if that was a good outcome or a bad one," said Rick.

Crispi watched the car disappear down the road. "She may break his other leg before the night's over." He pointed at the other car where the second policeman awaited them. "Get in, we'll go talk to your *capo*."

"I'm the one to get the threat, and the hotel calls the cops? What am I, chopped liver?"

Rick interpreted Rondini's second question as "I should have been told first"—not a direct translation, but it got his boss's point across. They sat on white leather chairs in a corner of the hotel lobby with Rick taking the interpreter position between the two of them. The policeman, who had little experience with Americans and even less with those raised on the East Coast, appeared intrigued by Rondini's manner. At least that's the way Rick interpreted the slight squint in Crispi's eyes.

The inspector did not attempt to justify the hotel management's decision. "Would you like me to assign a policeman to the hotel, Signor Rondini?"

Rick sensed that Crispi's offer was *pro forma*. He also expected Rondini to turn it down.

"Montoya will keep his eye on me. And my assistant is trained in the martial arts."

Another facet of the multifaceted Lexi Coleman, Rick thought as he interpreted.

"In addition, Inspector, I would not want to keep any manpower from helping you to solve my cousin's murder. Can I assume you believe these threats are connected to the crime?"

Crispi rubbed his stubble before replying. "You have declined my offer for protection, Mr. Rondini. Would you change your mind if I told you there is a connection? The fact is, I don't know. But if there are any other threats, no matter how they are delivered, you must promise to contact me immediately. Signor Montoya has my number."

"I will do that," said Rondini after getting it in English from Rick. "And you must promise to inform me if there are any developments in the investigation. You have Mr. Montoya's number."

In a battle of wills, Rick was certain that Rondini would come out on top. Inspector Crispi was good, but out of his league.

"Signor Rondini, I have just told Signor Montoya what I know, he will be pleased to inform you and we won't have to go through the translation. I really must return to the *questura*. Please be careful." Crispi didn't wait for Rick, but got to his feet, bowed stiffly, and walked to the door, leaving Rick and Angelo seated.

"Is he pissed off?" Rondini asked after the policeman had left.

"His manner is always the same, so it's difficult to tell. Are you sure you don't want police protection? It might be a good idea since someone appears to be unhappy with your presence in Mantova."

"We don't need a cop getting underfoot. If you have to take down some kook who attacks me, I'll pay you extra. You look like you could handle it."

"Is bodyguard part of Lexi's job description?"

"It could be, Language Man, it could be. Which reminds me that she should be made aware of what is going on. I didn't want to say anything, since she has enough to do, but you'd better tell her all about it."

"Me?"

"Yes, you. After that big lunch, I'm staying in tonight, so you are again assigned to take her to dinner. Tell her everything." He removed his glasses, took out a handkerchief, and started to clean the lenses carefully. "Now what does that cop know about the murder of my cousin?"

Rick was initially surprised by what got Lexi's attention, but when he thought about it, it made sense. She was, after all, Angelo's assistant, and her main focus would be on the business, not on possible murder suspects.

"Do you think Angelo's niece asked him to come here because he develops shopping centers?" she asked.

"I really don't know. She knows what his business is, but she could have found that out after she decided to track him down and invite him to the funeral. But the same thought crossed his mind."

"That doesn't surprise me. I told you he's very suspicious of people's motives."

"Or perhaps it's just his Italian genes," Rick said.

She had requested a less formal restaurant than the previous night, wanting to see "the real Italy," as if affluent people eating in an upscale ambiance wasn't really Italian. It was something about many American tourists that intrigued Rick, their idea that rustic meant genuine. The place this evening was brightly lit, noisy, and small, its wooden tables squeezed into a long, rectangular room that ended in the door to the kitchen. A few shelves built into niches were lined with dusty wine bottles, and the rest of the bright red walls were covered with art by local amateurs. No tablecloths this time, only brown paper place mats stamped with the restaurant logo, a plump goose. The menus were hand-written and stained. Strong aromas, which would have stayed in the kitchen in most restaurants, floated through the air. Lexi loved it.

"So the two threats could be connected to the possible murder of Roberto Rondini."

"I don't see how, Lexi, but it's too much of a coincidence to discount. And Inspector Crispi did offer your boss police protection, so the cops are taking it seriously."

The waiter arrived at the table with a bottle of mineral water in one hand and a basket of crusty bread in the other. He set both on the table and deftly popped the cap off the water with an opener he had in his pocket.

"*Un litro del vostro rosso*," Rick said to him, and the man walked away.

"What was that?" Lexi asked.

"I ordered a bottle of the house red. You want to eat like the locals, you have to drink like them, too. Do you want me to order for you tonight?"

She pushed away her menu. "I can't read this anyway. Go for it. Just don't order anything that comes from inside the animal."

"I'm with you on that. You know, when I first saw you I feared that you might be a vegetarian. You looked like the type."

"I was a vegan for a while in college, but it didn't last long."

"What made you change your mind?"

"Bacon."

"Ah."

The wine, dark and crimson, arrived in a decorated ceramic pitcher. Rick filled their glasses and they toasted their absent host and looked around the room, which was beginning to fill with a clientele distinctly different from the previous evening. Most of the diners chatted with the waitstaff like they ate there often. Many only gave the menu a cursory glance before ordering. Greetings were exchanged between tables. This was a neighborhood hangout.

"Tell me, Rick," Lexi began after taking a long pull on her wine, "is it Richard or Riccardo? I heard the driver calling you Riccardo."

"It's Rick. But for the full name, it depends on which side of the Atlantic I find myself. By chance my two grandfathers shared the name—Riccardo Fontana and Richard Montoya—so when I was born, the decision was easy for my parents. In both countries kids are often named after grandparents, of course. My American passport has Richard, and my Italian one Riccardo. What about Alexis?"

"I think it was an aunt. But maybe some TV star. My mother watched a lot of soap operas when she was carrying me."

The waiter appeared and Rick made a quick study of the menu before giving their order. "Be surprised," he said to Lexi. "Good peasant food, all."

"I'm for that. You wouldn't think that working on a computer and a telephone would give me such an appetite, but it does." She pulled a piece of bread from the basket. It was mostly holes and had a thick crust darkened by the oven. "Do you think Angelo is really in danger, Rick?"

"I think that if someone wanted to do him harm it would

have already happened. But there's no doubt in my mind of a connection between the demise of his cousin and those threats, and that connection is probably the infamous plot of land. That's what draws in your boss."

Lexi bit down on the bread with a crunch and chewed. "There must be somewhere in Chicago where I can get bread like this." She swallowed and took another drink of wine. "I'm worried. Tell me I shouldn't worry, Rick."

"Wish I could."

"You said you have an uncle who's a cop. What did he think of the threats?"

"I haven't talked to him since the first one, but he'll probably just tell me to be careful. That's what he's always said in such situations."

"Did you?"

"Most of the time."

A large platter of sliced *salumi* came to the table along with two plates that the waiter put in front of them. He pointed out *culatello*, *coppa*, and *bresaola* before wishing them *buon appetito* and retiring.

"This looks great," said Lexi as she picked up her fork. "Which should I try first?"

"The *culatello* is the king of local cured meats, but you shouldn't choke on the other two either."

They speared slices on their forks and transferred them to their own plates before cutting and eating. The bread served as a palate clearer between tastes of the three types, along with sips of the red wine. When the plate was empty they agreed that the *culatello* was the best, but the other two were in a tie for second place.

Conversation returned to the murder and Rick told her about the possible suspects: Livia's husband, Francesco; the farm manager, Carlo Zucari; Emilio Fiore, the gruff neighbor; and now perhaps one of the protesters outside the farm gate.

"Not just random, or a mugging gone bad, or a nutcase?

That's what many of the Chicago murders turn out to be."

"Mantova isn't Chicago, Lexi. There's something behind this one. My uncle always tells me that there are very few motives when it comes to murder. Revenge, sex, and money are the big three. Vendetta is an Italian word, of course, so revenge could be the motive, but revenge for what? And sex? A widower with a girlfriend a few years younger? Doesn't seem that that one flies either. Money is what I would bet on at this point, and that plot of land is worth a lot of it. Ah, the *pasta* has arrived."

The *salumi* plates had been cleared, and in their place the waiter set a large bowl filled halfway with thin ribbons of pasta coated by a dark sauce. Next to it was a single dish. The waiter took a fork and spoon, stirred the pasta a few times, and transferred half of it to the dish before saying something to Rick. Rick inclined his head toward Lexi.

"He seems to have forgotten the other plate, Rick."

The waiter picked up the serving bowl and placed it in front of Lexi. Rick got the plate.

"There was a restaurant in Rome near the embassy that used to serve *spaghetti alla carbonara* this way," he said. "My sister and I would order it and argue over who got the bowl. Used to drive my parents crazy. This is *papardelle al sugo d'anatra*, ribbon pasta with duck sauce." He peered at her portion. "I think he gave you more."

"You're not getting my bowl." She took a bite and her eyes widened. "I think I'll just let you order for me from now on."

Talking was put on pause to allow enjoyment of the *papardelle*, but then it returned to less pleasant issues than food. Rick was regretting he'd had to tell Lexi about the murder. It was causing her daytime personality to creep into her evening breeziness. It showed a protective side in her as well. Angelo had told Rick he was concerned about Lexi's social life, and now she was worried about her boss's safety. Like father and daughter, these two.

After a simple green salad to help digest the earlier two courses, they decided to call it an evening, with a stop for coffee on the way back to the hotel. Once again the chill of the air greeted them as they stepped into the street, but instead of snow, the stones were coated with the moisture of the evening fog. It was a cold, penetrating fog that went deep into their lungs with every breath. Its invisible droplets were bent on cleansing the city, pushing against doors and windows and wafting through the leafless branches of trees. Halfway to the hotel they spotted the defused yellow light of a bar still open despite the hour. Rick opened the door and Lexi hurried in.

It must have been one of the few establishments in the city that was both open and serving warm drinks, since the small room was almost filled to capacity. He guessed that a movie had just let out nearby, and a controversial one, since most of the customers were in animated conversations. Many of them sipped from small glasses, but cups were the container of choice, and the one man behind the bar banged away at his coffee machine to keep up with demand. Customers stood two deep at the bar, and around small tables that stood on one side of the room.

"What would you like, Lexi? An Italian would never order a *cappuccino* at this hour, but you're a tourist, so you are allowed. With the chill it might be just what you need."

"It does sound perfect."

"Go over and guard that last table while I get it." Rick worked his way through the people and got the attention of the barman. "*Un cappuccio e un caffè macchiato.*" The man was pouring two shots of *grappa* but nodded to confirm that he'd gotten the order. Rick looked back to see Lexi standing patiently next to the table, ready to repel any interlopers.

The barman was fast, despite the volume of orders. After leaving a good tip, Rick picked up the two cups and saucers and squeezed back through the people to get to their table. A bowl of sugar awaited their coffee. Rick set the *cappuccino* in front of Lexi and spooned sugar into his coffee. She picked up her cup, held it in both hands to absorb the warmth, and took a sip. No sugar for her.

"Excellent, Rick." She looked around after a second swallow. "I feel like I'm really in Italy on this trip." She glanced back at him. "I know. Where else would I be? But you know what I mean."

He finished his coffee in one swig. "I know exactly what you mean. It is the advantage of getting off the tourist track, coming in the off season, and most importantly, seeing someplace other than the big cities."

"Speaking Italian helps. Or traveling with someone who does."

He shrugged. "I'm sure you could learn it easily. Do you speak another language?"

"College French."

"Better than nothing."

She finished her coffee and rubbed her fingers over the window, wiping away the moisture caused by the heat of the room. The street was narrow, but the building on the other side was barely visible through the fog. "We'd better get back, Rick. There will be e-mails waiting for me to answer and reports to read."

"Let me get rid of these so they can use the table."

Lexi watched as he picked up their cups and saucers and carefully worked his way through the crowd. After placing them at one corner of the bar he turned and found himself hemmed in by a man who was carrying on an animated conversation with the woman next to him. Rick tapped the man on the shoulder to get by. The man turned, said something to Rick and shook his hand. The man introduced Rick to the woman and they shook hands. After a minute of conversation, Rick gestured toward Lexi, tapped his finger on his wrist where a watch would be, and took his leave. Lexi was waiting for him at the door.

"Someone you know?" she asked.

Rick pushed open the door and they stepped back into the cold arms of Mantova's fog. They both pulled their coats tighter around them as they started in the direction of the hotel.

"One of them. Carlo Zucari, the manager of the Rondini dairy. He reiterated the invitation to tour the operation. You are invited, too, of course."

"I'd enjoy that. Is that his wife?"

They turned the corner and Lexi tucked her arm under Rick's. The street was deserted save for a line of cars parked along one side. Fog and cold had scared away any cats which normally might have prowled at this hour. They were indoors, on something warmer than the dark cobblestones.

"That's the interesting part. He introduced me to her. I don't know if he's married or not, but that's not his wife."

"Why is that interesting?"

"Her name is Letizia Bentivoglio. If I remember correctly, she is the one Inspector Crispi said is the lady friend of the recently deceased Roberto Rondini."

"Hmm. As they say in mystery novels, the plot thickens."

"Lexi, no mystery author worth his salt would ever write that." From deep inside his coat pocket he felt the vibration of his phone. He unhooked his arm from Lexi's and extracted it with some difficulty, squinting to read the number. "I'll call them back." He quickly returned it to his pocket.

Despite the chill, he was perspiring. The evening had not gone well, continuing a pattern of the last few weeks. He knew he should have concentrated on the business at hand and not be distracted, but for him that seemed impossible. Where had he left his car? He took in a breath of the night air and coughed when the cold exploded in his lungs. Damn this fog. He looked up and down the street, trying to remember where he'd parked, and decided it had to be just ahead. His footsteps echoed along the narrow street as he searched the line of cars. Darkness took away the features of everything on the street. All the buildings looked the same: flat, two-storied fronts, silent and shuttered.

The cars, no matter what their daytime color had been, were black. A few streetlamps, unable to penetrate the heavy fog, left weak circles on the stone pavement or on the roofs of vehicles. Finally, he spotted his Alfa three cars ahead and increased his pace, pulling out his keys as he went.

Just as he reached the car the attacker struck.

He screamed in pain and fell forward toward the curb, his hands instinctively extended to stop the fall. The palms slid off the wet metal of the car's hood and his forehead slammed into the glass of the windshield. As he slid into the gutter he reached for the back of his head where he had been struck. Warm blood covered his hand and seeped into the cuff of his shirt. He was on his knees now, grasping the fender of the car parked behind his. A second blow hit him, but the thick collar of his overcoat rendered it harmless. His body stiffened in preparation for a third, but instead he heard a voice and the rattle of a shutter opening above them. Thank God, someone had heard him cry out. The weapon clattered to the ground and his assailant took off running. Running fast. He got to his feet and peered through the fog at the sound, but could see nothing. On the ground next to him was a thick piece of wood. An axe handle? Whatever it was he didn't care, his only thought now was escape. He pulled out a handkerchief and pressed it to his neck before opening his car door and dropping into the seat behind the steering wheel.

When the old man looked down from the open window, all he saw was fog and a pair of red tail lights disappearing into the darkness.

Chapter Seven

After a final pandiculation, Rick was ready to go. He was never one for extensive warm-up, even on cold days like this one, but Lexi apparently felt differently. She placed her left heel on the rim of the tall flowerpot in front of the hotel and bent her head down to touch her extended leg. She repeated the stretch with the other leg, then did several knee bends. Rick bounced in place and watched her, trying to remember the word for "tights" in Italian. It wasn't something that came up often in translating articles for academic journals.

"Lead the way." She made a few jumps on the balls of her feet.

The streetlamps had just clicked off when they came out of the hotel, but one car that passed them still had its headlights lit, though more for the fog than the darkness. They ran shoulder to shoulder along the narrow sidewalk, keeping to the curb so as not to knock down anyone who might emerge from one of the buildings. There was not much chance of that; the city was just beginning to wake up and this section of town was mostly residential. Only the bars would be open at this hour, dispensing strong coffee to those who couldn't sleep or had the bad fortune of working an early shift. Stores and other businesses would not open for three hours, and most of their clients would arrive well after that.

They crossed the small canal that cut across the southern

part of the town center and turned east toward the lake. A wide path ran above the water's edge, a promenade where the families of Mantova strolled on Sundays and holidays. Without saying anything to Rick, Lexi took the lead. This morning the fog wafted in off the lake, cutting the visibility of both path and water, and bringing with it a humid chill. They didn't feel the cold; if anything, it added to the pleasure of the run. Rick took in gulps of the air and noted its difference from what he was used to breathing on his morning runs in downtown Rome. Perhaps Lexi was noticing the same contrast with Chicago, though, like Mantova, it had its own lake. She ran like she was by herself, and thanks to a long stride, that was just what was happening. Rick watched as she steadily lengthened the distance between them.

The castle loomed up on the left. Floodlights which lit the walls each night had been shut off, and there was not yet enough natural light to bring out the texture of the stone, leaving the walls a uniform dark gray. The path dropped lower, closer to the surface of the lake, running along the initial section of the causeway before looping down beneath it. A truck rumbled overhead as Rick turned under the roadway and continued along the path which now rose back to its former level. A male runner, dressed for the cold, passed him going in the opposite direction, nodding a silent greeting. Lexi was now about twenty yards ahead, and the path was flat and straight. The grassy area between it and the street widened, and the occasional wood table and benches appeared, waiting for good weather to bring picnickers. On the other side of the street, the city's northern wall stretched for a few hundred yards before being replaced by the side of a more modern building. Lexi, then Rick, passed three fishermen seated on metal lawn chairs and bundled against the morning chill. They kept their eyes on the lake, seemingly oblivious to the runners as well as to each other. Rick looked up and saw that Lexi was running in place in front of a tunnel that went under the road.

"Time to turn back?" she asked when he reached her side.

"Good idea," Rick said while breathing heavily. "I've studied the map and I'm pretty sure this doesn't go anywhere except up to a busy street." As they turned, his phone rang.

Lexi raised her eyebrows. "You better get that, it could be your policeman."

After pulling the cell phone from the small pocket with difficulty, he saw the number and realized he hadn't called back last night. "I'd better take this, Lexi. It'll only be a minute."

She gestured that it was fine, and wandered toward the water, pulling her knees up as she went so they wouldn't stiffen up in the cold. Rick switched to Italian.

"*Ciao*, Betta. Sorry I didn't get back to you last night."

"You sound out of breath."

"Out for a morning run along the lake. It's beautiful. How is your, uh, case going?"

"We're going to be wrapping it up this morning. I thought I might take a couple days off, catch a train up to Mantova this afternoon. I'd love to see the Mantegnas again."

So the draw for a trip to Mantova would be the art. Very typical of the Betta of late. He glanced at Lexi, who was still pulling her knees up to her chest to stay loose. "Betta, this is a fascinating job, but the guy is keeping me busy day and night, I wouldn't have any time to spend with you."

There was hesitation before she replied. "*Va bene*. I understand. Have you been to the castle?"

"Yes, it turns out Signor Rondini is an art collector, so we went yesterday and saw the Mantegna masterpiece. Today we're going to learn about cheese production. It's nonstop with him."

"I'll be anxious to hear all about it when you get back to Rome."

"And you can tell me about your case."

"Yes. Yes, I'll do that. Call me when you're back."

"Will do. *Ciao*, Betta."

He took a deep breath and squeezed the phone back into the pocket.

"We'd better get going or you're going to stiffen up from the cold." Lexi was running in place. "Everything all right?"

"Yes, everything's fine. It was a friend from Rome checking up on me." He wondered if she could hear that it was a female voice on the other end of the call.

"It's good having friends who care about you, Rick. Same way back?"

Before he could answer, she was off, quickly up to regular speed, making long, smooth strides. He started running, maintaining the same distance behind her as before, moving his eyes between the grassy scenery, the lake, and her figure. The runner they had passed earlier was on his return loop, and smiled again at Rick. Three others came behind him and also waved, indicating that this was a popular morning route for the locals, despite the fog which was again wafting off the water, occasionally obscuring Lexi's form just ahead of him. They passed the castle and turned into the small square that would take them to the hotel's street. He was almost even with her now.

As Lexi approached the corner, a male figure with gray facial hair appeared around it, looked at Rick, and raised his arm. The man was close to Lexi, and she took the gesture as menacing. After a quick lash with her leg and a chop of her arm, he was on the ground looking up with a dazed expression on his face. She stood over him, arms raised and body tense. Rick reached them a moment later.

"Easy, Lexi, I know who this guy is."

"You do?" She was taking in short breaths. "I'm from Chicago, Rick. It was a reflex reaction. Hope I haven't caused an international incident."

"Probably not." He switched to Italian. "You can get up, Signor Folengo. I'll protect you against her. You shouldn't go around making threatening moves at people, especially those who know how to defend themselves."

The man got slowly to his feet, pushing back the long gray

hair that had fallen across his face. He looked like he had not
bathed since snarling through the window of the car at the
Rondini farm gate. He tried to brush off a patch of mud from
his knee, but only succeeded in spreading it over his already
dirty jeans and hand. "I recognized you and was calling for
you to stop. She could have hurt me, and then you both would
have been in great trouble with the police. But how do you
know my name?" He was standing now, and edging back from
Lexi, who continued to stand her ground.

"Somehow, I don't think the police would take your side."
Rick purposely did not answer his question.

"Who is this creep, Rick?"

He told her, then returned to Italian and Folengo. "Why
would you want to talk to me?"

"It was your employer I wanted to talk to. I assumed that
the rich relative from America would be staying at the most
expensive hotel in the city, and I was on my way there."

"Do you really think, after that scene at the farm, that Mr.
Rondini would want to talk to you?"

"Perhaps not, but I also have a petition to leave with him.
We are a large group, and we want to have our voices heard.
The very well-being of the Po Valley depends on our message
getting through."

"Rick?" She had her hands on her hips.

"Oh, sorry Lexi. The guy wants to give your boss a petition."

"For that he had to attack me? Take it and we'll see what it
says." A touch of her businesswoman persona had crept into
her voice.

He turned to Folengo, who, from his expression, did not
appear to understand English. "Give me the petition, and I'll
see that he knows about it. I can't promise he'll read it. I assume
this is about the sale of the land, like your protests?"

"You assume correctly." He pulled an envelope out of his
pocket and passed it to Rick. He was about to speak when Lexi
raised a hand.

"*Basta*," she said, to which the man froze, then turned and hurried off. They watched him disappear around the corner.

"*Basta*? So you do speak Italian, Lexi."

"Really? I thought it was Spanish. That makes me bilingual."

"Let's get back to the hotel before we catch a chill."

Angelo was in a more talkative mood. Instead of staring out of the car windows, as he'd done on previous drives into the Lombard countryside, he grilled Rick and Lexi about their encounter with the "ecofreak," as he characterized Folengo. Not that there was much to see from the Mercedes; the fog that had obscured the views of the lake for the morning runners had settled over the fields. As soon as the car emerged into some sunshine, it would be engulfed again. Marco kept the speed low, and he had turned on the car's penetrating, red fog light on the rear to make it visible to any traffic approaching from behind. As everyone living in the Po Valley knew, pileups caused by low visibility could happen at any time, but especially on the autostrada where too many drivers insisted on high speeds, despite the conditions. There was little traffic this morning on the two-lane road from Mantova to the Rondini dairy, but Marco took no chances.

Angelo was laughing. "Lexi, you did well to take that creep down. I wish I could have been there to see it. I hope he's there when we get to the gate so I can catch the look on his face when he sees you sitting in the back seat." He chuckled. "What a bunch of garbage in that letter. I think I'll tell Livia to sell the farm to a developer, just to piss off the guy."

There were no protesters at the gate. Marco slowed and turned in before pulling up to the house. The driver hopped out to open Angelo's door, and Rick did the same for Lexi. They walked up the steps to the house, but before reaching the door, Livia opened it and gave Angelo a welcoming hug. She greeted Rick and shook hands with Lexi.

"It's good to see you again."

"Thank you for inviting me along, Mrs. Guarino," said Lexi.

"Please call me Livia. Come in, everyone. Can I offer you coffee before you take the tour?"

"We just had some at the hotel with breakfast," answered Angelo. "Whenever you're ready, we are."

Livia's fingers brushed her face. "I won't be going with you on the tour. Francesco had an accident last night on the way home from the office. Nothing serious, but he's upstairs and I want to keep an eye on him. I've asked Carlo to show you around."

"I'm sorry to hear that," said Angelo. "Is there something I can do?"

"No, no. We'll be fine. I hope you'll enjoy seeing how the cheese is made." She opened the door and walked out to the porch with them. "Carlo will be there at the office." She pointed at a low structure a hundred yards away, visible behind the row of trees. The fog had lifted enough to see it and the other buildings of the dairy. "Come back when you're finished, and I'll offer you that coffee again."

"We'll do that."

They descended from the porch to the car and the driver got out to open the rear door.

"Over to that building, Marco," said Angelo as he stuffed himself into the back. Rick and Lexi took their assigned seats.

They drove slowly along the gravel road between two fenced fields, cows in one, open grass in the other, to reach the connected buildings. They were made with prefabricated cement, the lines of the ribbed walls interrupted only by small, high, windows, or by doors that rolled up to open. A shiny steel tank, which Rick assumed held milk, towered over the parking area, next to machinery that looked to be for cooling, something not needed on a day like this one. This outside view gave Rick the impression of a fanatical cleanliness. The cement walls were scrubbed and the stainless steel storage tank looked like it had been polished that morning. He could imagine what it was going to be like inside.

The car drove onto the pavement that surrounded the building and up to the door which Livia had pointed to from the house. Parked in front was a pickup truck which looked vaguely familiar to Rick. He remembered where he'd seen it when Zucari came out of the office with Emilio Fiore, the neighbor from across the road. The manager noticed the arriving Mercedes and said something quickly to Fiore, who nodded and walked toward the far end of the building. By the time Rick was opening the passenger-side door, Fiore had disappeared around the corner of the building and Zucari was walking toward the arriving car.

Knowing that the manager spoke no English, Rick prepared to earn his pay. After greetings were exchanged and Lexi introduced, they moved inside, leaving Marco leaning against his car. The entrance door brought them into a small waiting room outside the office of the Rondini dairy. Through glass partitions they could see two women working at computers in cubicles that took up half the room, the rest of it filled with files and office machines. As in the office itself, decoration in the waiting area was minimal; on the wall behind three chairs hung a company calendar, a map of northern Italy, and two posters from the Parmigiano-Reggiano Consortium. While they stood in the outer room, Zucari began his explanation of the process. He spoke in short sentences, which made it easier for Rick to interpret, but also gave Angelo and Lexi the impression the man was annoyed that he was taking time away from his real work.

He began by pointing to the map and explaining that Parmigiano-Reggiano cheese, by law, was produced only in certain geographical areas within the regions of Emilia Romagna and Lombardy, a system similar to the geographic designations for wines. Within those areas, thanks to the climate and soil, the quality of the milk was unique, and milk was, of course, the most important factor in making the end product. The diet of their cows was strictly controlled, never included silage or fermented feed, and the milk was always fresh from the previous evening. No additives or preservatives were ever used to make the cheese. The process followed a strict procedure beginning with the milking of the cows and ending more than a year later when the cheese was ready to be tested, certified, and finally put on the market.

"Follow me, please, and I'll show you how it all begins." He opened a heavy door with a small window, and motioned them to follow him.

The change from a small, drab, office of paper and computers to a bright, spacious workroom of milk and cheese was overwhelming to the senses, beginning with a strong odor of fermentation. The room held a dozen copper cauldrons, each the size of a large, round bathtub. They were filled with a white mixture and watched over by men dressed completely in white, including their caps. Everything was immaculate: white tiled floor, steel pipes, cauldrons, and workers.

"The milk from the late afternoon has been resting through the night," Zucari explained, with Rick interpreting, "and in the morning it is put into these cauldrons and mixed with other natural ingredients to curdle and ferment it. With the heat of the cauldron it begins to coagulate almost immediately. As it cooks, it is stirred with mixers." He pointed to machines that looked like small outboard motors, clamped to the side of each cauldron. "During the process he tests the mixture using a *spino*, a tool that goes back centuries."

Rick did not attempt to translate the word, but simply pointed to what the man at the cauldron closest to them was using. It looked like a small, round, birdcage on the end of a thick wooden pole. The worker stirred it slowly in the milky mixture that was thickening into cheese as they watched.

"With the price of copper, these kettles must have cost a fortune," said Angelo. He walked to one of the cauldrons and peered into the glutinous mixture, with Lexi at his side.

Rick stood back with the manager. "Wasn't that Emilio Fiore who just left?"

Zucari looked at him with a penetrating frown. "You met him after the funeral, Signor Montoya, and you know his farm is across the road."

"I did meet him, and he told me himself that he and Roberto Rondini didn't get along well at all."

"I've never had a quarrel with the man. He's here to look at some equipment we have which he's thinking about purchasing for himself. When he asked to see it, I was glad to help."

New management. Rick tried to figure out a way to ask about the woman Zucari was with the previous evening, without revealing that he knew she had been the mistress of his deceased boss. Before he could come up with something, Angelo and Lexi walked back to join them.

"Quite an operation," Angelo said, and Rick translated for the manager, who appeared glad to leave aside talk of the neighbor and continue his description of the process.

"Once the milk has coagulated enough, two of the men dip into the cauldron using those cloths." He nodded toward a shiny table loosely piled with large rectangles of white material. "A ball of the cheese mixture is lifted out and hung over the cauldron to drip out excess liquid, then wrapped in its cloth to be fitted in those molds." He pointed to another table with a row of ring-shaped pieces of plastic that looked like huge cookie cutters. "With experience they can tell just how much will fit into the molds. They wrap the cheese in the cloth, squeeze it inside the molds, and label them with the month and year." He walked to a long metal table on wheels where another row of molds was lined up. The rings enclosed the newly formed cheeses, wrapped inside their white cloths and marked with small, round stickers. "They will rest here for several days and harden into the wheels whose shape and size are the hallmarks of Parmigiano-Reggiano."

"It's not cheese yet?" said Angelo, tapping on the plastic ring.

"It's not the finished product yet," Zucari answered.

"How much milk does it take to make a wheel of the cheese, and how much will it weigh?"

Rick translated the answer, then made the conversions from liters to gallons, and kilos to pounds. "So about a hundred-fifty gallons of milk, and each wheel weighs about eighty-five pounds."

"This way, please," said Zucari when Rick was finished.

The three visitors followed him to the far end of the room under the eyes of a half dozen white-clad workers. He pushed through a set of swinging metal doors, once again polished to a glossy sheen. The room they entered now was equally large, but in contrast to the bright light of the cauldron room, it was dimly lit. Most of its space was taken up by long rectangular troughs filled with bobbing wheels of cheese. At the far end of the room, a man dressed in the standard white outfit walked along, slowly turning them in the liquid. Unlike the other room where the air was filled with the noise of pumps and other machines, here the only sound was the sloshing of the white wheels in the water.

"The cheese stays in this salt solution for several weeks, continuing the maturation process and absorbing the salt. The forms are regularly turned by hand to give the surfaces a uniform consistency."

Once again Angelo and Lexi wandered off to get a closer look.

"How long have you been working here, Signor Zucari?"

The manager watched Angelo as he answered. "About twenty years."

"How did you get the job? If you don't mind me asking."

"Why should I? My father knew Roberto Rondini and asked him to take me on, as a favor. That's the way things work here in Italy, Signor Montoya. I worked my way up to become manager."

"Things work that way in America, as well, Signor Zucari.

Clearly you had an aptitude for the work, or you wouldn't have ended up where you are."

"I'd like to think that."

The floating wheels of cheese were too much for Angelo to resist. He pushed one below the surface and watched it bob up and down, earning a smile from Lexi but an annoyed look from the room's lone worker. The two visitors rejoined Rick and Zucari.

"What's next?" Angelo asked.

"From here the wheels go into the aging room for the final step in the process. The rooms are kept at a precise temperature and humidity, and the wheels are periodically turned to assure that the aging is uniform throughout. They will be on the shelves for a minimum of twelve months, but up to and exceeding twenty-four. They are then tested by specialists from the consortium, first by tapping on them with a small, steel hammer, and then, if necessary with a needle, and at last resort a sampling dowel. When the quality of the cheese is confirmed, then, and only then, is it branded with the seal of Parmigiano-Reggiano and can be sold as such."

Zucari's eyes darted to a large metal clock on the wall and then to his own watch. He turned to Rick. "I'm afraid I forgot that I must deal with an issue of importance. It should take only a moment. Please tell Signor Rondini that I regret the interruption. You can go through those doors to the aging rooms."

He nodded at Rondini, walked quickly back toward the first room, pushing through the swinging doors. Rick told them what he'd said.

"I guess he didn't find out until this morning about having to show us around," said Rondini. He leaned over the pool and pushed another cheese wheel. "I saw that you were talking to him while Lexi and I were wandering about."

"I asked him what Emilio Fiore was doing here."

"Ah, Fiore. Lexi, that was the guy getting into the pickup.

He has the farm across the road and did not exactly get along with my cousin."

Lexi nodded. "I see. And now that your cousin is gone, the neighbor and the foreman are on friendly terms. Curious."

"Zucari told me that he's always gotten along with the neighbor," said Rick. "I also asked him how he got his job, and he said Roberto Rondini was a friend of his father."

"It's not what you know, but who you know," said Rondini. "It's the same everywhere. But in order to keep the job, and move up, you have to be good at it. Having an in with the owner only gets you so far. Isn't that right, Lexi?"

She smiled. "If you say so, Mr. Rondini."

Rick pointed to the doors at the opposite end of the room. "Shall we go into the aging room?"

"Lead the way, Language Man."

They walked between the troughs under the gaze of the worker, and past a row of steel trolleys ready to transport the cheese to its next location. Rick pushed through the doors and they found themselves in a room with a ceiling three times as high as the one they'd just left. Rows of shelves, separated by narrow aisles, towered above them. It was like the inner sanctum of some huge library, dimly lit and musty. But instead of ancient books, the shelves held wheels of light brown cheese, and the mustiness was the pungent odor of aging Parmigiano-Reggiano.

"Wow," said Lexi. "This is impressive. There are thousands of these wheels in here. It must be worth a fortune." She pulled out her smartphone and ran her thumbs quickly over the screen. "Nine dollars a pound in the States." She looked up at the rows. "It's like being in Fort Knox."

"*Grana* is a slang word for money in Italian," Rick said. "Which is the same word used for this kind of hard cheese."

"I can see why," said Angelo. He walked to the end of one of the rows and touched a wheel of cheese. "It's like an assembly line printing money. Every time you put a new row of cheese up to age you pull off another row and sell it. With a capable manager keeping an eye on things, my cousin could just let the process take care of itself and spend his time fishing. Not bad at all."

"What about marketing and sales?" Lexi said.

"Sales must be easy," answered Rick, "when only a relatively few producers, by Italian and European law, can make Parmigiano-Reggiano cheese. The consortium, which was created by the dairies, protects the geographic monopoly and does a lot of the marketing and public relations, so that helps too." He ran his hand along the shelf. "But it wouldn't work if they didn't have a good product."

They started up one of the narrow aisles, Rick first, followed by Angelo and Lexi. Hundreds of round sides peered down at them from the shelves, the top rows barely visible from below. The silence was broken only by their footsteps, and then by the faint opening and closing of a door somewhere behind them. Zucari must have returned, Rick thought, but after ten seconds the manager had not appeared. Rick listened for footsteps and decided that the sound of the door must have carried from a different part of the factory. Then he heard another noise.

It sounded like scraping or sliding, and it coincided with the slightest movement of the shelf on the right side of the aisle. He looked up and noticed a slight teetering of the cheese stacked five feet above them. One of the wheels began to slide slowly forward. From the next aisle over he thought he heard a low grunt just as another of the wheels started creeping toward the edge of its shelf. Then another began to move.

Rick spun around. "Go back! They're going to come down!"

Angelo's head shot upward, but he was mesmerized by the moving cheese and his body froze. Three of the wheels at the very top were almost halfway to the edge and the entire shelf rocked slowly and steadily. Fortunately, Lexi understood immediately.

"Get his left arm," she yelled.

They picked up Angelo and dragged him backward just as the first wheel of cheese hit the floor and smashed into pieces behind them. It was followed by another, and another, until most of the top shelf's contents was crashing to the floor. Rick and Lexi had almost gotten Angelo to the end of the aisle when one of the wheels glanced off the shelf on the other side and struck Rick just above his right knee. He let go of Angelo and dropped to the ground while Lexi kept pulling her boss until the two were safely against the wall near the door. Rick looked up to see another eighty-five pounds of cheese starting to tip off a top shelf above. He rolled over and it exploded next to him. On his hands and knees, he scrambled to the end of the row and out of harm's way.

"Somebody was pushing the shelf from the next row," he said to Lexi and Angelo, who were huddled against the wall. "Stay there, I'll get him." Rick pulled himself to his feet but immediately crashed back to the ground, holding his knee. "I guess I won't get him."

At that moment Carlo Zucari appeared, followed by a slew of white-clad workers. Rick looked up at the manager.

"Too late. You missed all the excitement."

Chapter Eight

The broken shards of cheese that covered the floor added new pungency to the air of the curing room. Only by counting the empty spaces on the shelves could Zucari calculate how many wheels had been lost. He was overseeing the salvage operation under the eyes of Rick, Angelo, and Lexi. The three of them stood back against the wall and watched two workers put chunks of cheese on wheeled trolleys. A third worker, raised up by a narrow forklift, was checking the shelving and adjusting cheeses that were still on it.

"I told Signor Rondini that we needed to replace these shelves," Zucari muttered to nobody in particular. Only Rick, among the three standing against the wall, understood him. He translated for Angelo and Lexi.

"Don't say anything about it being pushed," Angelo ordered. "Livia has enough to worry about; she doesn't need to think someone is trying to bump off her uncle."

"It could have been Rick they were after," said Lexi as she poked him without Angelo noticing.

Rick poked back. "Perhaps Folengo wanted to get back at Lexi for attacking him this morning, and he sneaked onto the farm under the cover of fog. But another possibility is that it could have been meant for our friend here." He inclined his head toward Zucari, who was directing the man working on the top shelf. "Don't forget that he slipped off just before it happened, and the person who did it may have been expecting him to be with us."

"The other scenario is that Zucari himself pushed the shelves," Angelo said. "Or it was done by his friend, Fiore, who was here looking at equipment he wants to buy."

"Mr. Rondini, Rick should report this to the police."

Angelo took in a deep breath and let it out slowly. "I suppose so. You're due to talk to him anyway, aren't you, Language Man? He may have some news about the investigation. Do you think you can make it out to the car?"

Rick rubbed his knee. "I'll be fine. It's just a flesh wound."

"Then let's get that coffee from Livia. It's going to taste good after this. And I have something important to tell her."

Inspector Crispi glanced at the array of food behind the *vetrina* before pushing open the glass door and entering the shop. A mixture of smells coming from all manner of fresh delicacies assaulted his senses, causing his thoughts about homicide to be momentarily pushed aside. The *salumaio* was laid out in typical Italian fashion: a refrigerated display case ran the length of the space, and behind it shelves were crowded with less perishable food. *Mortadella* and other meats and cheeses hung from hooks above the shelves, waiting their turn to be taken down and sliced. Bottles of wine, in twos and threes, were squeezed in everywhere. To the right was a small counter that held a cash register. Behind it stood the man Crispi assumed was Sandro Bastoncini. He looked up when the policeman entered.

Bastoncini wore the white coat that was standard for his profession, one which could have been that of a druggist, had it not been for traces of food near one of the buttons. Thanks to sprinkles of salt that had crept into the pepper of the man's well-trimmed hair, Crispi calculated him to be in his early fifties. The face was ruddy, no doubt due to his hours catching fish rather than those spent slicing salami. He squinted down his nose over a pair of reading glasses, not happy to see his visitor yet curious as to the reason for the visit. When he'd called, Crispi had purposely not told Bastoncini why he needed to see him.

"Inspector Crispi?"

"Yes. Thank you for seeing me, Signor Bastoncini." He didn't feel the need to show his identification, and it wasn't requested. "I only have a few questions. It shouldn't take very long."

"I hope not. My assistant called in sick today so I'm by myself until my son comes in after school to help. What's this about?" He folded his arms across his chest.

"I'll be brief. We're doing a routine investigation into the death of Roberto Rondini, and—"

"Rondini? I wouldn't be surprised if someone did him in, having known the man. But from what I read in the paper it was an accidental death."

Crispi's expression stayed the same. "Every indication points to an accident, yes. You knew Signor Rondini through your fishing association, I understand?"

"That's correct."

"From what you just said, can I conclude that you did not get along well with the deceased?"

"You can well conclude that, Inspector, though that was years ago. It was not a secret that we had some disagreements, but I was not the only one, I can assure you. It all came to a head when I was running for re-election on the board of the association, and Rondini spread false rumors about me to the members."

The door opened and a woman entered carrying a cloth shopping bag that was partially filled. She looked at Bastoncini and smiled. A regular.

"*Ciao*, Sandro."

"*Buon giorno*, Signora. I'll be with you in a moment."

Crispi made a gesture to indicate he should take care of the customer and Bastoncini walked behind the counter in front of where the woman was now standing. She ordered four *etti* of sliced *prosciutto*, but with as little fat as possible, unlike the last time she was in. With two hands he pulled out a leg of the ham and held up the end that would be sliced. He said something that Crispi couldn't hear, which made her giggle, and dropped it in the slicer. He turned the blade on and cut off several paper-thin slices, which he carried to the scale. It was a bit more than the four hundred grams she'd requested but she didn't mind. She then asked for a ball of *mozzarella* and a portion of the Russian salad, and chatted while he got them for her. That was all for today. He brought the three items to the cash register where he totaled them up and carefully put them into the bag she held open for him. After paying, she looked Crispi up and down and departed.

"What kind of rumors?" asked Crispi.

"I beg your pardon?"

"You said Rondini spread rumors about you."

"Oh, yes, of course." He wiped his hands on a cloth from under the counter. "Things which would seem unimportant to non-fishermen, but are very significant for us. Like what kinds of lures I used to win our competitions or even whether I was the one who actually caught the fish. Unfortunately, there were those gullible enough to believe his nonsense." He again folded his arms across his chest. "But, as I said, Inspector, the incident was years ago. I have gone beyond it and am involved in the association. I can't say I'd forgiven Roberto, but it just stopped being an issue. I was even in attendance a few days ago at his funeral."

Crispi tried to recall the face of Bastoncini among the mourners, but since he had sat at the rear of the church, he'd seen mostly the backs of people's heads. "I am not a fisherman, Signor Bastoncini, so I can ask you a basic question. Was it strange that he was fishing at that hour of the day?"

"Not at all, Inspector. The early morning hours are usually the best time to catch fish. They are ready for their breakfast, you might say. Those of us who work don't have the luxury of being able to fish every morning, like Rondini could."

"Everyone knew he was usually on the river at that hour?"

"He enjoyed telling all of us in the association how often he was on the river, and I'm sure he said the same to his non-fishing acquaintances. Being seen as a wealthy man of leisure was extremely important to Roberto Rondini, especially by those of us who have to work most days."

"What mornings do you fish?"

"You know the days the shops are open in this province, Inspector."

Crispi made a mental note to check the day of the week Rondini's body was found.

●●●●●

The coffee Livia served was dark *espresso* in small cups. A dish of cookies sat on the tray, decorated with colored icing and sugar, but she appeared not to have noticed them. She talked in short sentences as she poured each cup, interrupting herself to ask each of her three visitors how much sugar or cream they wished.

"I'm mortified that you were in there when the shelf broke. Carlo says that only a dozen wheels were damaged. It could have been much worse. When we had the earthquake a few years ago, it was terrible. Some dairies were almost put out of business. The worst damage was well south of here. Carlo will have to check all the shelving now. Oh, the cookies. Alexis, please try one."

Lexi took one of the cookies from the tray and stirred her *espresso*. "Touring the dairy was fascinating, Mrs. Guarino. I will appreciate the cheese even more now that I've seen how it's made."

"Lexi is right," said Angelo. He stirred his coffee and sat back into the cushions of the sofa where he and Lexi sat. The other three people sensed that he was not finished, and waited in silence for him to arrange his thoughts.

"I want you to know, Livia, that coming to Mantova, and especially to this farm, has made me more appreciative of my own roots. Meeting you, of course, is a great part of it, but just being in the land of my parents, where I was born, has opened my eyes to so much. Breathing the air here, seeing the fields, watching the river flow past…" He stopped to take a sip from his cup. "My great regret is that I did not come here sooner in my life."

At first Rick thought his boss was simply trying to get Livia's mind off the accident, since she was already upset about her husband and the falling cheese hadn't helped. A kind gesture, of the type Rondini was not likely to be known for in the competitive world of business. He hadn't gotten this far with kindness. Yet Rick sensed that Angelo's little speech was more than an attempt to comfort his niece. He'd spent relatively few total hours with the man since picking him up at the airport, but somehow Rick thought that something new was going on. It was a different side of Angelo Rondini, or perhaps a side that hadn't existed before. A quick glance at the puzzled expression on Lexi's face convinced Rick that he was correct.

Angelo continued.

"I'd like to make a gesture, Livia, to honor the memory of my cousin. In his death he did me a great favor by pulling me back to the land of my birth. I will be forever indebted to him for that, and want to do something to honor his memory." He saw that Livia was about to speak, and held up his hand. "I would like to have a small memorial made, something in stone. It would be placed near the dock, overlooking the river. With your permission, of course. When I visited it yesterday I was impressed by the beauty and tranquility of the spot. I understood why your father spent so much time there—I could almost feel his presence."

"Uncle, that would be wonderful. Of course you have my permission." The smile on her face disappeared as she looked past Angelo toward the hallway behind him. "Francesco, are you feeling better?" She spoke in Italian.

The others turned to see her husband standing in the hallway. Unlike the day of the funeral, he was dressed informally and was in need of a shave. An ugly, red bruise covered half his forehead, and he brought up a hand to cover it while his eyes squinted at the visitors.

"I didn't know they were here."

"I told you this morning, dear. You must not have heard."

"I'm sorry, Livia. The pain pills I took are making me groggy."

Angelo glanced at Rick, as if silently reminding him to remember what was being said so he could tell him later. The two men stood as Francesco approached them unsteadily.

"You will forgive me, I hope," he said. "An unfortunate accident last evening. I am in no condition to be sociable, I'm afraid, but Livia is capable of extending the hospitality for both of us."

Rick interpreted his words for Angelo and Lexi, and transmitted the answer in return.

"Mr. Rondini hopes you feel better soon."

Francesco nodded and shuffled off. A small bandage was visible on the back of his head. Whether he was coming into or about to leave the house was unclear. Had the farm manager called him about the falling cheese? Rick decided there was no way to know, and certainly no way to find out. The group in the living room settled back into their chairs, and Livia was anxious to move the subject away from her husband.

"Uncle, you are very kind to think of a memorial to my father. I know just the place you are thinking of, an open area overlooking the river and the dock. When I was a girl I used to sit there and watch the Mincio flow past."

He placed his empty cup on the tray. "Then it's done. Montoya will help me find someplace that can do the work quickly. There is something else I'd like to do, Livia, and perhaps you can help."

"Of course, Uncle."

Angelo leaned back against the cushions and adjusted his tie. Since the day of the arrival, except for the funeral, he had worn the same light-gray wool suit, but always with a different tie. Today it had a red-and-blue-stripe pattern.

"Where would I find records of my own birth? I know that my parents emigrated to America when I was an infant, but there must be something written somewhere. My birthplace was Voglia, which I think is just south of here."

"It is. It's in the area called Virgilio, named for Mantova's most famous native son. Voglia is where my grandfather Enzo lived when he was young."

"Probably the whole Rondini family lived there, including my parents. Your father wasn't born in Voglia, was he?"

"No, in Mantova at the same hospital where I was born. I've driven through Voglia a few times, and I can tell you there isn't much to it. You should try the *municipio*, where births and deaths are recorded, but also the parish church, where you'd find records of baptisms."

Later Rick, Angelo, and Lexi stopped halfway down the path in front of the Rondini home. They had said their good-byes to Livia, who reminded them of the event in honor of her father that evening. The early fog had disappeared, leaving a sparkle on the ground from the rays of the late-morning sun. Along the fence next to the road, a worker perched on a mower was making his final turn in the direction of the dairy buildings. Ragged lines of grass-cuttings left by the machine sent off a rich smell that enveloped the three people standing on the path.

"We have enough things to keep us busy until that event this evening," said Angelo, talking like the CEO in a staff meeting. "Language Man, can you find someplace where I can order a monument? If we pay them enough, they should be able to do it on a rush basis. And you have to talk to your cop friend to find out what's going on with his investigation. You should also tell him about the falling cheese, though I don't want him pushing me again to have police protection. And let's see if we can get to that town of Voglia to look up my birth record. I think it would be fascinating to see."

"Lexi," said Rick, "if you can lend me your tablet, I'll look up some stone places and also find where Voglia is."

Lexi fished out the tablet from her bag, hit a button to turn it on, and passed it to Rick. "It automatically reset from Chicago to Italy when we got here, so any search you do will be based on this location."

Rick checked the screen and started tapping in letters.

Angelo took her elbow. "Lexi, while he's doing that, I need to talk to you about the Hawaii project. I read the notes you put on my breakfast tray, and I think I know what I want to do." They strolled down the path toward the car where the driver was waiting. Angelo talked and gestured as he walked, while Lexi made notes on the small pad she'd taken from her purse. A few minutes later Rick was walking toward them, holding up the tablet.

"This thing works great, Lexi. If I can ever afford it, I'll get one for myself." The two had paused next to the Mercedes, where Marco stood holding the door open. They watched Rick reach them. "I found what looks like the perfect place to buy stonework, including grave markers and other memorials. It's just south of Mantova. Marco, do you know where this place is?" He held the screen close to the driver.

"Yes, of course. It's in the *zona industriale* near the river."

Rick passed the tablet back to Lexi, who turned it off and stowed it in her purse. "Shall we go there now?" he asked.

"Yes," answered Angelo, "but we'll drop Lexi at the hotel first. She has to get on the phone and spoil the breakfast of a few people back in Chicago."

He dropped himself into the back seat of the car. Lexi flashed Rick a quick grin and took her place next to her boss.

Rick extended his leg onto the floor of the front seat but pulled it back slowly and eased into the seat from a different angle. Perhaps the flying cheeses had done more damage than he'd realized.

• ● ● ● •

The industrial zone just south of the city was not on any of the tourist itineraries. Not that it was especially unsightly; it had its own style of orderliness, one which marked a prosperous local economy. But rather than the tranquility of history and art found in the center of Mantova, the atmosphere here was movement and noise caused by metal and machinery. Small factories, service businesses, depots, and warehouses lined both sides of the street, its surface showing the wear that came from the traffic of large vehicles. Save for the license plates on the trucks and the gauge of the railroad tracks that cut across the street, it could have been an industrial park outside any small American city.

The Mercedes turned through the iron gate of the monument business and drove past stones of various sizes and shapes before coming to a stop in front of the low metal building that served as the office. When Rick and Angelo emerged from the sealed-in silence of the car they could hear the sound of metal against stone coming from a shed to one side. The door to the office opened and a young woman dressed in jeans and a sweater came out. A gust of wind caught her long hair and blew it in front of her face.

"Can I help you?" she asked in Italian while brushing the hair aside.

Rick stepped forward and got right to the point. "This is Signor Angelo Rondini, visiting from America. He is looking for a small stone memorial for his deceased cousin Roberto Rondini. My name is Montoya, I'm his interpreter."

She shook Rick's hand and then Angelo's. "I'm sorry I don't

speak English. We'll be glad to help, but there is something I don't understand. We did the gravestone for Roberto Rondini, so what is it this gentleman needs?"

Angelo listened without understanding, but knew from her body language that she had asked a question. "You know what I want, Language Man. Explain it to her." He walked off and began looking at the stone pieces that sat in the open air.

"He must be upset by the death of his cousin," she said when Angelo was some distance away.

Or something else is bothering him, Rick thought. Perhaps the Hawaii project, whatever that might be.

"Mr. Rondini would like to put up a small memorial along the river, near the place where his cousin loved to go fishing. Unfortunately, it is a rush job, since he would like it installed tomorrow. He will of course pay you extra to get it finished expeditiously. There would be some words carved into it, but a minimum. 'In Memory of Roberto Rondini,' is all."

"I think we can do it. People usually die suddenly, so we are used to working on short deadlines, and right now business is slow. If he can choose the stone, we can do the wording in a few hours and have it put in place in the morning."

They looked at Angelo, who had stopped in front of an ionic column about four feet high, its top broken off leaving a jagged surface.

"That one is very popular," she said. "The broken stone symbolizes a life cut short."

"Let's see what he thinks." They walked to Angelo, who continued to study the column, his hands deep in the pockets of his overcoat. "She can do it, Mr. Rondini. Is this column what you had in mind?"

"What? Oh, yeah. I think this would be fine. They can do it all by tomorrow morning, including the inscription?"

"Yes, sir."

Angelo nodded and waved his hand weakly to indicate it was a deal. The woman went inside to prepare the paperwork,

leaving the two men standing next to the column. They watched
a truck loaded with stone blocks drive in past the Mercedes
where Marco was standing, smoking a cigarette. With a loud
grinding of gears the truck shifted into reverse and backed
toward the shed. Two men in overalls came out, brushed gray
dust off themselves, and surveyed the shipment.

"They're going to need some equipment to unload those
pieces," said Angelo. He spoke the words but his mind was
elsewhere.

"You okay, Mr. Rondini?"

"Huh? Sure, I'm fine, Language Man. Got a lot on my
plate."

"Business issues?"

He shook his head. "No, that will work itself out. It's this
whole deal with my cousin. His death. A possible murder. And
then someone pushes the cheese on us. Add to that the whole
trip here, bringing me back for the first time to where I was
born. There's a lot for me to absorb. I'm glad you're here to
help."

"I haven't really done anything, Mr. Rondini."

"Yeah, you have." They watched as a small forklift came out
of the shed and pulled up behind the truck. The two workers
argued about what should come next in the process. "I suppose
you know all about your Italian family."

"My aunt and uncle have told me a bit. I probably should
pick their brains more about the Fontanas, and ask my mother
when I see her next. I was pretty young when my Italian
grandparents died, but I remember the funerals. Every once in
a while I think that I should make a visit to their graves, outside
of Rome, but I haven't yet."

The forklift driver had taken charge, slipping the metal
prongs under the pallet that held the stone. The hydraulic
motor groaned as it lifted its load from the bed of the truck.

"Do it," said Angelo. "Life is short." As if to make his point,
he checked his watch. "I had wanted to visit Voglia now, but

I'll tell Marco we'll do it tomorrow morning, since I have to get back to confer with Lexi on that project. We'll get lunch at the hotel. I want you to go to the newspaper again to find out more about the various Rondinis, including yours truly." He pulled a piece of paper from his pocket and passed it to Rick. "These are my parents' names. See if there's anything there about them. And I want you to go see your friend the cop and get an update from him. That should keep you busy until it's time to go to the event at the—what's the name of the place?"

"Palazzo Te."

"Kind of a strange name."

"I looked it up. Comes from the local word for huts, since apparently there were many of them on the acreage when the Gonzagas decided to build the *palazzo* there. Perhaps a bit of ironic humor on their part."

"So it's not a hut?"

"We'll see this evening."

Crispi had suggested they meet over lunch, which sounded good to Rick. There was something about being attacked by cheese that gave one an appetite. As would be expected for a restaurant only a few blocks from the *questura*, police sat at many of the tables, and the caste system of their profession was evident. Uniforms dined together. Plainclothes—many with pistols on their belts—sat separately. The clientele was mostly male, with a few women mixed in with the uniformed cops. The noise level was high, another indication that the place was filled with regulars, and the plain walls and stone floor did little to dampen the decibels. One of the waiters, who was clearly aware of Crispi's status, led the inspector and Rick to a quieter table in the corner and placed menus in front of them. He took their order for wine and mineral water and departed.

Rick had glanced at the tables as they'd walked to theirs, and most of the choices were what he had expected policemen to eat in cold weather: hearty, stick-to-the-ribs fare. He barely had time to study the choices when the waiter returned with a bottle of water and a liter of the house red. Crispi, who had made a cursory glance at the menu, passed it to the waiter and ordered *agnoli in brodo* followed by the *stracotto di manzo*. Rick listened and told the waiter he'd have the same. Stuffed pasta in broth was the perfect way to start a meal when there was a chill in the air. Then pot roast on a bed of *polenta*, likely enough food to last him through the rest of the day. He snapped off a crust of bread and took a sip of the wine.

"You have some information for me, Montoya? This investigation, such as it is, appears to be going nowhere. No more threats to your employer?"

"No more threats."

Strictly speaking, it was true. An actual attempt to harm someone was not a threat, after all. And Angelo, just before leaving Rick in the hotel lobby, had said that, on second thought, he didn't want Crispi to know about the incident in the cheese-aging room. The inspector would become more adamant about police protection, and Angelo still wanted no part of that. Rick rubbed his sore leg under the table and wondered if it was the right decision.

"We went to the dairy this morning on Livia Guarino's invitation and did a tour of the cheese-making operation."

"Did she say anything that might help with the investigation?"

"No. And in fact she didn't take us on the tour since her husband had an accident last night and she wanted to stay close to him."

Crispi frowned. "What kind of accident?"

"Hard to say. He made a brief appearance and I saw bruises on the front and back of his head, but they didn't elaborate on what actually happened. So the manager, Carlo Zucari, gave us the cheese tour. Something else. The guy who owns the dairy across the road, Emilio Fiore, was coming out of the plant when we drove up, so Zucari doesn't appear to hold the same antagonism toward the man that his late boss did."

The *agnoli* arrived, floating in shallow bowls of almost clear, capon broth. Lexi would be pleased. They sprinkled on Parmigiano-Reggiano, mixing its pungency with the rich flavor of the capon, before picking up their spoons and wishing each other a *buon appetito*.

"Perhaps the two were talking about that plot of land which appears to be the source of so much grief," said Crispi after eating a few *agnoli*. "I had one of my sergeants, who is good at such things, do a title search on that plot. I wondered why it has been left to seed."

"What did he find?"

"She. She found that it was originally owned, decades ago, by a farmer who couldn't pay his taxes. It was taken over by the province and then sold to Roberto Rondini's father."

"I read about that incident in the archives of the *Gazzetta*, but didn't know that it was the same piece of land that now may come up for sale."

"According to tax assessment records, the plot was never developed, even though it is part of the Rondini dairy farm. Neither the recently deceased Roberto Rondini, nor his father, ever did anything with it."

"Until, possibly, now." Rick finished the last of the *agnoli* and started on what was left of the broth with his spoon. "But why wouldn't they have used the plot to grow grass? I don't know anything about farming, but I would assume that it is efficient to rotate your cows among various pastures."

"That was my thought as well."

"Something else curious about Carlo Zucari, the manager. I ran into him last night when Lexi Coleman, Signor Rondini's assistant, and I were having coffee after dinner. He was with a woman, and he introduced me to her."

"And?"

"Letizia Bentivolgio. Isn't she the woman who Roberto Rondini was seeing in town?"

Crispi put his spoon inside the empty bowl. His expression hadn't changed. "Yes, she is, and yes, that is curious. When I interviewed her she told me she'd met Rondini when he and his manager had come to buy equipment where she worked. It should have occurred to me that it was Zucari. I'll have to think about that one for a while."

"Well, I've thought about it, and concluded that it gives Zucari a motive to murder his boss." Rick took Crispi's silent stare as an invitation to continue. "Zucari and Letizia were a couple, and then Roberto Rondini moved in on her. She goes with the rich owner instead of the manager. Motive. Now that Roberto is out of the picture, Zucari moves back into it."

Crispi drummed his fingers on the table. "We have quite a drama."

"Another member of the drama's cast showed up early this morning when I was doing a run with Lexi along the lake."

The bowls were taken away by one waiter seconds before another put down the dishes with their second course. Not exactly fast food, but the staff knew that most of the policemen had a limited time for lunch. Rich vapors wafted up from the pot roast served on a bed of *polenta*, the meat's dark red juices spreading over the yellow edges. Both men studied their plates for a moment before taking forks in hand.

"And which one of the *dramatis personae* would that be?" asked Crispi after his first bite.

Rick recounted the encounter with Domenico Folengo, describing in detail how the activist had confronted Lexi and had paid the price.

To Rick's surprise, Crispi actually smiled. "I wish I had been there to see it. What a shame Folengo didn't come running to my office to bring charges for assault. We could have used some levity this morning." He resumed his deadpan expression and tucked into his main dish. "What did his manifesto say?"

"What you would expect. Keep the environment natural, save the planet by starting with the Mincio River. It did not make much of an impression on Signor Rondini. In fact he said in the car on the way to the dairy that he might tell his niece to sell the land for development just to annoy Folengo." Rick noticed the puzzled look on the policeman's face. "He was joking, of course."

"I never understand your American humor."

Nor Italian humor, Rick decided. He took up a piece of the *stracotto* and dipped it in the *polenta*, recalling the *polenta* under Angelo's perch the day before at the elegant restaurant in Goito. His today had to be just as good. At half the price.

"Inspector, can I interrupt for a moment?" The man who spoke had been walking by the table toward the door when he saw Crispi. Now he noticed Rick and waved his hand. "Never mind, I can talk to you later."

"It's all right, Lanzi. What is it you wanted to say?"

Though not comfortable with a stranger listening, Lanzi continued. "The gambling investigation. As you suspected, it looks like it involves an out-of-town syndicate. Probably from Milan. I've got a call in to the *questura* there this afternoon."

"Good. Let me know the details."

The policeman joined his colleagues waiting for him at the door.

"Should you really be talking other police business with a civilian listening, Inspector?"

"If there's one civilian I'd trust to be discreet it would be the nephew of Commissario Fontana."

Rick suspected his status as a confidant was due more to uncle Piero's position than his own personal qualities, but he was pleased to accept it nonetheless. Now could he get the cop to lighten up a bit, so they might have a normal relationship? Not likely.

"Did you interview the man from the fishing society?"

Crispi finished a mouthful of food and patted his lips with the napkin before answering. "Signor Bastoncini. Yes. The only information I got was another confirmation that Roberto

Rondini was at times a difficult man. He claims that Rondini spread rumors which cast doubts as to the honesty of his fishing practices, something which resulted in Bastoncini leaving the board. Cutthroat politics in a fishing association—can you believe it? But why am I surprised? My mother tells me stories about her lace-making group where two women are always at each others' throats. Once, when one was in the bathroom, the other got into her basket and untwisted all the bobbins. Montoya, these are women in their seventies and eighties." He took a drink of wine. "And they meet in the basement of the church."

Rick had no way to top that story. "There's an event tonight at the Palazzo Te that the cheese consortium has organized to honor Roberto Rondini. I expect most of those in your investigation will be there, certainly the Rondini manager, Carlo Zucari, as well as the neighbor, Fiore."

"I would expect every producer of Parmigiano-Reggiano cheese in Lombardy will be in attendance. A good opportunity to get together and exchange gossip under the pretext of honoring one of their own." Crispi raised an index finger. "You'll let me know if Francesco Guarino appears, despite his injuries."

"Of course. And there's another event. My boss has ordered a small stone memorial to be put up along the river to honor his late cousin. The ceremony will be tomorrow afternoon. I don't know who will be there."

"Near the dock?"

"That's what Angelo wanted, and Livia Guarino agreed."

Crispi shook his head. "That's a bit tasteless, isn't it? Near the place where the man was murdered?"

"She thinks of it as a place where her father spent many pleasant hours."

The detective shrugged and put his fork on the empty plate. "You and your American employer will be busy. How long does he plan to stay in Mantova?"

"I'm not sure. Originally, I was told that he couldn't be away for more than a week, and the inference was that it would be less. So I would expect only a couple days more before he flies back. I don't think I'm betraying any confidences to say that the trip is having an effect on him...apart from the murder investigation, I mean. It has opened his eyes to his Italian past, even though he left this country as an infant. He's got me doing research on his family, but I'm not sure if he's pleased with what I'm finding out."

"You mean about Roberto Rondini's father?"

"Correct. His Uncle Enzo was no angel, and neither was Cousin Roberto. Mr. Rondini has a forceful personality himself, as you have witnessed. It's one reason why he's been such a successful businessman in America. But I sense he has mixed feelings about his family's reputation here."

"I fear that if we solve this murder, that reputation will not be improved."

● ● ● ● ●

Other than a small, red carnation in his lapel, Signor da Feltre looked the same. The tie was plain, as was the suit, and the day's newspaper was once again spread out on the desk in front of him. The only sound was a soft hum coming from the florescent lights in the low ceiling which gave everything in the room a faintly ghostlike hue. The archivist looked up and smiled when Rick pushed through the doors. As usual, they were alone.

"What's the occasion?" Rick asked, pointing to the flower. Not that he and da Feltre were now close buddies, but after two previous visits, the question did not seem impertinent. But he added, "If you don't mind me asking."

Signor da Feltre looked down as if noticing it for the first time. "This? I'm meeting a lady friend after work. Coffee. Or perhaps a glass of wine. Who knows what it could lead to?"

Was that a wink? At the very least it was a twinkle in the man's eye. Rick had hoped that the guy had some sort of life outside the crypt where he spent his days, and it now appeared that he did. Da Feltre made an "it's all yours" gesture toward the computers and Rick walked over to take his usual place. He sat down, pulled out the sheet Angelo had given him with his parents' names, and pushed the ON button.

What little information Rick found on Angelo's parents was noticeably different in both tone and quantity from what he'd read earlier about the uncle. Angelo's father was a graduate of the local *liceo* and worked as a clerk after getting his diploma. One story mentioned a scholastic award he had received on graduation. His employment at an insurance office was noted in the wedding announcement, but as would be expected of those times, no mention was made of the work status of the wife. She would become a *casalinga*, a housewife, and take care of the infant Angelo when he came along. The marriage took place in Voglia, where the Rondini clan had apparently lived at the time, and where Angelo was later born. There was one small story about membership in a fishing association, but it wasn't clear if this was the same one that Roberto Rondini would join decades later. Rick concluded that fishing, when Angelo's father was involved, was a relatively inexpensive pastime, and which brought some food to the table. It would be a natural hobby for a clerk on a limited budget. Would he have given it up completely when he emigrated to America? Fishing was not something Angelo had mentioned, even when they had visited the dock and seen Roberto's boat. Not that the man was sharing all his childhood memories with Rick. Far from it.

The only story that mentioned the family's departure for the States was a short piece on the social pages about the annual Christmas party of the insurance office, held at a local restaurant. It listed awards and bonuses handed out, including to Angelo's father, with a mention that he would be leaving the firm to take a position with an Italian export company in New York and would be sorely missed by his colleagues.

Rick let the wheels of the chair roll him back from the monitor. He meshed his fingers together and stretched them in front of him while pondering the information he'd found about Angelo's parents. The picture that formed of the elder Rondini was one of a solid citizen—hard-working and a follower of the rules. Perhaps even a bit dull, but that could be Rick wanting to read something into it that was not there. What was fascinating was the contrast between the two brothers, at least as described on the pages of the Gazzetta. Angelo's father, keeping a low profile, working hard, and always toeing the line. The father of the late Roberto Rondini, brash, highly political, and somewhat shady. This might have been due to the newspaper's political slant, but in addition they had given Enzo Rondini considerably more ink than given to the brother who had slipped off to America, never to be mentioned again. Rick scooted the chair to the keyboard and searched again for Enzo Rondini, Angelo's uncle. He might have missed something on his previous visits to the archive.

What he found was coverage of the man's marriage. It took place four years after the departure of baby Angelo and his parents for New York. Enzo Rondini and his young bride, Pina, were married in the cathedral at Mantova—not, like his brother, in the parish church in Voglia. The man had moved up in the world. Rick cross-checked the names of those in the wedding party and found several to be local political leaders. He found no mention of the brother who had left for America several years earlier. Either Angelo's parents were not invited to the wedding or maybe it was too expensive for the young family to travel back to Italy for it. Either way, it appeared that the two Rondini brothers from the little town of Voglia were living very different lives, and not just because they found themselves on opposite sides of the ocean.

Rick folded his notes and slipped them into his pocket before turning off the computer and getting to his feet.

Signor da Feltre looked up from his paper. "Did you find what you were looking for?"

"I did. Thank you for your help." The man hadn't helped at all, but it seemed like the correct thing to say. He looked at the carnation and was going to add "I hope you get lucky," but decided against it. A minute later, as he was emerging from the building into the sunlight, he realized that there was one name that had not come up in his searches, and that was Angelo Rondini.

Chapter Nine

Covered with a greenish hue, the robed figure of the most famous Mantovano looked out over the park, past the bench where Rick and Angelo sat. Virgil held a scroll under his arm, perhaps a copy of his "Aeneid," and extended the other in a dramatic oratorical gesture. Adding to the classical stereotype, the sculptor had given the poet a long, flowing robe and conferred well-earned laureate status with a crown of laurel leaves. Though the metal Virgil was oblivious to the light wind that blew along the paths of the park, causing the stubby topiary to vibrate slightly, the two men on the bench felt it. Angelo adjusted his scarf and Rick buttoned his overcoat. The park was deserted save for an older couple who were walking the rectangular path around its grass center. Their serious faces and lack of conversation gave the impression it was their daily exercise, to be completed, no matter what the weather. Angelo and Rick watched the two pass their bench for the third time.

"What you've found about my father is what I would have expected. He was not the most outgoing of personalities. I'd always thought it was because he remained uncomfortable speaking English, despite reasonable fluency, or that he was ashamed of keeping his Italian accent. But I suppose he was just that kind of person, a bit introverted and more interested in numbers and spreadsheets than people. My mother was more outgoing than he was, but even she was pretty quiet.

When it was just the two of them they spoke Italian, of course. I'd overhear them, and just by a process of osmosis was able to understand a few words. I definitely could tell, from their voices, if it was an argument, even without knowing what they were saying. Not that there were many arguments."

"They must have kept in contact with your uncle. Letters, phone calls?"

Angelo looked up at Virgil and pondered the question before answering. "I knew I had an aunt and uncle in Italy, and a cousin, but it just didn't come up very often. My parents were Americans by then, and proud of it, and it simply wasn't something they dwelt on." He rubbed his chin in thought. "Strange. Talking about this makes me remember one night when I was about ten. I was in bed and heard my parents talking. It wasn't an argument, but they were clearly upset about something. I heard the name Enzo, so I knew they were talking about my uncle. I cracked open the door to my room, and when they saw me my mother rushed over and hugged me and I could see tears in her eyes. Funny the things you remember from your childhood."

"I can see how that would have made an impression on a kid."

Angelo nodded, his eyes still on the statue. "Now that you've told me all this, my guess is that they'd heard about my uncle Enzo's activities and were glad they were in the States and had no part of it."

"And were very relieved that you weren't exposed to it."

"Exactly. That must be why they didn't talk about Italy that much, they were not proud of what my uncle was up to here. And why not say it—the two brothers likely didn't get along very well when they were growing up. That happens in families."

Rick thought of his sister and was thankful that they always had been, and always would be, the best of friends. Moving around frequently as foreign service brats had forged that bond.

There were new cities, sometimes new local languages to learn, and the formidable task of making friends in a new school, but they always knew they had each other to face it with. The idea that they would not have been close was unthinkable.

Rondini tilted his head as he looked up at the statue, past a round fountain that had been drained for the winter. "Did you ever read anything by this guy, Language Man?"

"I had to read some of "The Aeneid" for a course in college."

"You read it in the original Italian?"

"The original was Latin, but no, I read an English translation."

Rondini didn't appear to mind being corrected. Even though he was looking at Virgil, his mind was elsewhere. "So your buddy the cop didn't tell you much of anything new when you had lunch with him. He seems to be ready to move this murder to the cold case file."

"I don't think I'd go that far, Mr. Rondini, though he is frustrated that not much new has surfaced. It's difficult to read the guy, if I might understate."

Rondini grunted. "I'm starting to think that this investigation won't be resolved before I fly back to Chicago. You think something might come up at this event we're going to tonight?"

"Hard to say. I expect that it will be attended by the usual suspects, along with lots of others."

"I want you to poke around as much as you can. I should be able to find enough people who speak English to talk with. Put on your detective hat and detect. Did your uncle the cop issue you a badge?"

"No, just a building pass to get into his office."

"That would get you a job on the police force in Chicago." He rose from the bench, and a gust of wind off the lake pushed open his overcoat. "Let's get back to the hotel, I need to have a shower before we go. I probably smell like cheese, though that would make me fit right in with this crowd."

Rick didn't need to be reminded of the encounter with the cheese wheels. The cold air was making his sore leg worse.

• ● ● ● •

As he drove, Marco gave his three passengers an introduction to what they were going to see. He spoke quickly, since the Palazzo Te was not far from the hotel. Nothing in a town this size was very far from anything else, even a building that had been built as a country villa and was, at that time, outside the walls of Mantova.

"Palazzo Te is considered Giulio Romano's masterpiece, one of the gems of the Mannerism movement, not only for its architectural style but for the paintings found on the walls of its many rooms, several done by Romano himself. It was built by the Gonzagas, of course, specifically Federico the Second, between 1525 and 1535. The building has been described as a pleasure palace, which was certainly the case with Federico, since it started as an extension of his stables and was enlarged to include living space for his mistress."

Angelo tapped Rick on the shoulder from his place in the backseat. "Are you familiar with Mannerism, Language Man?"

"I had a friend in Rome who is an art history professor, Mr. Rondini. Her specialty is Mannerism, so she talked about it a lot. Some of it rubbed off, I suppose." Rick looked back at Lexi, who had a slight smile on her face. "She lives in the States, now," he added, and Lexi raised an eyebrow.

Rondini didn't notice the exchange. "Well, you can be my guide when we're inside."

"I'm sure many of the people in attendance will be glad to explain the artwork, and can do a better job than I could," said Rick.

The car had been navigating the narrow streets of the city, but now the lines of buildings had given way to open space, a reminder that Palazzo Te had been built so the Gonzagas could escape to the country. Late afternoon light glistened off flat athletic fields visible through a long row of trees, and in the distance to the left they could barely make out the outline of the city's soccer stadium. After a few turns the car slowed and turned into a parking lot next to their destination. It pulled up to a low stone structure with the classical decoration to be expected for a palazzo of the early sixteenth century in Italy.

Rick helped Lexi out of the back seat, noticing the shapely leg as she stepped to the ground. She wore a simple black dress under her wool coat. Very little wind was getting through the protective line of trees, but overcoats were still needed, even for the short distance between the car and the door. The three walked to the entrance, their shoes crunching on the gravel path.

From the outside, it was unclear if the building was one story or two, which Rick suspected Giulio Romano had done on purpose to confuse. The Mannerists, his art historian friend, Erica, always said, liked to show that they knew the rules but enjoyed bending them. A sign outside the door announced that the museum would be closed to the public for a private event. The Parmigiano-Reggiano Consortium had some pull, as well as the cash to pony up for the rental.

Inside they were met by a young woman who took their coats before pointing them toward a doorway. "The ceremonies will take place in the Sala dei Cavalli," she said.

The spacious, rectangular Hall of the Horses was aptly named. Wide panels set high around walls were painted with images of horses—the pride of the Gonzaga stables—looking sleek and bored as they posed for the artist. Perhaps several centuries earlier sawdust had covered the floor and those very animals had been brought into the room for show, but this evening the only horseflesh lay in the art. The room was set with a long table along one side, and a small podium with a microphone stood against the opposite wall in front of a tall, gaping fireplace, its spotlessness indicating it hadn't been used in centuries. The table, covered with a linen cloth, held platter after platter of food, with the emphasis, not unexpectedly, on cheese. Wheels of Parmigiano-Reggiano sat regally at the

146 David P. Wagner

ends, a quarter of each one sliced out and arranged on a board with a number of their signature teardrop knives at the ready. The invitees, though mostly dairy operators who saw the stuff every day, were wedging off small chunks and popping them into their mouths. Other hors d'oeuvres were displayed on elegant dishes between the cheese, all against a background of soft-hued flowers. From a distance Rick was able to identify *prosciutto* wrapped around cheese strips, miniature pizzas, rice croquettes, and *crostini* spread with pâté and other toppings. He was beginning to wish he had skipped lunch. White-coated waiters circulated with trays of fluted glassware that had been filled from a bar behind the food table. The gathered friends and colleagues of the late Roberto Rondini, many with their spouses, talked in low voices, as appropriate for the occasion, but Rick had the sense they were talking business rather than sharing recollections of the dearly departed. Livia Guarino stood in the midst of a small group who were taking turns giving her embraces of condolence. She wore a gray dress accented by black lace around the sleeves and neck. Her husband was nowhere to be seen. When she spotted the three new arrivals she excused herself and hurried over. The men in the group looked to see where she was going and when they did, their eyes stayed on Lexi.

"Uncle, so good to see you." They exchanged air kisses and she shook hands with Rick and Lexi. "Thank you for coming. Had you already visited the Palazzo Te?"

Angelo looked around, his eyes raised to the wall paintings and the highly decorated boxes inserted into the ceiling. "No, and this is quite a place."

"The other rooms are open, you will have to see them all. I'm told the program will be short, with very few people speaking, so you'll have time to wander around. Unless you'd prefer to talk about local politics and cheese. That's all these people are interested in." She glanced over Angelo's shoulder. "Some people just arrived I must talk to, Uncle. Please get yourself something to eat and drink, the three of you."

They promised they would. Livia walked over to meet the new arrivals just as a waiter stepped up to them with a tray of glasses. Angelo and Rick waited for Lexi to take one before they served themselves.

"Here's to Federico Gonzaga," said Rick. "He knew how to build them to last."

"Almost five hundred years," said Lexi, as she looked at the wine in her glass. "And still holding parties here." She surveyed the crowd. "There's the farm manager, Zucari. He must have cleaned up the broken cheese by now. Do you recognize anyone else, Rick?"

"I recognize who he's with. It's Letizia Bentivoglio."

Angelo, who had been studying the ornate designs in the ceiling, turned quickly in that direction. "Roberto's lady friend? I wonder if Livia realizes that she's here, or even knows who she is. She looks younger than I expected, given my cousin's age."

"Men at that age don't usually take up with women older than they are," said Lexi.

"That's true," said her boss. "Very cynical on your part, Lexi, but true."

Rick watched the people who were starting to drift toward the food table. One large man stood next to it, deftly balancing a wineglass and plate in one hand while eating with the other. "There's the guy who owns the dairy next to the Rondinis', Emilio Fiore."

Angelo frowned. "The one we met after the funeral who'd had too much wine, and then at the restaurant. It looks like he's at the grape again. Be sure to talk to him, Language Man."

At that point a man in a dark, tailored suit came up to Angelo and introduced himself as the president of the consortium. He spoke fluent English with a slight British accent. Rick realized that the presence in Mantova of the American cousin would have been common knowledge among this group. He took advantage of the situation to excuse himself and head for the food, even though he wasn't hungry.

Rick's father the diplomat was a master at working the crowd at a reception, but unfortunately he'd never schooled his son in the skill. The only time Rick had observed it closely was one time in high school when one of the waiters didn't show for an event in their home. Rick was given a white coat and a tray of food, and while he worked he observed the senior Montoya moving from one group to another, playing the perfect host. Fishing for clues to a murder was not exactly analogous, but it was close enough. He began with two couples standing close to one of the wheels of cheese, and introduced himself.

As he half expected, they knew about Angelo, the American cousin, but were unaware that he'd brought his own staff along on the trip. Rick explained that Angelo's assistant came from Chicago, but he was an interpreter based in Rome. He sensed that the four thought someone who lived in Rome to be even more exotic than an American from Chicago. Did they know the deceased well? The two men did—at least they claimed to, since they were connected in some unspecified way to the cheese business. Their wives shook their heads, though they exchanged looks that Rick read to mean they'd heard about Roberto, and what they'd heard may not have been flattering. He decided he wasn't going to get much out of them, excused himself on the pretext of getting something to eat, and moved on.

As he stood deciding which of the culinary treats to try, a man dressed in a dark suit approached him, his hands clasped against his chest.

"Can I help you?" the man asked, and then noticed Rick's puzzled expression. He held out his hand. "I'm Lorenzo Dini, I cater all the events for the Parmigiano-Reggiano Consortium. You look like you needed some guidance."

Rick shook Dini's hand. "Nice to meet you, Signor Dini. Riccardo Montoya, visiting from Rome. Everything here looks delicious. The consortium does a lot of receptions like this?"

"They keep us busy, not just here in the production area but all over the country. And a few events in other parts of Europe. I was in Munich last week. The Germans love cheese."

"I'm sure they do." It seemed like a good time to pick up a small chunk, which he popped into his mouth. "Did you know the honoree this evening? Signor Rondini?"

"Oh, yes."

Rick swallowed the cheese and paid closer attention. "From these kinds of affairs? I'd never met him, I'm just working here, like you. As an interpreter." He hoped his being an outsider would loosen the man's lips.

Dini looked to one side and then the other. "You can learn a lot about people from how they act in a social setting like this. I should not speak ill of the departed, but Roberto Rondini was the kind of person who would treat people differently depending on what he wanted from them. He was all smiles with foreign cheese buyers, but with others he could be quite different."

"That seems like a lot to conclude just from seeing him at receptions and dinners."

"You'd be surprised, Signor Montoya." Again he looked furtively before continuing. "Do you see that man over there? With the woman?"

Rick followed Dini's eye and came to the manager of the Rondini dairy, who was standing with Letizia Bentivoglio and three men. This could get interesting. "The man with the good tan?"

"Yes, that's the one. I've never seen the woman, but I remember him from a reception several months ago at the chamber of commerce for a group of Arab investors. That man and Rondini were speaking with members of the visiting delegation, all very polite, but a moment later the two of them were in a corner of the room arguing. They weren't raising their voices, but it was clearly an argument. Rondini was poking his finger into that man's chest, and from the look on the man's face I thought he was going react violently. Now what kind of a person would berate someone in public like that?"

Dini was apparently unaware that Zucari had been in Roberto Rondini's employ, and it was not Rick's place to tell him. "Were there other times you saw Rondini like that?"

"That's the one I recall."

So the man—a world-class eavesdropper—was basing his view of Roberto Rondini on one incident. It was better than nothing, and it did involve the manager of the Rondini dairy. What would they have been talking with a group of investors about that would cause such a flare-up? Rick's conjecturing was interrupted by a voice coming over the microphone of the man who had been talking with Angelo and Lexi. Rick walked over to his boss, ready to interpret, and as the crowd quieted, he positioned himself behind Angelo and Lexi so they both could hear his English playback.

The remarks about their departed colleague were bland and neutral, and likely could have been given about most of the people in the room. Roberto Rondini had been, the president said, a prominent member of the consortium, always supportive of its ideals and standards, helping to grow the industry and the reputation of Parmigiano-Reggiano cheese in Italy and abroad. His words were as much about the consortium as they were in praise of its departed member, and they were greeted with polite applause. Someone else, whose title Rick didn't catch, stood up and gave an equally bland discourse.

"These guys are going to put me to sleep," said Angelo after Rick finished his interpreting.

Livia was the last speaker, and the group appeared to pay closer attention to what she said. It may have been because she was Roberto's daughter, and as the grieving daughter she deserved deference, or perhaps they were trying to size up the new owner of the Rondini dairy. She thanked everyone for coming, and said how much the consortium had meant to her father. She recounted an anecdote about her father and Rondini cows that got smiles and warm applause, and ended by saying that the Rondini dairy would continue to be a loyal member of the consortium as it had been when her father was alive. More applause followed, and the president thanked those gathered for their presence and declared the ceremonies ended.

"She did well," said Angelo. "I could see it on everyone's faces. I wonder how many of the dairies are owned and run by women. My guess is very few."

"Very poised," Lexi noted, "given the circumstances. What is it they always say? For most people the two most stressful things in life are funerals and public speaking? She had both of those tonight."

Angelo nodded.

The crowd was moving toward the food table, ready to do it justice after the formalities had been dealt with. Rick scanned the group, looking for someone who might give him something, anything, to help shed some light on the investigation as Angelo had ordered. He spotted Emilio Fiore, the neighboring dairy farmer, still with a glass of wine in hand. He was in a circle of other men which included the Rondini dairy manager, Carlo Zucari. Rick immediately recalled when Fiore had come out of the dairy office just before the curious incident of the falling cheese. And that brought to mind the dull ache he still had in his leg. Something else occurred to him. If Zucari was in that group, where was his date? Rick's eyes moved through the people and spotted Letizia Bentivoglio standing apart, looking up at a dark brown horse depicted on the wall. He excused himself to Angelo and Lexi and walked to her.

"A stunning animal," said Rick when he got to her side. She turned around, and he could see she was trying to remember who he was.

"Yes. I've always loved horses." Her eyes widened slightly. "Now I recall where I saw you, in the bar last night. You're the one who's translating for the visiting American cousin."

"Interpreting," Rick said. He couldn't reveal that he knew about the relationship she had with the deceased Roberto Rondini, but why not ask about her present companion?

"Signor Zucari gave us an interesting tour of the cheese-making operation today. I must thank him again for it." Her face betrayed nothing, so Rick guessed she had not been told of the falling cheese. "Have you known Zucari long?" It was a lame question, but she didn't appear to notice. Her reply was equally lame, or perhaps purposely vague.

"Everyone knows everyone else in this city, either personally or by reputation."

A waiter appeared with a tray of glasses. Letizia's hand moved quickly to take one, and Rick joined her. They exchanged wishes of good health and she took a deep drink. Rick sipped his.

"I was under the assumption," he said, "given his present position, that he was from the country."

"You would think that," she said, wiping her lips with the paper napkin that came with the wine, "him being a manager of a farm. But in fact he grew up in Mantova. His was not an easy childhood." Her eyes darted to where Zucari was standing with the other men.

Rick had the impression that this was not her first glass of wine that evening. It would make sense that she needed to be fortified, attending a memorial for the man with whom she was romantically involved, and in the presence of the dead man's family. He was still unsure if Roberto's daughter knew about Letizia Bentivoglio, or if she did, whether she disapproved. It was something he would likely never know, but he also doubted it could have anything to do with the man's demise. He was trying to decide if he should ask her about Roberto Rondini when she abruptly excused herself and walked away. So that was all he was going to get from Letizia Bentivoglio. This was getting frustrating. Time for a break from investigating. He looked at Angelo, who was in deep conversation with two men. Lexi stood to one side, talking with two much younger men. As he watched, she took a sip from her wineglass and her eyes moved around the room before resting on Rick. He inclined his head in the direction of the far door, and she nodded before saying something to the two and walking off.

"Enjoying yourself, my dear?"

She made a face. "I was standing there trying to think of the last time I'd had this much fun. It's enough to make me swear off cheese."

"Somehow I think those two guys were interested in more than just your views of cheese production. Well, Lexi, while you were enjoying a chat with Mantova's rich bachelors, I pretty much came up dry with the people I've talked to. But I'm not done yet. Let's take a quick break and see what's in this next room. Then I'll get back to doing what Angelo ordered me to do, and you can...well, do what you were doing."

"Sounds good."

The next hall—every room in the Palazzo Te was a hall—formed one corner of the square main building. The decoration on its walls and ceiling was even more ornate than the horse room, but the theme was different. Rather than horseflesh, what covered these walls was just flesh, very pink and either muscular or plump. The note on a stand in the middle of the floor identified the room as the Sala de Psiche, and explained that the decoration recounted the mythological tale of Cupid and Psyche. Those two were featured in one of the panels, but everyone else depicted around the walls paid little attention to them. They were too busy having a good time.

"Well," said Lexi as her eyes moved around the room, "I guess we know what the Gonzagas used this room for. Did you bring me in here on purpose?"

Rick laughed. "I didn't know, I swear."

"Nobody seems to be wearing clothes."

"It's mythology, Lexi. And orgies are clothing-optional affairs. Thankfully, most of them are carefully draped."

"Most, but not all." She pointed at a chubby figure, one arm around a satyr, the other embracing a wine jug. "That guy seems to be enjoying himself the most."

"Bacchus. You can always spot him since he's drinking wine and wears grape leaves on his head. It's quite a banquet. Look at all that food."

"As if they all came for the food."

They were standing in one corner, the better to get the complete sweep of the paintings on the opposite walls. As they studied the art, two men walked resolutely in, crossed the room, and exited through the other doorway. One gestured as he spoke, while the other studied the floor. Neither one paid any attention to the decoration or noticed the two people standing in the corner.

"Wasn't that...?"

"Yes," Rick answered. "Carlo Zucari, our cheese guide, with Emilio Fiore. Fiore was coming out of the dairy this morning when we drove up. They keep getting more and more chummy, those two."

"Why don't we follow them? Maybe you can overhear what they're saying."

"I can follow them and you can stay here and enjoy the artwork."

"I'll come with you, thank you very much."

The two walked into the next highly decorated room, then into the next, still with no sign of the men. Rather than an open doorway at the other side of this room, there was a heavy door. Rick pushed it open and they found themselves enveloped by cold air, causing Rick to whip off his jacket and put it around Lexi's shoulders. They were in a covered portico that connected two open areas on either side, and in keeping with the other rooms, its vault was decorated within an inch of its life. To their right lay the grassy, square courtyard in the center of the building. In the opposite direction, past columns and arches, was a bridge over a pool, and beyond that stretched the Gonzaga formal gardens. Rick looked both ways while Lexi stood shivering, despite the jacket.

"They're not out there, they must have continued into the

next set of rooms." He pushed open another door and once again they were inside an ornate space, but this one with little color. An endless army of ancient warriors marched in two rows along a stucco frieze around the room just below the ceiling. More classical figures adorned the barrel vault, carved like large cameos and set inside the open boxes. It was all shades of white, with the occasional light blue, and after the other rooms the effect was striking. If the symmetry of the palazzo was to be maintained, there would be another room before getting to the one at the corner. In fact they could see a second and third room through the narrow doorways. They could also hear the voices of the two men, coming from the corner room.

Rick held his finger over his mouth and gestured for Lexi to follow him quietly into the next room. She handed back his jacket before they slipped through the doorway and moved to the opposite side, near the opening to the room where Fiore and Zucari were talking. The two kept their voices low, but the words were clear enough for Rick to understand.

"…you can't let her do that."

"What am I supposed to do? She owns it, she can do with it whatever she wants."

"But that's insanity. What does her husband think?"

"He had some kind of accident last night and hasn't made an appearance. You saw that he's not here tonight. So I haven't talked to him and I don't know where he stands, or if he even knows what she's decided to do. Knowing what a weakling he is, it wouldn't surprise me if he isn't even being consulted. I've always thought he married her to get control of the dairy one day, but now I don't think she's going to let that happen. She's changed a lot since Roberto died. Before she was content to stay in the background, but now she's become a different person. She's her father's daughter, Emilio, but we all had to wait until he died to find that out."

Lexi poked Rick in the ribs and put her ear close to his head. He twirled his finger in an "I'll tell you later" gesture.

"You don't think she—"

"No, no, of course not."

"I agree. I think it had to do with something that happened long ago."

A few seconds passed before the manager spoke. "We'd better get back."

Rick froze. He hadn't thought about the two men coming back through the room where they were listening in on the conversation. Lexi apparently realized their dilemma at the same time. She pulled him roughly into the corner. A few seconds later, when Zucari and Fiore stepped through the doorway, what they saw was a couple locked in embrace. The two men chuckled to each other and kept walking into the next room, then through the door out to the portico.

Lexi reached up and rubbed her smudged lipstick from Rick's mouth. "You can take your arms from around my waist now, Rick, they're gone."

"They might come back." He breathed in her perfume and tried to place it. A bit flowery but with a certain powdery aura. One of the Chanels?

"Rick."

"All right, all right." He let his arms drop, but didn't step away from her.

Nor did she from him. "We should return to the other room—Angelo may be wondering what happened to us. But first tell me what they were saying."

"Let's go into the next room to do that. I think it may be the famous Hall of the Giants that I read about. We shouldn't miss it."

As they walked through the doorway Rick told her about the conversation, recalling it as best he could. "They had to be talking about the land," she said when he'd finished. "It sounds like she's leaning toward selling it for development."

"I agree, and neither of those two will be pleased when that happens."

"And they will put two and two together and conclude that the American developer pushed her into the decision, which we know is not the case, at least from the conversations between Angelo and Livia that you and I have heard. Did Angelo ever nudge her toward that decision?"

"Not when the three of us had lunch, Lexi. They might have talked other times when you and I weren't around, or by phone, but I don't have the sense that your boss wanted to influence her one way or the other. I would guess the opposite."

"I agree." She had been concentrating on what Rick had been saying, and now she looked around the room. "This is quite a place, I can understand why it's so famous."

Rick read the panel that was attached to a stand in the center of the square room while Lexi craned her neck in an attempt to take it all in. The paintings recounted the mythological story of the revolt of the giants against the gods of Mount Olympus and the gods' brutal and decisive reaction to the uprising.

The scene was one of total chaos.

Perched on a ring of clouds in the center of the round ceiling, the gods of Olympus looked down in fear and surprise. On one side, Zeus, larger than the others, was about to unleash another string of lightning bolts which had already begun to have their deadly effect on Earth. The columns, arches and walls of stone buildings on the ground had broken into huge pieces, crushing the rebellious giants whose ugly, contorted faces cried out in pain and anguish. The beautiful figures of the gods in the heavens contrasted with the brutish, deformed bodies writhing amidst the rubble on the Earth below.

Rick took his eyes from the panel and looked at the walls. "It says that at the time this work was finished, about 1535, people would surely have been reminded of the sack of Rome a decade earlier." He moved his head slowly to take it all in. "Makes you realize that having a few wheels of cheese fall on you is not that big a deal."

She took his elbow. "Time to get back, Rick, our boss may

be wondering what's become of us. Keep your eyes averted when we go through the cupid room."

Rick did as he was told, and when they emerged back into the Sala dei Cavalli they found that the group had thinned out along with the amount of food on the table. He spotted Angelo talking with two men near the food table. He appeared to be understanding them, so Rick decided his interpreting wasn't needed. Instead he whispered something to Lexi and walked to a man standing almost in the corner, holding a wineglass and staring blankly at the brown horse on the wall above him. Emilio Fiore looked up and focused on Rick's face for a few moments before there was recognition.

"Ah, Signor Montoya. I saw you here earlier with that lovely young lady. She's Angelo Rondini's assistant, I've been told." He chuckled and took a long pull from his wineglass.

Rick was unsure if Fiore was referring to seeing them in this room or the other one, not that it mattered. "Was it you we saw coming out of the dairy this morning, Signor Fiore?"

There was a puzzled frown, but the question finally registered. The wine was having its effect. "Oh, yes, this morning. I had just stopped in to ask Carlo something. He told me you all were going to tour the cheese-making process. You were, I trust, duly impressed?"

Rick thought for an instant that Fiore knew about the falling cheese and the question was intentionally and cleverly double-edged. If he did know, the dairy manager must have told him. Or else he was the one who tried to push over the shelves. But it wouldn't make sense for the perpetrator to make jokes about it, even after a few glasses of wine, when it could bring suspicion on himself. But Fiore could also believe everyone had decided it was a terrible accident and nothing more, and he was not under suspicion. Or, Rick finally concluded, he was reading too much into Fiore's words and the question was posed in total innocence.

"We were fascinated. The aging room was especially interesting."

"Yes. As quiet as a morgue."

A curious analogy. "Is your cheese production similar, Signor Fiore?"

"I don't turn out as much cheese as the Rondini dairy, but we are at full capacity. If I had more pasturage I could increase it, but that doesn't appear to be in the cards." He checked his wineglass, realized it was getting low, and looked around for a waiter.

"Is your dairy a family business, like the Rondini's?"

Fiore thought about the question longer than Rick expected. "Well, I own it, if that's what you mean, but not by inheritance. Unlike with Roberto, it was not handed to me by my father. I bought it about a dozen years ago when it came on the market. Not cheap, but it was worth it to me. Anyone in your family own farm land, Signor Montoya?"

A passing waiter took Fiore's empty glass and gave him one that was full. Rick declined the offer.

"I have an uncle in America who raises chiles. He has a few horses and chickens, but I didn't see any cows the last time I visited him several years ago. So no cheese."

"That is unfortunate. Cheese is one of man's greatest creations, and transforming a simple product like milk into something so delicious is almost like performing magic. You must have felt that when you did the tour with Carlo."

It wasn't the only thing I felt, Rick was tempted to say. Instead, he decided to go right to the point. "Signor Fiore, I've heard that some people think Roberto Rondini's death was not an accident. What is your opinion?"

The glass stopped inches from his lips and slowly lowered. "I have heard the same thing, Signor Montoya, but have no way of knowing. The police investigated it immediately after his body was found, so I assume that their conclusion was that Roberto was the victim of an accident. Unless they are still investigating, of course. Have you heard anything in that regard?" As he took a drink his eyes stayed on Rick.

"You should probably ask the local police, not an outsider like me."

Fiore shrugged, then noticed something over Rick's shoulder. "Your employer is looking this way, so he may be requesting your presence. Perhaps he's heard enough stories about cheese for the evening."

He turned and caught Angelo's eyes before they moved back to the people with him, which Rick took to mean that his boss approved of his conversing with Fiore. "Mr. Rondini seems to be holding his own. Tell me something, Signor Fiore. I trust you know about the acreage that lies between the Rondini dairy and the river. It does not appear to have ever been planted, or if so, it's been many years since. Do you know why the late Roberto Rondini never did anything with it?"

Fiore took the small paper napkin in his hand and passed it roughly over his mouth. "Your employer is curious about that, I suppose. Has he ever seen a plot of land that he didn't want to develop?"

Rick could have pointed out that Angelo had no interest in this plot, but thought it better to keep the man in doubt. He recalled the day of the funeral when they had walked through the field and someone he assumed was Fiore had been watching them from a distance.

"You haven't answered my question."

"No, Signor Montoya I haven't, and it is because I don't know the answer. That piece of land was like that when I bought my farm, and my relationship with Roberto, as I told you, was not the best. I did make it known to him that I would be interested in purchasing the plot, but as a rule we didn't share secrets. So I never found out the reason for leaving such prime real estate purely for the enjoyment of the birds and insects. It is unfortunate that you didn't have time to ask that question of Carlo Zucari when you were touring the dairy."

"From what you said about reaching your full capacity, I take it you could put that land to good use."

Fiore's mouth turned up slightly, as much a sneer as a smile. "That would be the case."

Chapter Ten

The Mercedes pulled slowly out of its parking space and started down the path to the street. Darkness had overtaken the green area around the Palazzo Te, but invisible floodlights spread wide yellow beams along its stone sides, picking up the texture of the design.

"You enjoyed seeing the rooms, Signor Rondini?" The driver kept his eyes on the road as he made the turn onto the pavement. There were no cars on the street except those parked silently along the side.

"Yes we did, Marco," answered Angelo. "I didn't get into any except the horse room where the event took place, but that was very impressive. I believe Lexi and Rick saw more of the place, am I right, Lexi?"

"Yes, we did get into the other rooms. The most interesting was the one with the giants, don't you think so, Rick?"

"I liked the cupid room, and especially the one just before the giants." Rick glanced back at Lexi, who was staring out the window.

"The Sala dei Giganti is the most famous room," the driver said, picking up on Lexi's comment. "The lower figures, the giants, were done by Rinaldo Mantovano, a local artist, but Giulio Romano himself painted the gods on the ceiling and oversaw the whole work."

"Next time we'll take you inside, Marco, and you can explain it all." Angelo tapped Rick on the shoulder. "I hope you were able to find out something, Language Man. I saw you talking to people. Are we closer to solving this mystery?"

"We might be," Rick answered, thinking it wasn't something to discuss with the driver listening. "I'll tell you about it when we get back to the hotel."

Angelo looked out his window but didn't appear to be focusing on the passing building. "I had a couple invitations at the reception to have dinner later, but I told them I needed to have a business meal with my assistant. Lexi, we really have to go over those three new proposals."

"Of course, Mr. Rondini. I'll pull up the files on my tablet when we get to the hotel."

Angelo leaned forward and tapped the driver's shoulder. "Marco, you can take the night off again. We'll go somewhere we can walk to from the hotel. I got some suggestions at the reception."

"Yes, sir," Marco answered, keeping his eyes on the road.

Ten minutes later Angelo, Lexi, and Rick sat around a small round table in the bar of the hotel. In front of Angelo was an empty coffee cup. Rick and Lexi sipped white wine but eschewed the small, marinated *mozzarella* balls the waiter had brought to the table.

"The friendship between Fiore and Zucari does seem curious, given that my cousin wasn't on the best of terms with his neighbor. When you overheard them, the two of them must have been talking about the infamous plot of land, and the manager appears to know what Livia has decided to do with it. We talked at length this evening, but she didn't mention that issue, not that she needs to share her business with the uncle from America. She did appear to be more upbeat, but I thought that she was just starting to come to terms with her father's passing. Perhaps there is something else going on here. Maybe we'll find out tomorrow when we gather at the river." He looked at his empty *espresso* cup as if deciding whether to have another. "She has invited other people to the unveiling of the column tomorrow, if that's the right word for the event. I'm glad I decided to make this gesture, it may help her to get over her grief. The more ceremonies of remembrance the better, in my experience."

Lexi looked at Rick, and her expression told him that Angelo was referring to his own grief in the loss of his wife. He tried to remember from the bio he'd read just how long it had been.

"It doesn't appear that this case is going to be resolved any time soon," Angelo continued. "And we will be flying home the day after tomorrow, when the flight crew's vacation in Verona will end. Maybe your uncle can keep an eye on the investigation, and you can let us know if anything happens."

"Of course, Mr. Rondini."

Angelo raised himself slowly to his feet. Fatigue lined his features. "Let's postpone our business dinner, Lexi. I got enough to eat at the reception. I thought I was getting over the jet lag, but it seems to be hitting me again. You two go out for something."

Rick and Lexi exchanged glances. "Of course, Mr. Rondini," she said. "You can have something sent up to your suite if you get hungry."

"I'll do that." He shuffled toward the elevator as they watched.

"I think it's more than jet lag," said Lexi when her boss was out of earshot. "It's like he's got the weight of the world on him. The only other time I saw him like this was after Mrs. Rondini passed away."

They sat in silence for a few moments before Rick spoke. "The upside is that I get to have another meal with Alexis Coleman. Did you partake too much at the reception or are you up for another restaurant meal in Mantova?"

"I could use something," said Lexi. "Maybe a salad." She looked at Rick. "Is there somewhere we can get a light meal?"

"Light. Heavy. Whatever you want."

• ● ● ● •

Lexi did order a salad, but it was a second course after a bowl of *stracciatella*, chicken broth swirled with egg and grated Parmigiano-Reggiano, topped with a slice of toast. Rick convinced her that it was a simple peasant dish. The salad was fresh greens lightly coated with oil and vinegar. He explained that Italians are minimalists when it comes to salads. He, too, went with lighter fare, though if pushed, he would have ordered pasta. *Minestrone* was first—fresh vegetables in the same broth as Lexi's—and for *secondo*, asparagus that had been cooked and then topped with Parmigiano-Reggiano and run under the broiler. Lexi's spoon, and then her fork, had darted across the table to sample both. The dishes now were gone, as was an empty wine bottle, and they were sipping *espressi* while nibbling on pieces of *torta sbrisolona*, which the waiter said was a specialty of the city. It turned out to be something between a cookie and a cake—flat, crunchy, and flavored with almonds. It was so perfect with coffee that they ordered second cups after Rick convinced her that *espresso* wouldn't keep her awake.

"I have to get some of this to take back to Chicago. It looks like it would travel well." She picked up and quickly ate the last of the crumbled pieces, one with a whole almond.

"There's a bakery I passed on the way to the police station that will have it for sure. We'll pick some up tomorrow. I'd like to take some back to Rome as well." He took his last sip of coffee. "Italian regional cooking is always full of surprises. I'd never heard of this stuff and I doubt if I can find it in Rome. I'll just have to come up here every few months and stock up."

Lexi inclined her head and smiled. "You can come up with that friend of yours who's an art historian and she can explain the paintings."

"She really is in the States now. And married."

"I'm sure you can find someone else to keep you company, Rick."

"Mantova would never be the same without you, Lexi." He reached across the table and squeezed her hand. "And without Angelo paying for it, of course."

She laughed, pulled her hand away, and slapped his. "You are terrible. But that reminds me who we are both working for, and that I should be getting back to the hotel to go through my e-mails. Angelo will want a complete report at breakfast. And speaking of breakfast, I must check that buffet at the hotel more carefully. Will they have *torta*...?"

"*Sbrisolona*. If they don't, we'll demand it."

"It will taste good after our morning run."

Rick rubbed his leg. "Lexi, I don't know about that. I'm still pretty sore and shouldn't push it."

"First a dusting of snow stops you and now some minor discomfort in your leg? What kind of an athlete are you, Mr. Montoya?"

"A fair weather and injured one, it appears. Have you ever worked as a personal trainer? You sound like it."

"No, but at Northwestern the track team had a trainer. He was tough."

Rick shook his head and signaled for the bill. "The many facets of Alexis Coleman."

A few minutes later they emerged into the Mantova night. The restaurant was a few blocks from the hotel on a quiet side street, though almost all the streets in the city's historic center were silent at that time of night. As they walked they heard only an occasional TV voice muffled by wooden and metal shutters closed tight to keep out the cold. They walked in silence, arm in arm, enjoying the stillness of the medieval surroundings, when Rick's phone rang. He fumbled and brought it from his jacket pocket.

"It's my Uncle Piero, I'd better take it." He pressed the screen. "*Zio, buona sera.*"

"Good evening to you, Riccardo. I hope I am not interrupting dinner."

"No, we're just walking back to the hotel from the restaurant."

"One always eats well in Mantova. I was wondering if there is any news on your investigation. I didn't want to call Inspector Crispi, but I trust you are *aggiornato* on everything."

"As up-to-date as Crispi, unless he's learned something new since the last time we met. At this point we're stuck in a rut, but we're both convinced that the murder was connected to a plot of land."

"Land owned by the dead man?"

"Correct, and now by his daughter. It was acquired decades ago by less-than-honorable means, which probably has nothing to do with it. The issue seems to be whether the victim was going to sell it to someone who would develop it in ways not connected to the traditional agriculture of the area. There is no lack of people who are against such development."

"So, no lack of people with a motive to murder."

"That's right. The deceased was not universally loved, as I've found out, but I doubt his personality was malevolent enough to be the only factor in his murder. There had to be something else, and this land appears to be that something."

Lexi listened without understanding, waving to indicate that he should take his time.

"It wouldn't be the first time someone was killed over a land dispute," said Piero. "You'll remember Romulus and Remus."

Uncle Piero, the true Roman, Rick thought. For them there was nothing new under the sun.

"Was this land acquired recently?"

"No, Uncle. It was decades ago. I think the issue is what should be done with it now."

"People can have long memories, Riccardo."

Though she was trying to hide it, Rick read Lexi's body language, and it was saying that she was anxious to get back to the hotel and get to work. "That's where we stand, *Zio*. I'm not optimistic that a murderer will be found, certainly not before

Mr. Rondini flies back to the States and I return to Rome, the day after tomorrow."

"You're walking with your employer?"

"No, he stayed in. I'm with his assistant. She's standing here but doesn't understand Italian."

There was a pause before Piero replied. "I suppose this assistant is aged and walks with the aid of a cane."

"Not exactly, *Zio*."

"I see. Then I should not be taking your time. Call me if anything comes up, otherwise I'll see you when you get home."

They said their good-byes and Rick returned the phone to his pocket, realizing he hadn't mentioned the threats. "My uncle the cop. He wanted to know if anything was happening in the case." They had come to a corner and he pointed to a very narrow and straight alley. "If I have it right, this should bring us out at the street our hotel is on."

"It doesn't look very inviting, but lead away." Lexi again took his arm.

As they started down the pavement it became obvious that they were walking past the backs of residences and businesses. Doors were metal, some with multiple locks, and bars covered every window at street level. It must have been pick-up day, since metal garbage cans sat empty at intervals, some turned on their sides. The street was so narrow a parked car would have blocked another trying to pass, and signs with P crossed out appeared at intervals on the walls. With this parking prohibition, other than the garbage cans, it was empty. To match the lack of traffic was a lack of lighting; only a few dim lamps attached to buildings lit the way. In Rome at night on a street like this Rick would have at least seen a cat or two creeping under the shadows, but here there were none. About a hundred meters in the distance they could see the bright lights of the hotel's street.

"I could tell by the way you talked that you're very close to your uncle."

"Are you starting to pick up some Italian, Lexi?"

"No, of course not. It was the tone of voice, and your body language."

"You're very perceptive. Piero and I get along very well. He always tells me the truth, without preaching to me, and I'm always honest with him. And he's a pretty impressive guy. I wish you could meet him sometime."

"What kind of preparation do cops in Italy need?"

They moved together to one side in order to avoid a garbage can that had rolled into the center of the alley. Rick pushed it to the side with his foot as they passed.

"My uncle has a degree in law from *La Sapienza,* that's Rome's state university. I think a law degree is a pretty common career path. Then they do their own training, of course."

"*La Sapienza?*"

"It means 'wisdom,' or 'knowledge.' An appropriate name for an institution of higher learning, wouldn't you say? Has a much classier ring to it than the 'University of New Mexico,' where I went."

"Or my Northwestern, which isn't even in the Northwest. Of course it was in the northwest when it was founded in 1851, but then the Northwest moved northwest and Northwestern stayed where it was."

"It's not too late to move it to Washington or Oregon."

"I doubt if the board of trustees is considering that." She stopped and turned back. "What's that?"

Rick looked and saw that a car was slowly turning into the alley behind them. It backed up once and then squeezed through the opening of the buildings on either side of the corner. In the darkness he couldn't tell what kind of a car it was, but from the low pitch of the engine it sounded like an SUV or perhaps a small truck. Just into the alley it stopped.

"He's probably realizing it's too narrow and is now going to back out," Rick said.

They started walking again but were stopped by the sound of the revving engine behind them. Along with hitting the gas pedal, the driver had switched to high beams, sending a blinding light toward them that bounced off the bare walls of the buildings.

"I don't like the looks of this, Lexi." He tried to calculate the distance to the end of the alley and safety. It looked like about fifty yards. At that moment they could hear the car shifting into gear and starting toward them. "Let's go."

Lexi unbuttoned her long wool coat so that she could run more easily, and Rick did the same. Fortunately she wore slacks and low heeled shoes, and was able to get up to a stride quickly. Rick, for one of the first times in his life, cursed his cowboy boots. He also immediately started feeling the pain in his leg from the falling cheese. Lexi might make it, but he was beginning to doubt if he could.

The sound of a garbage can hitting the bumper and bouncing off a wall temporarily cut into the growl of the engine, along with a high squeal of tires. Perhaps the can had slowed down the driver enough to give them enough time to escape. The hope disappeared when Rick heard the car roar back to full power. The light from the high beams was getting stronger, throwing Rick's long shadow ahead of him as he followed Lexi.

"Look for a doorway!" he shouted. Why hadn't he taken her up a wide street?

All the doors they passed were flush with their buildings, and the one garage door was the same. No indoor space would be wasted in an alley, the niched entrance-ways would be on the opposite side of the building, the street address.

The car was fifty yards away and closing.

"Up on the right!" shouted Lexi, pointing ahead. There was a small indentation in the back of the building, but it was filled with two plastic garbage cans. Lexi reached it and grabbed one of the cans, flinging it across the pavement. Rick was right behind her and pushed the other one into the beams of headlights coming at them. Lexi squeezed into the space and pulled him in next to her. They had to bend slightly to get their heads inside, but there was enough room to get them out of the car's path. Lexi put her arms around Rick's waist and squeezed close to him just as the car was about to pass.

It didn't slow down, even when it hit the plastic can that Rick had pushed into its way. The empty can careened off the bumper with a thump and slammed into Rick's leg as the car sped past the two huddled figures. A moment later it was gone and the silence returned.

"You know, Lexi, I love holding you in my arms, but next time, let's pick a more comfortable location." They disentangled. "Are you okay?"

"I'm fine. What about you? Did that thing hit you?"

Emerging from the niche, Rick picked up the two garbage bins and put them back where they had been before the incident. "In the leg. But fortunately it was the other leg."

"So now you have two excuses for skipping our run tomorrow morning." She watched as he pulled out his cell phone. "Who are you calling?"

"Crispi. I got the license plate." He scrolled and pressed the screen. After two rings the call was answered. "Inspector? Can you have someone look something up for me?"

As in any five-star hotel, there was someone on duty at the bar, even at the late hour. In one corner was a gray-haired man with a woman who could have been his daughter, but wasn't. They were working through a bottle of something bubbly that nestled in an ice bucket. Rick and Lexi sat at a small table at the opposite end of the room. Their two small glasses, containing a caramel-brown liquid, were being carefully nursed. Next to the glasses was Rick's cell phone, still warm.

"The car belongs to a man who lives just across the river. When the police called him he said that was ridiculous, his car was parked in front of the house, and started complaining about police inefficiency and getting him out of bed for nothing. Of course when he looked outside, his car wasn't there."

Lexi finished a sip of her brandy. "Stolen vehicle."

"Exactly. They're looking for it now. But more importantly for us, Crispi is not happy that this happened after Angelo turned down police protection."

"But the car tried to run us down. Angelo wasn't the target."

Rick shrugged. "Of that I'm not sure. But the bottom line is that Crispi is insisting we have a police escort for the rest of the time you're in Mantova, and won't take no for an answer. Your boss won't be happy. I'm not happy. Nobody is happy."

"I'm happy the two of us got out of that alley in one piece."

"Between my bad leg and these boots, I almost didn't make it."

"You need a good massage."

He took her hand in both of his. "What a great idea, Lexi."

"The hotel spa opens tomorrow at seven a.m. I'm sure they can get you in."

Rick smiled. "You're good." He leaned closer. "There's something I couldn't help thinking, both when we were outside the giants hall, and later in the alley when we ducked to get away from the car."

"You mean when you had me in your arms?"

"Right."

"I'm afraid to ask."

He leaned closer and sniffed. "I kept thinking, what is that perfume she's wearing?"

Lexi laughed. "What are you, some kind of perfume expert?"

Rick's response was an offended frown. "Well, as a matter of fact, I do know a thing or two about perfume, my dear. When I lived in Albuquerque, I had a friend who worked at the perfume counter at our big department store. While waiting for her to get off work, I used the time to familiarize myself with the various scents."

Lexi stared at him. "You're not joking."

"Certainly not. It's become kind of a hobby."

"I'm impressed. Well, I wear—"

"No. Don't tell me. I'm still trying to place it. I'm narrowing it down."

"I suppose you need more time and more whiffs of it."

"That would be very helpful."

She leaned over and kissed him on the cheek before finishing her brandy and getting to her feet. "There. Hold that memory. Thanks for a wonderful dinner and an exciting walk home, Rick. Sorry we can't go for a run tomorrow. I'll see you at breakfast."

He watched her slacks as she walked to the lobby, remembering how those long legs looked in running tights. Then he rubbed his thigh and cursed the fates.

● ● ● ● ●

They could not see the water of the Po River as the car went over the long, double-lane bridge. After reaching the southern bank, visibility improved, but Marco still made his turns with care. The morning fog, which had been heavy since leaving Mantova, was showing signs of lifting, thanks to a tenacious, probing sun. As the car got farther from the bridge, what had been a heavy curtain of gray was turning to wisps of vapor, revealing the drab, flat landscape. On the left side of the road any view of the river was blocked by a thick grove of trees, planted decades earlier for flood control and now leafless in the fall chill. To the right, dark dirt stretched from the pavement to the horizon. At the far edge of the field, at the end of a row of high trees, the white walls and red roofs of houses offered the eye a slight contrast to the brown earth and cloudy sky. The driver slowed and signaled for a turn. Angelo twisted to look out of the rear window at the police car that was keeping a discreet distance behind them.

"Maybe we can get Marco to lose the tail on the way back. It could be fun."

Rick, who sat next to him in the backseat, wasn't sure if his boss was joking, so he decided to ignore the suggestion and change the subject. "We're coming into your place of birth, Mr. Rondini."

They had just passed the sign announcing their entry into Voglia, followed by another sign mandating a reduction in speed, not that they were going at all fast. Tall trees lined both sides of the straight two-lane road. The open field continued to stream by on the right, but a combination of brick wall and tall hedge began along the left, hiding either a residence, farm, or both. They passed a gate but were unable to catch a view of what was inside. When the hedge ended, they were into the town itself. Standing under two pine trees in the center of a square of gravel was a statue of a soldier. A wreath, its white ribbon blowing slightly in the wind, was affixed to the pedestal. The soldier, dressed for the First World War, held a rifle in one hand and saluted the horizon with the other. The memorial indicated they had come upon civic center of town, and the two buildings on the opposite side of the street confirmed it. They had the architecture of the late nineteenth century, as well as the light-yellow color and white trim used so often in government buildings. Each flew the Italian flag from its center balcony and was marked by raised letters: *Scuola* and *Municipio*. There were likely classes going on behind the shutters of the school, but it was not evident from the street. City Hall showed some activity; people were entering the building and the shutters were raised. Most of the movement on this street, however, was in a large parking lot across from the municipal building and next to the church. It was full of canopied vehicles, each in an assigned spot and decked out to sell food, clothing, hardware, and sundries. Locals, bundled against the chill and armed with shopping bags, walked the aisles among them.

"It appears that we're here on market day," said Rick. "They must have planned it that way so you could get some local color."

In fact, the stands and the people were as drab and gray as the weather. This was not a market like Campo dei Fiori, near Rick's apartment in Rome, full of bright flowers, where the clients knew the sellers, traded daily greetings and jibes, and haggled over quality and price. But that was a permanent market. Voglia was this day's stop for the tireless itinerant vendors of the province. By midday they would pack up and drive to another town where they would set up again at dawn, work all morning, only to move again.

"This has to be the most inefficient system for the sale of goods in the western world," said Angelo. He pointed to a bar just down the street. "Can we get a coffee in there?"

The way Angelo said it made Rick wonder if this return to his home village had been a good idea. The man was cranky, which could have been the result of bad business news Lexi had given him in the morning briefing, or simply his annoyance at having a police escort. The other possibility was that he was having second thoughts about visiting Voglia. They parked the car and got out while the police vehicle slipped into the space next to them. The cop driving made a point of not meeting Angelo's eyes. Perhaps Inspector Crispi had told him that the American was not happy to be protected.

Angelo stopped in front of the car, took a deep breath, and looked up and down the street. "Not exactly the kind of place that's going to keep its young people from leaving for the big city, is it?"

They walked to the door of the bar, saw that it was open, and went inside. At one table a man whom Rick guessed to be one of the vendors had his hands around a large cup, absorbing its warmth. Otherwise, despite market day, the place was empty of clientele. They had likely been in earlier and would show up late. A woman stood behind the bar and sized up the two new arrivals. Rick assumed she was the owner, otherwise she would be enjoying her grandchildren in retirement. It was impossible to know how long her gray hair was since it had been tied up in a bun, but likely at least shoulder-length. The skin signaled smoker, and her voice, when she spoke, confirmed it.

"What can I get for you, *Signori*?"

Angelo understood without knowing the words. "Can she make me an American coffee?"

"*Per piacere, un caffè lungo per lui, un espresso per me.*"

She grunted and turned to the silver machine behind her while Angelo looked around the room. Under the glass display case were what was left of the morning pastries and a larger number of *panini* awaiting the lunch crowd. Lined up on the shelves behind the bar was a meager collection of *grappe* and *digestivi*, with one bottle of whiskey, unopened and gathering dust. Rick expected another disparaging comment from Angelo, but the man was silent, staring into the large mirror that ran the length of the back wall. The woman finished her preparations and put a large cup of black coffee in front of Angelo, a small one in front of Rick.

"Is this the rich American?" said the woman, stopping Rick's sugar spoon in mid-air.

"*Scusi*?" Rick asked.

"The American. Our mayor went to the funeral of Roberto Rondini a few days ago and said there was some rich American cousin there who was born here. I hear a lot in this place."

Angelo had caught the name when she spoke and asked Rick to interpret.

"She heard about the funeral, and that an American cousin of Roberto was there." He left out rich. "So she put two and two together and thought you might be him."

"Your cowboy boots blew my cover, Language Man." Rick was surprised to see his boss turn to the woman and extend his hand. "Angelo Rondini, my pleasure."

The woman shook the hand and introduced herself before giving Rick a questioning look.

"And I'm Riccardo Montoya, Signor Rondini's interpreter."

The woman pushed back a bit of hair that had escaped the

bun. "We have something in common. I was born here, too. But I stayed."

Rick went into his interpreting routine.

"Ask her if she knew the Rondini family."

Rick did, and got her answer. While she spoke, Angelo waited patiently, stirring sugar into his coffee and tasting it.

"She was young when Enzo Rondini, your uncle, moved to Mantova. She never knew Roberto, and says neither of them ever came back to visit, despite being so close. She thinks the Rondinis didn't want to be associated with the place, and people here were fine with that."

Angelo looked at the woman while he listened, nodding his head. She stared back.

"Looking at this place, I can understand why my uncle stayed away. Don't translate that, just tell her I found what she said interesting. Then let's get out of here and visit the church."

Rick complied.

A few minutes later they were back on the street. Marco was chatting with the policeman between their two cars when they noticed Rick and Angelo starting to cross the street. The cop watched them cross and then left the driver to follow at a distance. A light wind blew in from the west, taking away any vestige of the morning fog but bringing with it an equally humid chill off the river. It was like a silent signal that the market would soon be packing up, and the sound of metal canopy poles clanging to the ground followed, though a few women still poked around the open stalls for last-minute bargains.

Angelo pushed open the door to the church and was followed in by Rick, who dipped his fingers into the small font just inside and crossed himself. Angelo didn't seem to notice; he stepped in and squinted at the darkened space. Vertical windows were cut high up into the walls, but little light was getting in thanks to the clouds, or perhaps too-long-postponed cleaning. Two small bulbs illuminated a tiered table of votive candles, some lit and adding a fluttering, eerie light to that side of the church. The only decoration on the walls was a set of stations of the cross, hung at intervals on bare nails. Rick counted eight rows of empty wooden pews, a number which likely was enough to accommodate the town's faithful for mass. They fit easily into a single open space that lacked columns and side chapels. The only ornamentation was on the altar, raised by a few steps from the cement floor of the main church. A gold crucifix hung from the ceiling over the cloth-covered altar, flanked by silver candlesticks. Had he not known better, Rick might have thought they'd wandered into a Protestant church.

"So you think this was where I'd have been baptized?"

"There could be another church, but I doubt it. This is the only game in town, and from the exterior, I'd guess it's been here since the nineteenth century. So, unless they took you into Mantova, which was unlikely, you were baptized right there." He pointed to a stone font on a pedestal at one side of the altar area.

Angelo walked along one side past the pews, pausing briefly at the table of candles before coming to the altar and crossing himself. Rick watched, wondering what was going through the man's head. In Rome, he still attended the small church where he'd been baptized—though not with enough frequency to satisfy his mother—and his Roman priest today was the same man who had sprinkled water on his head back then. Between all the diplomatic assignments of his father, the family always made regular trips back to Rome to visit relatives and attend mass in the family church. His mother insisted on it, a continuity in Rick's life that he'd never thought much about, that he took for granted. Angelo Rondini was not as fortunate. Now he was returning to a church he never knew in a town he'd left as an infant, trying to decide what it meant for his life now. Or if it even meant anything.

A door slammed on the right side of the chancel and a bent balding man appeared, dressed in black with a stained apron and carrying a broom and dustpan. When he saw the two men standing below him, his face turned to a puzzled and annoyed frown. After a moment of thought he put down the dustpan, walked to a corner, and began sweeping as if he were the only person in the church.

"Ask him if he can show us the baptism records," said Angelo, his voice lowered as if the man understood English.

Rick walked up the three steps and approached the sweeper. "Excuse me, we're visiting Voglia and would like, if it's possible, to look up a name in the records of baptism. Would that be possible?"

The man stopped and stared, making Rick wonder for a moment if he was one of the many immigrants who had come to Italy from Eastern Europe, whose Italian was not up to the task. Then the man spoke.

"That's impossible. I'm here by myself. You'll have to come back another day."

Rick interpreted for his boss.

"You know the local culture, Language Man. Work some magic."

Rick turned back to the custodian, opened his overcoat, and reached into his pants pocket. From it he pulled his money clip and took two ten-Euro notes from it. "I'm sorry you are so busy, and we don't want to take you from such important work. By the way, is that the donation box over there?"

The man looked at the money and back at Rick before nodding. Rick walked to the box, slipped the two folded notes through the slot, and walked back to Angelo.

The man held up a hand. "Perhaps I can find the time for such a good friend of the church." He scurried over and leaned his broom against the wall. "Come this way, please."

"Well done," said Angelo.

"I'll put it on my expense account."

The door took them from the old church to a more recent addition, though still old by American standards. After passing a kitchen and large meeting hall, they came to a closed door where the man stopped to reach into his apron and pull out a set of keys. He found the one he was looking for, and with some difficulty got the lock open. If there were windows, they were shuttered, since the room was as dark as an ancient closet, with a musty smell to match. He reached inside the doorway and found the light switch. After some buzzing from the ceiling, an uncovered florescent tube came to life, revealing a small rectangular space, not quite a room but more than a cubicle. A wood desk was wedged between rows of stuffed shelves, but no chair. On the desk stood a single lamp with a parchment shade that looked like it had come with the original building. The custodian looked at the floor, perhaps realizing that it had been too long since it had last been swept, and then pointed to the shelves, now bathed in a pale yellow light.

"They're by year," he said. "Turn out the light and close the door when you leave. It locks itself." He disappeared down the hall and Rick wondered if he was on the way to empty the donation box.

"If they really are in chronological order, you should be easy to find," said Rick as he stepped to the shelf. The first book he pulled down was a ledger that had been filled in by hand and dated to the year 1756. So there must have been another church on this site, or somewhere else in Voglia, before the present one. The items listed showed church income from donations and fees for marriages and other services, as well as expenses, everything from fixing the roof to stipends for the priest. Rick found it fascinating, but it wasn't what they were looking for. He replaced the ledger, brushed the dust off his hands, and moved to another section of shelves. Here he found the baptism records. Angelo told him his birth date, and Rick started pulling down books.

In the period just after the war they changed from bound volumes to hole-punched sheets kept in notebooks, but still handwritten. Everything was recorded in the elaborate script of the time, full of curls and loops. He found the year, then the month, and began leafing carefully through the pages, each with columns for the date, name of the child, names of the parents and godparents, and the officiating priest.

"Here you are. It was about three weeks after your birthday." Rick held his finger on the page and Angelo bent closer.

"It's hard to read in this light."

Rick pulled out his phone and activated the flashlight mode. The page came to life.

"There are my parents. Who are the other names?"

"These two are your godparents, the other is the priest." He read the names.

"My mother's sister and her husband, I think. They lived in Milan. I haven't heard those names in years, since I was a kid."

What would have made more sense would be that the brother from right there in Voglia, Enzo Rondini, had been Angelo's godfather. But then Rick remembered his research in the archives of the *Gazzetta*. Angelo's uncle wasn't married yet. It would be logical that a married couple be godparents. Rick turned off the bright light but kept the phone in his hand. He aimed and clicked, and the flash momentarily lit up the page again.

"For your records, Mr. Rondini."

"Good idea."

Rick closed the book and returned it to its slot on the shelf. "Now to City Hall to find the actual birth record?"

"Lead the way."

They followed the instructions they'd been given, turning out the light and closing the door behind them, before retracing their steps back to the door off the altar. The custodian was not immediately visible, but when they stepped down onto the floor, he could be seen along the side wall, putting his broom to use with slow, deliberate sweeps. Rick walked over and thanked him for the help. When he turned back he saw Angelo standing directly in front of the crucifix, his hands clasped across his chest, head bowed. After a few moments he raised his eyes and he crossed himself slowly. Was Angelo Rondini a religious man? It was not something that had come up in the few days they had been together and perhaps, because of that, Rick assumed the man was not a regular at mass. But why assume that? Your faith was not something that you chatted about, especially with someone you had just met. From what Rick just witnessed, Angelo appeared to be a practicing Catholic...or had decided to become one again.

The temperature had dropped since they'd gone into the church. The sky was blocked by a pewter layer of clouds which stopped any beams of sun from reaching the ground. Rick and Angelo buttoned their overcoats and walked to the curb. A battered car passed in front of them, coming from the market. The man driving was arguing with the woman next to him, and in the rear seat a small boy looked through the car window, trying to ignore the dispute. His grim eyes moved quickly from Rick to Angelo to the church behind them. Rick watched the car as it turned off the street into a road through the fields.

They crossed the street to where Marco and the policeman stood next to their respective vehicles. Rick told the two men where he and Angelo were going next and the policeman gave him a loose salute, as if he didn't take this bodyguard duty very seriously. Marco, in contrast, was somber, reflecting the mood of his boss. The *Municipio* was only a few doors down, confirming that most community activity was conveniently located on this one street. Government, church, a bar, and a market— on this day, it was all a resident would need. On side streets, houses and the occasional two-story duplex had been built on acreage that had been open fields. There had to be a *pizzeria*, a requirement for a population this size, but likely it was somewhere on the periphery along with a small agribusiness or two. The people living in this town had to work somewhere; they couldn't all be public employees or pensioners.

The municipal building had a yellowed drabness that went

with its vocation. Two of the parking spaces in front of it, reserved for city vehicles, were empty. Of the other four, two held small sedans: a shiny red Mini and a Fiat *Cinquecento*. They were dwarfed by two pickup trucks next to them, their fenders and tires caked with dark mud. Rick and Angelo went up the steps, through the door, and into a large room that served as a waiting area. Wooden chairs, perhaps dating to the inaugural year, ran along one side, their line broken only by a door in the middle. Two men who were dressed like they belonged with the trucks, sat and talked quietly, each with an official-looking folder in hand. The opposite wall was taken up by two more doors and a long bulletin board cluttered with decrees, announcements, and other official government business. Rick wondered if anyone ever read them. Maybe, when people got bored waiting for their bureaucrat, they got up and wandered over. At the opposite wall from the entrance sat a man in a blue uniform. The desk in front of him was bare except for a telephone with a rotary dial, another vestige of the building's inauguration. Rick walked to the desk.

"Birth records?"

The man jerked a thumb toward a stairwell at the corner of the room. "Second floor."

There was no elevator, and Angelo took his time climbing the flights of steps, stopping at the top to catch his breath. The stairs had brought them to another room equal in size to the foyer directly below it, but with a lower ceiling. Here only a few empty chairs rested against the walls. There were more doors than on the first floor and they were all closed. The side of the room facing the street was made up of windows as well as a glass door that led to a small balcony, giving the room most of its light. The balcony must have been used at one time for political speeches, but that custom had gone out of fashion and now it served as a place to anchor the flag. Rick scanned the names on the door and found the one he was looking for: *Anagrafe.*

Followed by Angelo, he pushed open the door and almost immediately was stopped by a counter that ran the length of the room. Behind it were shelves filled with records, as would be expected in the office that kept track of the community's marriages, births, and deaths. He expected a cranky clerk to go along with the atmosphere of the place, but instead a woman appeared from behind the shelves, a kindly smile on her face. She was dressed in clerkly fashion in a blue skirt topped by a white blouse and dark cardigan sweater. Her glasses hung from leashes around her neck.

"Can I help you?"

"Thank you, yes," answered Rick. "We would like to look up a birth record."

She looked at Angelo and back at Rick, not understanding why the older man wasn't talking. "Doing some genealogical research? I get that on occasion."

"You could say so, yes. Signor Rondini is visiting from America, and he doesn't speak Italian. I'm assisting him."

"Ah." She looked at Angelo as if he was unable to speak at all, then turned back to Rick. "You wanted to look up a birth record? Everything is by year, of course, there is no way to search for specific names. Do you have the dates in mind?"

Rick told her.

"Interesting. There was a man in here recently looking for the same year." Before Rick could respond, she disappeared behind the shelves.

"No problem?"

"No problem. She's going to get the register from the year you were born." He decided it wasn't worth mentioning what she'd said. It was likely just a coincidence.

Angelo took a deep breath and leaned his elbows on the counter. "I had mixed feelings about coming to this town. It was something I had to do if I was going to return to Italy. My daughter insisted on it. But what I'm finding is a depressing village with not much past and a questionable future." He took off his glasses and rubbed his eyes. "Maybe I'm reading too much into what we've seen so far."

"You may well be, sir. This is a prosperous area. A bit drab, perhaps, especially on a day like this, but—"

"Drab? Tell me about it. This woman's the first person we've seen who smiled. But I suppose it's just as well. If it had been bustling and exciting, I might have wondered why my parents ever left."

They heard some noise from behind the shelves and the clerk emerged carrying four books that she eased down onto the counter. The word "births" was written in faded lettering on the cover of the top one, under which were two dates indicating the period covered inside. She brushed dust from her fingers.

"These are the four for that year." She pointed to the top of the stack. "This first one is from December of the previous year until mid-March. You can see how it's arranged." She smiled at Angelo. "You can take them to the end of the counter to read them. I'm sorry we don't have room in here for a desk."

"That will be fine," said Rick, "thank you." She returned to her hiding place and he slid the books down to the far end of the wood counter, under one of the ceiling lamps. The lighting was better than in the church archives, and he'd need it to read words that had lightened on the pages over time. Angelo stood next to him as he checked the dates on the covers and set aside the three not needed. "Month and day, when written, are switched in Italy. It will be in this one." He pointed to the dates on the outside and opened the book.

The pages were thick, and the entries written in the same elaborate script as they'd seen in the baptism records. Even if cursive wasn't being taught in the schools by then, the persons writing had been old enough to practice the old ways. Perhaps the woman who was helping them still did, but Rick doubted it. Everything on computers by now, even in a small town like Voglia. Like in the church, each page was carefully lined with columns. Date. Name of the child. Names and ages of the parents. Their places of birth and present residence. Rick explained the system as he turned the pages.

"Here it is. Rondini." Rick put his finger about halfway down the page.

Angelo adjusted his glasses and leaned forward to read. Suddenly he stiffened and bent his head closer to the page. His breath came in short gasps, like Rick had heard on the stairway.

"Mr. Rondini, are you all right?"

He ignored the question. "That's impossible. It just couldn't be."

Rick looked closer and realized what Angelo had read. There was his name, the A and R written with a flourish next to the birth date. In the next column, under the designation for parents, were two names: Enzo Rondini and Giuseppina Bardi.

"Why did they never tell me the truth?"

Chapter Eleven

Lexi shuddered. "Good Lord, that's horrible. What a way to find out you're adopted. Poor Angelo. Poor, dear Angelo." She and Rick stood in the doorway of her hotel room. "Why am I making you stand out here? Come in and sit down. I'm ready to go, I was just finishing up an e-mail, though that seems so unimportant now."

"He's pretty tough, Lexi. He'll sort it all out and get over it."

Her room was larger than his, and laid out differently. Unlike American hotels, built to order with every room a clone of the next, Italian hotels were often converted historic buildings like this one. Rooms had different sizes and shapes, each with its own charm. Lexi's had been rectangular, but when a bathroom was added it became L-shaped. Arranged around the space was a double bed, a couch, and a glass breakfast table with two chairs. One wall had a built-in desk with a comfortable leather chair. Lexi's laptop was centered on the desk next to a neat stack of papers, a legal pad, and pens, all under the light of a recessed lamp underneath the desk's shelving. Very neat and businesslike, as would be expected for Angelo Rondini's special assistant. He looked at the dresser near the bed, hoping to see a bottle of her perfume and was disappointed. It was in the bathroom.

He pulled off his overcoat, lay it over one of the chairs, and sat in the other. "What makes it harder to take, of course, is just who his biological parents were. Enzo Rondini, who Angelo thought was his uncle, is in fact his father, and his father is really his uncle. Enzo, who was not married at the time, must have talked his older brother and his wife into taking their child."

"And sending them off to America."

"I suspect they had been planning to emigrate before this happened. But with the same last name, Rondini, it must have been easy to take baby Angelo to the States as their own son. Enzo, even then, was ambitious, and didn't want the stigma of fathering a child when he wasn't married, though later he did marry Giuseppina. I recall reading the name Pina in the news stories of the time."

Lexi settled into the sofa, crossed her ankles, and stretched her legs. She was dressed in an off-white turtleneck sweater and black slacks. Gold rings again dangled from her ears. As always, her makeup was perfect, with just a hint of blush on her smooth, brown skin.

"Rick, I just realized something. Roberto Rondini was Angelo's brother."

"Exactly. He was coming to terms with that in the car as we drove back. Lexi, he was already depressed about his birthplace before all this happened. It's not exactly a charming town to begin with, and the weather didn't help. The discovery turned out to be the end to a perfect visit."

"What can we do, Rick?"

"I was hoping you would have some suggestions, though I'm not sure if there is anything we can do. You know him much better than I. Is he the kind of person who likes to talk things out with someone, or work problems out on his own?"

"More the latter."

"Then we leave him alone."

Lexi leaned forward on the sofa. "This couldn't have anything to do with the murder, could it?"

"No, I'm sure it doesn't. It happened so long ago." He closed his eyes. "Wait a minute."

"Rick, what is it?"

"Just thinking of something. Two things, in fact. I just said that what we discovered today about Angelo happened long ago, which is of course true. But my uncle said something when I first talked to him about the case and it just popped back in my head. People have long memories, is what Piero said." He closed his eyes again and rubbed them with his fingers. Then he opened them wide and smiled. "The kid in the car."

"What are you talking about?"

He fumbled in his pocket for his phone, scrolled quickly through the numbers and hit one. "I have to call Crispi." A voice answered on the third ring and Rick switched to Italian. Lexi watched.

"Inspector? This is Montoya."

"What is it?"

Mr. Personality, as always. "Can you check on something for me, or have that sergeant who is good with public records do a check?" When he got no reply, he continued. "When I was at the *Gazzetta* there was a story about the family whose land had been expropriated."

"You mean—"

"Correct, the same land, I'm quite sure. Could she check the name of that family? I'm interested in the person who owned it before foreclosure, before it was taken by the province and then purchased by Enzo Rondini."

"Montoya, that was fifty years ago. Is this connected to our case?"

Rick was tempted to revert to sarcasm, but resisted. "I believe it is."

Even over the phone Rick could hear Crispi's slow exhale. "All right, I'll get her on it, and call you back. Not sure how long it will take."

"I'm going to be out at the river, the memorial for Roberto Rondini, with my ringer turned off. Can you just text me the name?"

"As you wish."

"Thank you, Inspector." Rick was about to hang up when Crispi stopped him.

"Montoya, something else has come up, involving Francesco Guarino. Is he going to be at this memorial at the river?"

"Livia's husband? Yes, I assume so, if he's recovered from his accident."

"I'll tell you about it later. Is the corporal I assigned to you doing his job?"

It took Rick a moment to understand that he meant the bodyguard. "We're all still in one piece, Inspector."

"Glad to hear it. Don't say anything to your boss about Guarino. It may be nothing."

The call ended just as they heard a knock at the door. Rick and Lexi exchanged glances. "Come in," she called out.

Angelo opened the door, dressed in his overcoat, ready for the drive to the river. "Lexi? Did you hear back from—oh, you're here, Language Man."

Rick got to his feet, as did Lexi. "Mr. Rondini, Rick told me what happened. I don't know what else to say except that I'm so sorry."

Rick noticed that his boss was in better shape than when he'd seen him last. When they had arrived in the hotel, Angelo had walked slowly across the lobby, head bent, eyes staring at the floor. He stayed that way until Rick got off the elevator and the doors closed. Rick got to his room, checked his e-mails, and wondered what, if anything, he could do. Was it a good idea to leave Angelo alone, or did he need to talk it out? Only Lexi would have the answer, if there was one. That was when he'd walked up one flight of stairs and knocked on her door. Looking at the man now, it was evident that he'd come to grips with the news. Or put it away in some compartment to deal with later.

"Thank you, Lexi. It's been quite a shock. Not like anything I've been through before. I just got off the phone with Nikki, and as always, she was very supportive. She's the only one I can talk to about family matters since her mother died."

"I've unburdened myself on Nikki a few times," Lexi said. "She's a good listener."

"She wasn't very happy that I woke her up. In my state I'd forgotten about the time difference, but she forgave me when I told her why I was calling." He looked at Rick, as if noticing for the first time that he was present. "Do you think your policeman friend is going to discover who killed my brother?"

The question, and the tone of voice, jolted Rick. The investigation had risen to a new level of interest for Angelo Rondini, or focusing on it may have been a way to put aside the shock he'd received in Voglia.

"I just spoke with him and asked him to check on something that came to me as a result of our visit today. It has to do with the previous ownership of that tract of land."

"That damn land again? The Rondinis have owned it for decades, I don't see how that could be of any help in finding Roberto's murderer."

"Crispi thinks it might," Rick said, stretching the truth somewhat.

"No way. It has to be someone who doesn't want that land developed, or more likely wants it for himself. If property is involved, the issue is going to be money. I can tell you that from personal experience."

"That may well be, sir. But this thread should be followed and then checked off if it leads nowhere." What Rick didn't say, was that if his hunch was correct, among those gathering at the river to honor Roberto Rondini could be the very person responsible for his murder.

"It's getting late, Mr. Rondini." Lexi rose to her feet and picked up her coat. "We don't want to keep all those people waiting."

• • ● • •

Thunderstorms had rumbled through the Trentino region the previous day, swelling the creeks that snaked through the steep hills surrounding the Lago di Garda. The streams dropped from cliffs around the lake, creating spectacular but temporary waterfalls. The water level rose, lifting the pleasure boats that had not yet been put into storage for the winter. At the southern end of the lake the shore squeezed into a funnel at the town of Peschiera, pushing the overflow from the rains into the start of the Mincio. The new river was allowed to meander for only a few kilometers. A short distance from the lake, canals began stealing from the main course, sending water east and west where it would be partitioned among farms and towns. Though diminished, the river kept flowing. At Borgetto, as it had for more than six hundred years, it passed under the bridge built by the Duke of Milan when the Visconti controlled the land on both banks. On the river ran, cutting through Goito before entering a nature preserve where birds—in air, perched and wading—watched it pass. By the time it lapped the outer edge of the Rondini property, the Mincio was calm and wide.

The Mercedes was not the first car to arrive. When it pulled into the open area above the river bank, followed by the police escort, Livia and Francesco Guarino were standing next to one of the dairy's Land Rovers, deep in conversation. She wore leather boots for the wet ground and a wool coat for the weather. He was bundled in a heavy overcoat, and his head was covered by a hat which conveniently hid any marks of his accident. It was not a friendly conversation. When Livia saw the other car pull in she said something to her husband and walked to where Angelo had opened his door and stepped to the ground. They embraced before she greeted Lexi and Rick.

"Uncle, the monument is beautiful, just perfect in its simplicity. It is so appropriate that it overlooks the river where my father spent so many hours."

"I'm glad you approve, Livia," said Angelo. "They did a good job installing it?"

"They came early this morning, and Francesco helped them place it." They all looked down at the patch of grass on which the column rested. "You can see that they put paving stones around it, which was a perfect touch. The inscription faces the river, as it should."

"So the fish can look up and remember their tormentor."

She laughed. "I never thought of that, Uncle, but yes, it's true."

Rick watched the exchange and wondered why her husband was hanging back when he should have come over to greet Angelo. Was it due to their argument? Or could it have something to do with the cryptic comment by Inspector Crispi about the man? Rick also wondered when Angelo would tell his niece, now a true niece, what he had learned that morning on the visit to Voglia. It had to come out eventually, but this was not the time to get into delicate family matters, what with the arrival of guests. And they were beginning to arrive.

The pickup truck that Rick had seen on two occasions drove up and parked several spaces away. From the driver's seat emerged Emilio Fiore, dressed in a leather jacket over jeans, like he had just come from feeding his cows. Carlo Zucari got out of the other side, dressed more formally, but with a practical pair of boots for the terrain. He opened the extended cab rear door and helped a woman step to the ground. Rick was surprised to see the face of Letizia Bentivoglio, and glanced at Livia who was watching the trio's arrival.

"Letizia was a friend of my father," she said to Angelo without prompting. "I don't suppose you talked to her last night at the Palazzo Te. We had a nice conversation and I invited her here today."

If Angelo put the name with the story of his brother's mistress, he didn't let on to Livia. Another car pulled up with the president of the cheese consortium and two other men Rick had seen the previous night. Livia excused herself and went to greet them.

"Is she who I think she is?" Angelo asked.

"Yes, Mr. Rondini," Rick answered. "I spoke with her last night, but she didn't have much to say. Certainly nothing that could help with the investigation."

Lexi made a small cough. "I noticed her last night as well. And we saw her having coffee with Zucari after dinner, didn't we Rick?"

"She's the one."

"Well, I'm glad she's here," said Angelo. "She obviously was important to my brother in his last days, and that's enough for me. Who are they?"

A light green pickup truck had driven up and parked with the other vehicles. Rick was too far from it to read the logo on the doors, so he decided it was either from another dairy, or perhaps a government entity. Two men got out whom he didn't recognize.

"I don't know, Mr. Rondini. Someone else Livia invited, I assume."

"Let's go down to the dock while Livia sorts it all out. It's her land, after all." He called to the driver, who was standing with the cop. "Marco, keep your friend from getting bored. There shouldn't be much danger for us with this group"

The driver nodded. "Yes, sir, I will."

The three of them walked down the gentle slope, stopped for a moment to look at the column, and continued to the river's edge. Angelo plunged his hands into his pockets and looked out over the water. On the far side a lone boat ran slowly along the shore, its motor barely audible. "Here we all are, coming down to the river, like some kind of story from the Bible. Everything happened here, next to this water, both the good and the bad. And now we're all back, like my brother somehow planned it this way." His smile was weary. "Let's join the others."

Everyone who'd been expected must have arrived, since Livia was inviting them to gather around the monument. Rick watched the policeman, who had been chatting with Marco, come down from the parking area and position himself on a small rise just to one side. It was a perfect place to stay out of the way while still keeping an eye on the Americans, as well as everyone else, indicating the cop was taking his assignment seriously. Nobody seemed to be surprised by his presence, or even notice it. They were too busy chatting with each other or admiring the clean, white stone of the column.

Rick looked at the gathering and wondered how long it would take Crispi to look up the name he'd requested. Maybe the records didn't go back that far, or had been lost in a fire. Records were always being lost in fires in Italy, which often was very convenient if they contained information that someone didn't want made public. He was doing it again, thinking like an Italian, something his uncle had been accusing him of lately.

A soft putter sound drifted over the scene before the mo-ped causing it came through the opening in the trees and approached the parking lot. Only Rick and the policeman seemed to notice, and they watched as a man parked, pulled out the key, and stepped to the ground. He wore a battered helmet which he unsnapped and pulled off with difficulty due to the quantity of hair. Placing the helmet on the seat, he walked briskly down the hill while trying unsuccessfully to push his hair into place.

"Look who's here, Lexi," said Rick.

Both she and Angelo looked up.

"That's the nut that was demonstrating at the gate," said Angelo. "Tell the cop to get rid of him, Language Man."

"Curiously enough, Mr. Rondini, your niece just noticed him and waved. I have to believe she invited him."

"I don't get it."

"We should get it soon," said Lexi, "she's about to start the proceedings."

Livia stood in front of the column with her back to the river. The invitees gathered on the other three sides of the monument, while Angelo, Rick, and Lexi stood behind her, back a sufficient distance so that Rick's interpreting would not be too distracting.

"Thank you all for coming," she began.

Rick placed himself between and just behind Lexi and Angelo, then went to work.

"We are here thanks to the generosity of Signor Angelo Rondini, who has put this monument here to honor the memory of my father." She turned and smiled at Angelo. "I could not imagine a more appropriate place. It was here that Roberto Rondini came when he wanted to forget the problems of the moment, and as you can see and feel, the tranquility of the river has the power to do just that. I recall one time when my father was starting to bring me into the family business..."

Livia spoke, and Rick translated in a low voice for Angelo and Lexi. When she was in the middle of her story, he felt the vibration of his phone, and without stopping his interpreting, he pulled it from his pocket. It was a three-sentence text from Crispi. When he was doing simultaneous interpreting, Rick put himself into an intense, concentrative zone; all that existed was the voice he heard in one language and the words in the other that he spoke in response. The message he glanced at on the screen of his phone broke his concentration. Angelo noticed and turned around.

"What's going on?"

"Sorry, Mr. Rondini." He pointed to the phone and kept his voice low. "The message came in from the inspector. It's not what I expected."

"Let me see." Rick showed him the small screen of his cell. Lexi bent to see it as well.

Rick whispered as he pointed. "This is the man who owned the land when it was taken by the government for unpaid taxes." His finger moved. "This is the name of his son, who was a boy at the time. Crispi did a check of this name and found that he died recently. And this last name is the grandson of the original owner and son of the man who just died."

Angelo's eyes darted from the phone to the people gathered around the monument. "That son of a bitch."

"Crispi is on his way," Rick said. "He'll probably be here before this ends."

"I want to get my hands on the guy before that."

"Mr. Rondini," said Lexi, her voice almost inaudible, "be reasonable. This is something for the police to handle."

To get Angelo's mind off revenge, if that was possible, Rick returned to interpreting Livia's remarks. She had finished the story about her father and was on a new topic.

"...the land that extends from the Mincio to the edge of our pasture land. It has not been used by my family for many years, but I have decided it is time to determine its future. I have received many purchase offers for those who wish to develop it in one way or another: luxury housing overlooking the river, a factory, a shopping center. I weighed all the possibilities and have made a decision."

The group was silent. The only sound, other than the low hum of Rick's voice, was the ripple of the river as it ran under the wooden dock behind them. Livia looked at the monument in front of her before going on.

"It was thinking about my father coming here that helped me decide what should happen to this land. I could not destroy the tranquility of this place with construction and development, it would be an affront to the memory of my father. Instead I will be donating the land to the Mincio River Nature Reserve, so that it can revert to its most natural state, and be available for the enjoyment of the public."

She smiled at the two men who had arrived in the green truck, and they began to clap. They were joined by an enthusiastic Domenico Folengo, after which came the more subdued applause of the others. The expressions Rick saw on the faces of the invitees betrayed their opinion of her decision. The men from the cheese consortium exchanged glances, now understanding that a large amount of acreage would not be used in competition with other dairies, and the equilibrium of power within their organization would remain stable. The two men from the nature reserve were still clapping as they exchanged words. Fiore and Zucari showed only grim frowns and ignored each other. Letizia Bentivoglio had a tearful smile and kept her eyes on the column inscribed with Roberto Rondini's name. Francesco Guarino, unlike the others, displayed only stunned surprise. Was it possible that Livia had not told her own husband beforehand? She waited for the clapping to subside and continued.

"I would like now to ask the person we can thank for this beautiful memorial, Angelo Rondini, to say a few words." She turned. "Riccardo, can you do the interpreting, *per favore?*"

If Angelo was surprised by the invitation, he didn't show it. He and Rick stepped forward and Livia moved to one side. The faces on the others showed curiosity. All of them, save the invitees from the nature reserve, knew who Angelo was, and of those, many had met him. Despite that, he was still a curiosity in the closed circle that was any Italian city. That he had been born here just added to the exotic quality of the man.

"We are here today," he began, "to remember Roberto Rondini. While our gathering is about him, I cannot help but tell you about how my life has been changed by his death. As many of you know, I never met Livia's father, and that will be one of my greatest regrets until the day I die. But I have him to thank for bringing me back to the place where I was born. I should have done it earlier in my life, I know that now. But it isn't too late for me to reconnect to my roots, and to my family."

While he listened to the Italian, Angelo squeezed his niece's hand. The only sound was Rick's voice, until the faint bleat of a siren floated over the fields toward the river. Lexi noticed it and looked anxiously at the people gathered around the stone column. Angelo apparently heard it as well, as his next words indicated.

"Regretfully, Roberto's death was not an accident." He paused and waited for Rick to interpret.

The reaction from the group was immediate. They stiffened, exchanged puzzled frowns, but stayed silent, no doubt wondering what was coming next from the American.

"And now we know who was responsible."

Rick turned to his boss. "Mr. Rondini, do you really think this—"

A sharp cry of pain came from where the policeman had been standing, causing everyone's head to turn in his direction. The cop was on his knees, a stunned look on his face. Blood seeped around fingers pressed against a wound on his forehead, but he was alert enough to reach for his holster with the free hand. The holster was empty.

Marco stood above him and waved the gun at the crowd, but his eyes were on Livia.

"You think you're so noble, donating the land to the people," he said in a quivering voice. "But you can't give away land that doesn't belong to you." His eyes darted to the stricken faces of the others. "Enzo Rondini stole it from my grandfather. Her father knew. Yes, Roberto Rondini knew the whole sordid story. And yet he came to my father's funeral, so what was I to think? Perhaps the man had some decency, something that his father lacked. Perhaps he was ready to make amends for stealing this land from my grandfather. But when I came here—to this very place—to talk with him, he laughed at me." He looked nervously back at the line of trees which separated the river from the Rondini property as the gun wobbled in his hand. His eyes moved from person to person but ended on Livia's face. "You were my last chance. Surely you would see things differently. But now I know I was wrong, you decided to give the land away, land which rightfully belongs to my family."

The sound of the siren had grown stronger. Rick calculated that Crispi was passing the gate of the dairy and would be appearing within minutes. Which might be too late. He started walking slowly toward the driver, holding up his hands.

"Marco, don't do this. No one here had anything to do with taking that land. It was decades ago. Everyone here is innocent."

"Stay where you are, Riccardo." The hand shook as he gripped the pistol. Again he looked quickly back, hearing the siren. His voice, which had been a plaintive wail, now turned icy cold. "The police won't get me, I promise you that. But there is some unfinished business I have to take care of."

He raised the pistol and moved its barrel between Livia and Angelo. His eyes darted from one face to the other, trying to decide which to aim at first. Lexi took advantage of the hesitation, grabbed Livia by the shoulders and pushed her to the ground behind the column. Marco's reaction was immediate. He jerked the gun in their direction and the barrel exploded. The bullet hit the column and small chunks of stone flew into the air. Everyone fell to the ground and instinctively covered their heads. Rick had dropped to one knee on his bad leg and winced in pain. He looked back and saw that Lexi and Livia huddled, unhurt, behind the column.

The sound of a second shot echoed across the water.

Marco began swaying. The gun was still held tightly in one hand, but his arms had dropped to his sides. His unfocused eyes rolled skyward as the pistol slipped from his grip and fell to the ground. He clawed at a dark red spot below his collar, then looked in disbelief at the blood on his fingers. Slowly his knees bent, and he crumpled to the ground.

Rick looked back. Angelo stood stiffly, arms extended and legs spread, like he was on a firing range. The small pistol was pointed at the body of the driver. Only when Rick reached Marco did the pistol disappear into Angelo's overcoat pocket.

Two police cars burst through the opening in the trees.

● ● ● ● ●

"Angelo's got a concealed-carry permit, Rick."

"Somehow I doubt it's valid here in Italy, Lexi. But since Crispi's man was lax in allowing Marco to grab his gun, and your boss saved the day, the inspector may look benignly on the transgression."

"I hope so. Angelo never goes anywhere without it. Another advantage of having one's own airplane."

Rick glanced at the memorial, where the farm manager and Letizia Bentivoglio stood reading the inscription. She was holding tightly to Zucari's arm, and her face was streaked by tears as she stared at the letters etched into the stone. Her hand reached out and touched the cold surface when Zucari noticed Rick watching them. Gently but firmly he led her from the column toward Rick and Lexi.

"That was very courageous of you to try to stop him from shooting," said Zucari.

"I wasn't successful," Rick answered.

"Never the less, my *cugina* and I are very appreciative of your effort." She nodded silently, tugged at Zucari's arm, and they walked away quickly.

"What's the matter, Rick?" said Lexi. "You look stunned."

"Zucari and Letizia Bentivoglio. They're cousins. I thought…"

He was interrupted by the brusque appearance of Emilio Fiore. Livia's neighbor ignored Lexi and spoke to Rick. "Well, Montoya, your boss didn't get what he wanted, did he? A nice international contract would have been so nice, an excuse to fly over here and eat in our restaurants." He pointed a calloused index finger at Rick's chest. "But I would have preferred even a shopping center to this insane decision by Livia. If only Carlo and I could have talked her out of it. We didn't care who got the land, as long as it was used for cattle. Now nobody is happy except those eco-freaks." He shook his head and strode off.

Rick turned to Lexi. "He's not happy about the donation," he said.

The invitees milled around, talking in low voices. They studiously averted their eyes from the prostrate figure of an unconscious Marco Bertani. One of the policemen who had arrived with Crispi was applying first aid as best he could, after having covered the bleeding driver with a blanket. In the distance another faint siren could be heard, this one that of an ambulance.

After tending to the fallen man, Crispi had spoken first with Livia, since it was her property, then with the shaken policeman who gestured nervously as he talked and held a bandage to his head. Then the inspector had pulled out his cell phone and spent at least ten minutes in conversation before striding toward Rick. Lexi saw him approach.

"I'd better let you two talk."

"Thanks, Lexi." He watched her walk quickly to Angelo, who was standing with Livia and her husband.

Crispi did not bother to shake hands. He glanced again at the man on the ground, looked out over the water, and then faced Rick. "This place is cursed, Montoya. She told me she's going to turn it into a nature reserve, but I'm thinking nobody will want to come here. One person killed and his murderer shot, in almost the same spot? They'll be afraid to get near this shore."

"Or they'll come out of morbid curiosity."

The detective nodded. "I suppose you could be correct." He paused and rubbed his chin. "I just had a long conversation with my boss and explained to him what happened."

Rick studied Crispi's face, and as always it revealed nothing. "You told the *questore* what Mr. Rondini did?"

"Of course. He was pleased he'd made the decision to allow Mr. Rondini to be armed, after those threats."

It took an instant to understand, then Rick smiled. "I had forgotten that."

"So had the *questore*. It took some convincing since his first reaction was to prosecute your Mr. Rondini for illegal possession of a firearm. But I reminded him of another investigation I've been doing."

Rick couldn't resist. "Lando up the windmill again?"

"No."

Still no change of expression. The man was a robot.

"I refer to that illegal gambling operation," Crispi said. "You may remember one of my men said something to me when we had lunch."

"I remember," said Rick. "But I don't understand how that would convince your boss to look the other way with Mr. Rondini."

"Let's just say that the *questore* himself is very fond of games of chance. He was pleased when I told him that the investigation into the local operation will be going nowhere."

Crispi may not have all the social graces needed in office politics, Rick decided, but he knows how to work the system. Uncle Piero will be pleased.

"I will not give Mr. Rondini the details behind the decision, but he will be very appreciative."

"It also affects Signor Guarino."

"Livia's husband? You have lost me again, Inspector."

"Signor Guarino also enjoys the occasional wager. More than occasional, apparently. He was rather heavily in debt."

Rick glanced over at Francesco Guarino, who was talking with one of the men from the cheese consortium. "So his injury may not have been from an accident?"

Crispi's answer was a shrug.

The ambulance pulled up and turned off its siren, but the flashing lights stayed on. A woman in white carrying a small bag got out of the passenger side and ran down to where Marco lay. Two men dressed the same followed seconds later, bumping a stretcher on wheels down the hill. The gathered group, ordered to stay by Crispi, was being interviewed by the inspector's men. They had avoided looking at the man who had been shot, but now stopped and watched the emergency crew work. The policeman who had worked on the driver walked to where Crispi and Rick were standing.

"He's in bad shape, sir, but they can probably save him. I didn't see a slug, so it must still be lodged in his upper chest.

The shooter was a good marksman, but if he'd aimed just a bit lower, the man would be dead."

"You did well, Corporal. Now help the others take statements from the witnesses. Just the Italians."

"Yes, sir." He walked to the group. They were still watching the medical technicians work.

"I assume you'll be talking to Rondini and Signora Coleman, Inspector. Do you want me to interpret when you do?"

Crispi pondered the question. "Your statement should be enough," he said finally.

The EMTs lifted Marco to the stretcher and carefully strapped him in.

Rick thought back to when the man had met him at the train station. Nothing in the way he'd acted that day, or since, had betrayed what must have been simmering inside. Even as he resorted to violence against Angelo, Marco kept on playing his part, holding out hope that the Rondini family would finally make amends for the sins of the past. Was that hope so unreasonable? But Roberto Rondini's daughter had other plans for the land, and when that became clear, the explosion was inevitable.

Rick's thoughts were interrupted by the voice of Crispi.

"Tell me something, Montoya. What made you think that the previous owner of the property could have a connection with the murder? It was, after all, half a century ago that the land changed hands."

One man pulled the stretcher while the other pushed from behind, and they started back up the incline toward the ambulance. Their colleague walked next to it, keeping her eyes on the ashen face of the man wrapped the blanket. Crispi was the only one not watching Marco being taken away. He had turned to stare out over the water, which had become choppy thanks to a light wind. After a few seconds he looked back at Rick, who was deciding how to answer. Tell him about seeing the boy looking up from the back seat on that street in Voglio?

Mention the old newspaper photograph of Marco Bertani's father at about the same age, staring at the camera, perhaps on the same street?

"It was just a hunch, Inspector. My uncle told me that some crimes have roots going back many years. That made me think of it."

"Your uncle is an excellent policeman, Montoya."

● ● ● ● ●

The late afternoon sun had dropped below the level of the wall, casting a long shadow over the gravestones and making the temperature colder than it had been when they'd gotten out of Livia's vehicle. But at least the high wall sheltered them from a wind that blew over the fields around the cemetery, slowed only by the occasional line of trees. Winter was upon the Po Valley, and with it had come gray skies and shortened days. Snow, infrequent on the flat lands, would soon build up in the mountains to the north, a white cloak from the foothills to the Austrian border.

Rick and Lexi stopped just inside the gate and watched Angelo and Livia walk together to the grave of Roberto Rondini, she holding tightly to her uncle's arm. In her other hand she held a small bouquet. She knelt and placed it among the wilted flowers from the funeral, still arranged around the headstone. When she got to her feet, Angelo put his arm around her and began speaking quietly in her ear. They both looked down at the grave as he spoke.

"He must be telling her now," said Rick. Lexi gripped his arm as they watched.

Livia suddenly looked at her uncle, but he kept his eyes on the fresh grave. Her expression was one of shock, but it soon melted into a bitter smile, and she looked at Angelo's face as if seeing it for the first time. She reached up and touched his cheek, causing him to turn toward her. Her fingers moved around his face, like a blind person meeting a new friend. They stood over Roberto's grave for several minutes before he grasped her arm and they turned toward the gate.

After one step Angelo paused, took a breath, and looked down at two grave stones. With difficulty he got to one knee, rested his hand on the stone marked Giuseppina Rondini, and closed his eyes. When he opened them, he stared at the letters on the next grave for several minutes. He struggled slowly to his feet with the help of his niece, crossed himself, and the two of them walked arm in arm to the gate. Outside the wall, the nearly horizontal rays of the setting sun joined them together into a single, long shadow stretching over the rich soil of Lombardy.

Chapter Twelve

Angelo was his thoughtful self again on the drive from the hotel to the airport. Other than a crack about hoping that Renzo, the new driver, wouldn't try to kill them, he remained quiet in the comfortable back seat of the car that had picked them up just after dawn. Rick had his usual front passenger position, and Lexi sat behind him, clicking her fingernails on her tablet's keyboard. The day was clear and sunny, as if Mantova was telling the three visitors that they should stay longer. "There is more to see," the castle called out when they drove past it, "and my city is giving you such nice weather to help you enjoy it." The lake glistened as they drove over the causeway on their way to the *autostrada*. After taking the toll ticket, the car glided down the ramp and roared over to the left lane, passing a slow-moving truck like it was parked. The wine red Maserati Quattroporte acted like it knew about the Mercedes and wanted to put it to shame on the highway. The engine adopted a throaty growl after being taken through the gears and settling into cruising speed. The trip to Verona's Villafranca Airport, the driver had told Rick, was only about thirty kilometers, which at that hour would take twenty minutes. The way the Maserati was passing everything on A22, Rick thought it might be fifteen. He checked the clock on the dashboard when they arrived at the gate to the tarmac, and he was correct.

The airplane was parked in the same place. It's door was open, and through the cockpit window the pilot could be seen doing his pre-flight check. As the car drove up one of the flight crew appeared at the doorway and turned to alert the crew that the boss had arrived.

"I have to make a call to Livia," said Angelo as the driver started to open his door. They were the first words he'd uttered since they'd pulled into the street in front of the hotel. He got out, took a cell phone from his pocket, and walked toward the tail of the plane as he dialed. Rick and Lexi, standing next to the car, watched him stride away. They were both dressed for travel, Rick in blue jeans and a sweater under leather jacket, she in the same pants suit she'd worn when he'd watched her walk down the steps of the plane just a few days earlier.

"He's already back into his business mode," said Rick.

"He was never really out of it, Rick, even with all that's happened." She looked up as two crew members came down the steps. "There's something you never told me, Rick. What was it Marco shouted just before he got off that shot?"

"I didn't tell Angelo, either, come to think of it. Marco yelled that she had no right to give away the land since it didn't rightly belong to her, that her grandfather stole it, and that she was his last hope to make amends. He also said that Roberto had laughed at him. That must have happened when he confronted Roberto at the dock."

"And that enraged him enough to commit murder."

"I expect that was the scenario, yes. If Marco survives, the police will ask him."

They were interrupted by the arrival of Angelo, as well as one of the flight attendants ready to hoist the luggage up the steps to the plane. The new driver popped the trunk.

"By the way, Language Man. The driver is going to take you all the way to Rome."

Rick held up his hands. "I appreciate the offer, Mr. Rondini, but if he drops me at the train station in Verona, that will be fine."

"No, it's done. Call it an extra thank-you for your services. In addition to the outrageous fee I'm paying you, of course."

"I appreciate it." Rick glanced at the trident logo on the front of the Maserati. "With this car he could have me home in time for lunch."

"Better than airplane food, I'm sure. Now if you'll excuse us, we have a plane to catch."

Angelo and Lexi's bags were being taken up the steps, and Renzo was about to close the trunk when Lexi stopped him. She walked over, pulled out a large shopping bag, and handed it to her boss.

"What's this?"

"Your gift to Nikki. With all that was happening yesterday I thought you might not remember to pick up something for your daughter. It's her size and color."

"You're a lifesaver, Lexi. I talked to her last night and told her to start planning a trip, that she has to get to know her Italian cousin. The shopping here will give her even more incentive to visit." He turned around and faced Rick. "She said she wanted to see Rome, too, by the way. Maybe you could show her around, Language Man."

Lexi, who stood behind Rondini, shot Rick a big grin.

"I'd be glad to, sir."

Rondini took in a deep breath and looked up at the mountains where the sun sparkled off the distant snow. He reached out his hand. "Thank you for all you did, Rick. If you ever need a job back in the States, let me know."

Rick was momentarily without words. It was the first time Angelo had called him by his first name. "It was a pleasure working for you, Mr. Rondini."

"Come on, Lexi. Say your good-byes and let's get the wheels up." He got to the top of the stairs and gave Rick and the driver a presidential wave before going inside.

"He doesn't say that to just anyone, Rick."

"What, Lexi? Ask them to take care of his daughter?"

"Well, that too. I meant offering you a job. You're going to love meeting Nikki."

"You won't tell her anything bad about me, will you?"

"Only the good things, I promise." She put her arms around him and kissed him on the cheek. "Good-bye, Mr. Montoya."

He returned the kiss. "That would be *arrivederci*, Ms. Coleman."

Clutching her tablet bag, she hurried up to the door, waved, and disappeared. A crew member retracted the stairs and pulled the door closed just as one of the engines came to life. Then the second engine turned over with a high-pitched whine, and a ground crew member appeared and removed the chocks from the wheels. Sun reflected off the metal body of the plane, causing Rick to shade his eyes as he watched. He was lost in thought for a few minutes while the plane slowly began to move, then he pulled out his cell phone, checked the time, and turned to the driver.

"Renzo, if by some chance we can't make it all the way to Rome by lunchtime, there's a restaurant I know just off the *autostrada* near Orvieto that specializes in grilled meats."

"I certainly wouldn't want to get a speeding ticket, Signor Montoya."

Ten days later, at a few minutes before one in the afternoon, Rick made his way down a cobblestone street near the Chamber of Deputies. It was sunny, but a chilly front had dropped down off the Apennines and was holding the Eternal City in its grasp. The cashmere scarf around his neck felt good. As always, he looked forward to lunch with Commissario Fontana. Uncle Piero invariably had some fascinating story of his police work that he shared with Rick, and was a good listener if Rick needed advice. There was no one better than a policeman to explain Italians, and specifically Romans, to a newcomer, and though Rick spent much of his youth in Rome and spoke perfect Italian, he still had much to learn about what made the locals tick. It was an education that would never be complete.

Piero's choice of restaurant that day was non-traditional for their periodic lunches. Its menu featured regional specialties from around the country, brought in fresh daily, most famously *mozzarella* from the Campania region around Naples. Unlike their usual lunch spots, the place was extremely modern in décor, stainless steel and glass to the extreme. As Rick noticed when he pushed through the doors, the clientele was also younger than at the other restaurants. Roman yuppies sat at a long polished-wood bar, but instead of eating sushi they sipped wine and speared pieces of cheese and cured meats. He looked past the bar and saw his uncle sitting at a table next to the window. Piero got to his feet and gave his nephew a kiss on both cheeks, in the Italian family tradition. He was dressed more staidly than usual, a dark wool suit with a white shirt, the tie a conservative print. Perhaps he wanted to contrast himself with the youthful clientele of the place, including Rick who wore a blazer without a tie.

"I ordered a Langhe," Piero said, picking up the garnet wine bottle on the table. "Since we'll be eating *mozzarella* and *prosciutto*, it should be a good match."

"Perfect." Rick watched the wine flow into his glass. "Some good wine and cheese is just what I need. I've never been to this place, but heard a lot about it."

Piero glanced at his nephew's face, noticing faint circles under his eyes. "I'm glad you finally found the time to have lunch with your uncle."

Rick took a long sip of the wine. "I had a backlog of translations to do, and to make it worse, scientific articles. They're the most tedious. So I've been at my computer most of the day and into the night working on them. And I had a few last-minute interpreting jobs I had to squeeze in."

"You do look tired."

Rick rolled his eyes before scanning the menu. "Let's do the *mozzarella* sampler, I've heard it's the way to go in this place."

"And some *prosciutto*," said Piero. "They have their own producer of *San Daniele*. And a few artichokes. After that, if you're still hungry, we can decide." He waved over the waiter and gave him the order. "Now tell me what really happened up there. The report I saw from Crispi didn't give the impression it was complete."

Rick fortified himself with a bite of crusty bread and another sip of wine before giving his uncle a description of the investigation. He tried not to leave anything out, since he knew Piero would be interested in all the details. The policeman did not interrupt, but Rick knew he would have questions when he was finished.

He was just about done when the waiter arrived with their order and put empty plates in front of them. A rectangular white platter had the three unadorned *mozzarella* balls, and on a wood board lay paper-thin slices of reddish-pink *prosciutto*. In a bowl sat two small artichokes in oil, prepared Roman style.

"This one is the *delicata*," said the waiter, pointing to one of the balls. "It is sweeter than the middle one, the *intensa*, which has a stronger taste. The third is the *affumicata*, with a smoky flavor. *Buon appetito*." They thanked him, and after he departed decided to go from sweet to smoky. Each of them cut off a slice of the first and put it on his own plate, along with some of the *prosciutto*. The *carciofi* would wait.

"Your *capo* is quite the man," said Piero, after a bite. "But I wouldn't have been happy if someone involved in one of my cases was found to be carrying a weapon."

"Do you think Crispi did the right thing?"

"By closing an eye to it? Since your Mr. Rondini was an American, and one you said knows your ambassador, Crispi avoided a monumental headache by finessing it. But what fascinates me is how he handled it with his boss. It's a side of Crispi I hadn't seen before."

"Do you know the *questore* in Mantova, Zio?"

"I do." Two words, but Piero's tone of voice told Rick volumes about the Mantova chief of police. "He will be retiring soon, Riccardo, but don't tell that to Crispi. Which do you think is best?"

Piero's question referred to the *mozzarella*, since they had tasted pieces from all three, and eaten half the *prosciutto*.

"The smoked is definitely the winner. But they all melt in your mouth like pudding."

"I agree." Piero took two more slices of *prosciutto*, one of the artichokes, and another piece of bread. "Did you tell your boss about the gambling problem of his niece's husband?"

"No. I didn't think he needed to know, and he had enough on his mind. My guess is that Livia will deal with it. Just in the few days I was there I could see her changing, taking charge, becoming the head of the family. Francesco will be brought into line, I would be willing to bet on it." Rick put a piece of *prosciutto* on his fork. "No pun intended."

"What fascinates me," said Piero, "is that the plot of land was never used."

"I've thought about that myself," said Rick. "All those years ago Enzo Rondini may have bought it simply to demonstrate that he could, to show everyone that he had the power and the money, and leaving it fallow just added to that impression. At the time he was starting to have higher political ambitions, so acquiring land was the perfect way to show he was a force to be reckoned with. After that he may have lost interest."

"Or felt some guilt?"

"From what I read about him in the newspaper archives, he wasn't the kind of person who felt guilt, but one never knows what's in someone's head." Rick took the other artichoke. "The question is whether Enzo's son Roberto knew the whole story of the land, since it was only recently that he started thinking about selling it. That was about the time he appeared at the funeral of Marco's father. "

"That's a bit bizarre."

"Yes and no. The man at the newspaper archives told me someone else had been in doing a search on the Rondini's, and I suspect it was Roberto Rondini himself. His lady friend had told Crispi he had been doing a lot of thinking about his parents and his own mortality. He must have read about the land episode in the newspaper archives and found out that the descendants were not only still around, but one of them had just died. So he went to the funeral, perhaps to clear the air after all those years."

"If that was his intention, it backfired. Your man, the driver, must have found out who he was, wasn't happy, and then stalked Roberto, ending in a confrontation at the river."

"That's the scenario I came up with too."

Rick had more wine and looked out the window at a dark Mercedes passing slowly along the narrow street. "What bothers me in all this is why I didn't suspect Marco. I was so focused on all the other suspects—the neighbor, the manager, Livia's husband, even the demonstrator—that I didn't see what was right before my eyes. Every time something happened, from the first threatening note on the windshield, to the falling cheese, he was there, and yet it didn't cross my mind he could be involved."

Piero wiped up the oil from the artichoke with a piece of bread and popped it in his mouth. "Hiding in plain sight, so to speak."

"It's a cliché, *Zio*, but it's true. I've gone back over the days in my mind and recalled other things. Like when Marco dropped us at the church that first morning, mentioning that he'd been to a funeral recently, and later Crispi told me that Roberto Rondini had been to one as well. That should have at least made me wonder. And a couple days later Angelo made a comment in the car about how he was going to tell Livia to sell the land just to annoy Folengo, the demonstrator. He was joking, but our driver heard it and must have taken him seriously. What happened immediately after that? Someone tries to push thousands of pounds of cheese down on us."

Piero took the final slice of the first ball of cheese. "A waste of good Parmigiano-Reggiano."

"Especially since we escaped relatively unscathed." Rick had not told his uncle about the slight injury to his leg, which was now back to normal.

"*Zio*, I may not have mentioned about Marco trying to run us down."

Piero was about to take a drink of wine but stopped before the glass got to his lips. "No. I don't believe you did."

Rick recounted their exciting walk back from the restaurant. "Once again, I didn't see the obvious," he added when he'd finished. "Angelo had said that people at the reception suggested restaurants near the hotel where he could take Lexi to dinner."

"So you concluded that someone who was at the reception, who knew he was going to dinner on foot, was the one who tried to run you down."

"Exactly." Rick splashed some wine in his glass and drank it. "Which brought me back to the same list of suspects since they were almost all at the Palazzo Te. Instead it was Marco, who had been given the night off."

"And decided it would be a good opportunity to run Angelo down, though I'm not clear why the American was in his sights in the first place. What was the threat?"

"At first I thought it was because he didn't want the land developed, and Angelo appeared to be pushing her toward doing that. But then it occurred to me that Marco may have considered that Angelo could have some claim on the land."

"As a cousin? I don't think so. The property would have gone to the deceased's daughter."

"Ah, but when we went to the registry office in Voglia, the clerk said someone had been in checking on the same year's records. I would bet that was Marco. He knew the truth, that Angelo was in fact Roberto's brother. When Angelo said he wanted to go to his birthplace, Marco feared that Angelo would find out and try to claim the land for himself."

"So better to get rid of him that night rather than let him see the birth record the next day."

Rick's reply was a thoughtful nodding of his head. A minute

passed before Piero spoke, and the words jolted Rick out of his thoughts.

"Have you talked to Betta since you've been back?"

It was no secret that Piero thought highly of Betta Innocenti. She was the first of Rick's romantic attachments that he completely approved of, though he would never try to influence his nephew one way or another in such matters. More importantly, Piero stayed away from a discussion of Rick's relationships during those infrequent phone calls with his sister—Rick's mother—no matter how much she prodded him. Rick was grateful for his uncle's discretion.

"I talked to her once. She said she was working day and night on a new case with the art police. When I told her I was busy with translations she seemed almost relieved."

"How did that make you feel?"

"You're sounding like a psychiatrist, *Zio*."

The policeman drained his wine glass. "Sorry. It's better for us to talk about a funeral in Mantova."

"I agree. Which reminds me of a detail I may not have told you, about the case. A key detail, and I must give you credit for it. Something you said when we talked on the phone nudged my mind in a new direction which, as it turned out, helped solve the murder."

Piero carefully folded his napkin and placed it next to his empty plate. "And what would that have been, Riccardo?"

"You said people have long memories."

Commissario Fontana smiled and called for the check.

The Wines

For the readers who may be planning a trip to Mantova after reading this book, or would like to look in their local wine shop for some of the wines Rick drinks, here is a bit more information.

In one of the meals with Lexi, Rick orders an **Oltrepó Pavese Pinot Grigio.** The grapes are grown, as the name indicates, on "the far side of the Po" River from Pavia, a picturesque town famous for its medieval atmosphere and university. Besides Pinot Grigio, the Oltrepó appellation can be found on a number of red and white wines, including Chardonnay, Malvasia, Moscato, Barbera, and Cabernet Sauvignon. Production of DOC wines in this geographic area is the third largest in Italy, after Chianti and Asti, but the quality matches the quantity.

At the lunch with Angelo and his niece, they order **Lambrusco Mantovano**. Unfortunately, Lambrusco, which is more commonly associated with Emilia-Romagna than Lombardy, gets a bum rap from many American wine drinkers. This is unfortunate, since a dry Lambrusco, ruby red and lightly sparkling, is a wonderful accompaniment to many a meal. Also unfortunately, it is hard to find a good one in the States, but if you do, you will not regret it.

Rick's uncle orders an unnamed **Langhe** red for their meal at the end of the book. The Langhe is an area of rolling hills in south central Piemonte, the region which has Turin as its capital. Some of Italy's finest wines come from the Langhe, including perhaps the most famous, Barolo. But when you see the name Langhe on a bottle it can be one of various varieties, both red and white. The Langhe area, which does not get the tourist invasions like Tuscany and Umbria, is the place to go in the fall when you can sample both the wine and the truffles. Tasting shaved truffles on a cheesy gnocchi, along with a hearty red, can be a life-changing experience.

Mantova is on the eastern edge of Lombardy, but there are more Lombard wines than Rick could ever drink in one book. From the northern part of the region is **Valtellina**, noted in the second mystery in the series, *Death in the Dolomites*. Mantova is also close enough to the Veneto region, with its **Soaves, Bardolinos** and **Valpolicellas**, that they would be commonly found on wine lists in the city. They also show up in the third Rick Montoya book, *Murder Most Unfortunate*, which takes place in Bassano del Grappa, in central Veneto. That region also produces the best **Prosecco**, the bubbly which seems to find its way into every Rick Montoya mystery, including this one. Fortunately, Prosecco is available everywhere in the States.

I should note that in this book, as in others, Rick often orders the house wine, available in all but the highest-end restaurants in Italy. The house wine is usually local, reasonable, and good. You will seldom go wrong by ordering the *vino rosso* or *vino bianco della casa*.

Mille grazie to my good friend, John Myers, the knowledgeable owner of 80 Twenty Wines in Pueblo, Colorado, for his advice and assistance.

Author's Note

Many people have asked me where the best food in Italy is found. Such a judgment is subjective, of course, but that doesn't stop me from answering. What I tell them is to get a map of northern Italy and draw lines connecting three cities: Parma, Cremona and Mantova. That area in the heart of the Po River Valley produces a spectacular array of farm and dairy products, and over centuries has created memorable regional dishes using them. Many of my best culinary memories were made inside that triangle, and my wife and I still talk about dishes and restaurants from the area. The Lombard city featured in this book is especially rich in its gastronomic tradition, and as I have done with regional specialties in my other books, I've included foods unique to Mantova on these pages.

But the draw for the visitor to Mantova—as well as to the other cities in the area—is more than culinary. Its history and art, which are really inseparable, come at you from all sides, blending with the medieval atmosphere that permeates most of the downtown area. We have the Gonzagas to thank for that, since the dukes ran the place for three hundred years and were patrons of some of the most talented artists of the time, such as Raphael, Giulio Romano, Alberti, Mantegna, and Rubens. The Gonzaga court was also famous for the school run by humanist Vittorino da Feltre for both boys and girls, noble as well as poor. Much of the Gonzaga action took place in the massive complex that includes the Palazzo Ducale and the Castello San Giorgio, now a museum. It is inside the castle where Rick, Angelo, and Lexi see Mantegna's work on the walls and ceiling of the Bridal Chamber, one of the great masterpieces of the Renaissance. The Palazzo Te, which is featured in another scene of the book, is also a museum that should not be missed by anyone traveling to the city. The Gonzaga summer residence shows off Giulio Romano's then-controversial Mannerism in both architecture and painting.

Three of the restaurants where Rick eats in this book are real places that I had in mind when writing. His and Lexi's first dinner was at Il Cigno Trattoria dei Martini, which does two local specialties—pumpkin ravioli and capon salad—to perfection. It was the first place I dined at on my first visit to Mantova years ago, and we've been back many times since. Il Ponte in Goito is another excellent restaurant, with views of the river either through their picture window or from tables outside in the summer. And the place where Rick and his Uncle Piero lunch at the end of the book is Obicá, which has two locations in Rome as well as in other Italian cities. Be warned, however, that once you eat their fresh *mozzarella*, you will want to throw rocks at other *mozzarella*.

There's a lot of cheese in this book, and most of it is Parmigiano-Reggiano, which chef Mario Batali rightly calls "the undisputed king of cheeses." If you are curious to see more about how it is made, the producers consortium website, parmigianoreggiano.com, has an excellent video along with facts about the history and traditions of their product. I thank the consortium for information that was so helpful in writing this book.

As always, I am indebted to my wife, my most trusted adviser on food and fashion, for her support, ideas, and constructive criticism. My son, Max, once again gave me advice, this time on his favorite subject of cars, both German and Italian. And a thank you to my good friend, Bill Bode, for explaining the technical aspects of private jets, to make sure Angelo Rondini flew in style. Finally, since this is the fifth Rick Montoya Italian Mystery, I wish to express my appreciation to friends, old and new, who have encouraged me to continue turning them out. Hearing from readers is one of the most satisfying aspects of this writing thing, and I am grateful to all of you.

To see more Poisoned Pen Press titles:

Visit our website:
poisonedpenpress.com
Request a digital catalog:
info@poisonedpenpress.com